DOUBLE

01

AYAKO
NODA

TABLE OF CONTENTS

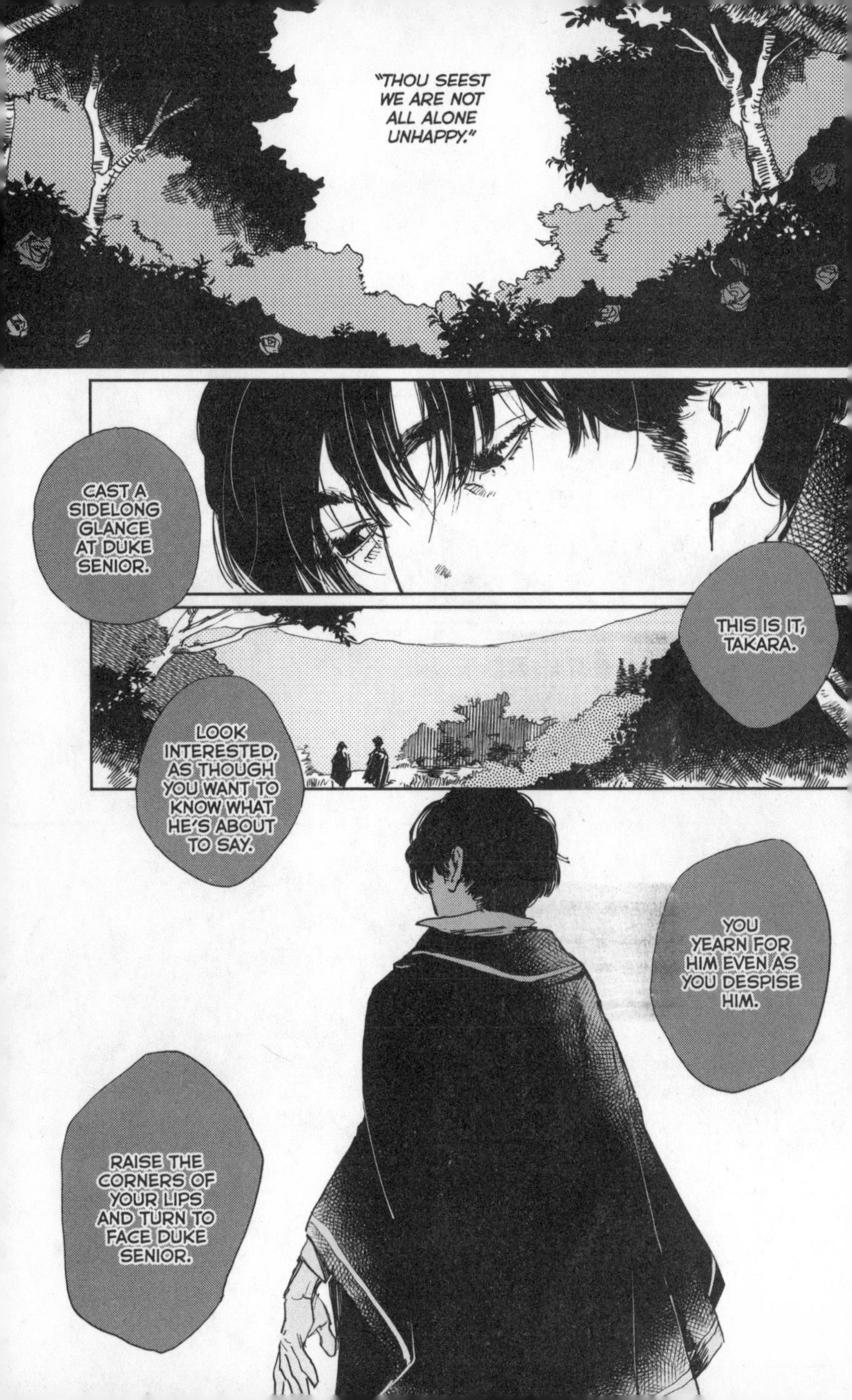
"THOU SEEST WE ARE NOT ALL ALONE UNHAPPY."
CAST A SIDELONG GLANCE AT DUKE SENIOR.
THIS IS IT, TAKARA.
LOOK INTERESTED, AS THOUGH YOU WANT TO KNOW WHAT HE'S ABOUT TO SAY.
YOU YEARN FOR HIM EVEN AS YOU DESPISE HIM.
RAISE THE CORNERS OF YOUR LIPS AND TURN TO FACE DUKE SENIOR.

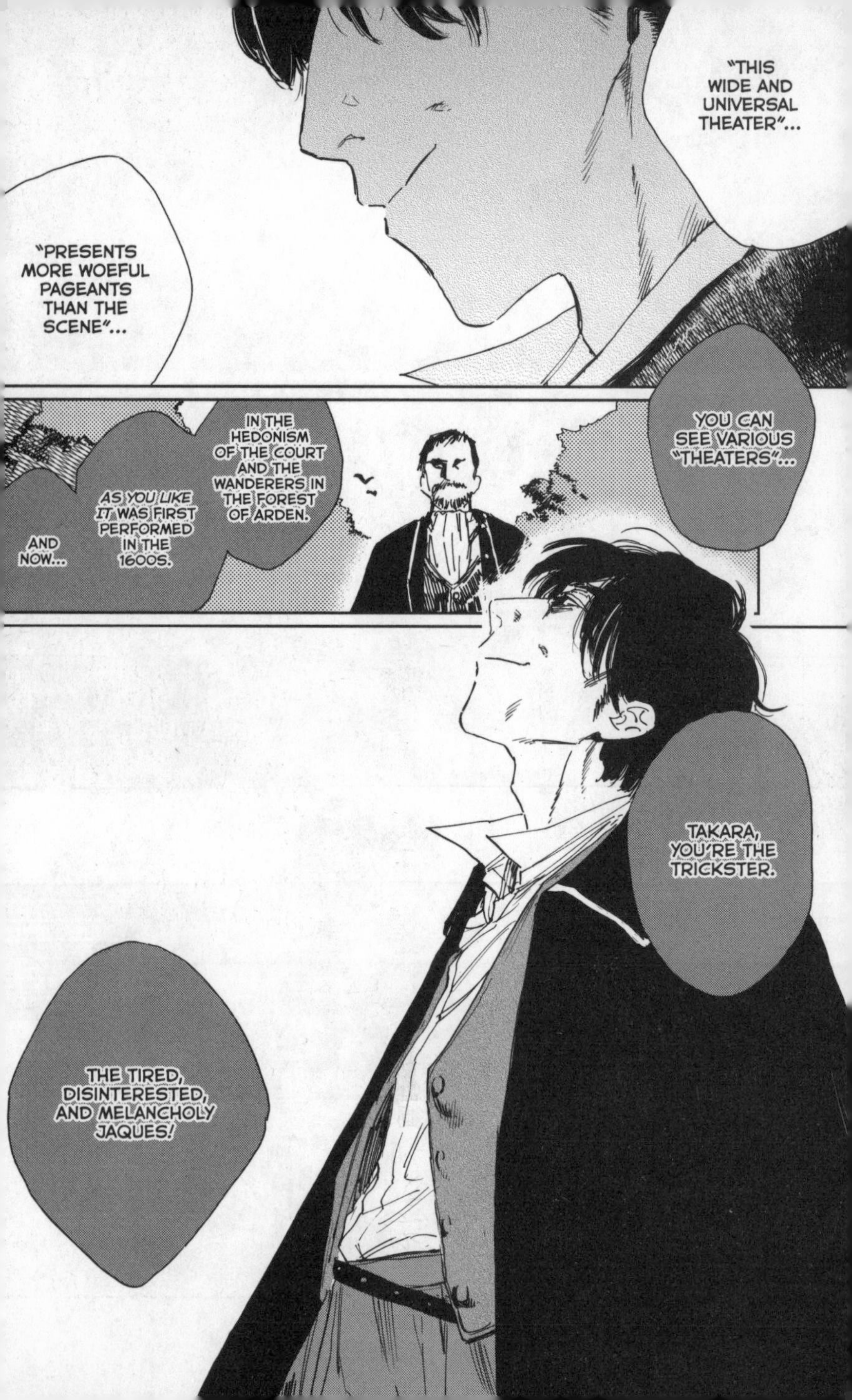
"THIS WIDE AND UNIVERSAL THEATER"...
"PRESENTS MORE WOEFUL PAGEANTS THAN THE SCENE"...
YOU CAN SEE VARIOUS "THEATERS"...
IN THE HEDONISM OF THE COURT AND THE WANDERERS IN THE FOREST OF ARDEN.
AS YOU LIKE IT WAS FIRST PERFORMED IN THE 1600S.
AND NOW...
TAKARA, YOU'RE THE TRICKSTER.
THE TIRED, DISINTERESTED, AND MELANCHOLY JAQUES!

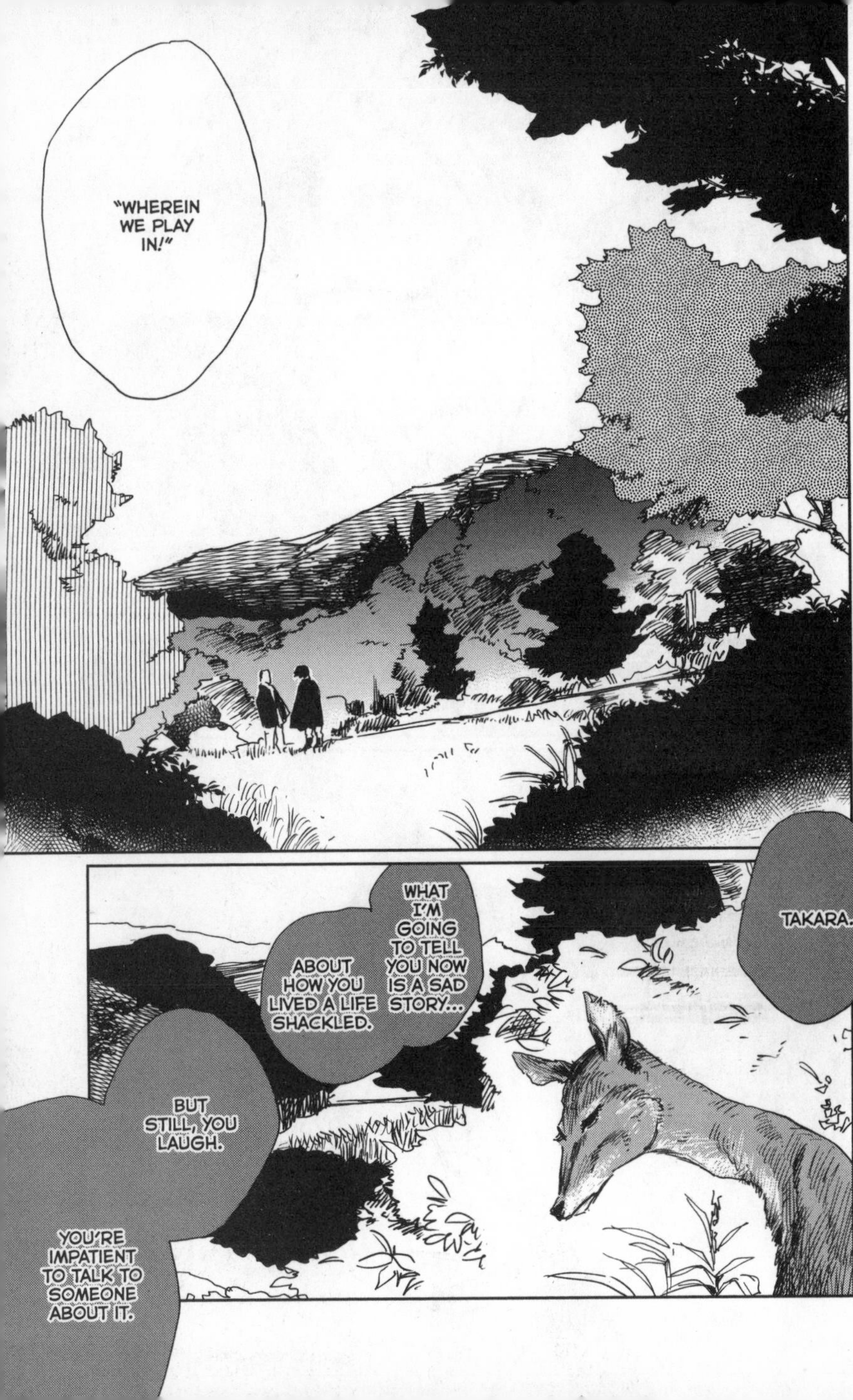
"WHEREIN WE PLAY IN!"
TAKARA.
WHAT I'M GOING TO TELL YOU NOW IS A SAD STORY...
ABOUT HOW YOU LIVED A LIFE SHACKLED.
BUT STILL, YOU LAUGH.
YOU'RE IMPATIENT TO TALK TO SOMEONE ABOUT IT.

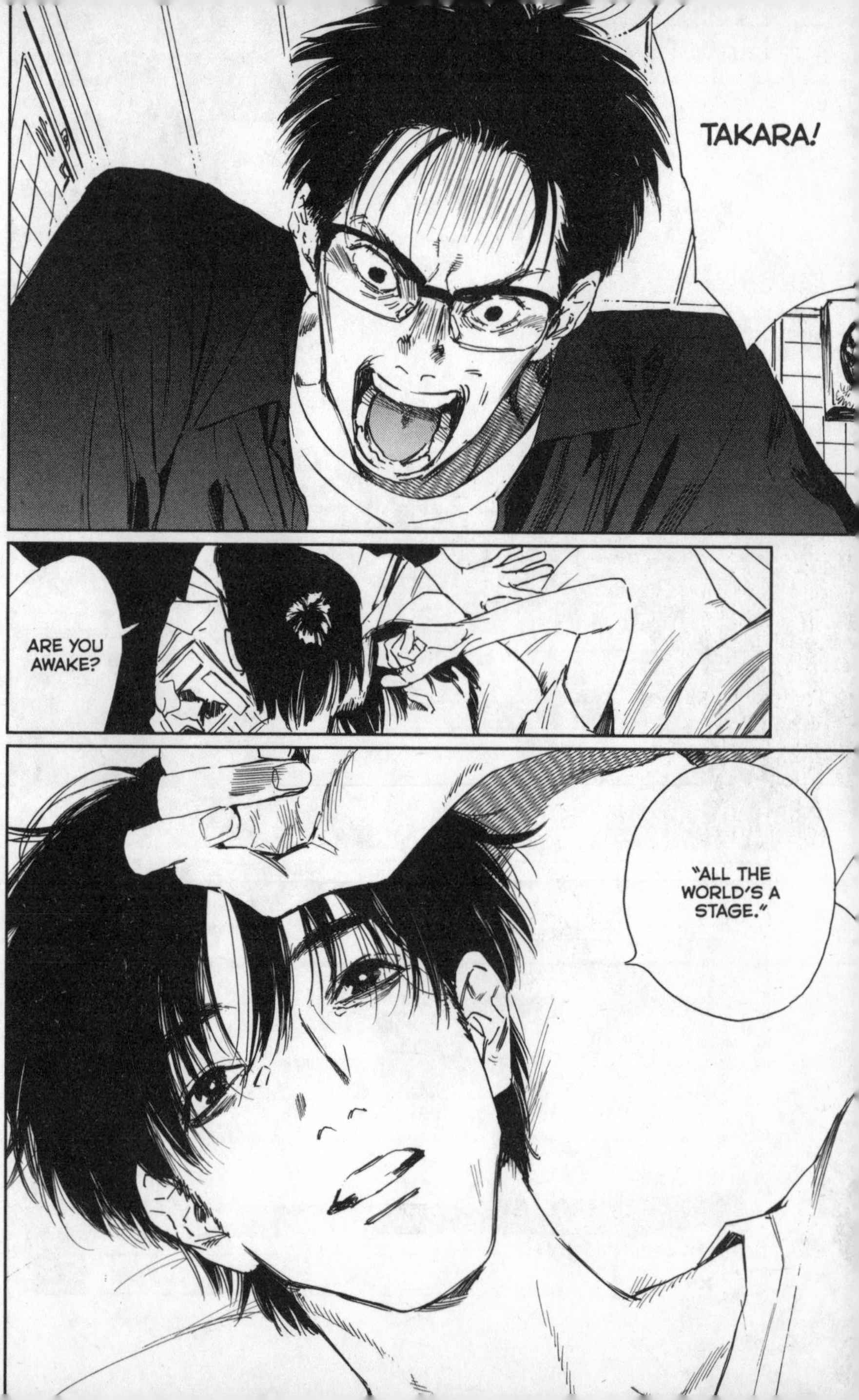
TAKARA!
ARE YOU AWAKE?
"ALL THE WORLD'S A STAGE."

CHAPTER 1 AS YOU LIKE IT

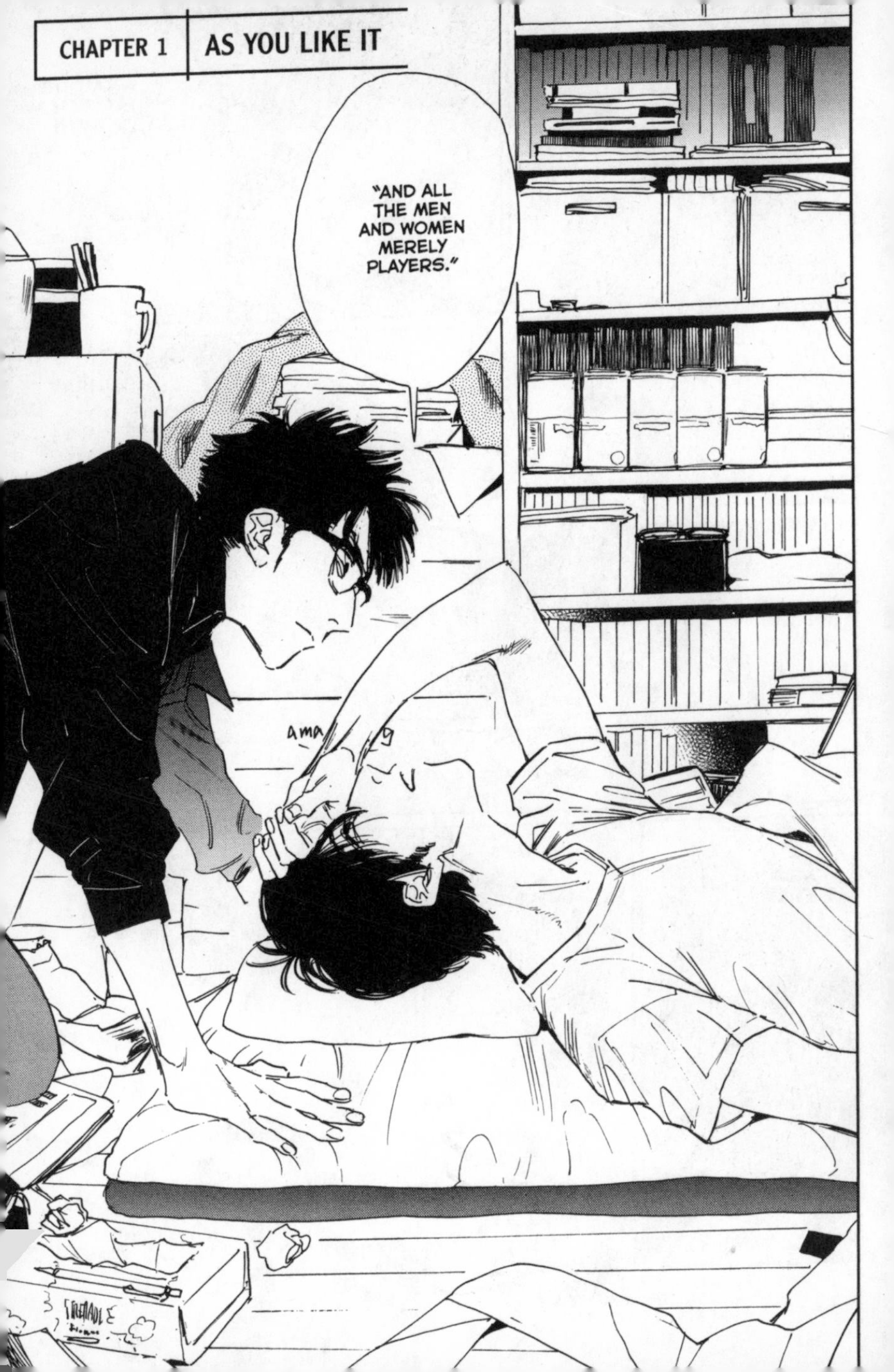
"AND ALL THE MEN AND WOMEN MERELY PLAYERS."
AMA

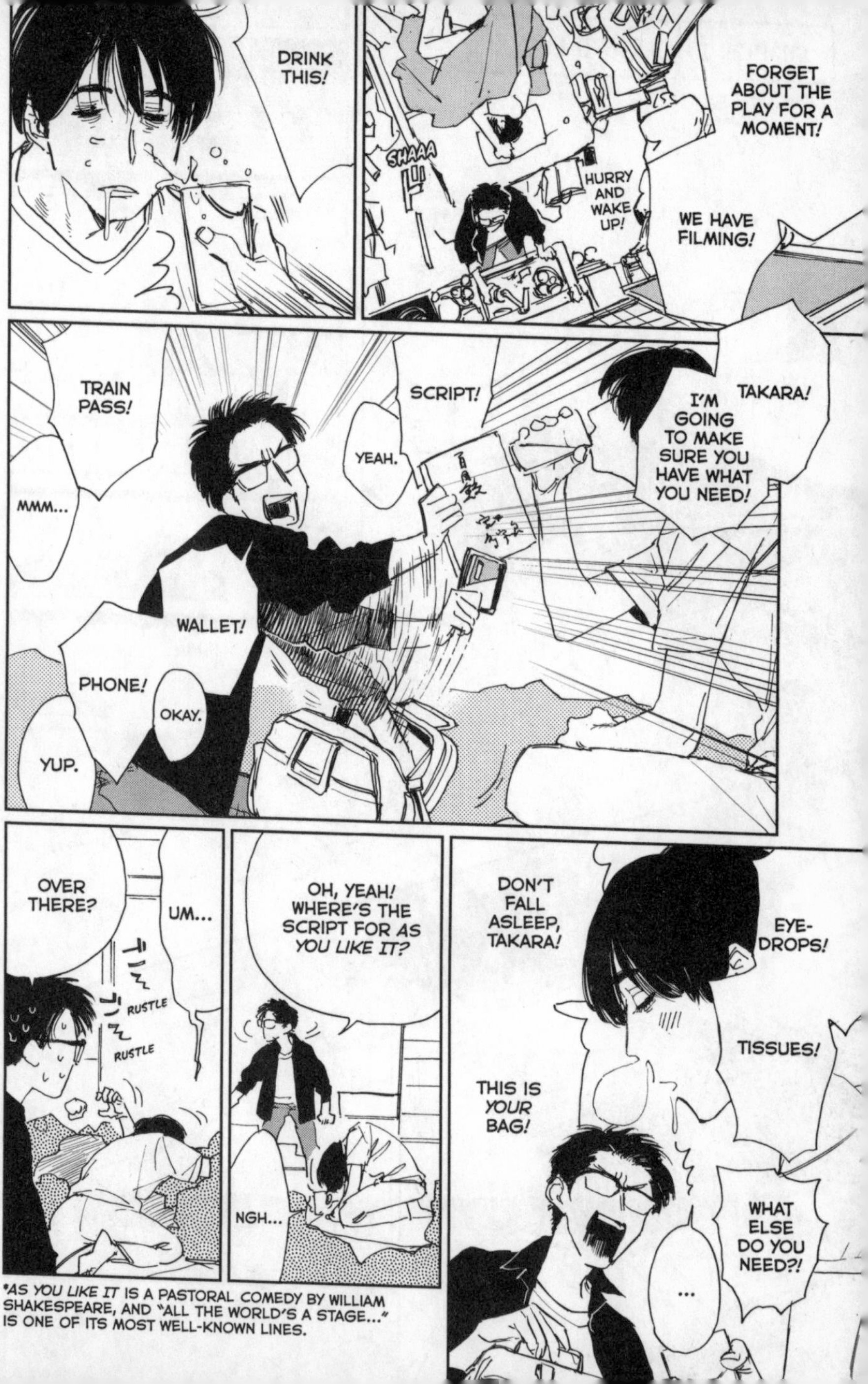
FORGET ABOUT THE PLAY FOR A MOMENT!
SHAAA
HURRY AND WAKE UP!
WE HAVE FILMING!
DRINK THIS!
TAKARA!
I'M GOING TO MAKE SURE YOU HAVE WHAT YOU NEED!
SCRIPT!
YEAH.
TRAIN PASS!
MMM...
WALLET!
OKAY.
PHONE!
YUP.
EYE-DROPS!
DON'T FALL ASLEEP, TAKARA!
TISSUES!
THIS IS *YOUR* BAG!
WHAT ELSE DO YOU NEED?!
...
OH, YEAH! WHERE'S THE SCRIPT FOR *AS YOU LIKE IT*?
NGH...
UM...
OVER THERE?
RUSTLE
RUSTLE

*AS YOU LIKE IT IS A PASTORAL COMEDY BY WILLIAM SHAKESPEARE, AND "ALL THE WORLD'S A STAGE..." IS ONE OF ITS MOST WELL-KNOWN LINES.

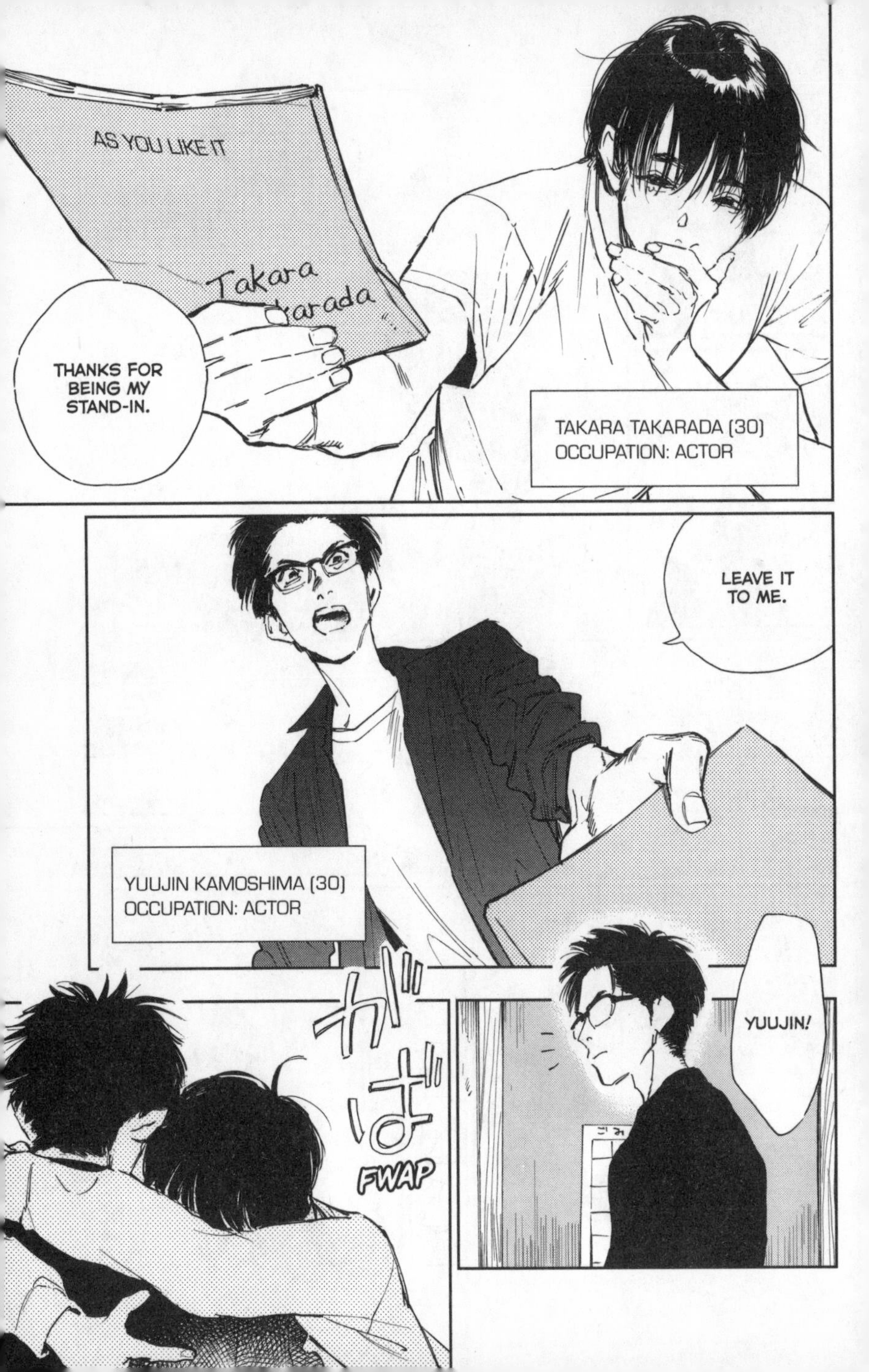
AS YOU LIKE IT
Takara Takarada
THANKS FOR BEING MY STAND-IN.
TAKARA TAKARADA (30)
OCCUPATION: ACTOR
LEAVE IT TO ME.
YUUJIN KAMOSHIMA (30)
OCCUPATION: ACTOR
YUUJIN!
ごみ
がば
FWAP

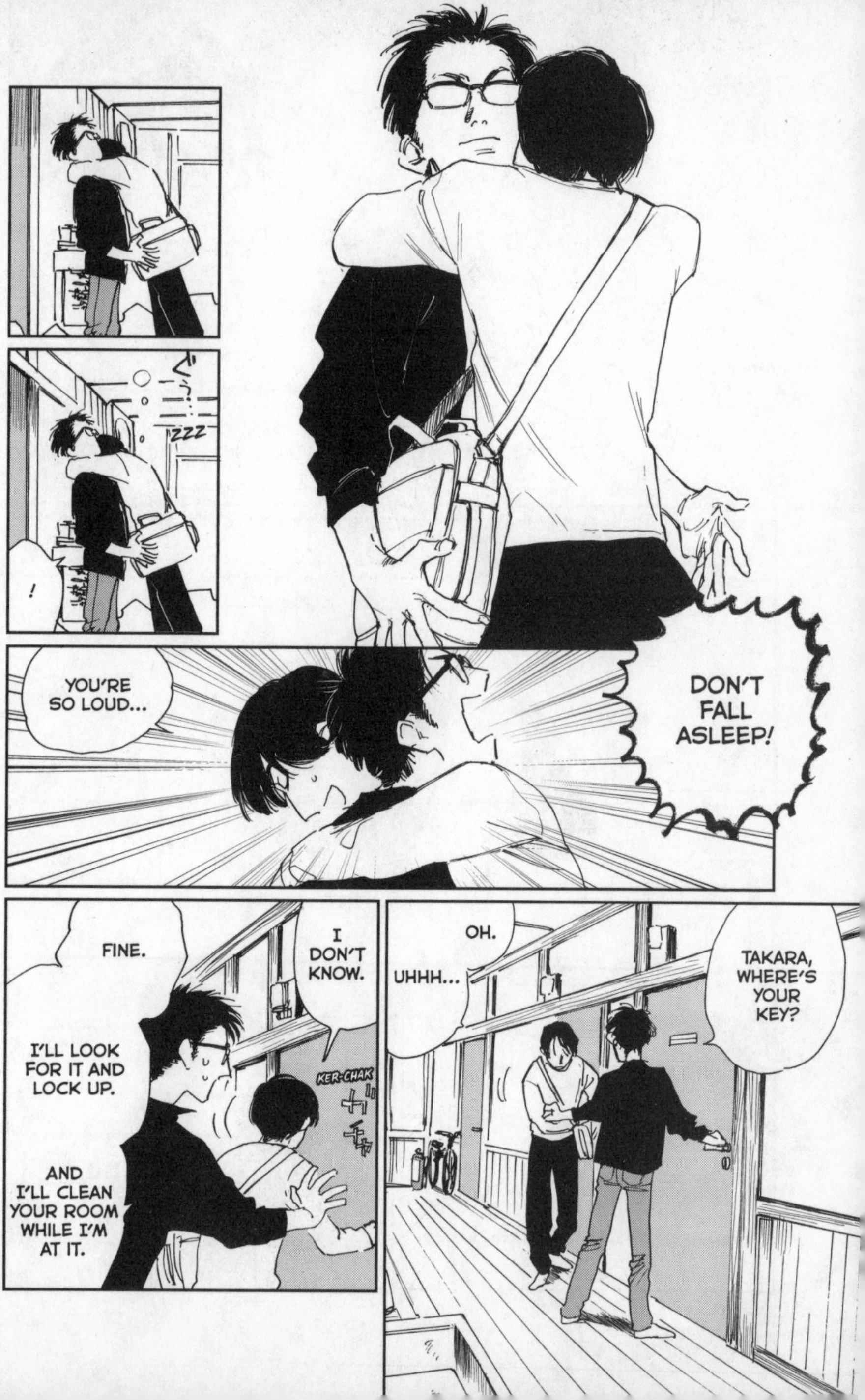
ZZZ
!
DON'T FALL ASLEEP!
YOU'RE SO LOUD...
TAKARA, WHERE'S YOUR KEY?
OH.
UHHH...
I DON'T KNOW.
KER-CHAK
FINE.
I'LL LOOK FOR IT AND LOCK UP.
AND I'LL CLEAN YOUR ROOM WHILE I'M AT IT.

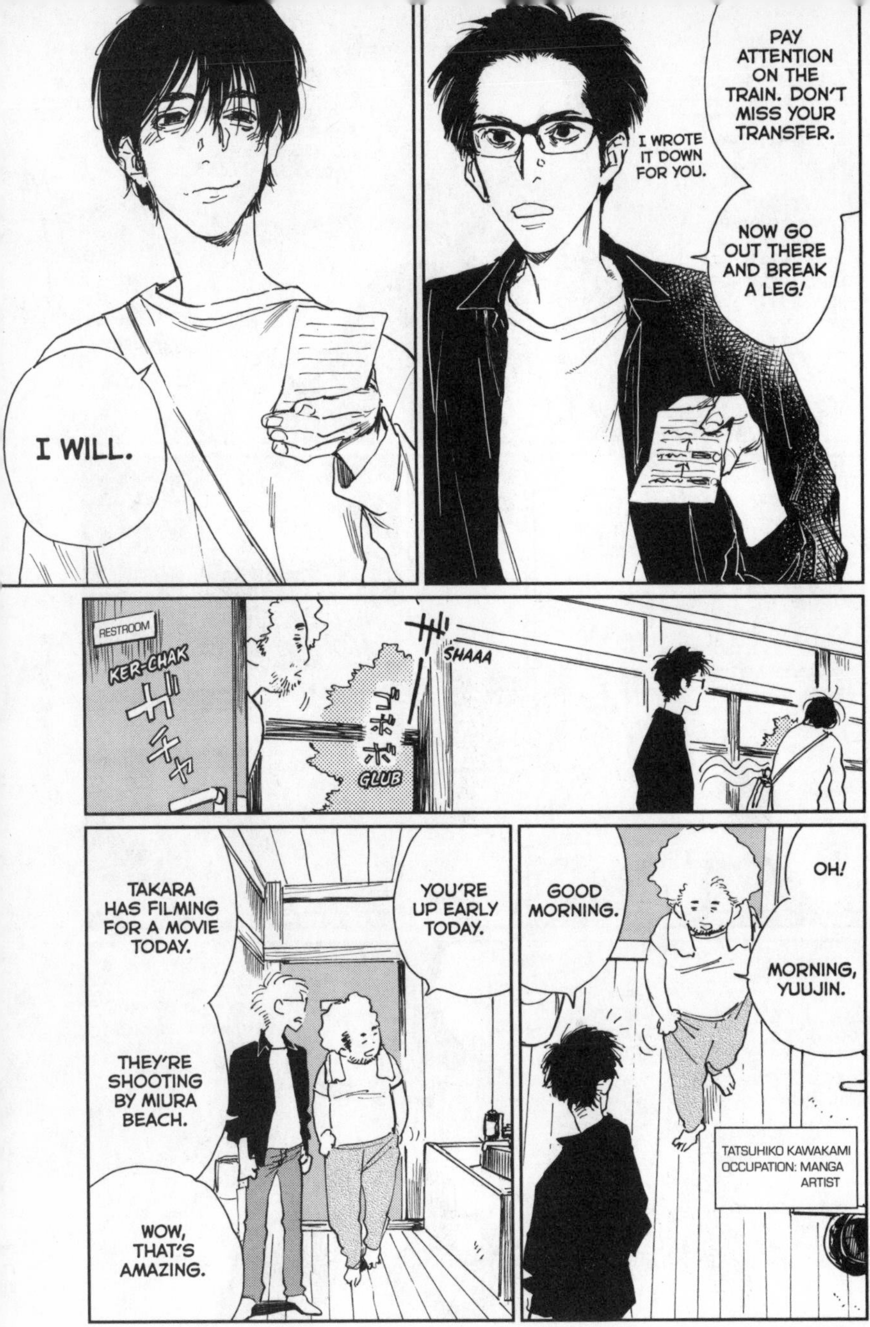
PAY ATTENTION ON THE TRAIN. DON'T MISS YOUR TRANSFER.
I WROTE IT DOWN FOR YOU.
NOW GO OUT THERE AND BREAK A LEG!
I WILL.
SHAAA
ゴボボ
GLUB
RESTROOM
KER-CHAK
ガチャ
OH!
MORNING, YUUJIN.
GOOD MORNING.
TATSUHIKO KAWAKAMI OCCUPATION: MANGA ARTIST
YOU'RE UP EARLY TODAY.
TAKARA HAS FILMING FOR A MOVIE TODAY.
THEY'RE SHOOTING BY MIURA BEACH.
WOW, THAT'S AMAZING.

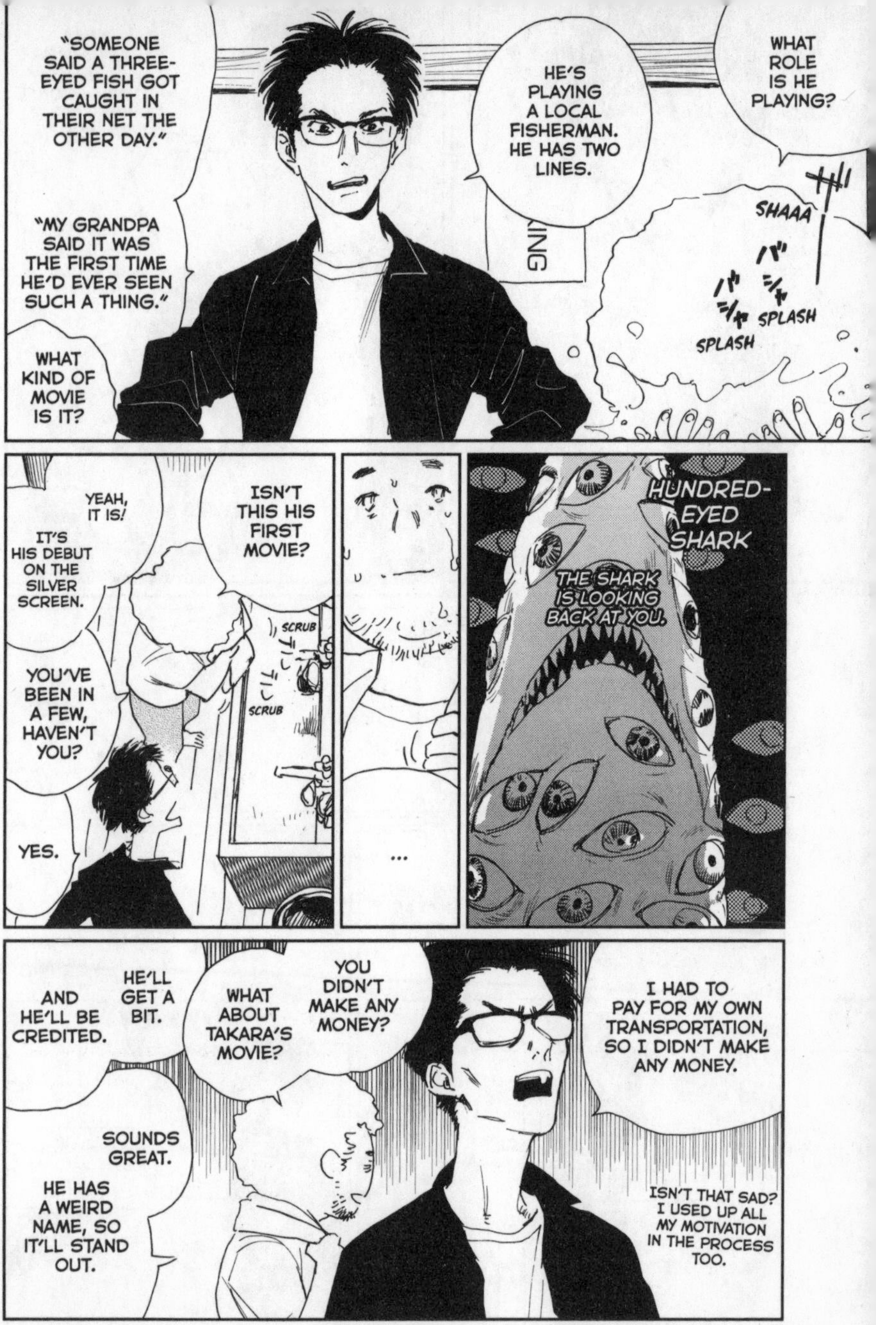
WHAT ROLE IS HE PLAYING?
HE'S PLAYING A LOCAL FISHERMAN. HE HAS TWO LINES.
SHAAA
SPLASH
SPLASH
"SOMEONE SAID A THREE-EYED FISH GOT CAUGHT IN THEIR NET THE OTHER DAY."
"MY GRANDPA SAID IT WAS THE FIRST TIME HE'D EVER SEEN SUCH A THING."
WHAT KIND OF MOVIE IS IT?
HUNDRED-EYED SHARK
THE SHARK IS LOOKING BACK AT YOU.
...
ISN'T THIS HIS FIRST MOVIE?
YEAH, IT IS!
IT'S HIS DEBUT ON THE SILVER SCREEN.
SCRUB
SCRUB
YOU'VE BEEN IN A FEW, HAVEN'T YOU?
YES.
I HAD TO PAY FOR MY OWN TRANSPORTATION, SO I DIDN'T MAKE ANY MONEY.
YOU DIDN'T MAKE ANY MONEY?
WHAT ABOUT TAKARA'S MOVIE?
HE'LL GET A BIT.
AND HE'LL BE CREDITED.
ISN'T THAT SAD? I USED UP ALL MY MOTIVATION IN THE PROCESS TOO.
SOUNDS GREAT.
HE HAS A WEIRD NAME, SO IT'LL STAND OUT.

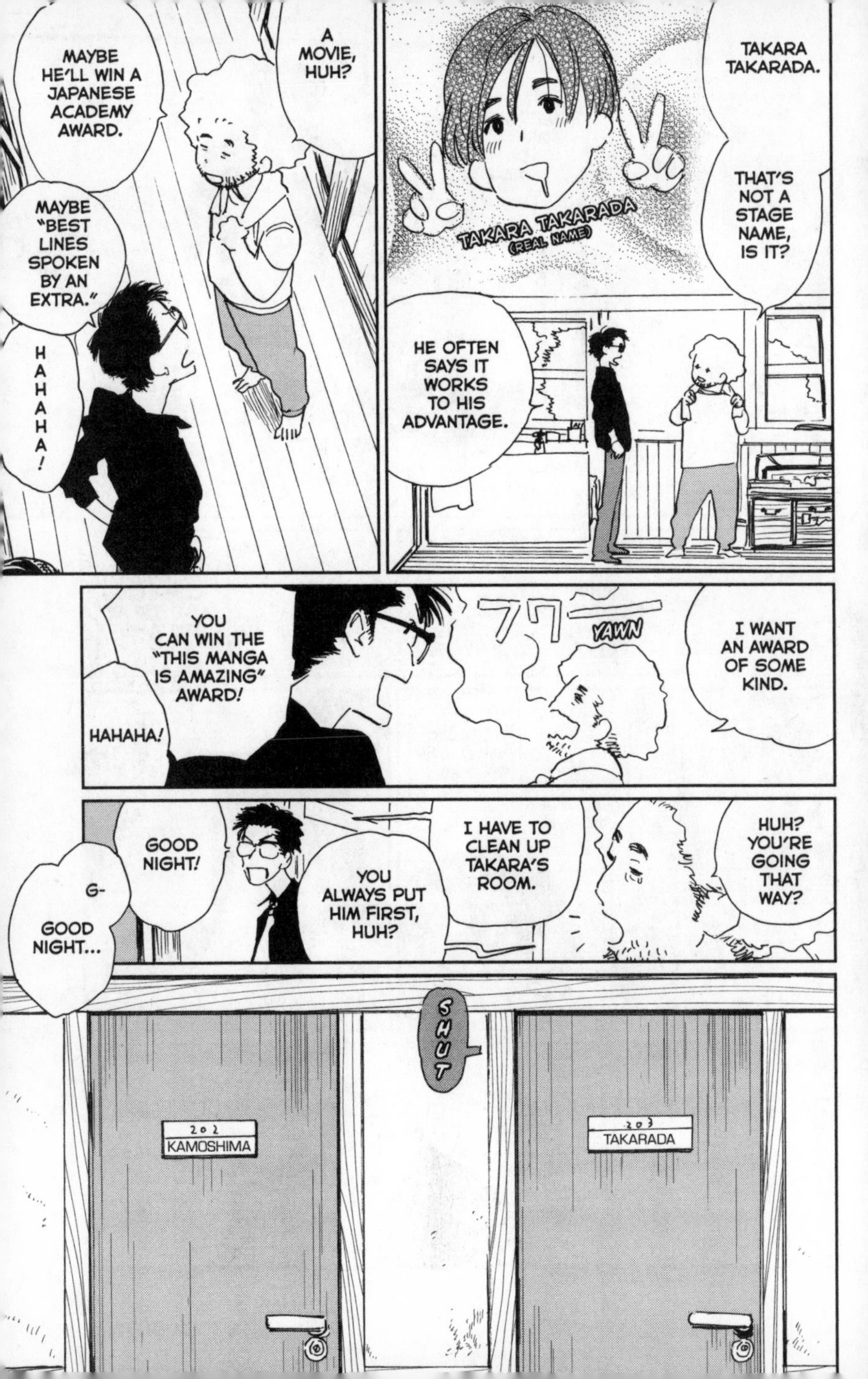
TAKARA TAKARADA.
THAT'S NOT A STAGE NAME, IS IT?
TAKARA TAKARADA (REAL NAME)
HE OFTEN SAYS IT WORKS TO HIS ADVANTAGE.
A MOVIE, HUH?
MAYBE HE'LL WIN A JAPANESE ACADEMY AWARD.
MAYBE "BEST LINES SPOKEN BY AN EXTRA."
HAHAHAHA!
YAWN
I WANT AN AWARD OF SOME KIND.
YOU CAN WIN THE "THIS MANGA IS AMAZING" AWARD!
HAHAHA!
HUH? YOU'RE GOING THAT WAY?
I HAVE TO CLEAN UP TAKARA'S ROOM.
YOU ALWAYS PUT HIM FIRST, HUH?
GOOD NIGHT!
G- GOOD NIGHT...
SHUT
203
TAKARADA
202
KAMOSHIMA

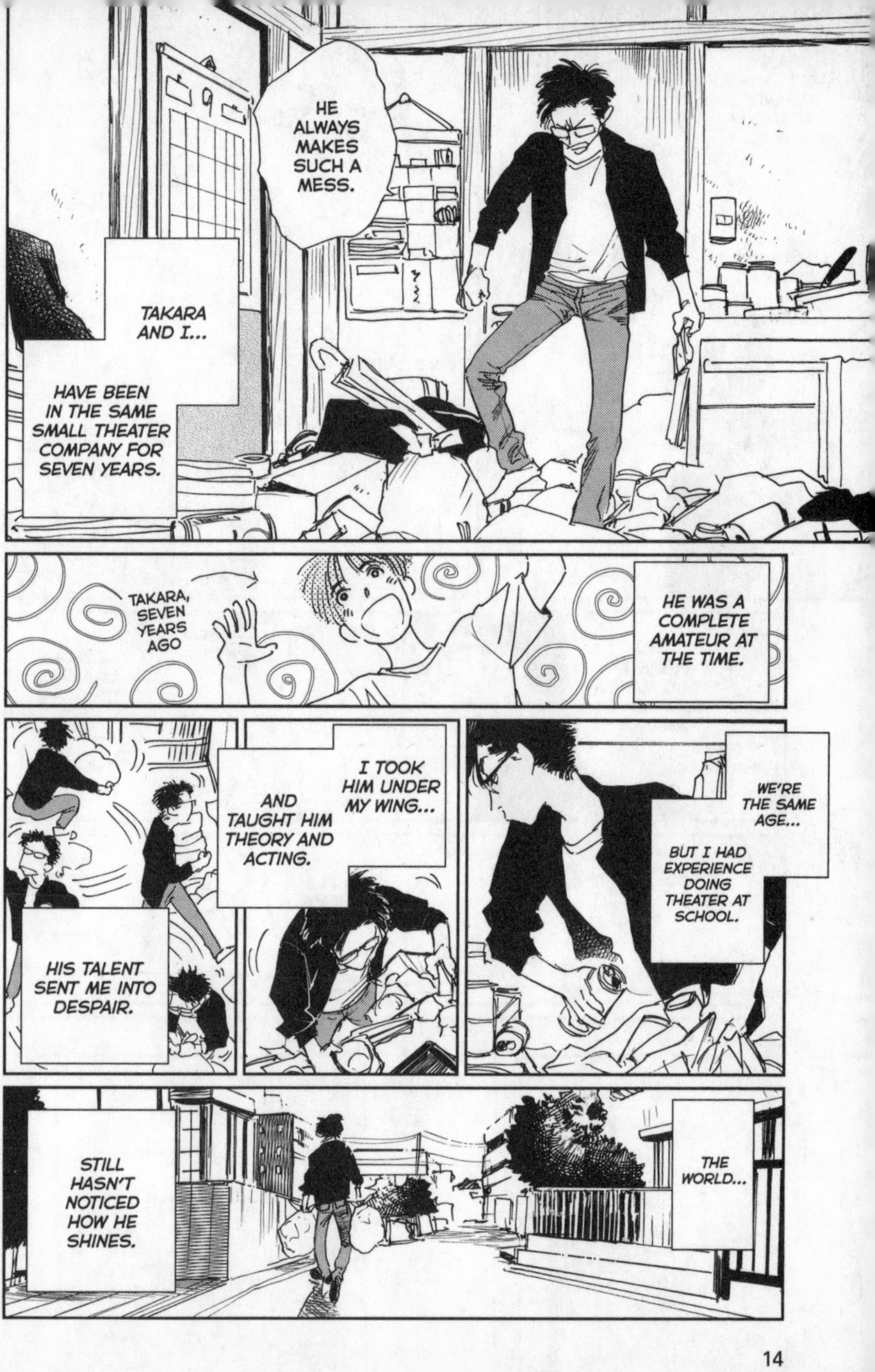
HE ALWAYS MAKES SUCH A MESS.
TAKARA AND I...
HAVE BEEN IN THE SAME SMALL THEATER COMPANY FOR SEVEN YEARS.
HE WAS A COMPLETE AMATEUR AT THE TIME.
TAKARA, SEVEN YEARS AGO
WE'RE THE SAME AGE...
BUT I HAD EXPERIENCE DOING THEATER AT SCHOOL.
I TOOK HIM UNDER MY WING...
AND TAUGHT HIM THEORY AND ACTING.
HIS TALENT SENT ME INTO DESPAIR.
THE WORLD...
STILL HASN'T NOTICED HOW HE SHINES.

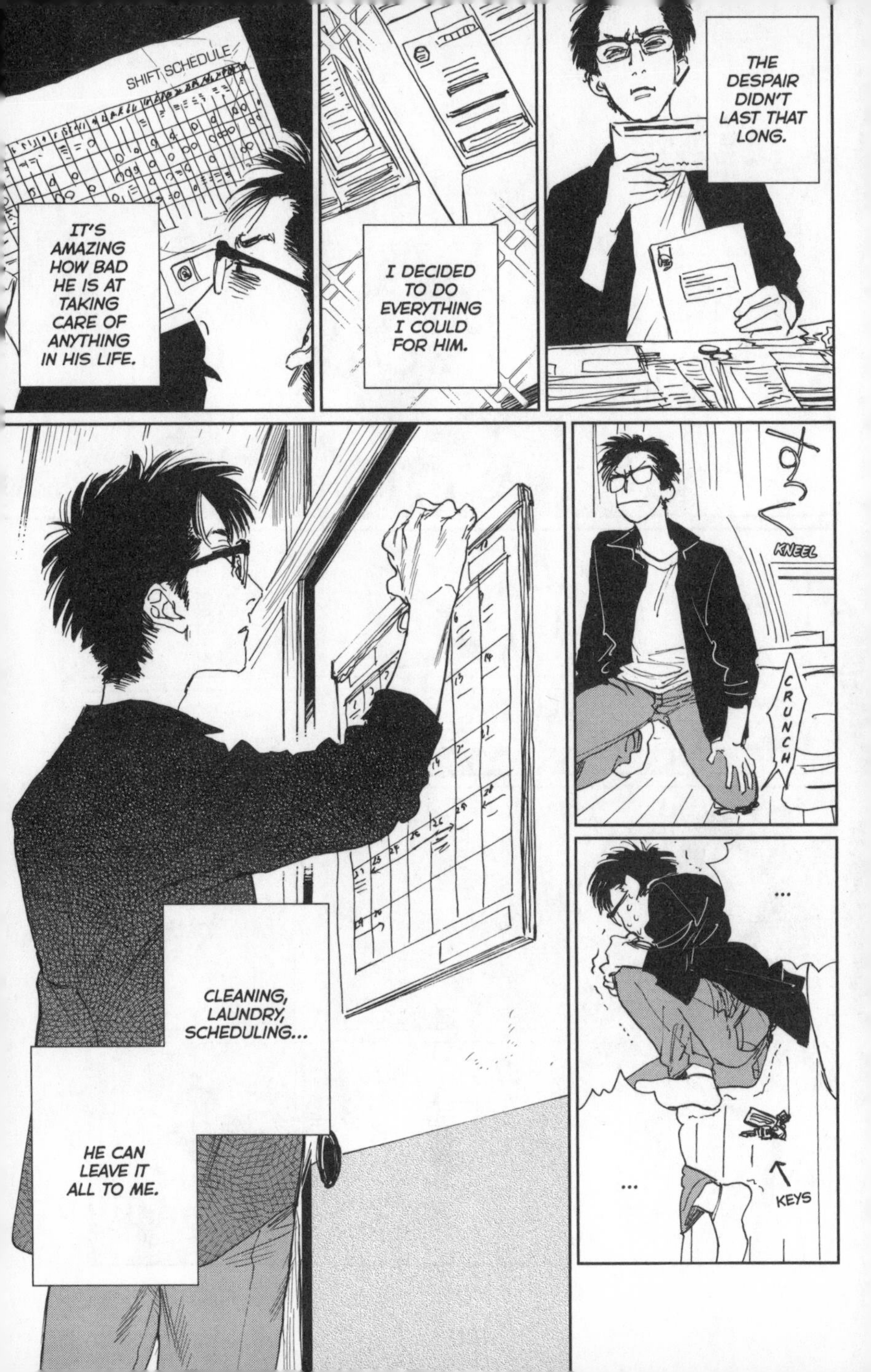
THE DESPAIR DIDN'T LAST THAT LONG.
I DECIDED TO DO EVERYTHING I COULD FOR HIM.
SHIFT SCHEDULE
IT'S AMAZING HOW BAD HE IS AT TAKING CARE OF ANYTHING IN HIS LIFE.
KNEEL
CRUNCH
...
...
KEYS
CLEANING, LAUNDRY, SCHEDULING...
HE CAN LEAVE IT ALL TO ME.

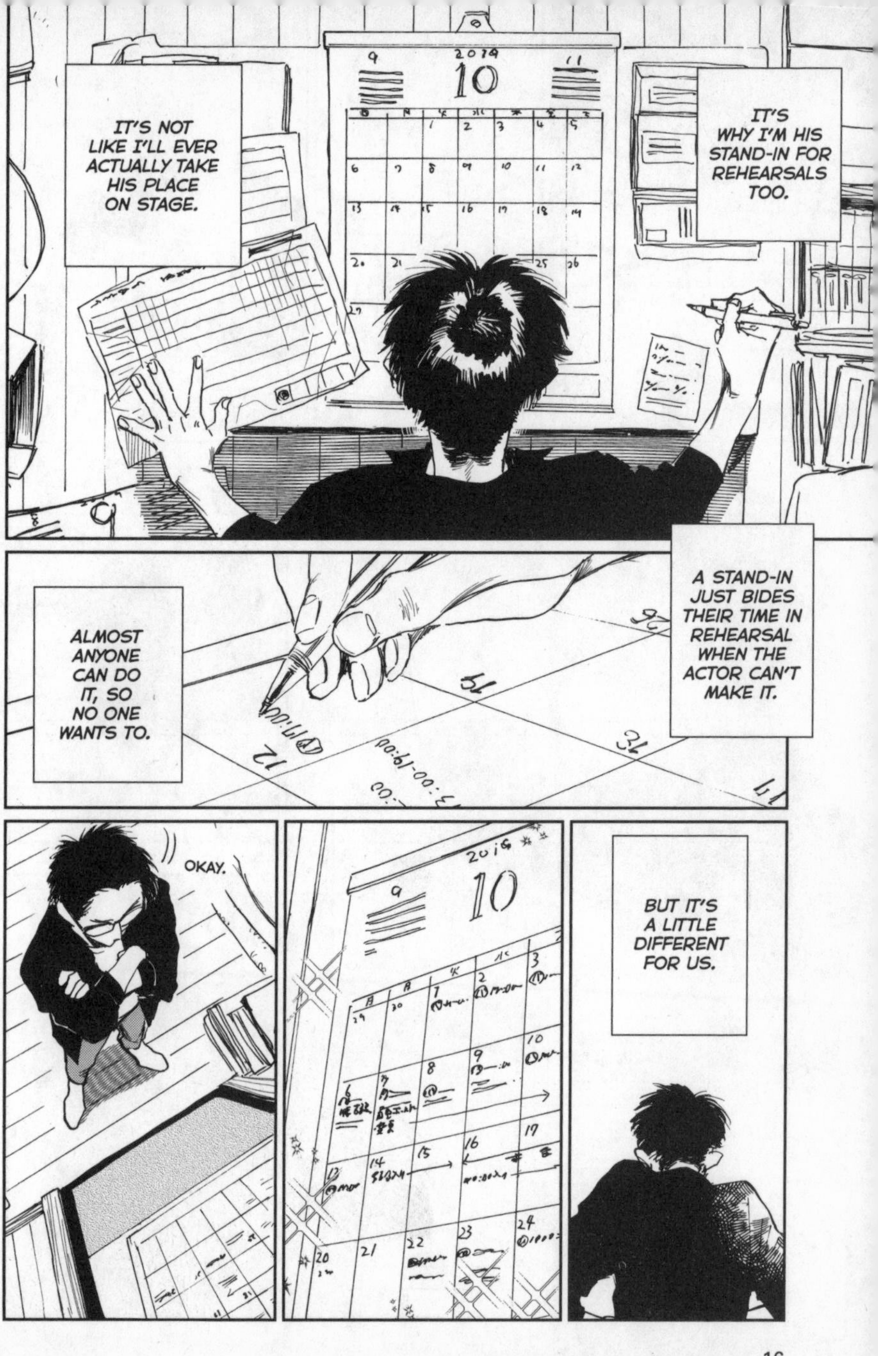
IT'S WHY I'M HIS STAND-IN FOR REHEARSALS TOO.
IT'S NOT LIKE I'LL EVER ACTUALLY TAKE HIS PLACE ON STAGE.
A STAND-IN JUST BIDES THEIR TIME IN REHEARSAL WHEN THE ACTOR CAN'T MAKE IT.
ALMOST ANYONE CAN DO IT, SO NO ONE WANTS TO.
BUT IT'S A LITTLE DIFFERENT FOR US.
OKAY.

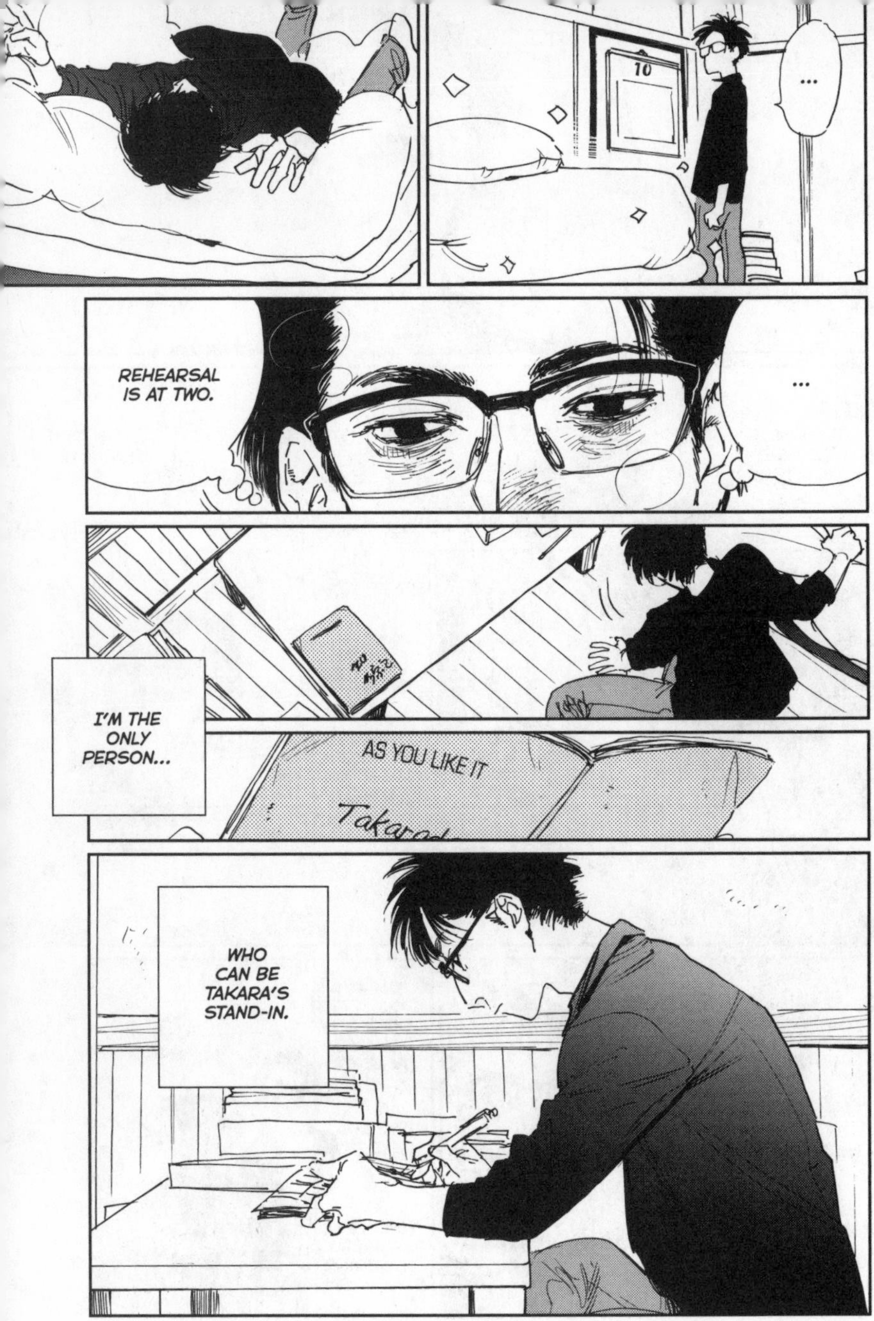
...
...
REHEARSAL IS AT TWO.
I'M THE ONLY PERSON...
AS YOU LIKE IT
WHO CAN BE TAKARA'S STAND-IN.

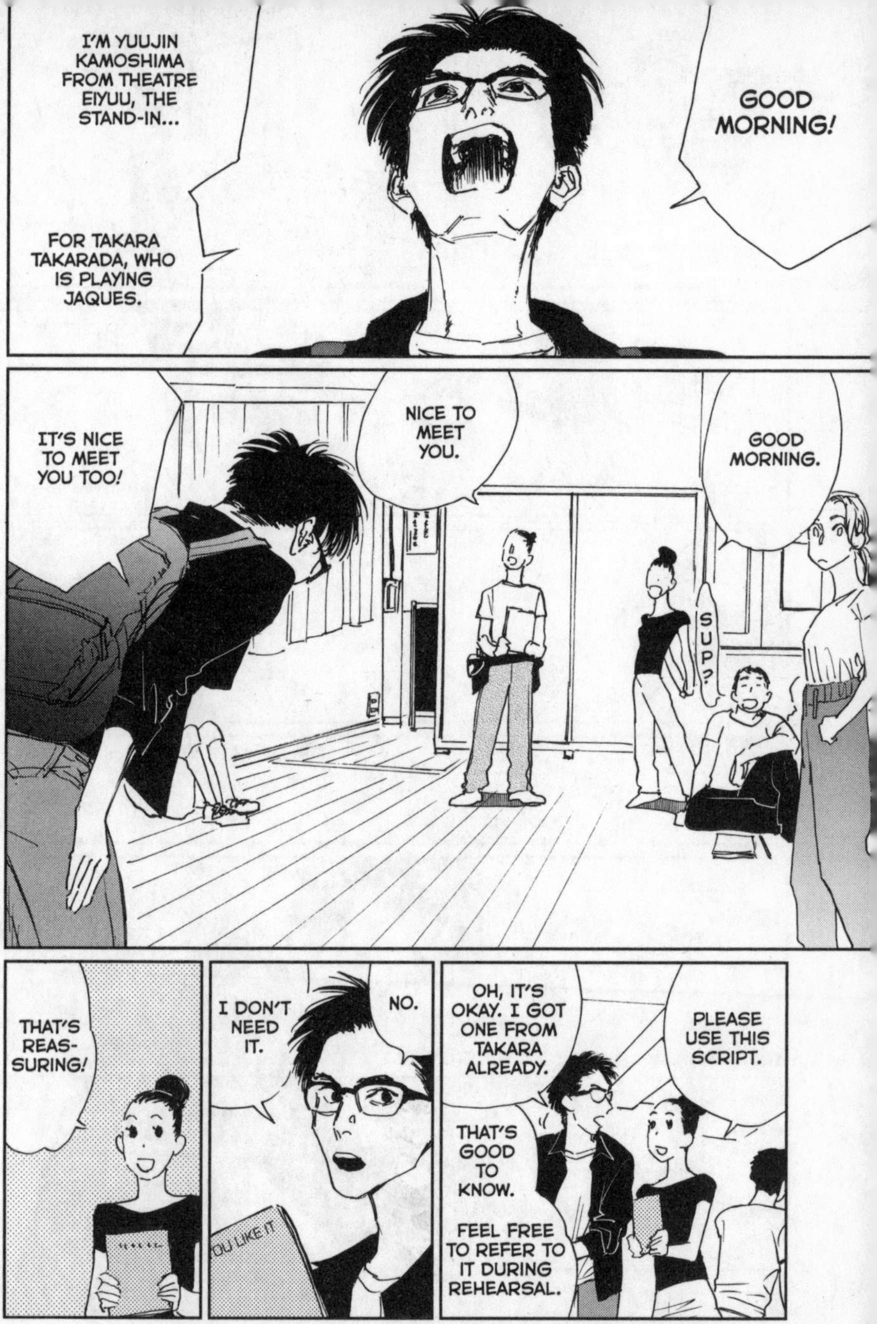
GOOD MORNING!
I'M YUUJIN KAMOSHIMA FROM THEATRE EIYUU, THE STAND-IN...
FOR TAKARA TAKARADA, WHO IS PLAYING JAQUES.
GOOD MORNING.
SUP?
NICE TO MEET YOU.
IT'S NICE TO MEET YOU TOO!
PLEASE USE THIS SCRIPT.
OH, IT'S OKAY. I GOT ONE FROM TAKARA ALREADY.
THAT'S GOOD TO KNOW.
FEEL FREE TO REFER TO IT DURING REHEARSAL.
NO.
I DON'T NEED IT.
OU LIKE IT
THAT'S REAS-SURING!

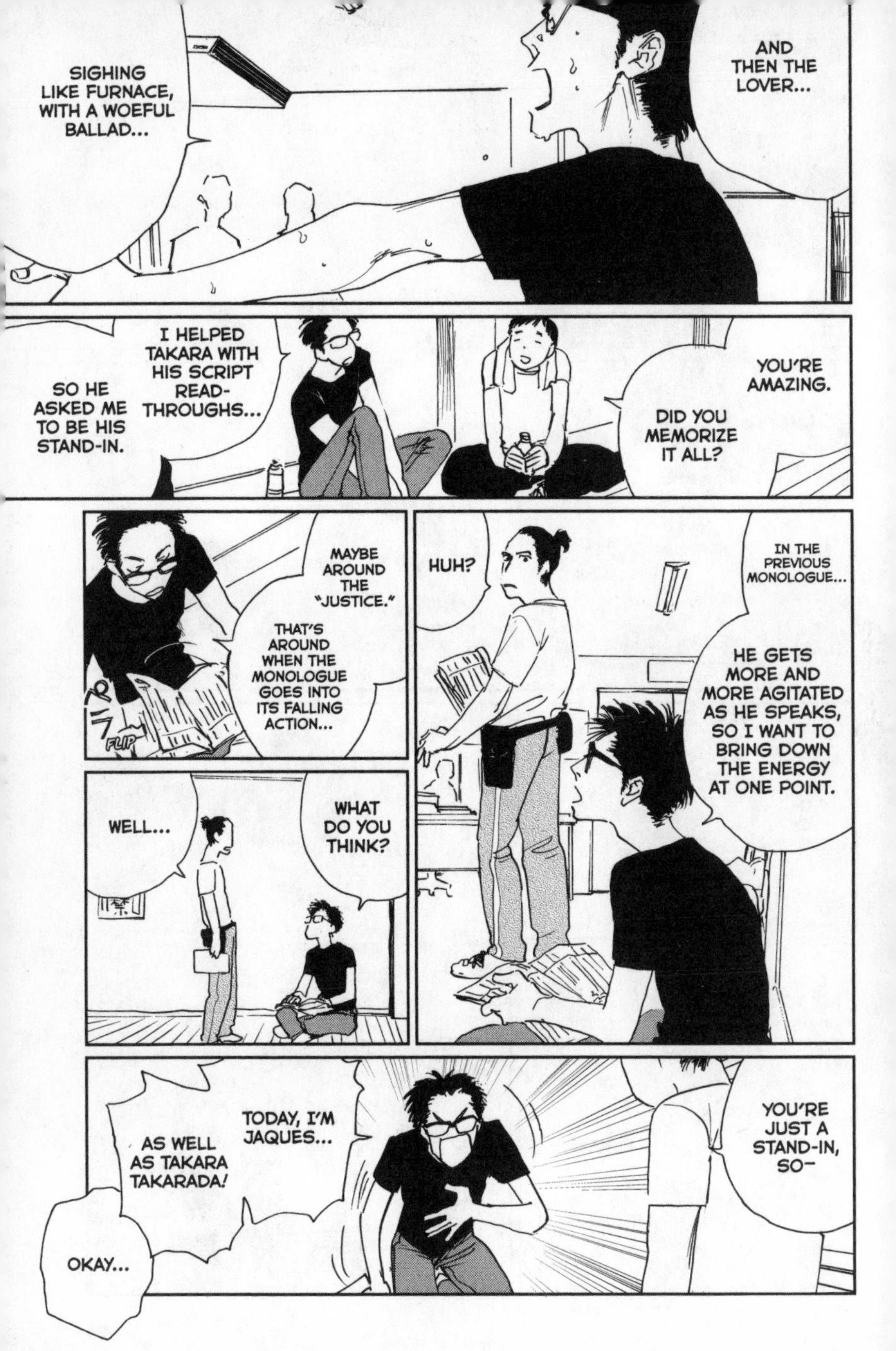
AND THEN THE LOVER...
SIGHING LIKE FURNACE, WITH A WOEFUL BALLAD...
YOU'RE AMAZING.
DID YOU MEMORIZE IT ALL?
I HELPED TAKARA WITH HIS SCRIPT READ-THROUGHS...
SO HE ASKED ME TO BE HIS STAND-IN.
IN THE PREVIOUS MONOLOGUE...
HUH?
HE GETS MORE AND MORE AGITATED AS HE SPEAKS, SO I WANT TO BRING DOWN THE ENERGY AT ONE POINT.
MAYBE AROUND THE "JUSTICE."
THAT'S AROUND WHEN THE MONOLOGUE GOES INTO ITS FALLING ACTION...
FLIP
WHAT DO YOU THINK?
WELL...
YOU'RE JUST A STAND-IN, SO—
TODAY, I'M JAQUES...
AS WELL AS TAKARA TAKARADA!
OKAY...

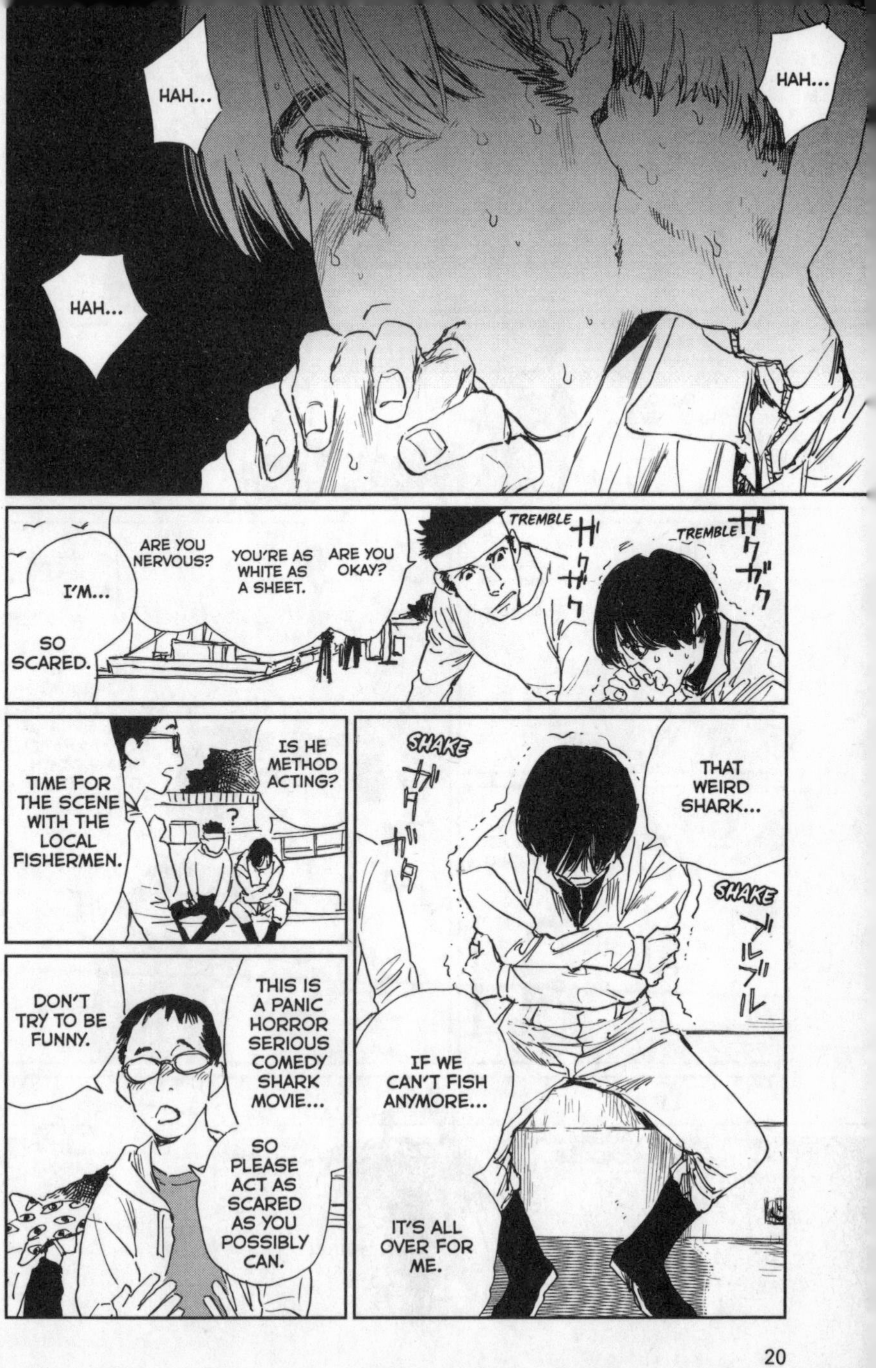
HAH...
HAH...
HAH...
TREMBLE
ガクガク
TREMBLE
ガクガク
ARE YOU OKAY?
YOU'RE AS WHITE AS A SHEET.
ARE YOU NERVOUS?
I'M...
SO SCARED.
THAT WEIRD SHARK...
SHAKE
ブルブル
SHAKE
ガタガタ
IF WE CAN'T FISH ANYMORE...
IT'S ALL OVER FOR ME.
IS HE METHOD ACTING?
TIME FOR THE SCENE WITH THE LOCAL FISHERMEN.
?
THIS IS A PANIC HORROR SERIOUS COMEDY SHARK MOVIE...
DON'T TRY TO BE FUNNY.
SO PLEASE ACT AS SCARED AS YOU POSSIBLY CAN.

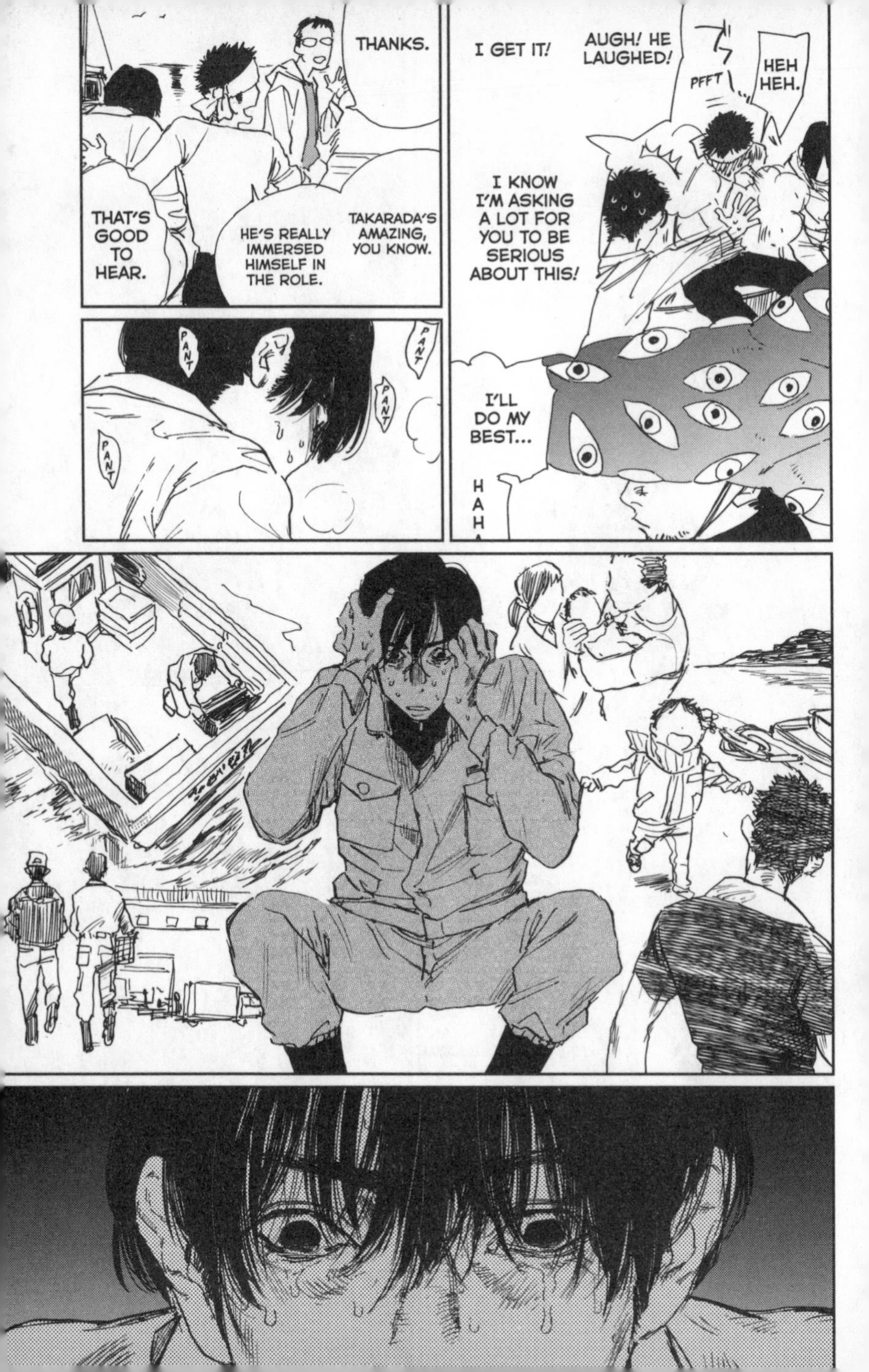
HEH HEH.
PFFT
AUGH! HE LAUGHED!
I GET IT!
I KNOW I'M ASKING A LOT FOR YOU TO BE SERIOUS ABOUT THIS!
I'LL DO MY BEST...
HAH
THANKS.
TAKARADA'S AMAZING, YOU KNOW.
HE'S REALLY IMMERSED HIMSELF IN THE ROLE.
THAT'S GOOD TO HEAR.
PANT
PANT
PANT

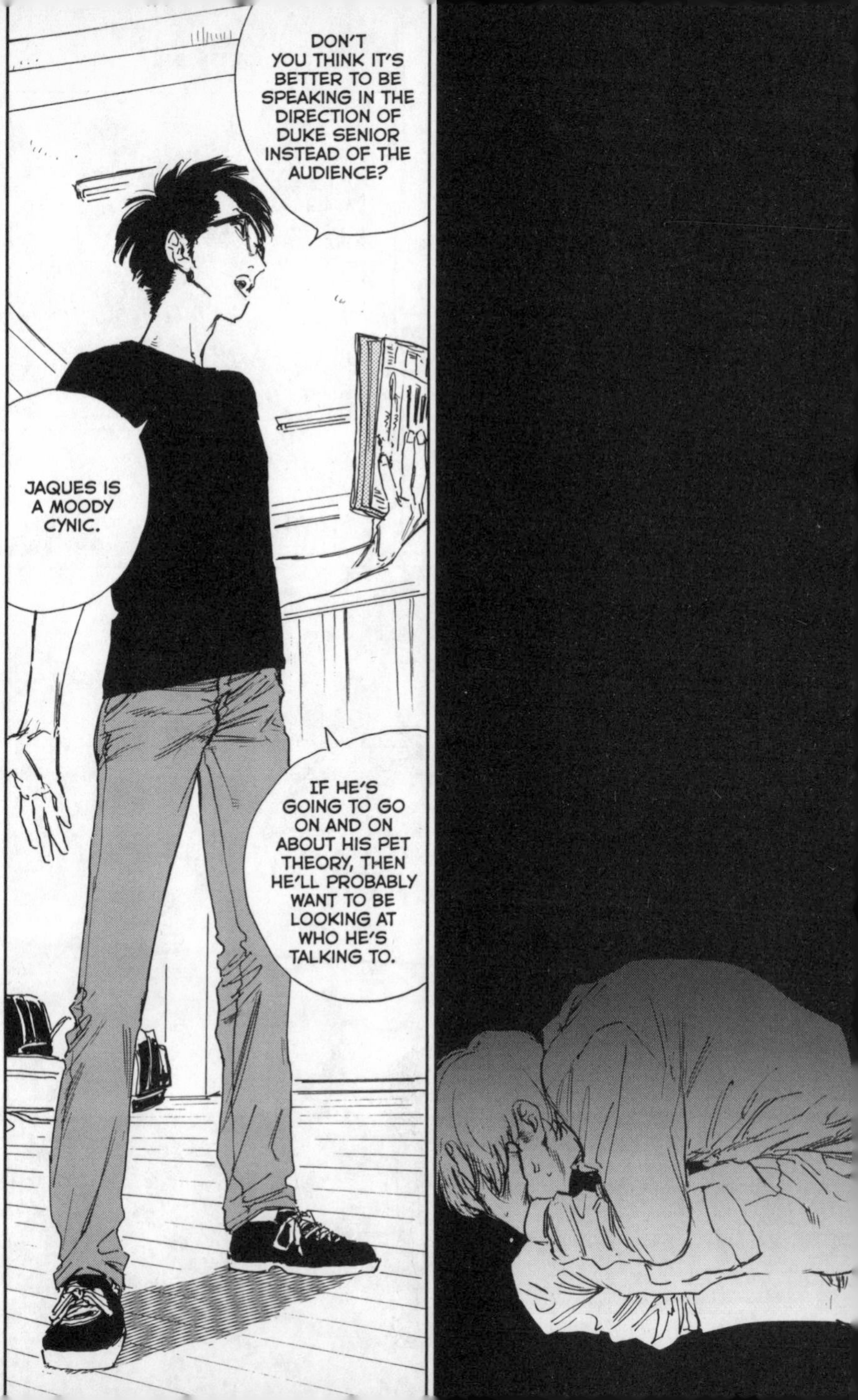
DON'T YOU THINK IT'S BETTER TO BE SPEAKING IN THE DIRECTION OF DUKE SENIOR INSTEAD OF THE AUDIENCE?
JAQUES IS A MOODY CYNIC.
IF HE'S GOING TO GO ON AND ON ABOUT HIS PET THEORY, THEN HE'LL PROBABLY WANT TO BE LOOKING AT WHO HE'S TALKING TO.

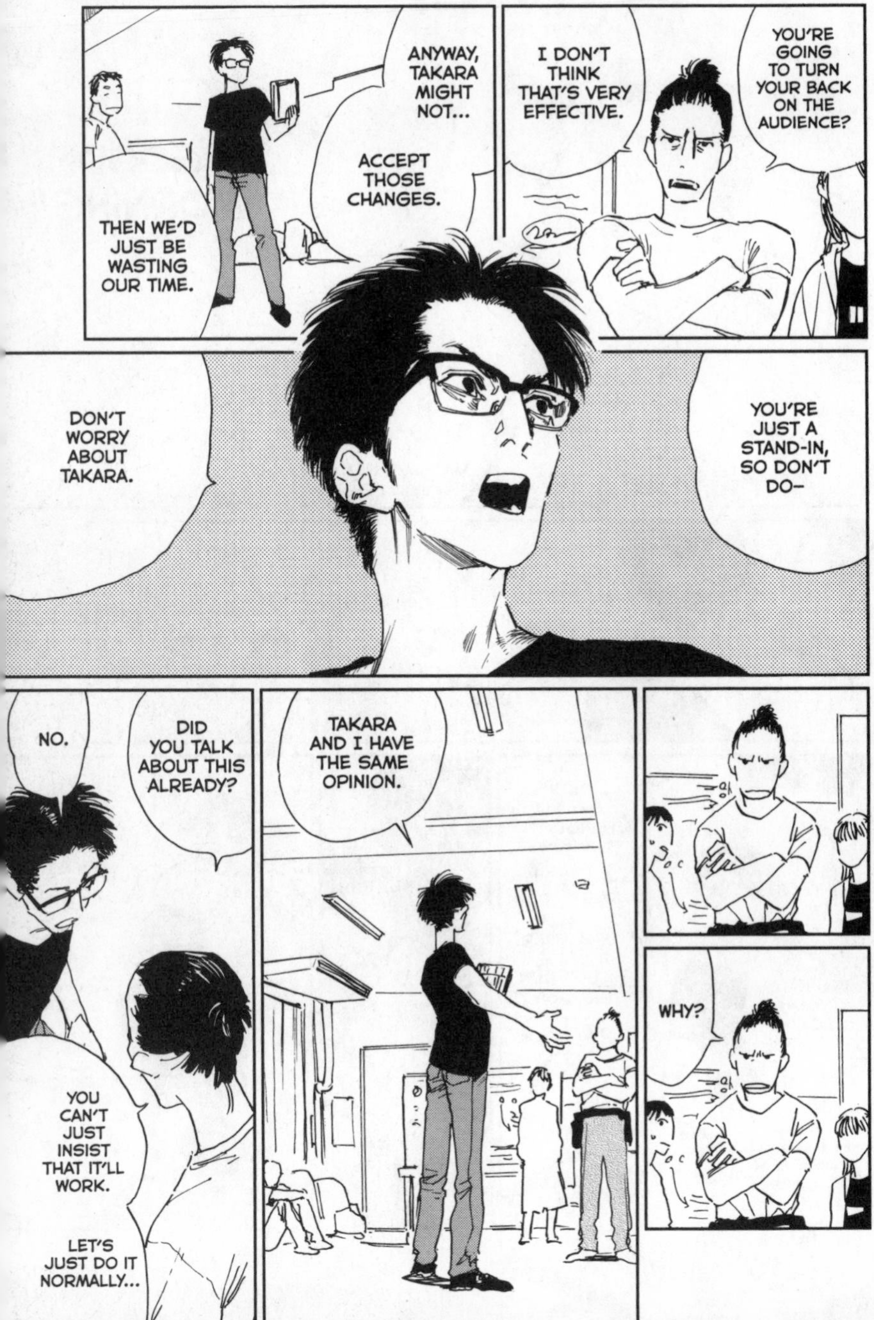
YOU'RE GOING TO TURN YOUR BACK ON THE AUDIENCE?
I DON'T THINK THAT'S VERY EFFECTIVE.
ANYWAY, TAKARA MIGHT NOT...
ACCEPT THOSE CHANGES.
THEN WE'D JUST BE WASTING OUR TIME.
YOU'RE JUST A STAND-IN, SO DON'T DO–
DON'T WORRY ABOUT TAKARA.
WHY?
TAKARA AND I HAVE THE SAME OPINION.
DID YOU TALK ABOUT THIS ALREADY?
NO.
YOU CAN'T JUST INSIST THAT IT'LL WORK.
LET'S JUST DO IT NORMALLY...

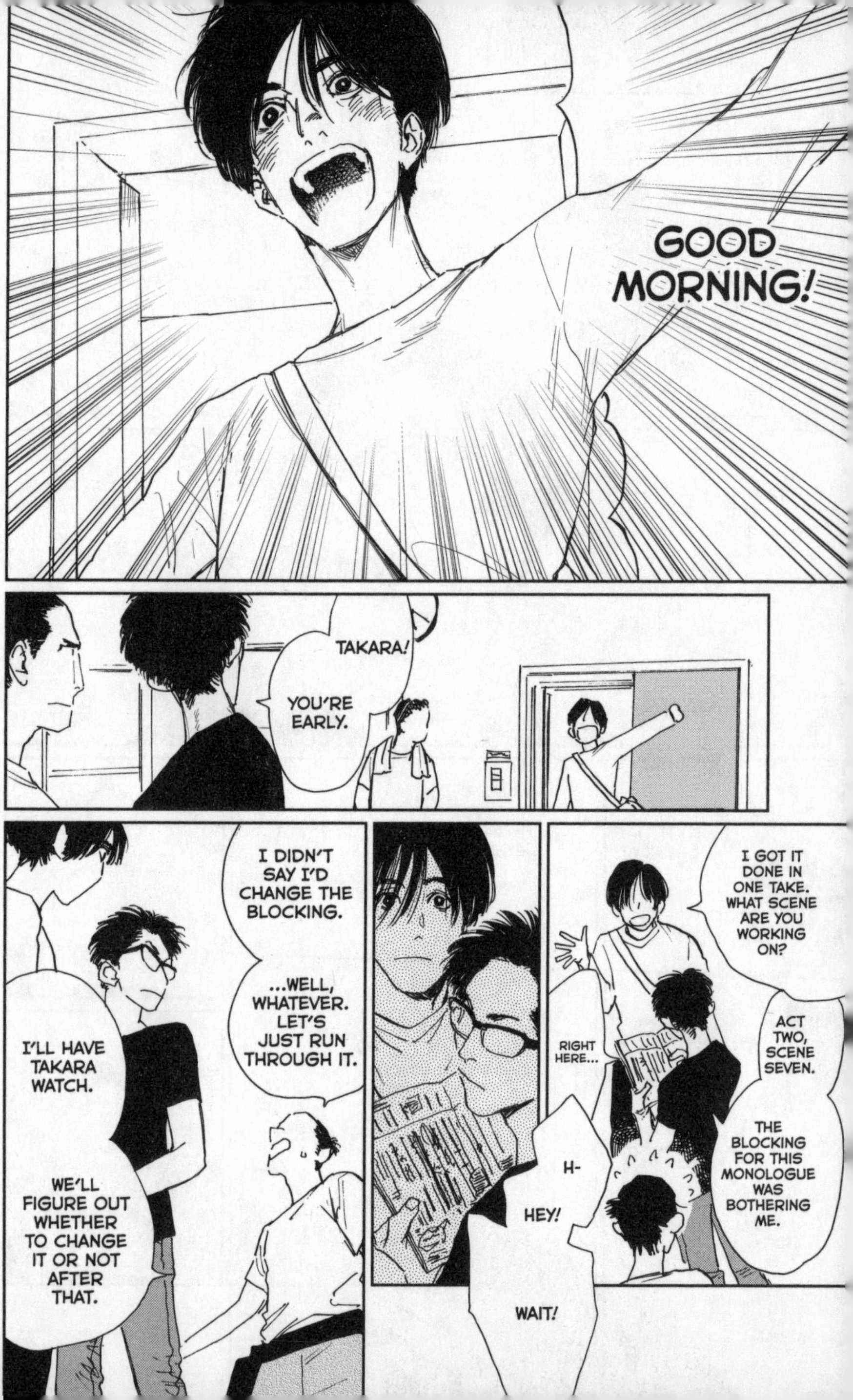
GOOD MORNING!
TAKARA!
YOU'RE EARLY.
I GOT IT DONE IN ONE TAKE. WHAT SCENE ARE YOU WORKING ON?
ACT TWO, SCENE SEVEN.
THE BLOCKING FOR THIS MONOLOGUE WAS BOTHERING ME.
RIGHT HERE...
H-
HEY!
WAIT!
I DIDN'T SAY I'D CHANGE THE BLOCKING.
...WELL, WHATEVER. LET'S JUST RUN THROUGH IT.
I'LL HAVE TAKARA WATCH.
WE'LL FIGURE OUT WHETHER TO CHANGE IT OR NOT AFTER THAT.

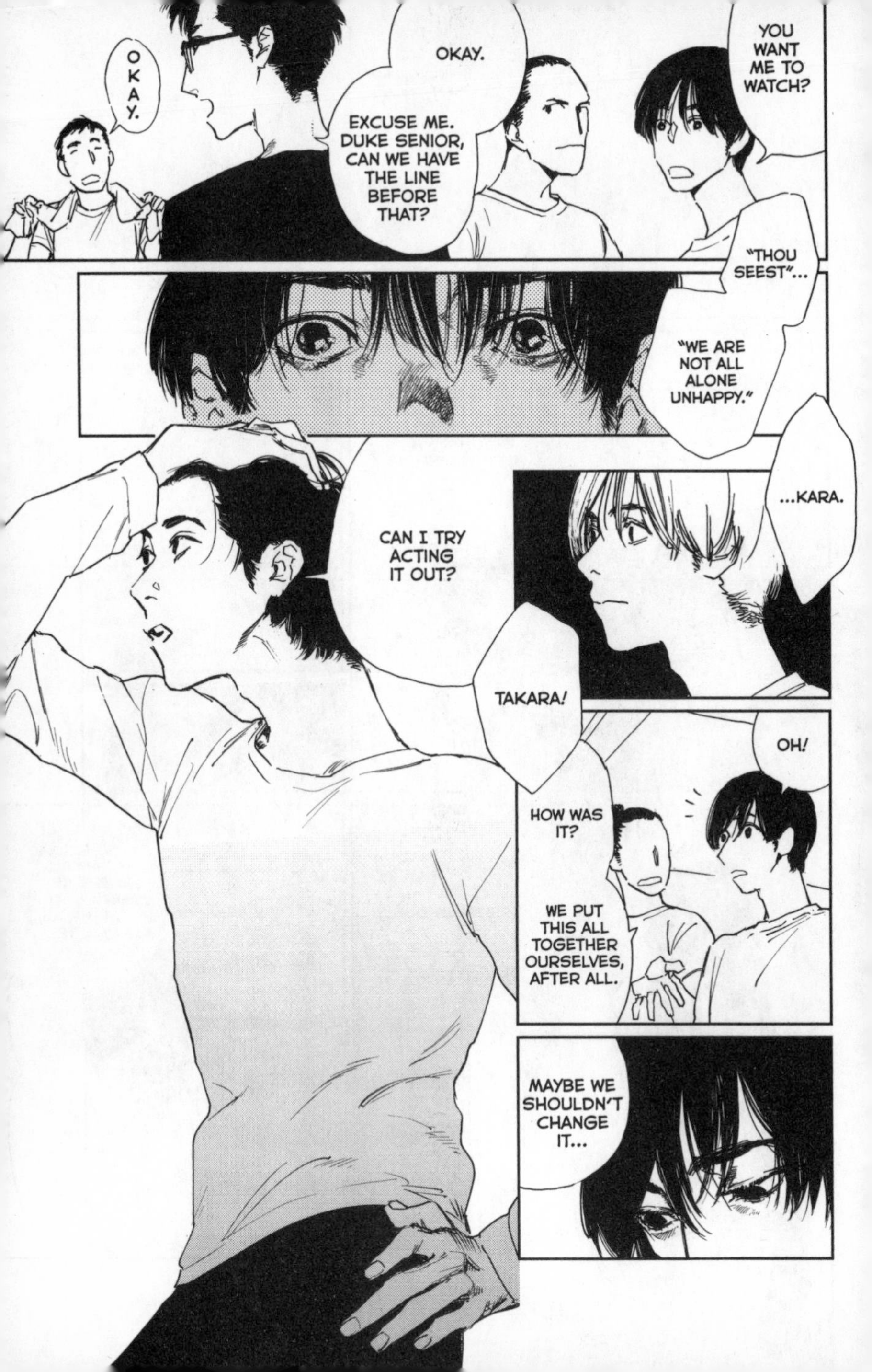
YOU WANT ME TO WATCH?
OKAY.
EXCUSE ME. DUKE SENIOR, CAN WE HAVE THE LINE BEFORE THAT?
OKAY.
"THOU SEEST"...
"WE ARE NOT ALL ALONE UNHAPPY."
...KARA.
TAKARA!
OH!
HOW WAS IT?
WE PUT THIS ALL TOGETHER OURSELVES, AFTER ALL.
MAYBE WE SHOULDN'T CHANGE IT...
CAN I TRY ACTING IT OUT?

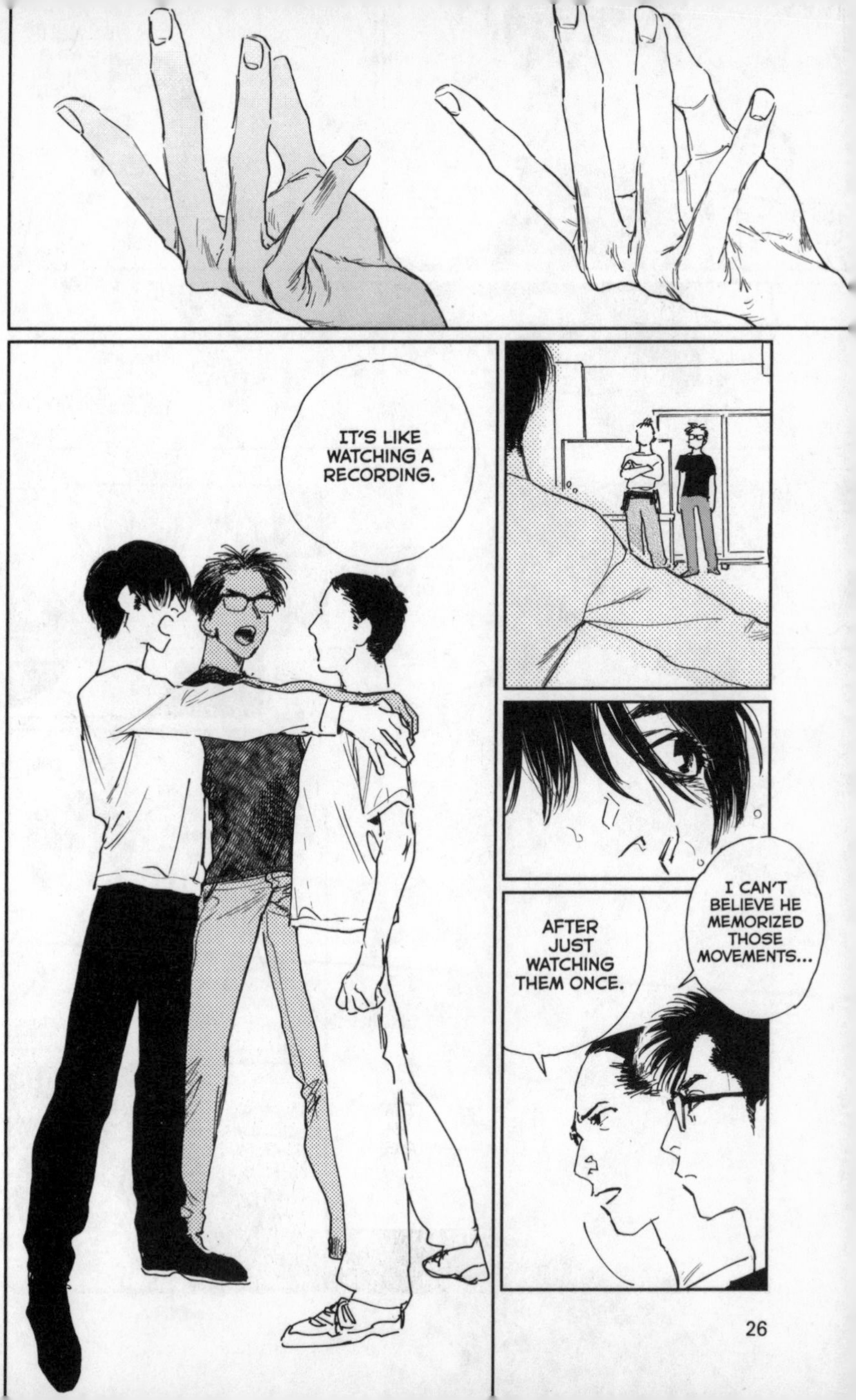
I CAN'T BELIEVE HE MEMORIZED THOSE MOVEMENTS...
AFTER JUST WATCHING THEM ONCE.
IT'S LIKE WATCHING A RECORDING.

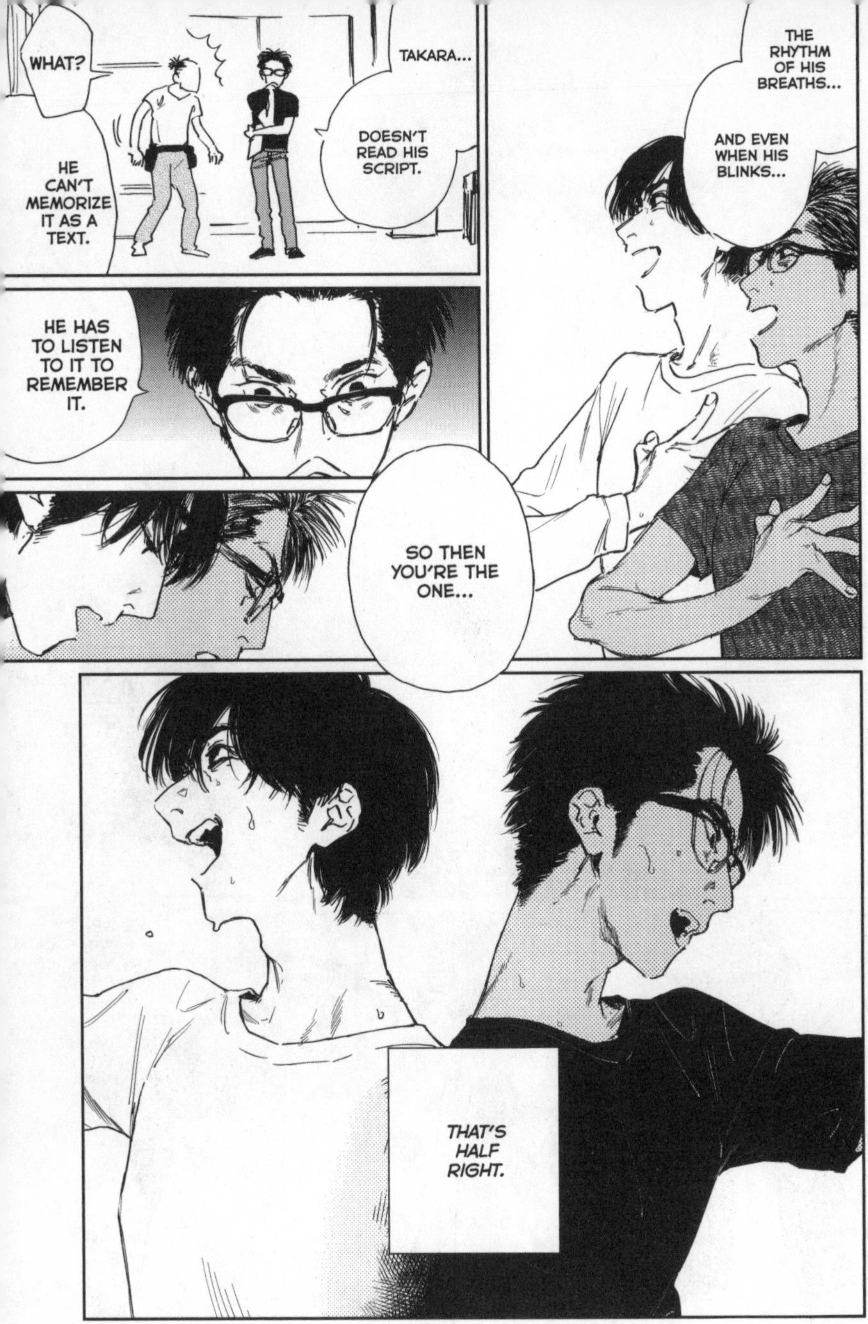
THE RHYTHM OF HIS BREATHS...
AND EVEN WHEN HIS BLINKS...
TAKARA...
DOESN'T READ HIS SCRIPT.
WHAT?
HE CAN'T MEMORIZE IT AS A TEXT.
HE HAS TO LISTEN TO IT TO REMEMBER IT.
SO THEN YOU'RE THE ONE...
THAT'S HALF RIGHT.

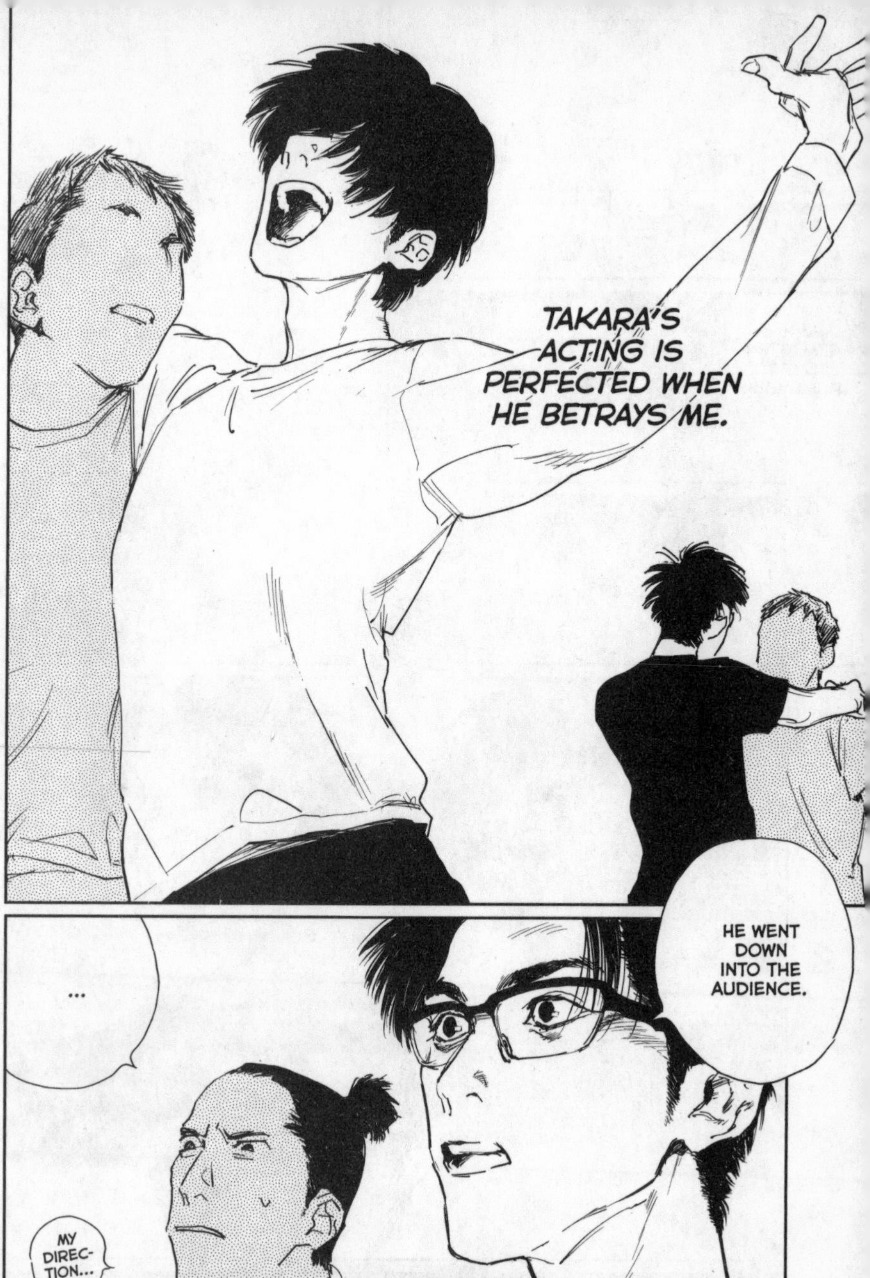
TAKARA'S ACTING IS PERFECTED WHEN HE BETRAYS ME.
HE WENT DOWN INTO THE AUDIENCE.
...
MY DIRECTION...

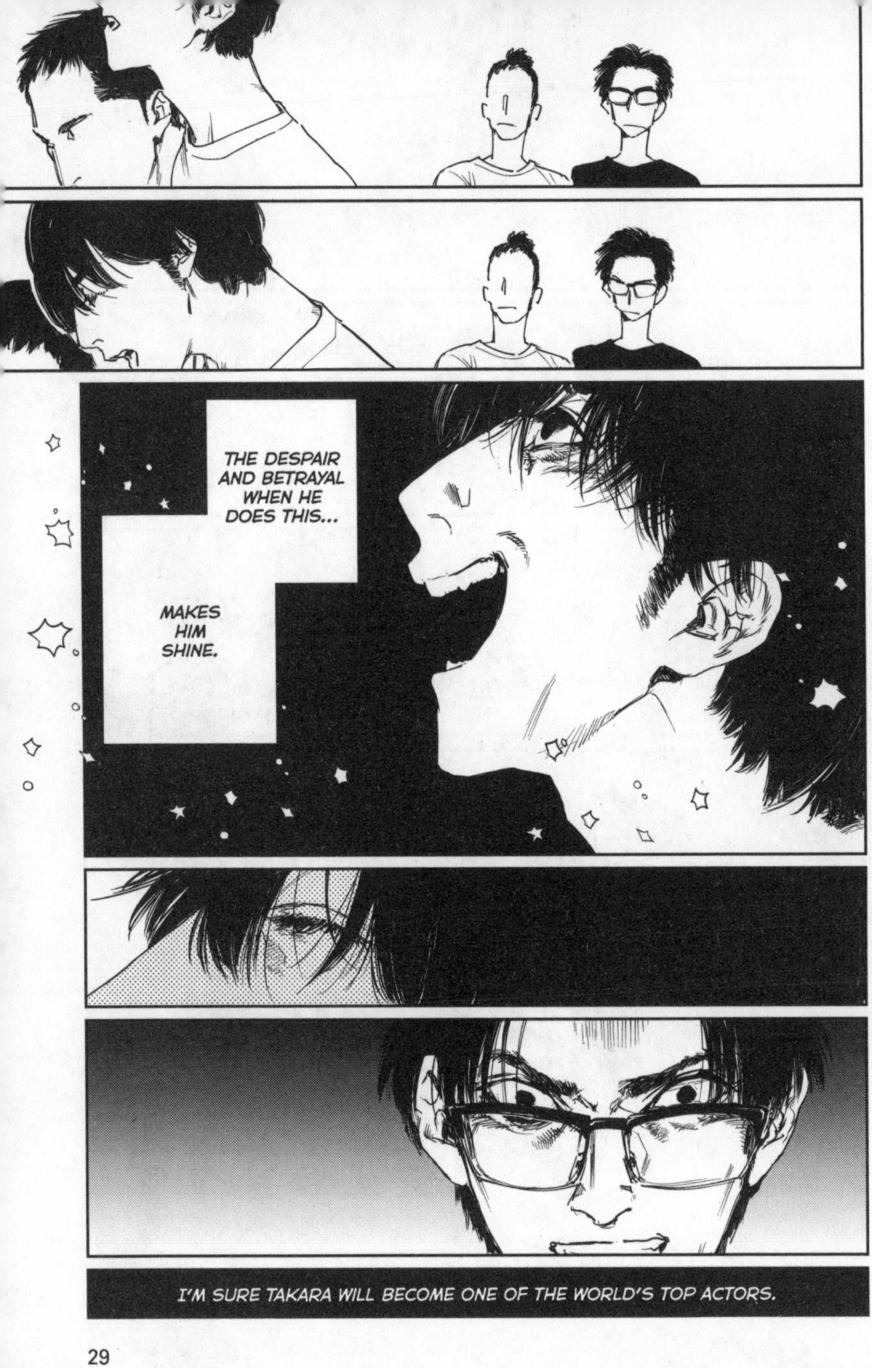
THE DESPAIR AND BETRAYAL WHEN HE DOES THIS...
MAKES HIM SHINE.
I'M SURE TAKARA WILL BECOME ONE OF THE WORLD'S TOP ACTORS.

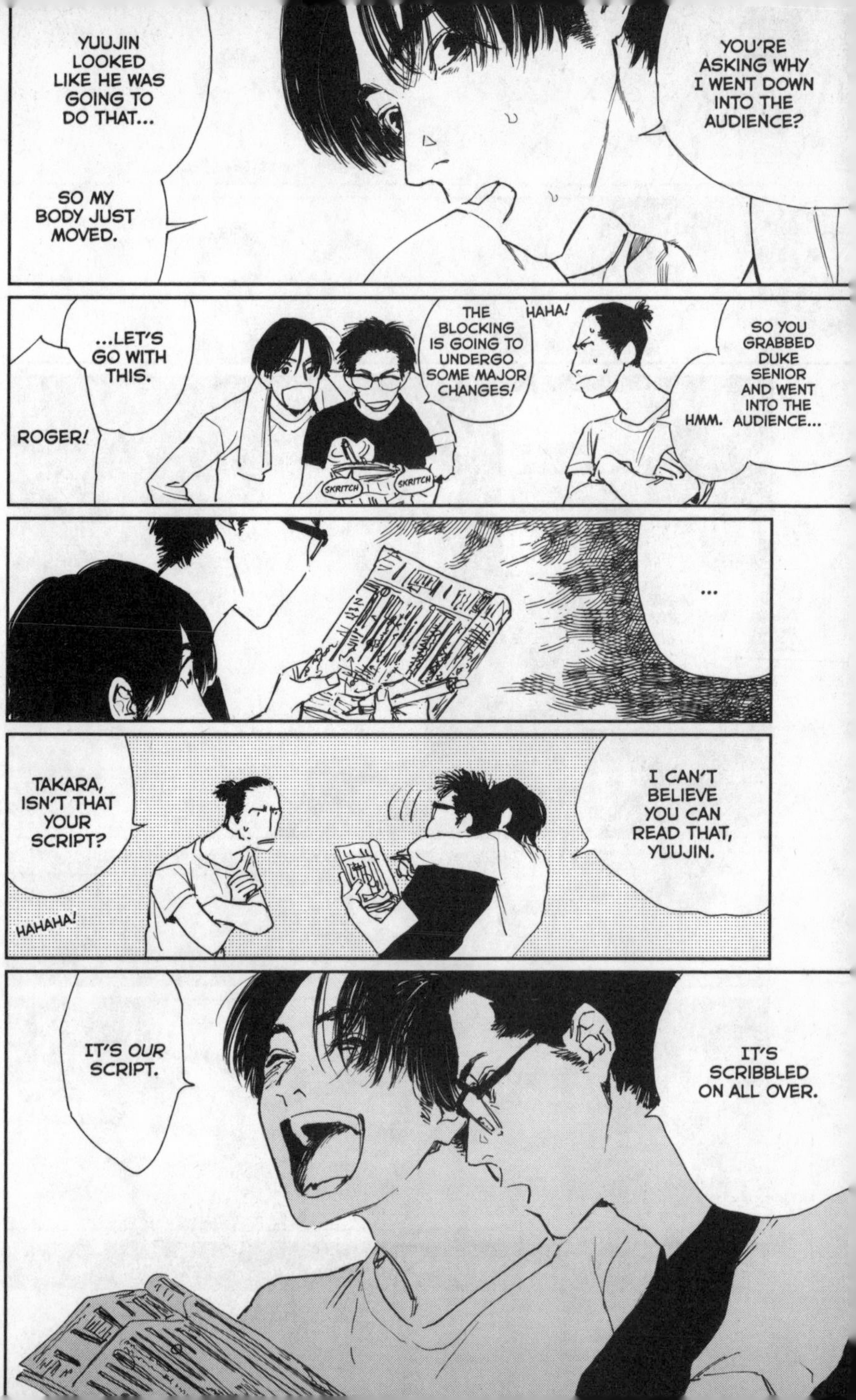
YOU'RE ASKING WHY I WENT DOWN INTO THE AUDIENCE?
YUUJIN LOOKED LIKE HE WAS GOING TO DO THAT...
SO MY BODY JUST MOVED.
SO YOU GRABBED DUKE SENIOR AND WENT INTO THE AUDIENCE...
HMM.
HAHA!
THE BLOCKING IS GOING TO UNDERGO SOME MAJOR CHANGES!
...LET'S GO WITH THIS.
ROGER!
SKRITCH
SKRITCH
...
I CAN'T BELIEVE YOU CAN READ THAT, YUUJIN.
TAKARA, ISN'T THAT YOUR SCRIPT?
HAHAHA!
IT'S SCRIBBLED ON ALL OVER.
IT'S *OUR* SCRIPT.

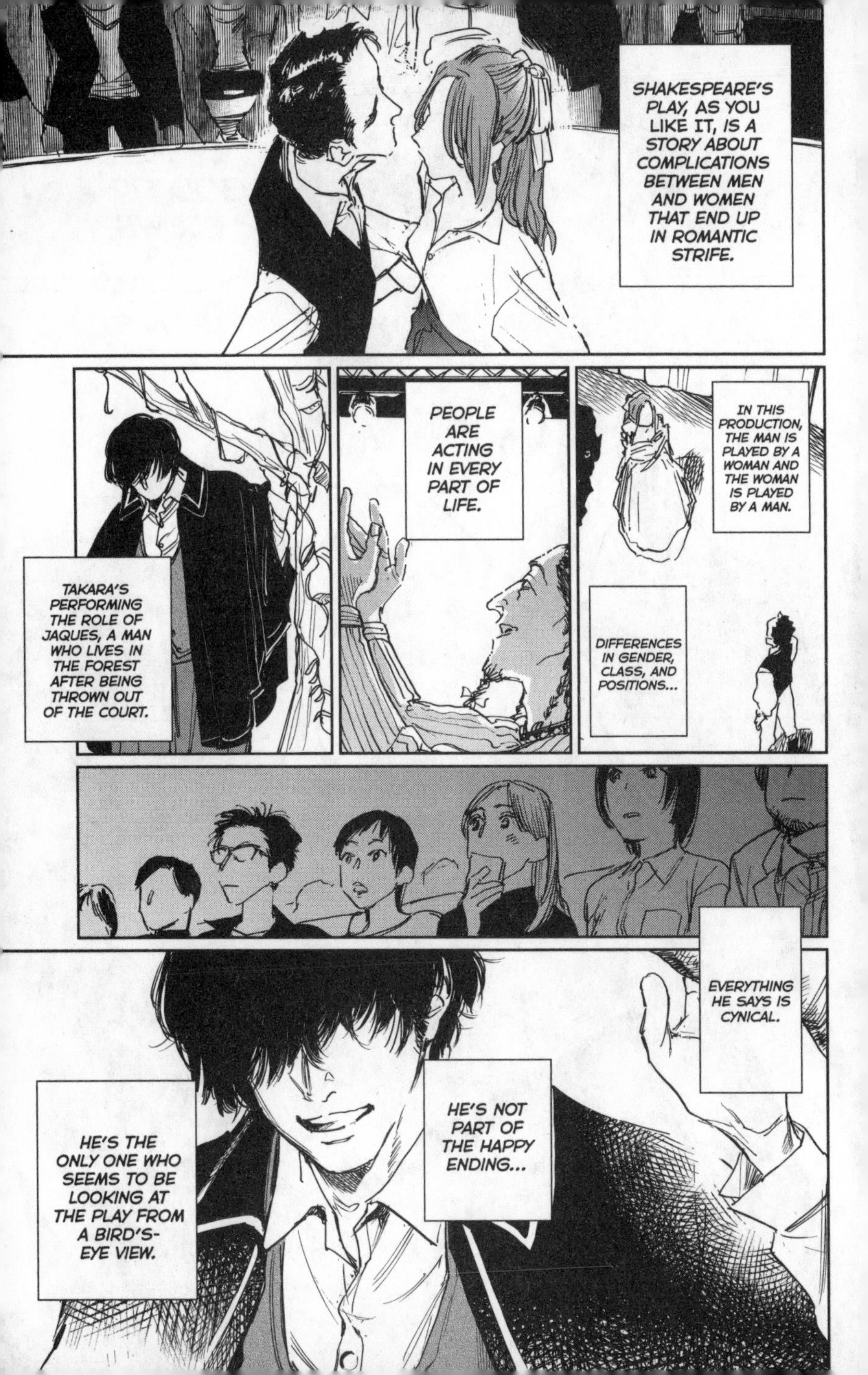
SHAKESPEARE'S PLAY, AS YOU LIKE IT, IS A STORY ABOUT COMPLICATIONS BETWEEN MEN AND WOMEN THAT END UP IN ROMANTIC STRIFE.
IN THIS PRODUCTION, THE MAN IS PLAYED BY A WOMAN AND THE WOMAN IS PLAYED BY A MAN.
DIFFERENCES IN GENDER, CLASS, AND POSITIONS...
PEOPLE ARE ACTING IN EVERY PART OF LIFE.
TAKARA'S PERFORMING THE ROLE OF JAQUES, A MAN WHO LIVES IN THE FOREST AFTER BEING THROWN OUT OF THE COURT.
EVERYTHING HE SAYS IS CYNICAL.
HE'S NOT PART OF THE HAPPY ENDING...
HE'S THE ONLY ONE WHO SEEMS TO BE LOOKING AT THE PLAY FROM A BIRD'S-EYE VIEW.

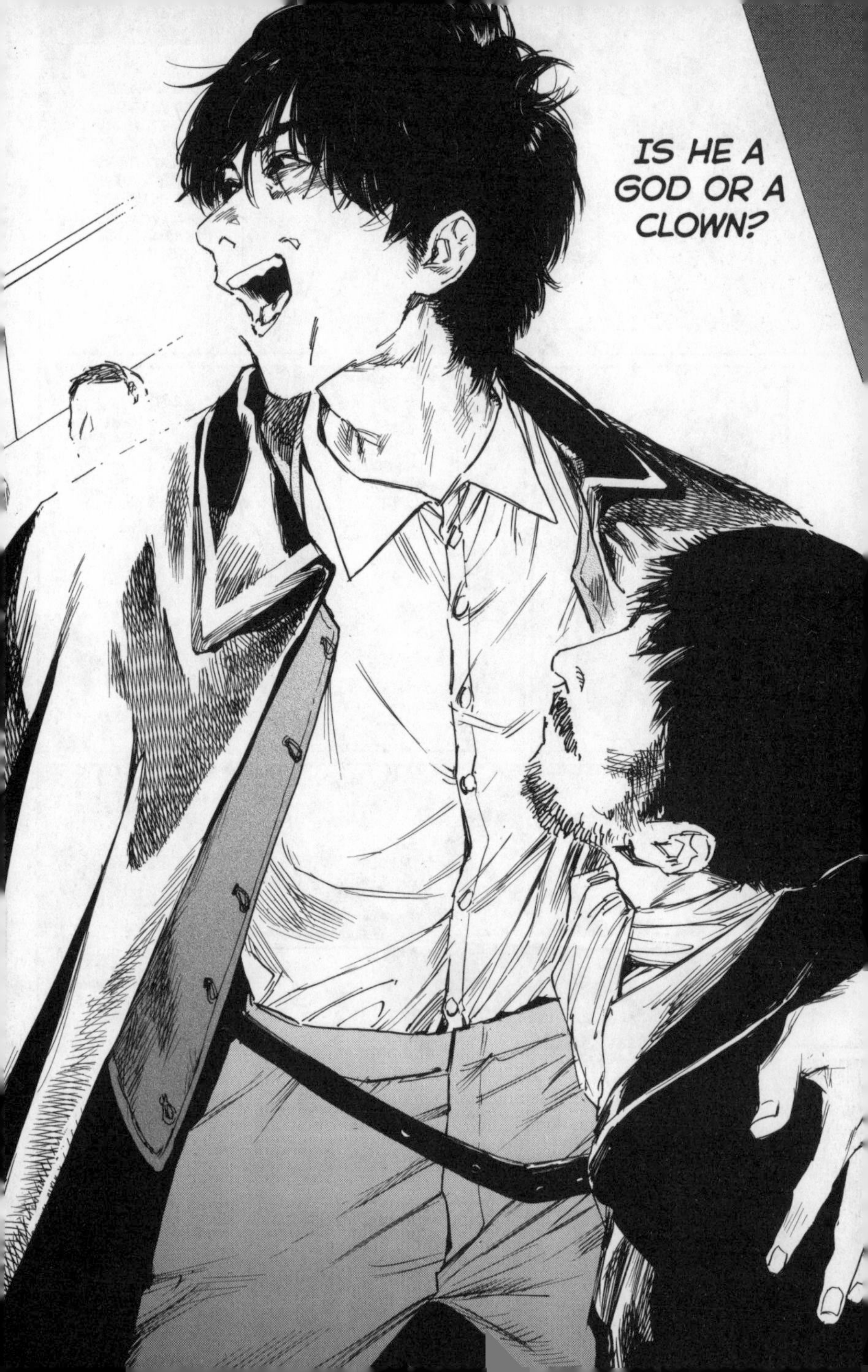
IS HE A GOD OR A CLOWN?

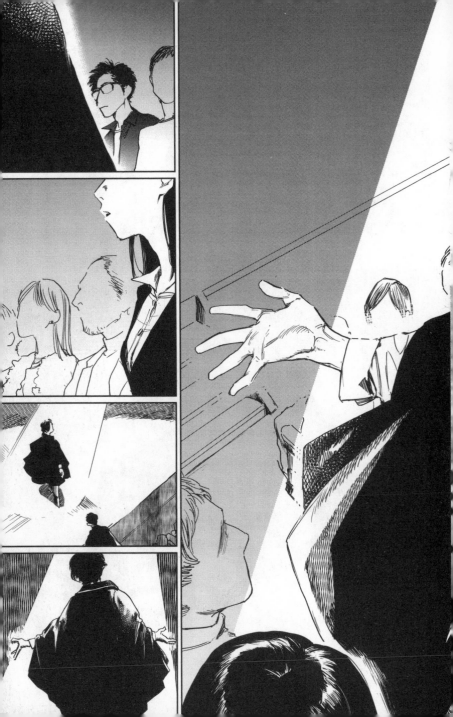

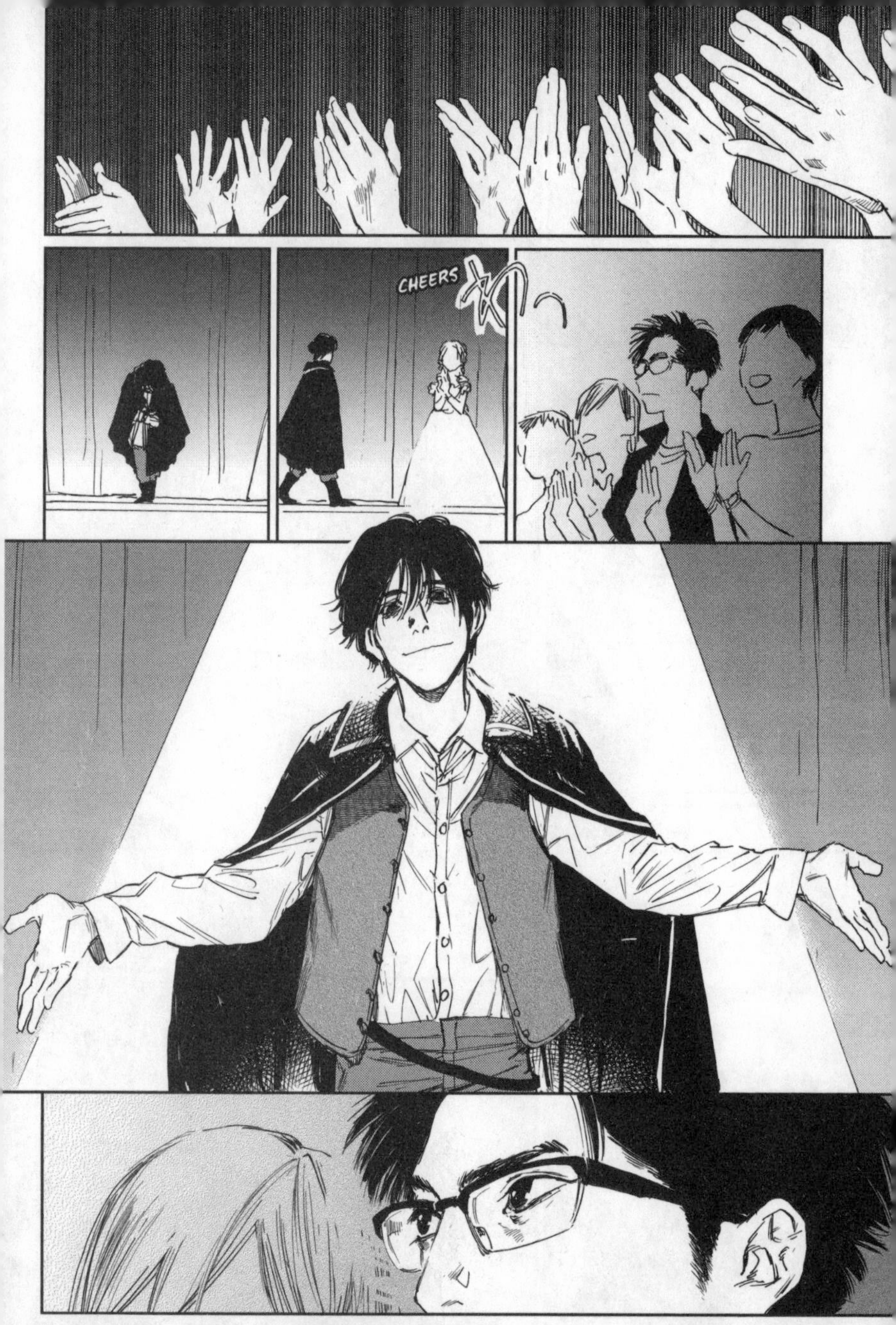
CHEERS

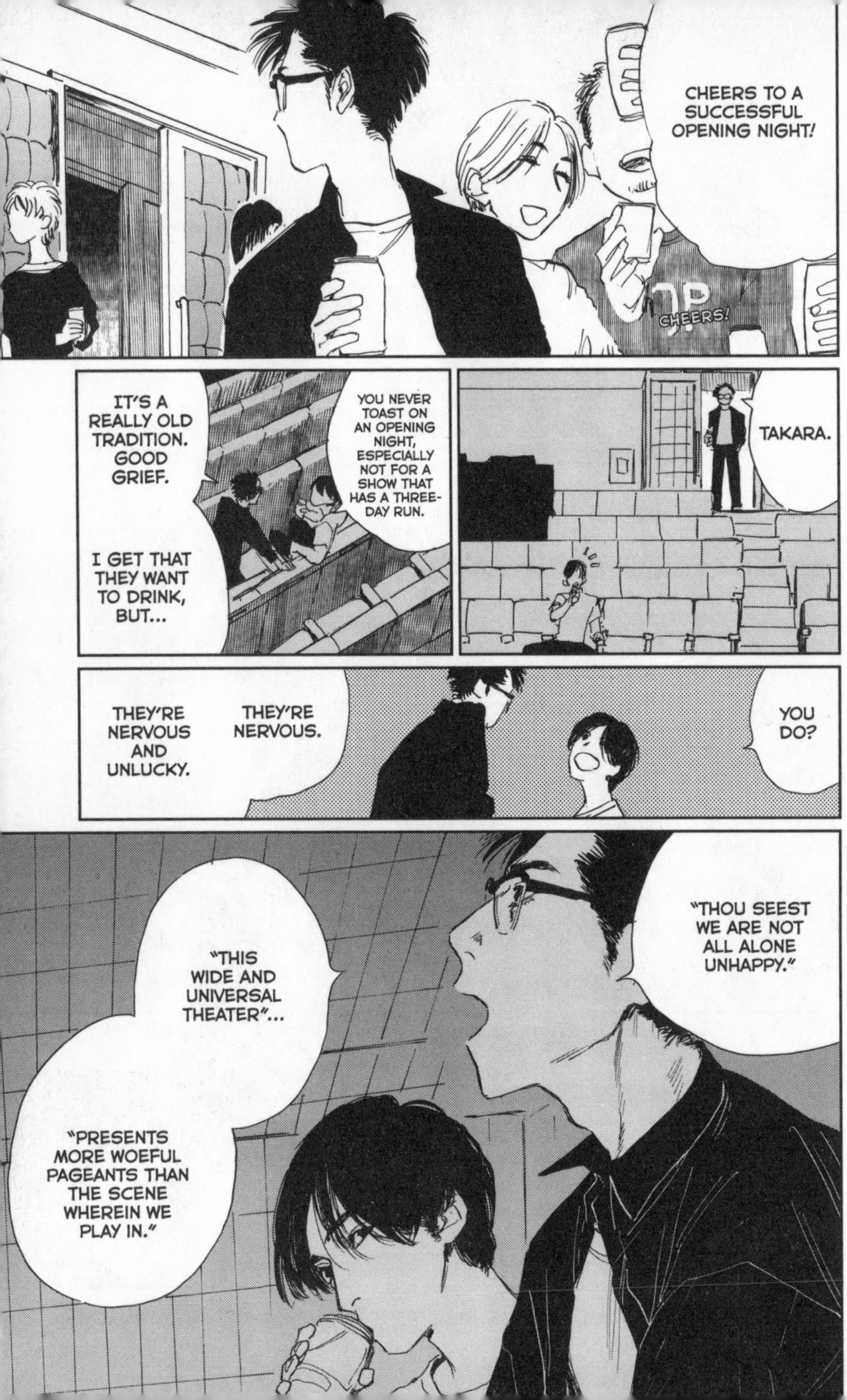
CHEERS TO A SUCCESSFUL OPENING NIGHT!
CHEERS!
TAKARA.
YOU NEVER TOAST ON AN OPENING NIGHT, ESPECIALLY NOT FOR A SHOW THAT HAS A THREE-DAY RUN.
IT'S A REALLY OLD TRADITION. GOOD GRIEF.
I GET THAT THEY WANT TO DRINK, BUT...
YOU DO?
THEY'RE NERVOUS.
THEY'RE NERVOUS AND UNLUCKY.
"THOU SEEST WE ARE NOT ALL ALONE UNHAPPY."
"THIS WIDE AND UNIVERSAL THEATER"...
"PRESENTS MORE WOEFUL PAGEANTS THAN THE SCENE WHEREIN WE PLAY IN."

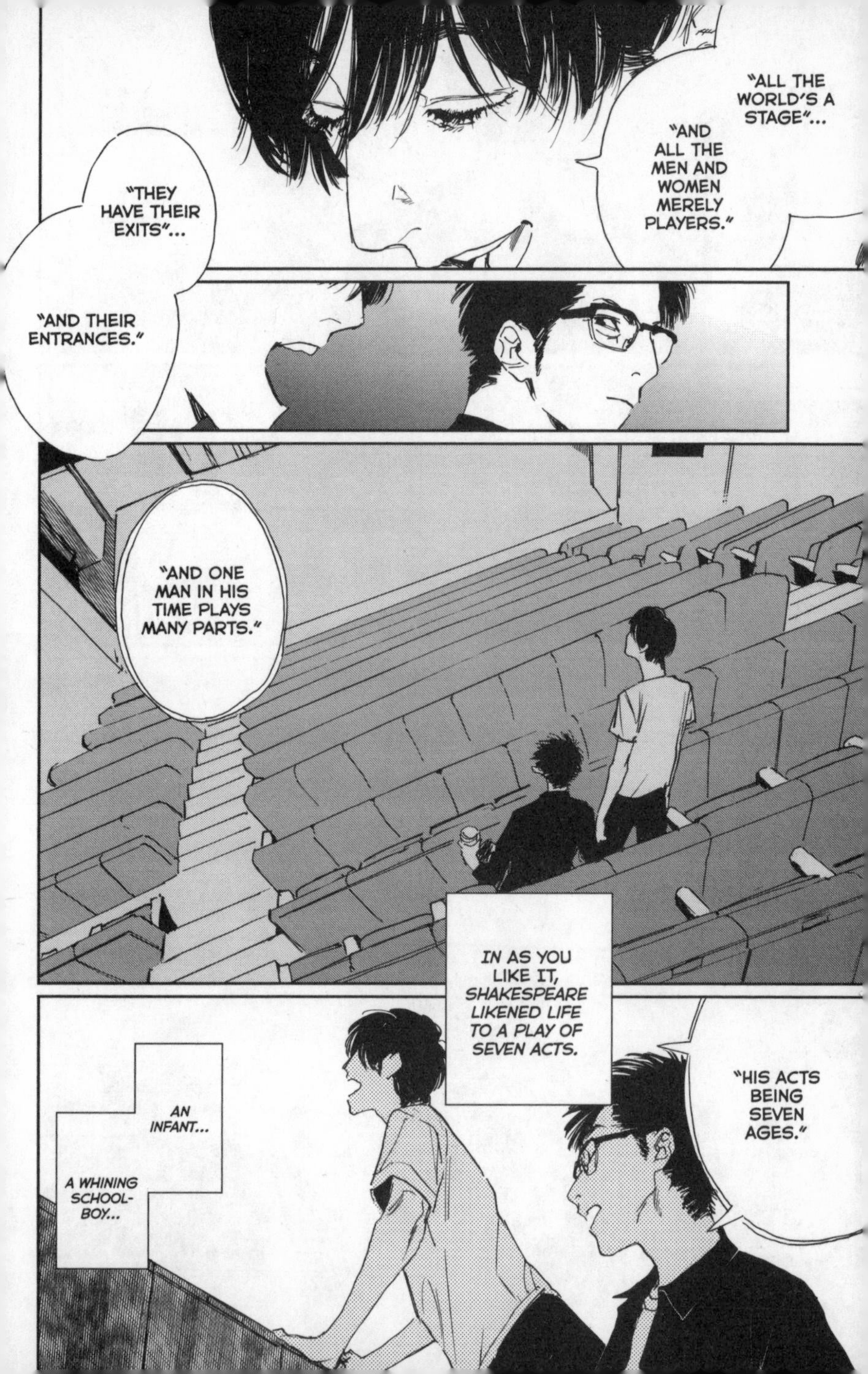
"ALL THE WORLD'S A STAGE"...
"AND ALL THE MEN AND WOMEN MERELY PLAYERS."
"THEY HAVE THEIR EXITS"...
"AND THEIR ENTRANCES."
"AND ONE MAN IN HIS TIME PLAYS MANY PARTS."
IN AS YOU LIKE IT, SHAKESPEARE LIKENED LIFE TO A PLAY OF SEVEN ACTS.
"HIS ACTS BEING SEVEN AGES."
AN INFANT...
A WHINING SCHOOL-BOY...

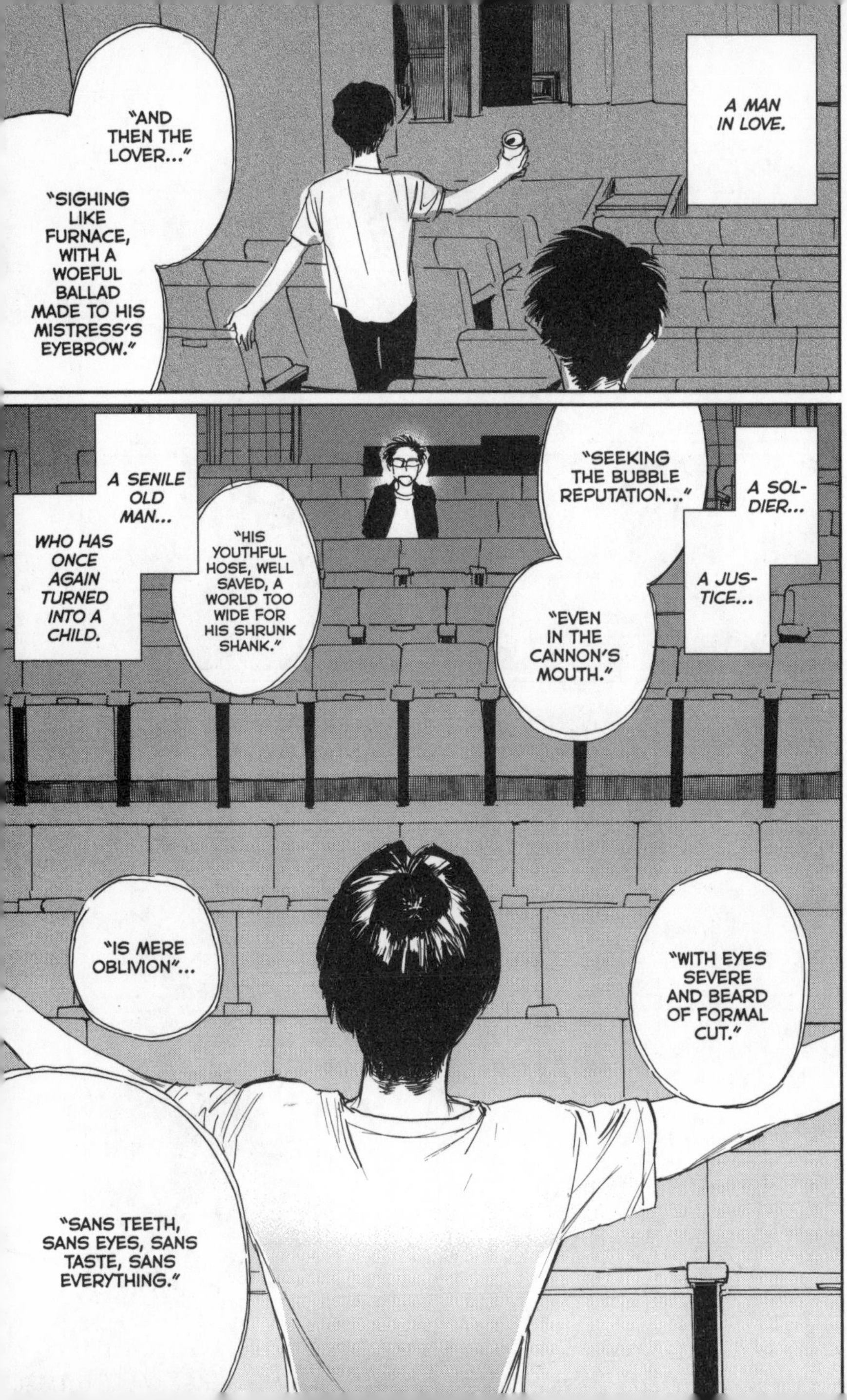
A MAN IN LOVE.
"AND THEN THE LOVER..."
"SIGHING LIKE FURNACE, WITH A WOEFUL BALLAD MADE TO HIS MISTRESS'S EYEBROW."
A SOL-DIER...
"SEEKING THE BUBBLE REPUTATION..."
A JUS-TICE...
"EVEN IN THE CANNON'S MOUTH."
A SENILE OLD MAN...
"HIS YOUTHFUL HOSE, WELL SAVED, A WORLD TOO WIDE FOR HIS SHRUNK SHANK."
WHO HAS ONCE AGAIN TURNED INTO A CHILD.
"WITH EYES SEVERE AND BEARD OF FORMAL CUT."
"IS MERE OBLIVION"...
"SANS TEETH, SANS EYES, SANS TASTE, SANS EVERYTHING."

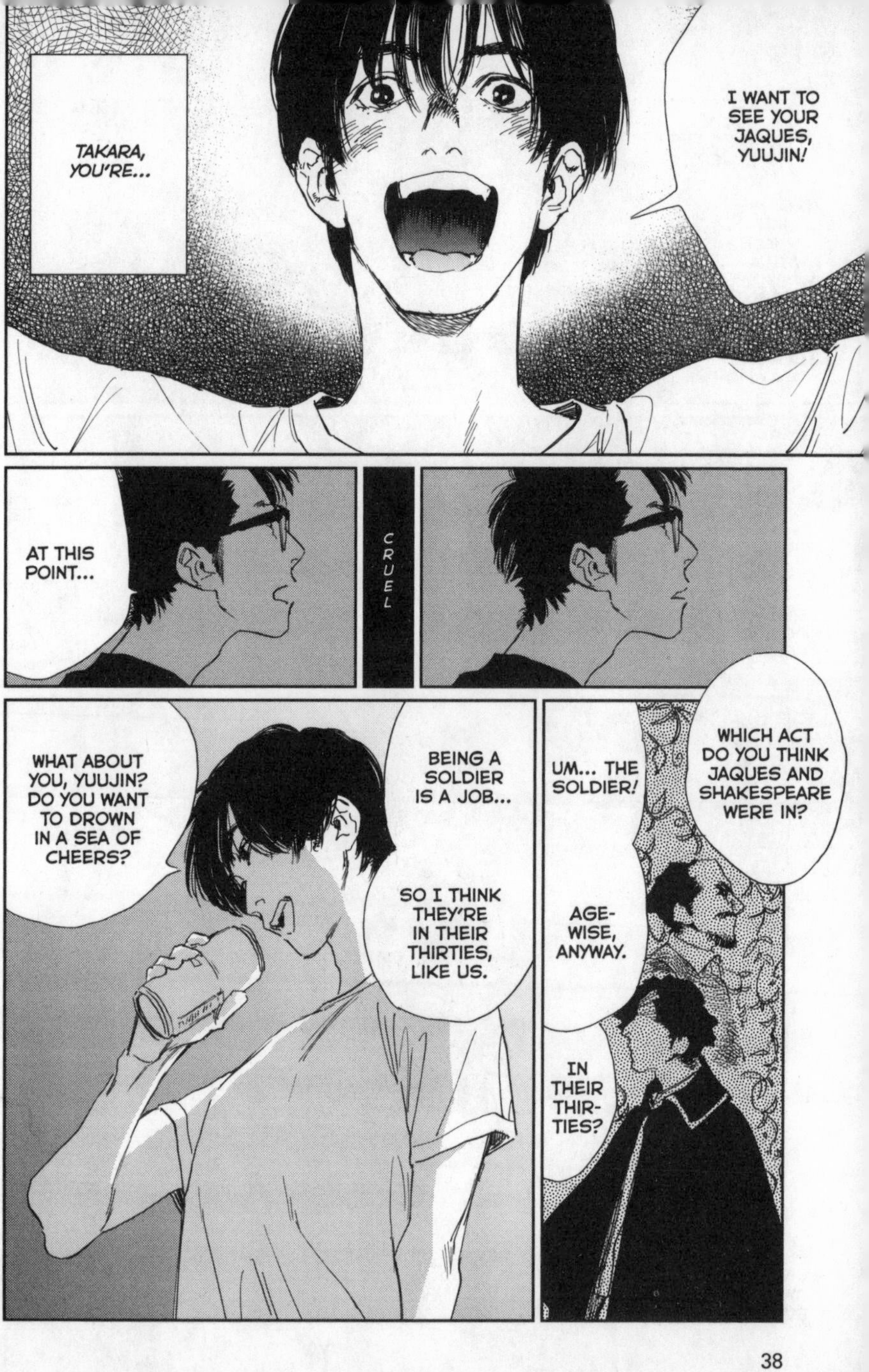
I WANT TO SEE YOUR JAQUES, YUUJIN!
TAKARA, YOU'RE...
CRUEL
AT THIS POINT...
WHICH ACT DO YOU THINK JAQUES AND SHAKESPEARE WERE IN?
UM... THE SOLDIER!
AGE-WISE, ANYWAY.
IN THEIR THIR-TIES?
BEING A SOLDIER IS A JOB...
SO I THINK THEY'RE IN THEIR THIRTIES, LIKE US.
WHAT ABOUT YOU, YUUJIN? DO YOU WANT TO DROWN IN A SEA OF CHEERS?

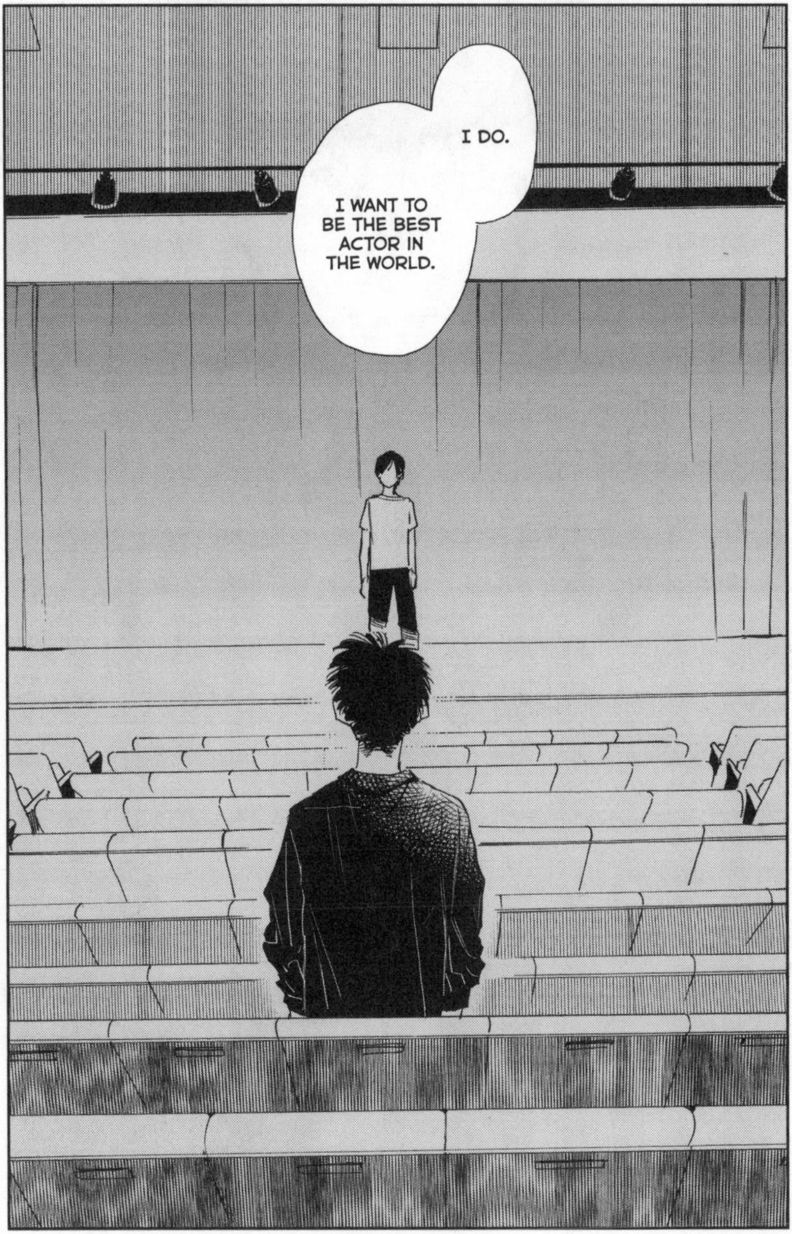
I DO.
I WANT TO BE THE BEST ACTOR IN THE WORLD.

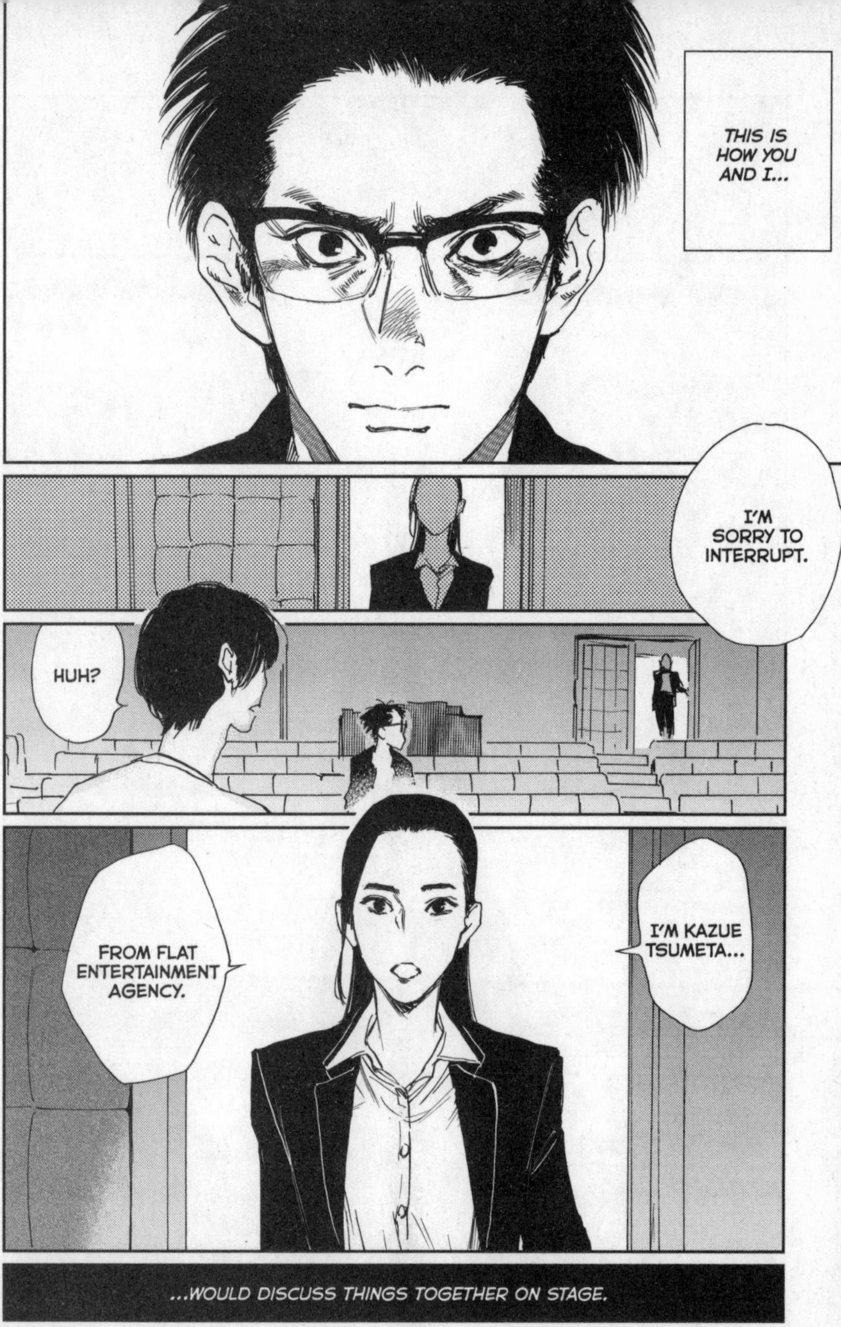
THIS IS HOW YOU AND I...
I'M SORRY TO INTERRUPT.
HUH?
I'M KAZUE TSUMETA...
FROM FLAT ENTERTAINMENT AGENCY.
...WOULD DISCUSS THINGS TOGETHER ON STAGE.

DOUBLE

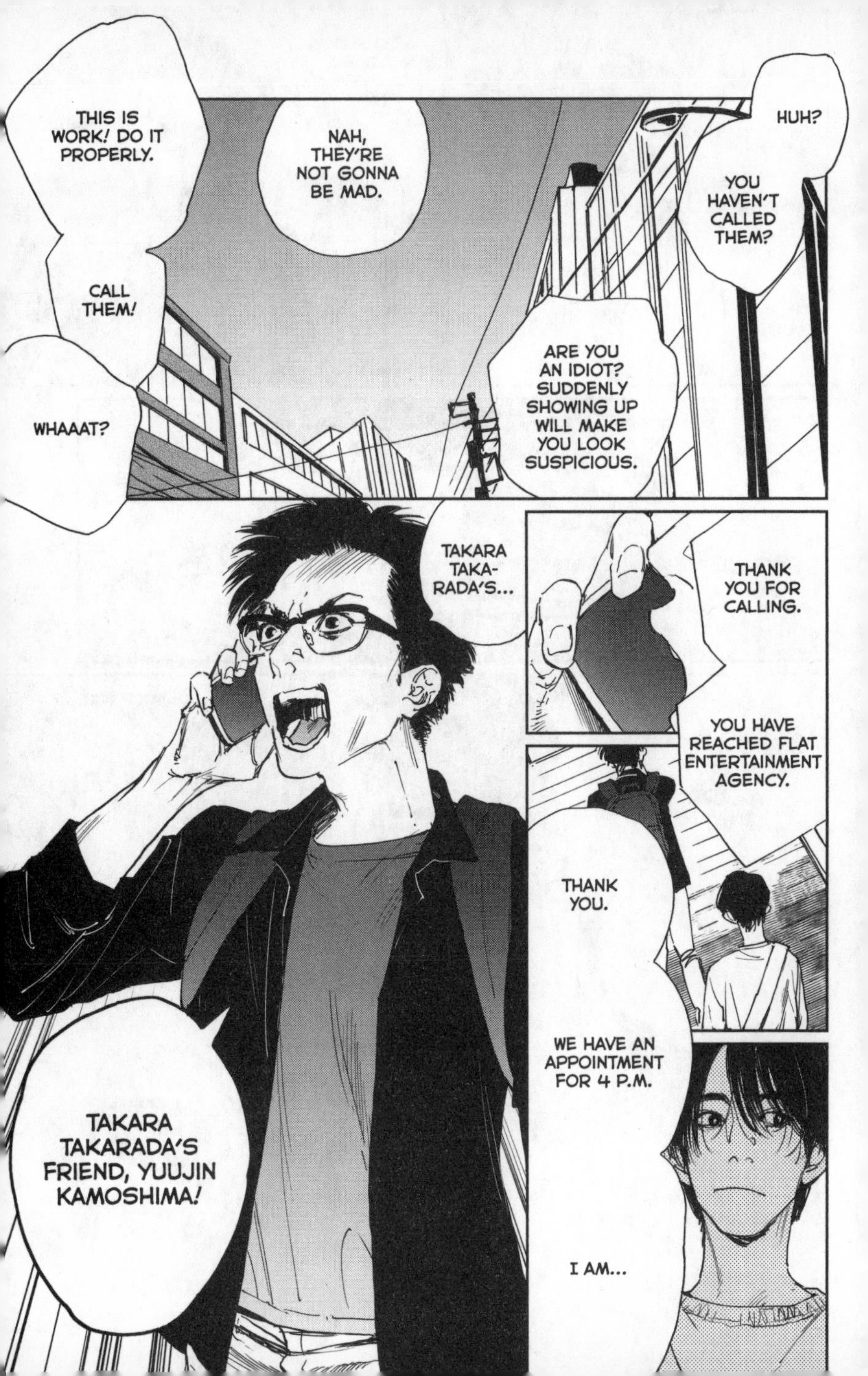
HUH?
YOU HAVEN'T CALLED THEM?
NAH, THEY'RE NOT GONNA BE MAD.
THIS IS WORK! DO IT PROPERLY.
CALL THEM!
WHAAAT?
ARE YOU AN IDIOT? SUDDENLY SHOWING UP WILL MAKE YOU LOOK SUSPICIOUS.
THANK YOU FOR CALLING.
YOU HAVE REACHED FLAT ENTERTAINMENT AGENCY.
THANK YOU.
WE HAVE AN APPOINTMENT FOR 4 P.M.
I AM...
TAKARA TAKA-RADA'S...
TAKARA TAKARADA'S FRIEND, YUUJIN KAMOSHIMA!

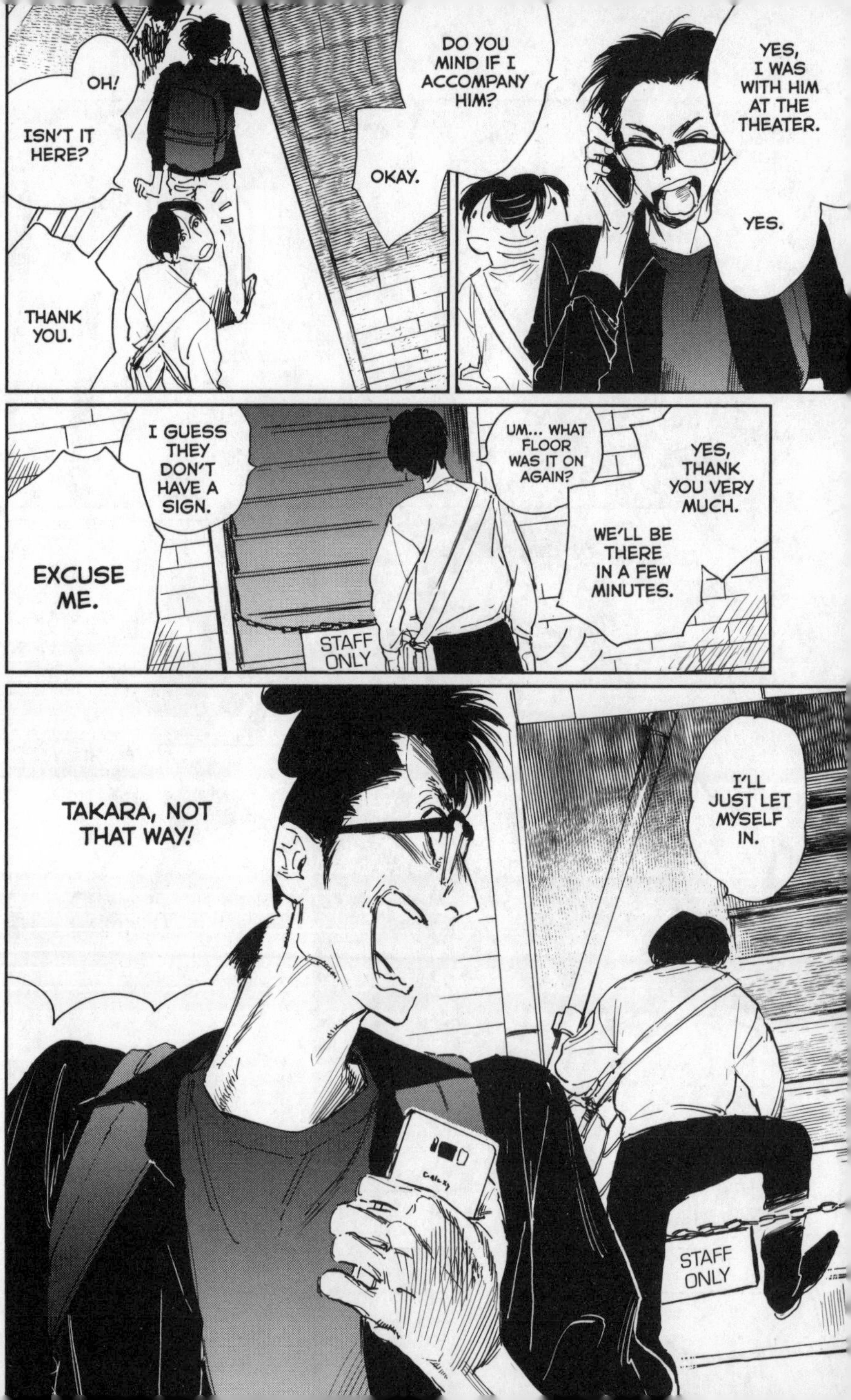
YES, I WAS WITH HIM AT THE THEATER.
DO YOU MIND IF I ACCOMPANY HIM?
YES.
OKAY.
OH!
ISN'T IT HERE?
THANK YOU.
YES, THANK YOU VERY MUCH.
UM... WHAT FLOOR WAS IT ON AGAIN?
WE'LL BE THERE IN A FEW MINUTES.
I GUESS THEY DON'T HAVE A SIGN.
EXCUSE ME.
STAFF ONLY
I'LL JUST LET MYSELF IN.
TAKARA, NOT THAT WAY!
STAFF ONLY

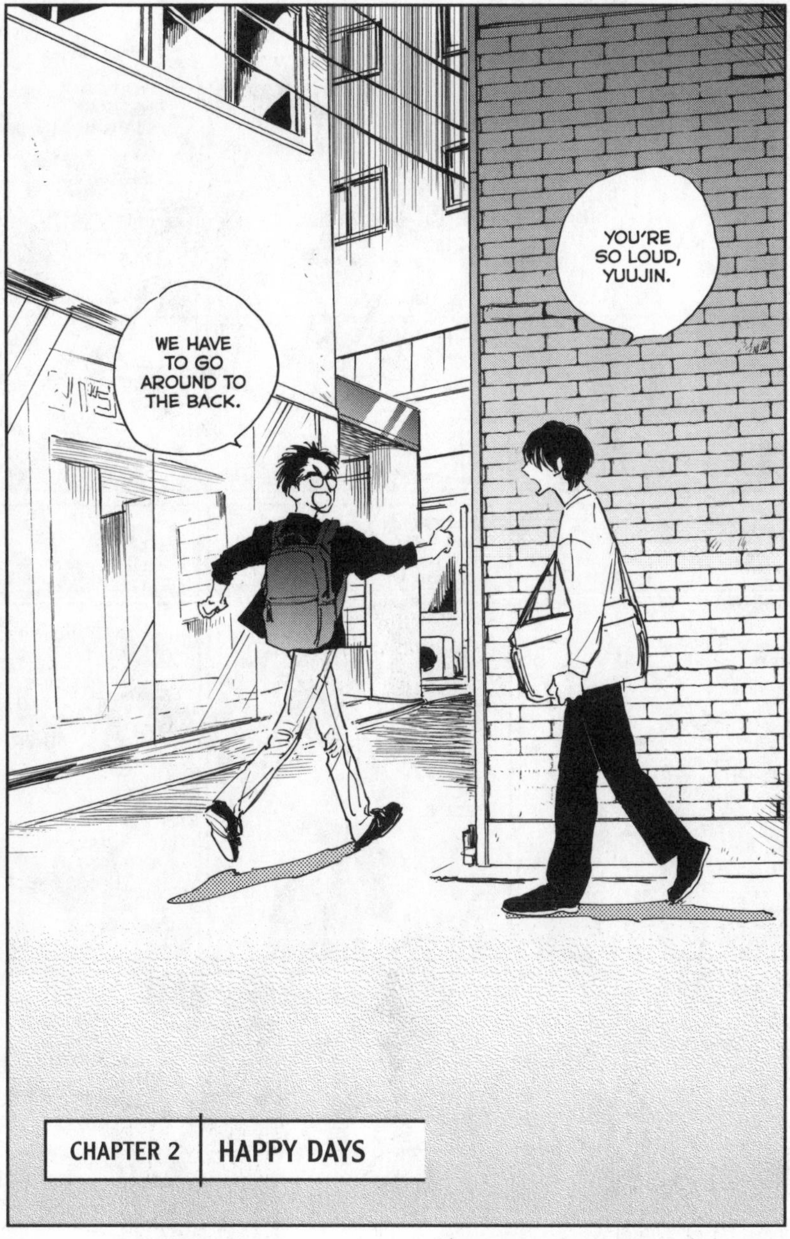
YOU'RE SO LOUD, YUUJIN.
WE HAVE TO GO AROUND TO THE BACK.
CHAPTER 2
HAPPY DAYS

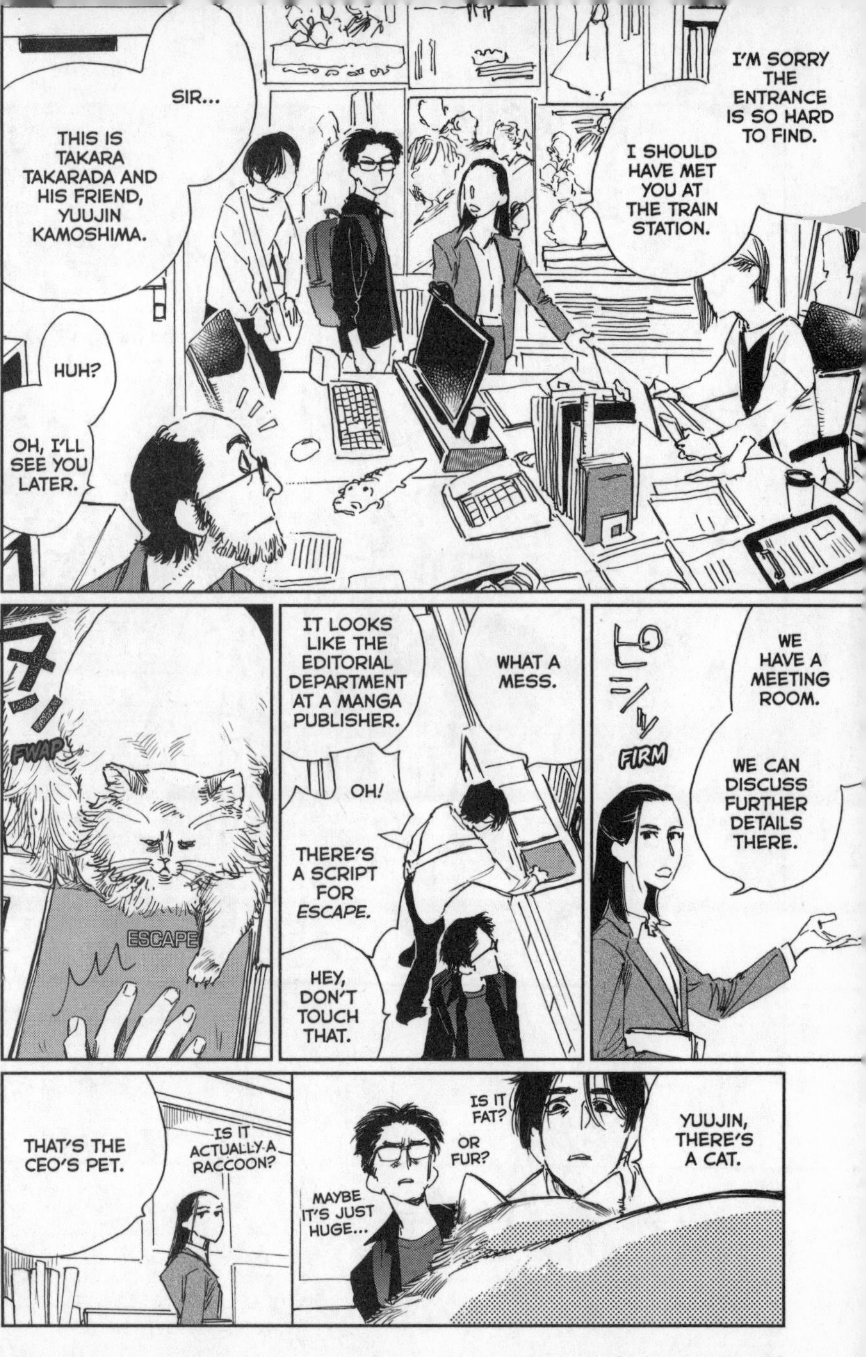
I'M SORRY THE ENTRANCE IS SO HARD TO FIND.
I SHOULD HAVE MET YOU AT THE TRAIN STATION.
SIR...
THIS IS TAKARA TAKARADA AND HIS FRIEND, YUUJIN KAMOSHIMA.
HUH?
OH, I'LL SEE YOU LATER.
FIRM
WE HAVE A MEETING ROOM.
WE CAN DISCUSS FURTHER DETAILS THERE.
WHAT A MESS.
IT LOOKS LIKE THE EDITORIAL DEPARTMENT AT A MANGA PUBLISHER.
OH!
THERE'S A SCRIPT FOR *ESCAPE*.
HEY, DON'T TOUCH THAT.
FWAP
ESCAPE
YUUJIN, THERE'S A CAT.
IS IT FAT?
OR FUR?
MAYBE IT'S JUST HUGE...
IS IT ACTUALLY A RACCOON?
THAT'S THE CEO'S PET.

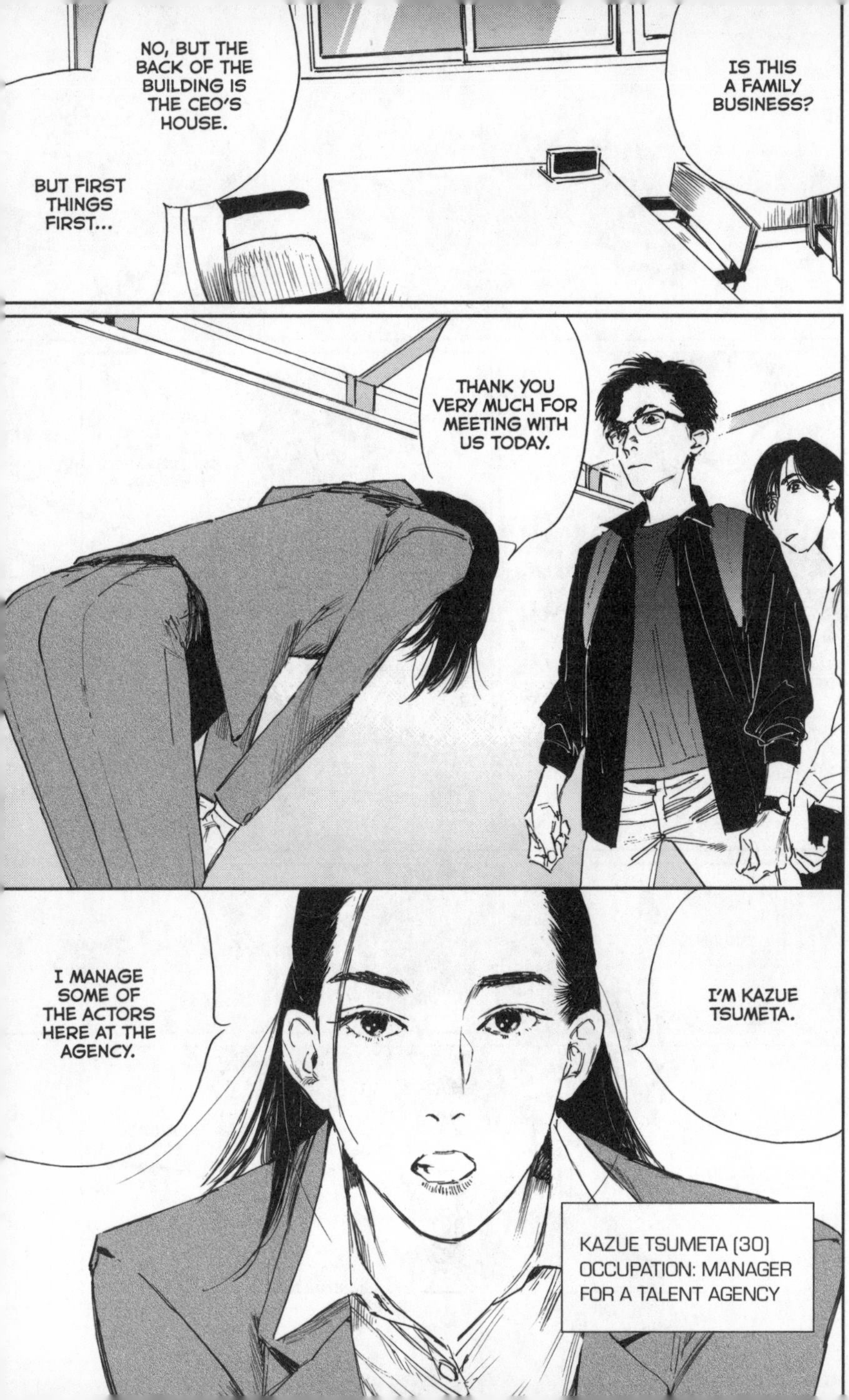
IS THIS A FAMILY BUSINESS?
NO, BUT THE BACK OF THE BUILDING IS THE CEO'S HOUSE.
BUT FIRST THINGS FIRST...
THANK YOU VERY MUCH FOR MEETING WITH US TODAY.
I'M KAZUE TSUMETA.
I MANAGE SOME OF THE ACTORS HERE AT THE AGENCY.
KAZUE TSUMETA (30)
OCCUPATION: MANAGER FOR A TALENT AGENCY

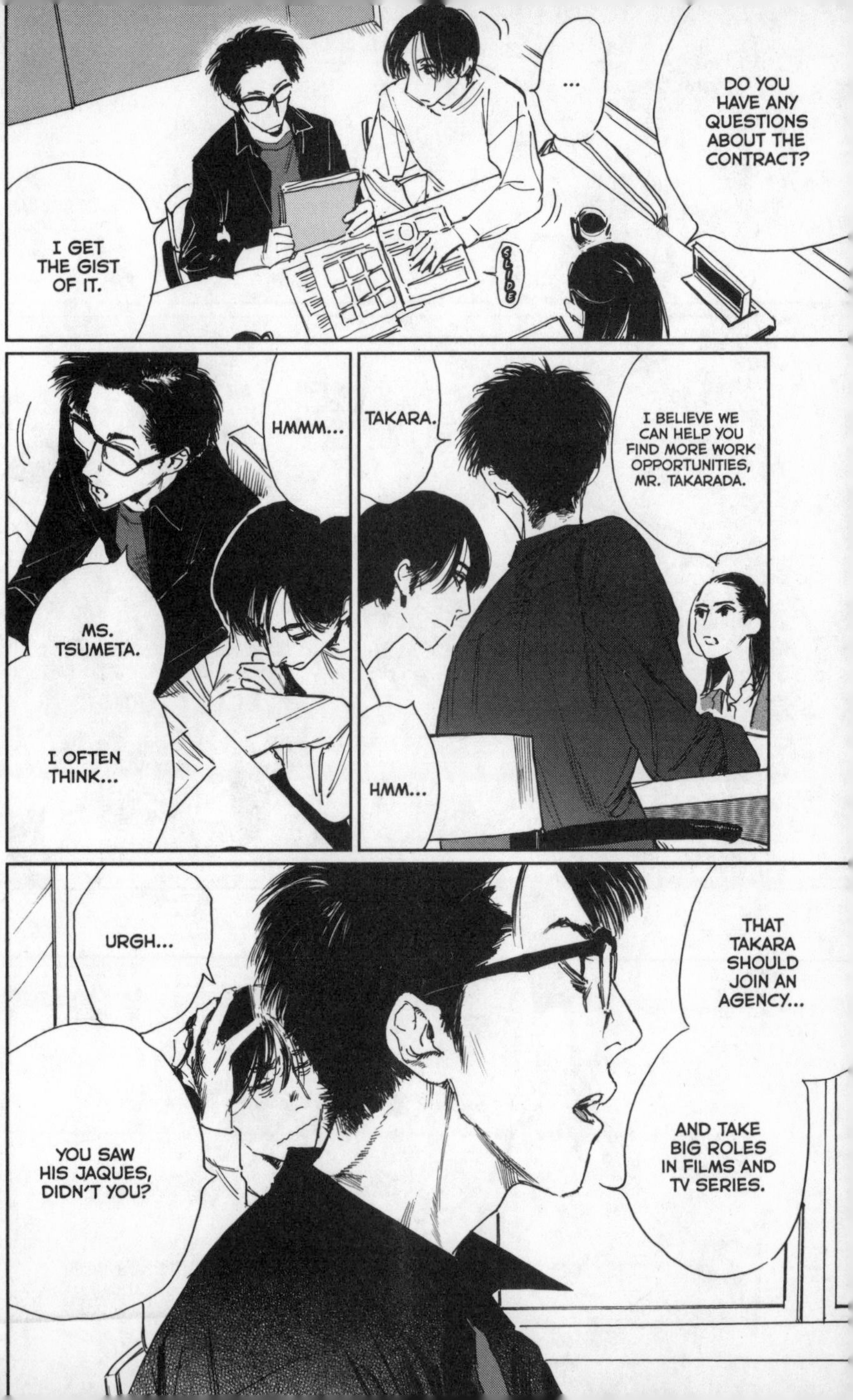
DO YOU HAVE ANY QUESTIONS ABOUT THE CONTRACT?
...
SLIDE
I GET THE GIST OF IT.
I BELIEVE WE CAN HELP YOU FIND MORE WORK OPPORTUNITIES, MR. TAKARADA.
TAKARA.
HMM...
HMMM...
MS. TSUMETA.
I OFTEN THINK...
THAT TAKARA SHOULD JOIN AN AGENCY...
AND TAKE BIG ROLES IN FILMS AND TV SERIES.
URGH...
YOU SAW HIS JAQUES, DIDN'T YOU?

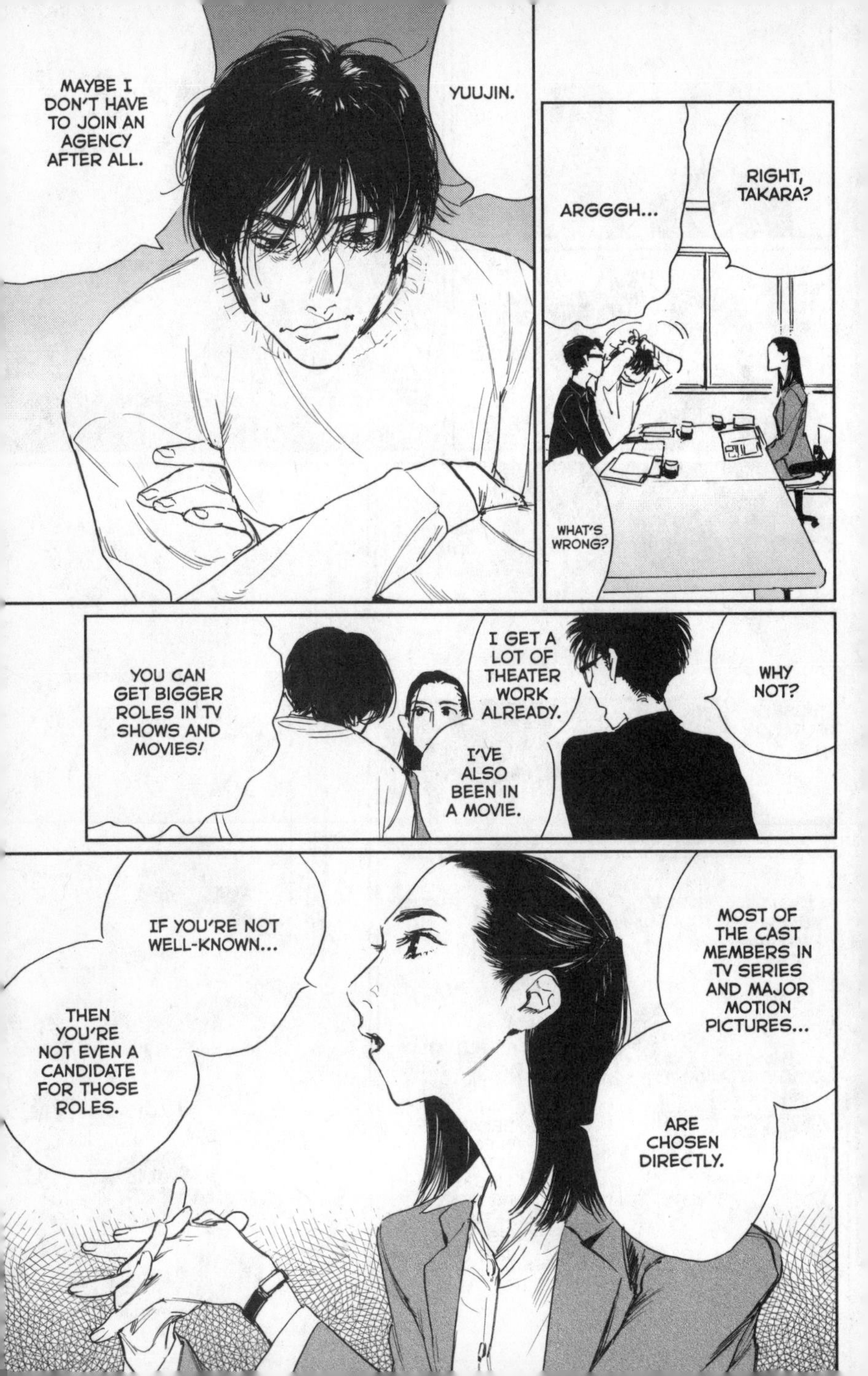
RIGHT, TAKARA?
ARGGGH...
WHAT'S WRONG?
YUUJIN.
MAYBE I DON'T HAVE TO JOIN AN AGENCY AFTER ALL.
WHY NOT?
I GET A LOT OF THEATER WORK ALREADY.
I'VE ALSO BEEN IN A MOVIE.
YOU CAN GET BIGGER ROLES IN TV SHOWS AND MOVIES!
MOST OF THE CAST MEMBERS IN TV SERIES AND MAJOR MOTION PICTURES...
ARE CHOSEN DIRECTLY.
IF YOU'RE NOT WELL-KNOWN...
THEN YOU'RE NOT EVEN A CANDIDATE FOR THOSE ROLES.

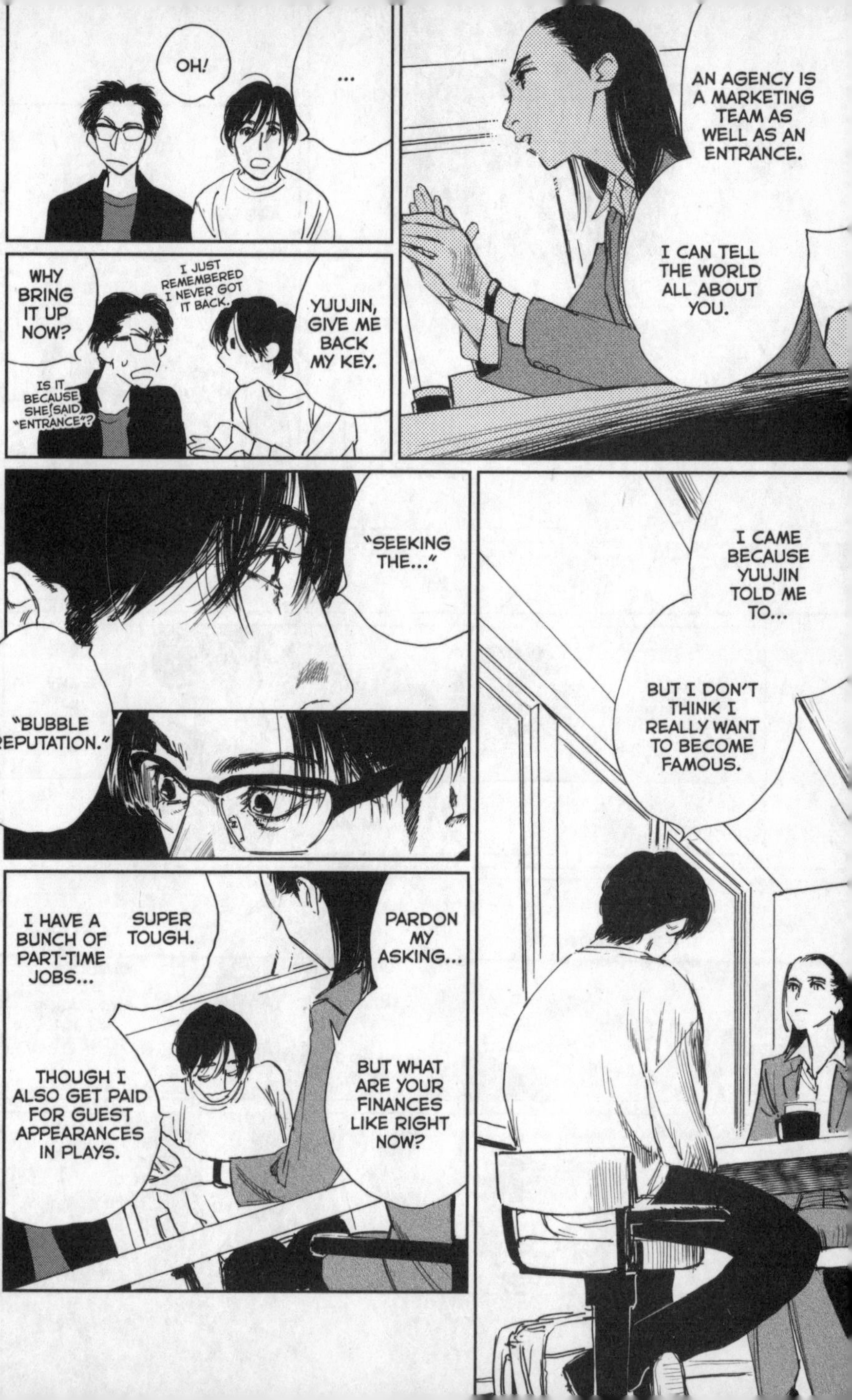
AN AGENCY IS A MARKETING TEAM AS WELL AS AN ENTRANCE.
I CAN TELL THE WORLD ALL ABOUT YOU.
...
OH!
YUUJIN, GIVE ME BACK MY KEY.
I JUST REMEMBERED I NEVER GOT IT BACK.
WHY BRING IT UP NOW?
IS IT BECAUSE SHE SAID "ENTRANCE"?
I CAME BECAUSE YUUJIN TOLD ME TO...
BUT I DON'T THINK I REALLY WANT TO BECOME FAMOUS.
"SEEKING THE..."
"BUBBLE REPUTATION."
PARDON MY ASKING...
BUT WHAT ARE YOUR FINANCES LIKE RIGHT NOW?
SUPER TOUGH.
I HAVE A BUNCH OF PART-TIME JOBS...
THOUGH I ALSO GET PAID FOR GUEST APPEARANCES IN PLAYS.

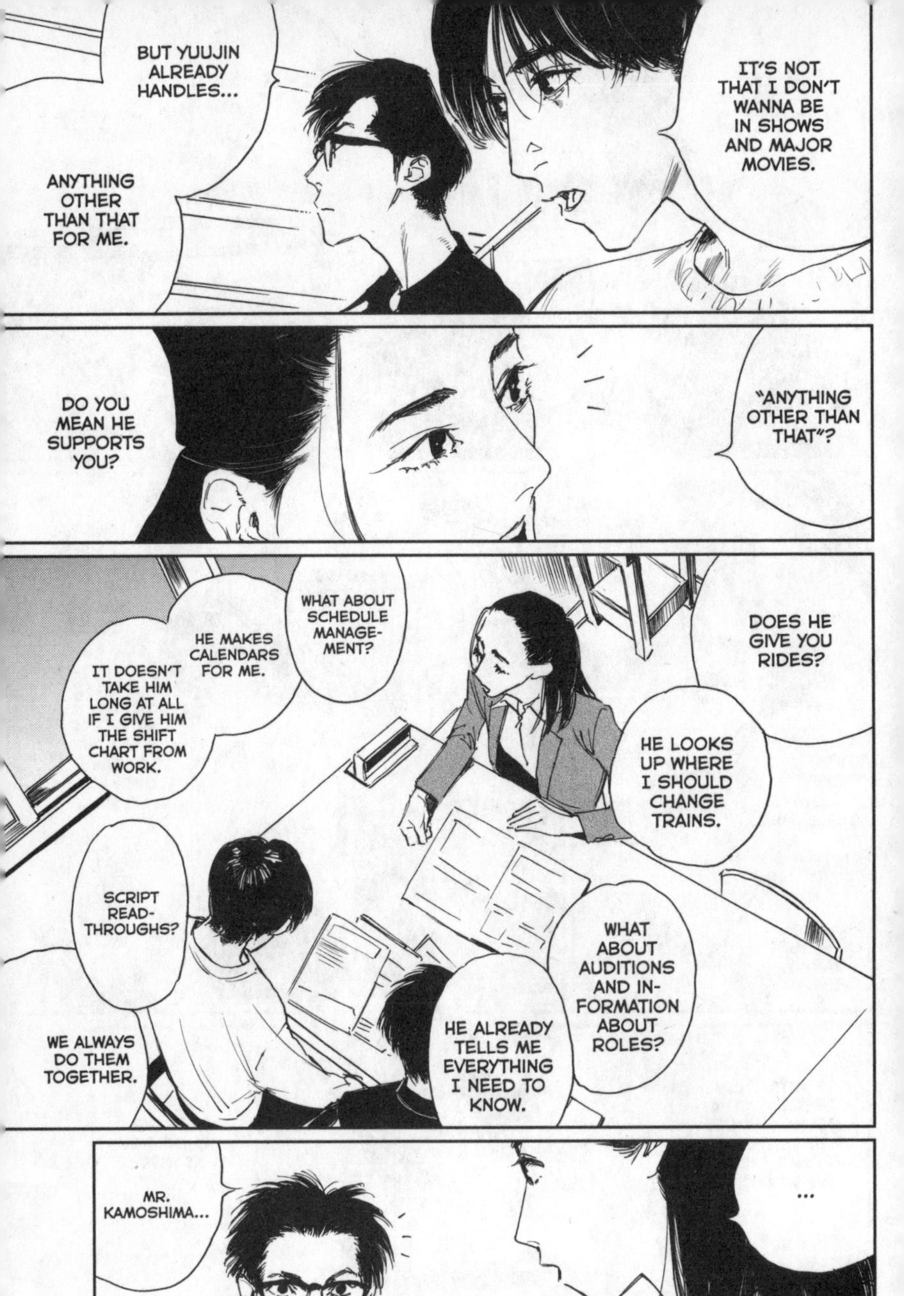
IT'S NOT THAT I DON'T WANNA BE IN SHOWS AND MAJOR MOVIES.
BUT YUUJIN ALREADY HANDLES...
ANYTHING OTHER THAN THAT FOR ME.
"ANYTHING OTHER THAN THAT"?
DO YOU MEAN HE SUPPORTS YOU?
DOES HE GIVE YOU RIDES?
HE LOOKS UP WHERE I SHOULD CHANGE TRAINS.
WHAT ABOUT SCHEDULE MANAGE-MENT?
HE MAKES CALENDARS FOR ME.
IT DOESN'T TAKE HIM LONG AT ALL IF I GIVE HIM THE SHIFT CHART FROM WORK.
WHAT ABOUT AUDITIONS AND IN-FORMATION ABOUT ROLES?
HE ALREADY TELLS ME EVERYTHING I NEED TO KNOW.
SCRIPT READ-THROUGHS?
WE ALWAYS DO THEM TOGETHER.
...
MR. KAMOSHIMA...

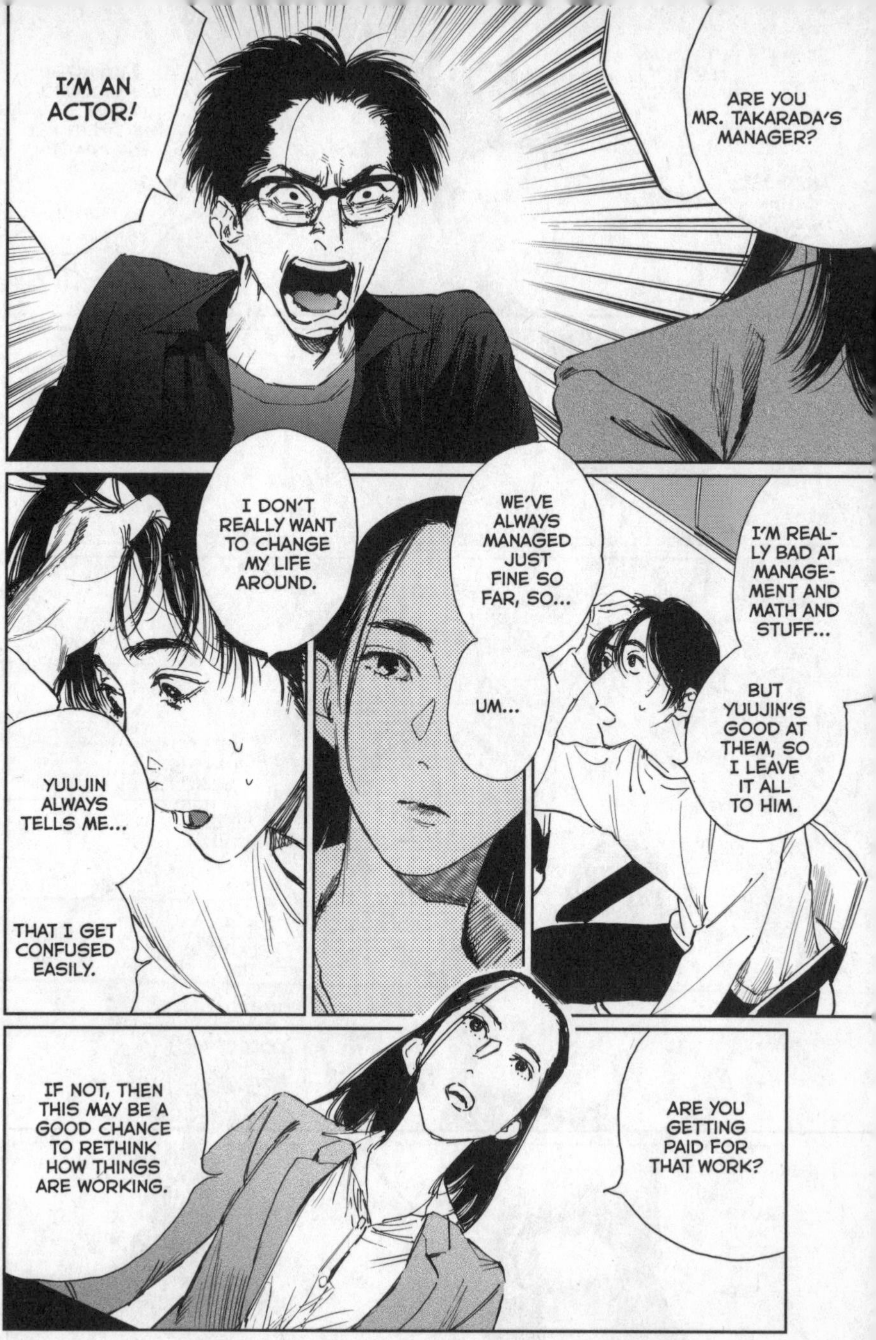
ARE YOU MR. TAKARADA'S MANAGER?
I'M AN ACTOR!
I'M REAL-LY BAD AT MANAGE-MENT AND MATH AND STUFF...
BUT YUUJIN'S GOOD AT THEM, SO I LEAVE IT ALL TO HIM.
WE'VE ALWAYS MANAGED JUST FINE SO FAR, SO...
UM...
I DON'T REALLY WANT TO CHANGE MY LIFE AROUND.
YUUJIN ALWAYS TELLS ME...
THAT I GET CONFUSED EASILY.
ARE YOU GETTING PAID FOR THAT WORK?
IF NOT, THEN THIS MAY BE A GOOD CHANCE TO RETHINK HOW THINGS ARE WORKING.

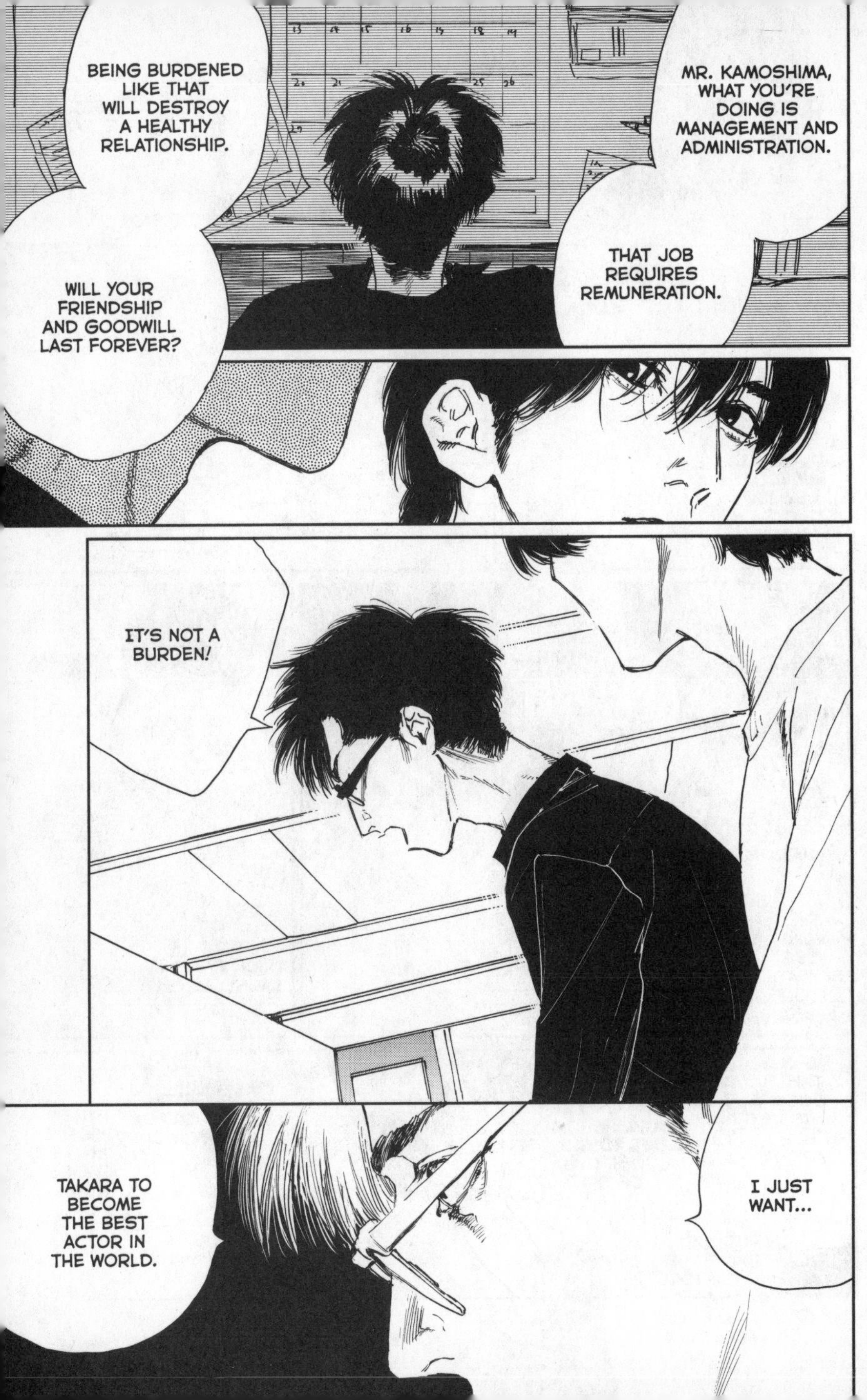
MR. KAMOSHIMA, WHAT YOU'RE DOING IS MANAGEMENT AND ADMINISTRATION.
THAT JOB REQUIRES REMUNERATION.
BEING BURDENED LIKE THAT WILL DESTROY A HEALTHY RELATIONSHIP.
WILL YOUR FRIENDSHIP AND GOODWILL LAST FOREVER?
IT'S NOT A BURDEN!
I JUST WANT...
TAKARA TO BECOME THE BEST ACTOR IN THE WORLD.

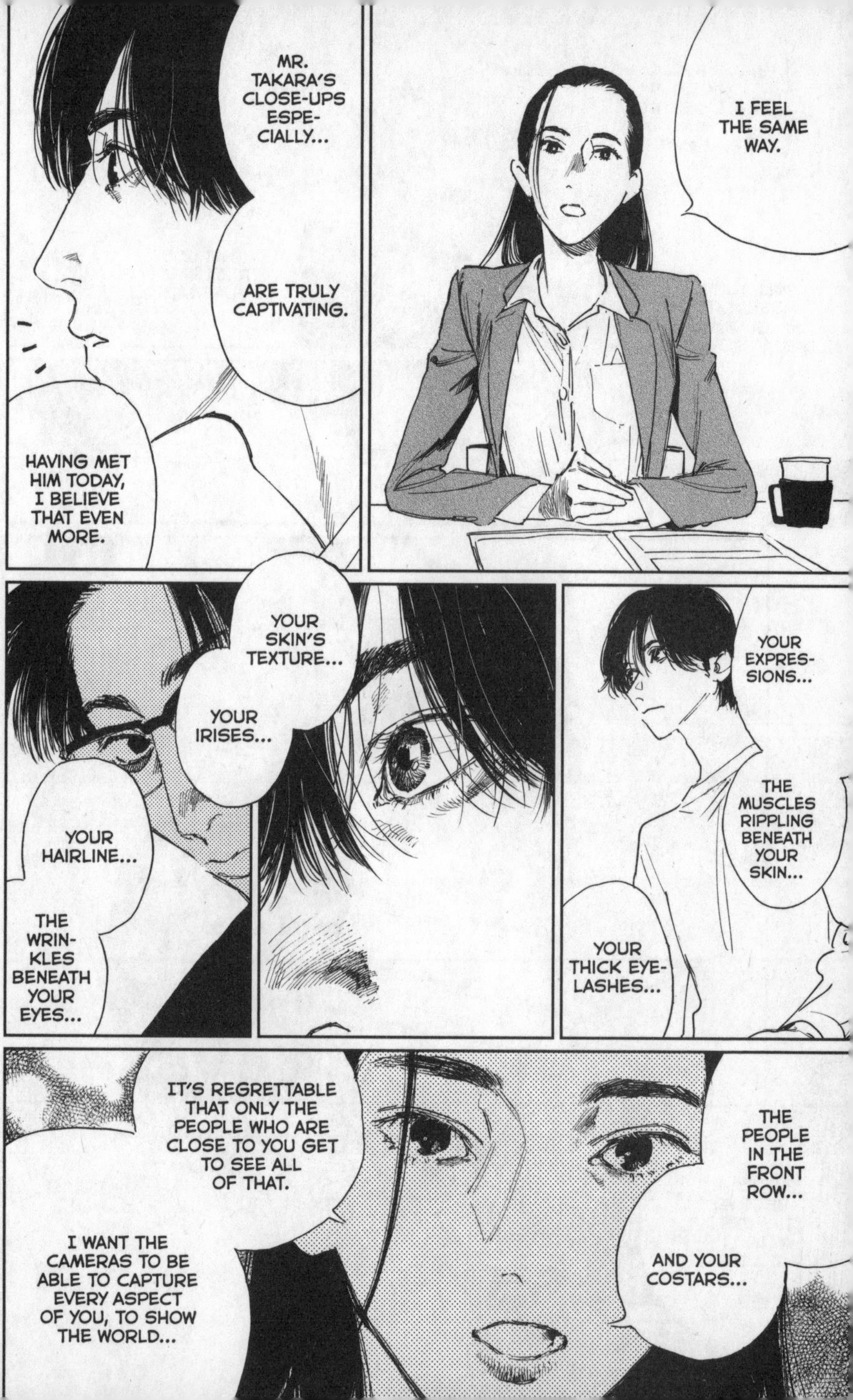
I FEEL THE SAME WAY.
MR. TAKARA'S CLOSE-UPS ESPECIALLY...
ARE TRULY CAPTIVATING.
HAVING MET HIM TODAY, I BELIEVE THAT EVEN MORE.
YOUR EXPRESSIONS...
THE MUSCLES RIPPLING BENEATH YOUR SKIN...
YOUR THICK EYELASHES...
YOUR SKIN'S TEXTURE...
YOUR IRISES...
YOUR HAIRLINE...
THE WRINKLES BENEATH YOUR EYES...
THE PEOPLE IN THE FRONT ROW...
AND YOUR COSTARS...
IT'S REGRETTABLE THAT ONLY THE PEOPLE WHO ARE CLOSE TO YOU GET TO SEE ALL OF THAT.
I WANT THE CAMERAS TO BE ABLE TO CAPTURE EVERY ASPECT OF YOU, TO SHOW THE WORLD...

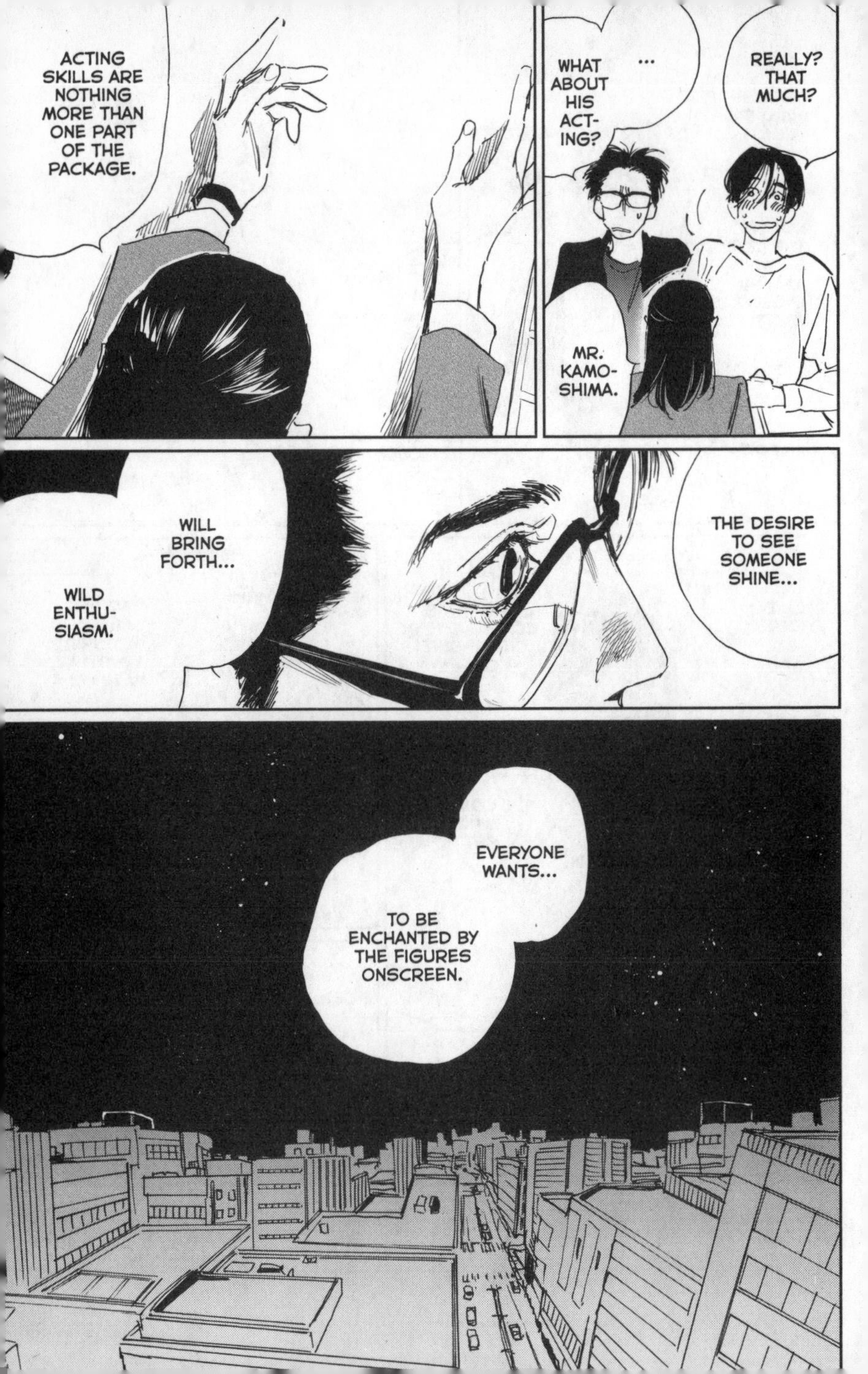
REALLY? THAT MUCH?
...
WHAT ABOUT HIS ACT-ING?
MR. KAMO-SHIMA.
ACTING SKILLS ARE NOTHING MORE THAN ONE PART OF THE PACKAGE.
THE DESIRE TO SEE SOMEONE SHINE...
WILL BRING FORTH...
WILD ENTHU-SIASM.
EVERYONE WANTS...
TO BE ENCHANTED BY THE FIGURES ONSCREEN.

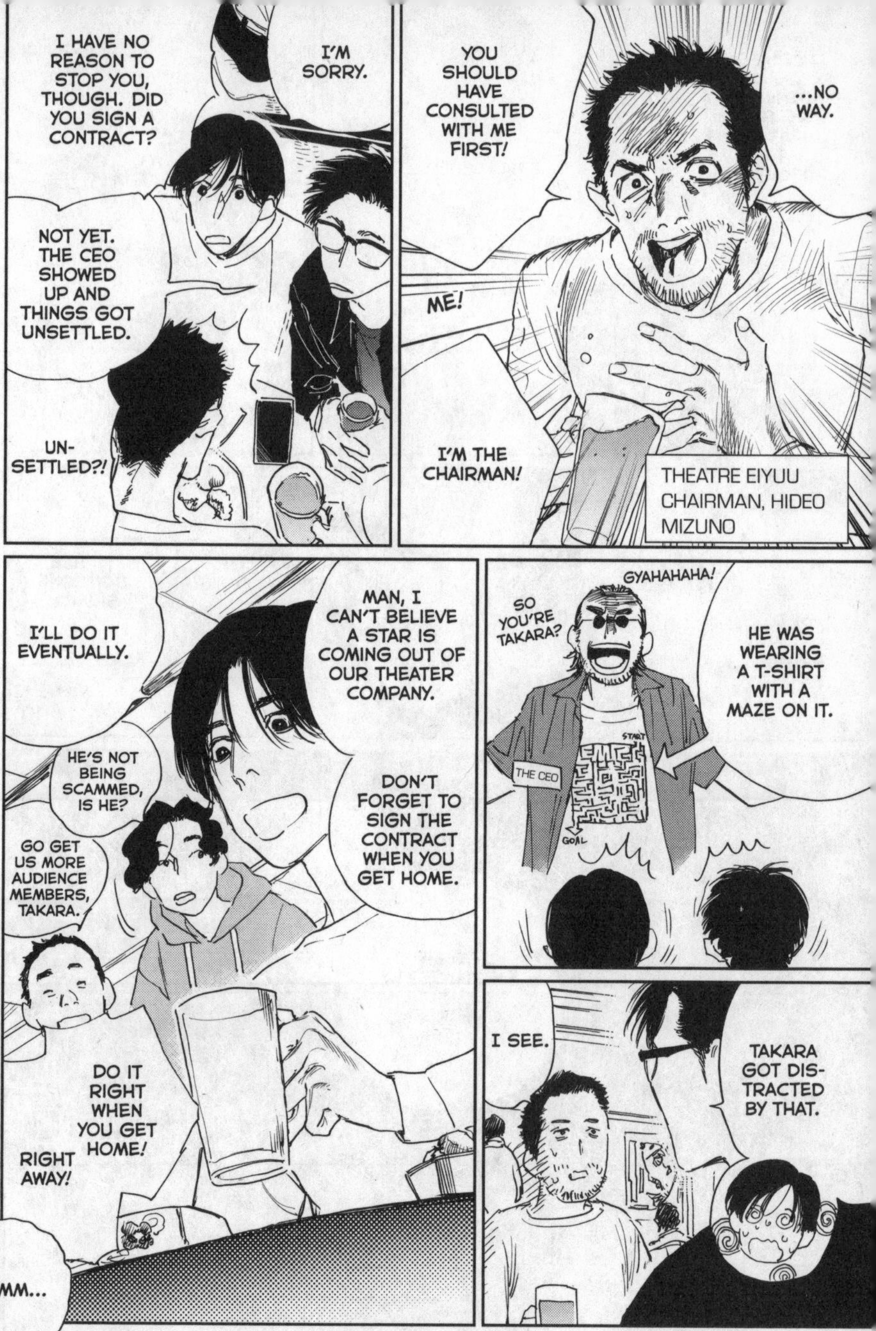
...NO WAY.
YOU SHOULD HAVE CONSULTED WITH ME FIRST!
ME!
I'M THE CHAIRMAN!
THEATRE EIYUU CHAIRMAN, HIDEO MIZUNO
I'M SORRY.
I HAVE NO REASON TO STOP YOU, THOUGH. DID YOU SIGN A CONTRACT?
NOT YET. THE CEO SHOWED UP AND THINGS GOT UNSETTLED.
UN-SETTLED?!
GYAHAHAHA!
HE WAS WEARING A T-SHIRT WITH A MAZE ON IT.
SO YOU'RE TAKARA?
START
THE CEO
GOAL
TAKARA GOT DIS-TRACTED BY THAT.
I SEE.
MAN, I CAN'T BELIEVE A STAR IS COMING OUT OF OUR THEATER COMPANY.
I'LL DO IT EVENTUALLY.
DON'T FORGET TO SIGN THE CONTRACT WHEN YOU GET HOME.
HE'S NOT BEING SCAMMED, IS HE?
GO GET US MORE AUDIENCE MEMBERS, TAKARA.
DO IT RIGHT WHEN YOU GET HOME!
RIGHT AWAY!
HMM...

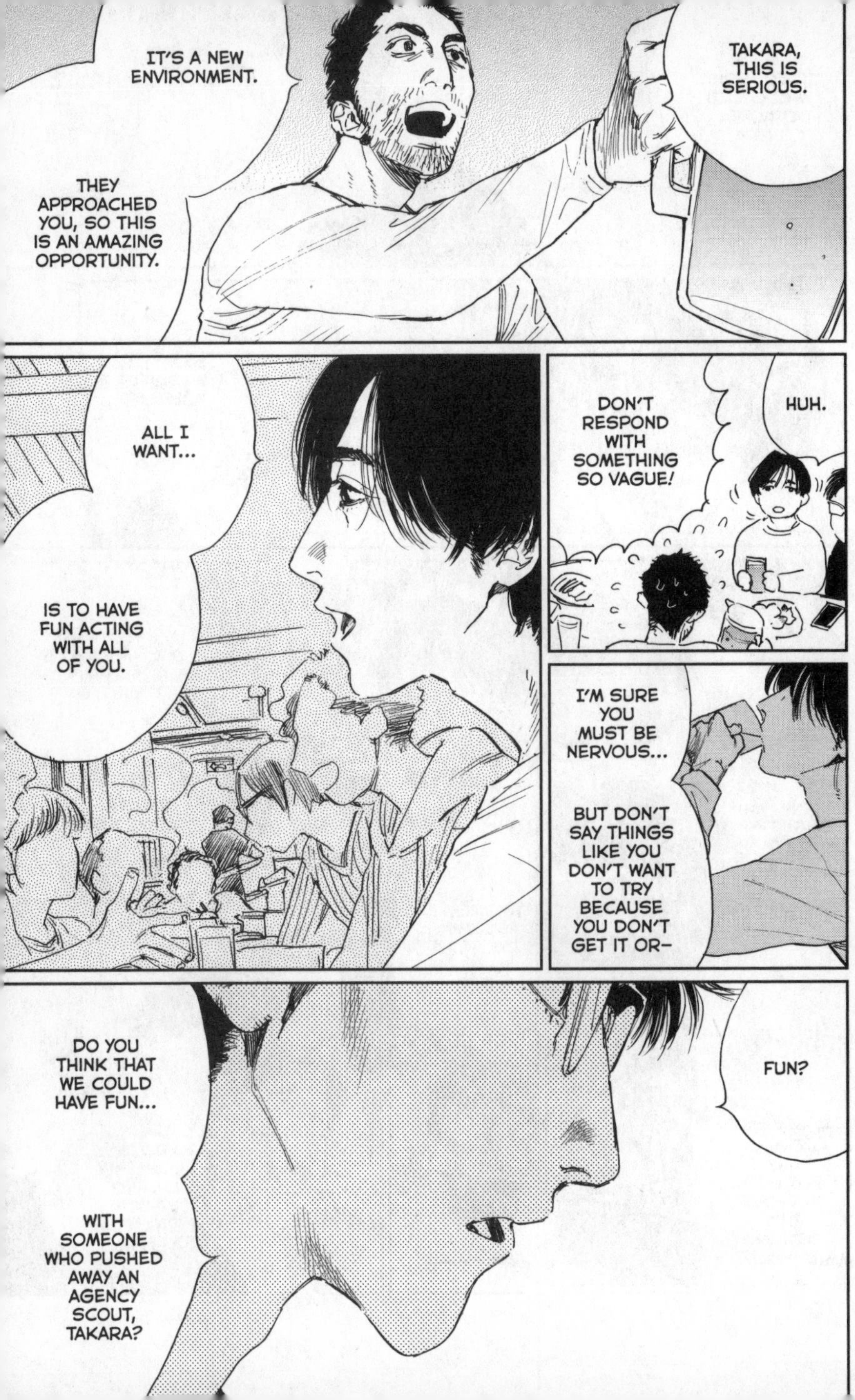
TAKARA, THIS IS SERIOUS.
IT'S A NEW ENVIRONMENT.
THEY APPROACHED YOU, SO THIS IS AN AMAZING OPPORTUNITY.
HUH.
DON'T RESPOND WITH SOMETHING SO VAGUE!
I'M SURE YOU MUST BE NERVOUS...
BUT DON'T SAY THINGS LIKE YOU DON'T WANT TO TRY BECAUSE YOU DON'T GET IT OR–
ALL I WANT...
IS TO HAVE FUN ACTING WITH ALL OF YOU.
FUN?
DO YOU THINK THAT WE COULD HAVE FUN...
WITH SOMEONE WHO PUSHED AWAY AN AGENCY SCOUT, TAKARA?

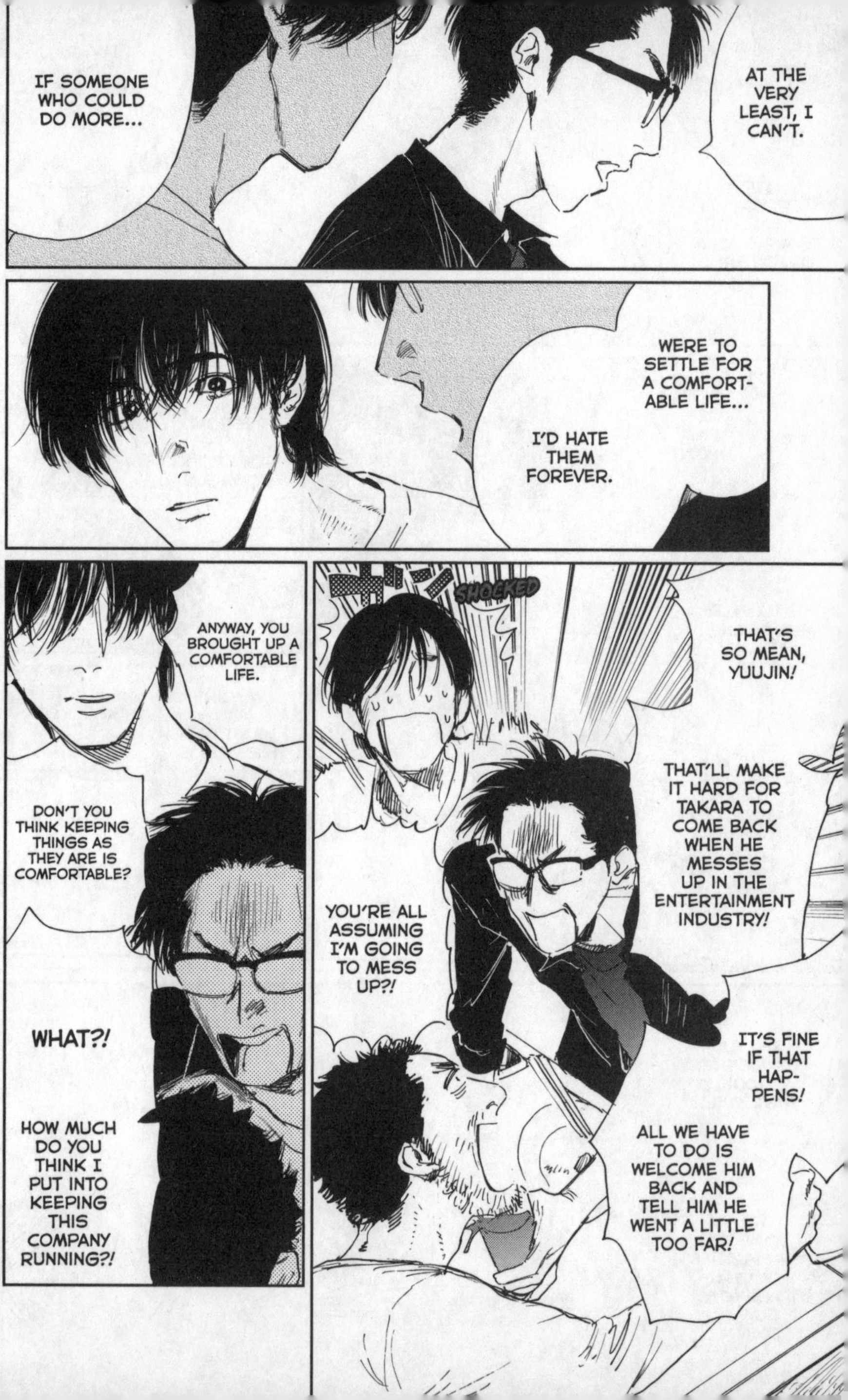
AT THE VERY LEAST, I CAN'T.
IF SOMEONE WHO COULD DO MORE...
WERE TO SETTLE FOR A COMFORTABLE LIFE...
I'D HATE THEM FOREVER.
SHOCKED
THAT'S SO MEAN, YUUJIN!
THAT'LL MAKE IT HARD FOR TAKARA TO COME BACK WHEN HE MESSES UP IN THE ENTERTAINMENT INDUSTRY!
YOU'RE ALL ASSUMING I'M GOING TO MESS UP?!
IT'S FINE IF THAT HAP-PENS!
ALL WE HAVE TO DO IS WELCOME HIM BACK AND TELL HIM HE WENT A LITTLE TOO FAR!
ANYWAY, YOU BROUGHT UP A COMFORTABLE LIFE.
DON'T YOU THINK KEEPING THINGS AS THEY ARE IS COMFORTABLE?
WHAT?!
HOW MUCH DO YOU THINK I PUT INTO KEEPING THIS COMPANY RUNNING?!

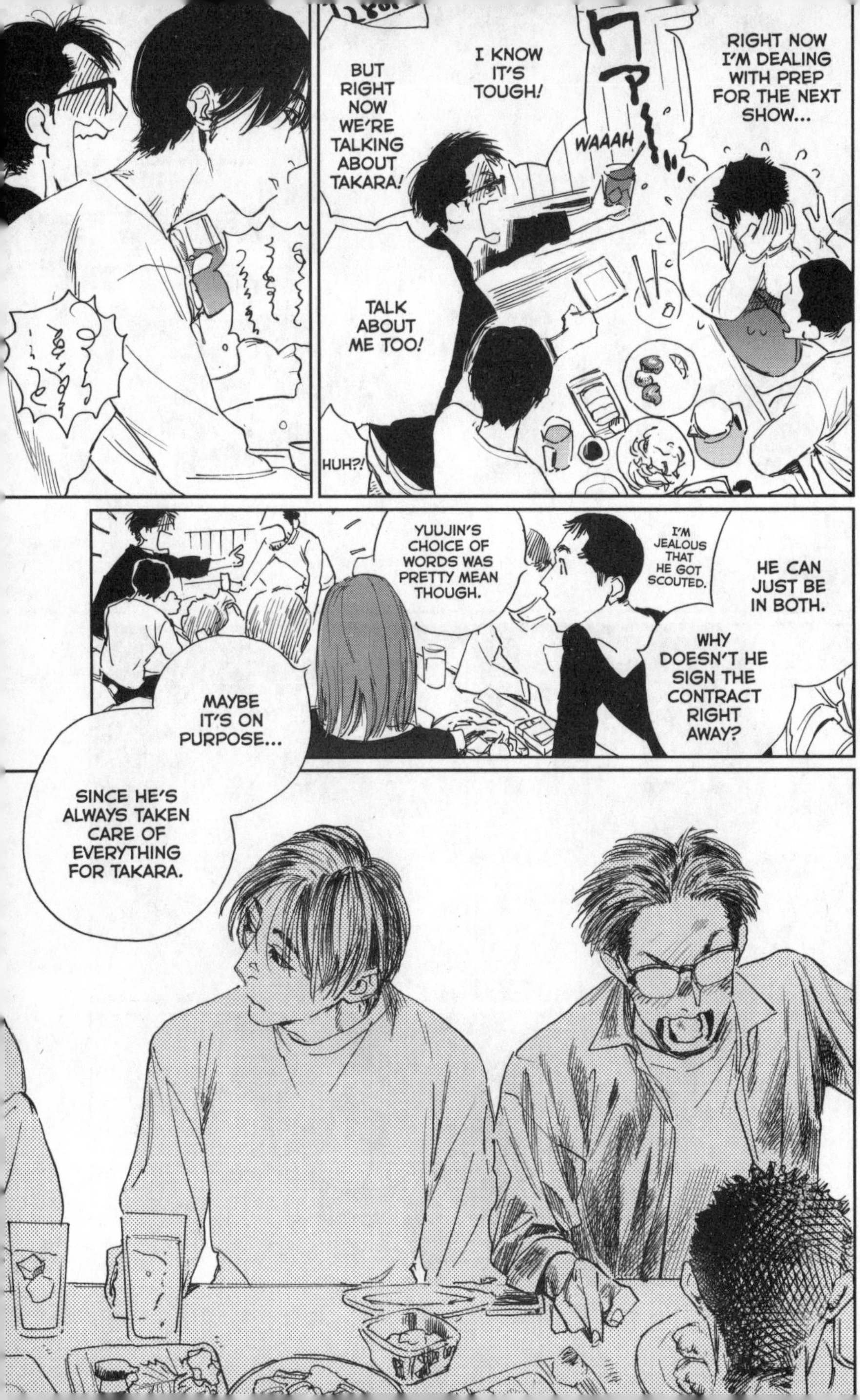
RIGHT NOW I'M DEALING WITH PREP FOR THE NEXT SHOW...
WAAAH
I KNOW IT'S TOUGH!
BUT RIGHT NOW WE'RE TALKING ABOUT TAKARA!
TALK ABOUT ME TOO!
HUH?!
HE CAN JUST BE IN BOTH.
I'M JEALOUS THAT HE GOT SCOUTED.
WHY DOESN'T HE SIGN THE CONTRACT RIGHT AWAY?
YUUJIN'S CHOICE OF WORDS WAS PRETTY MEAN THOUGH.
MAYBE IT'S ON PURPOSE...
SINCE HE'S ALWAYS TAKEN CARE OF EVERYTHING FOR TAKARA.

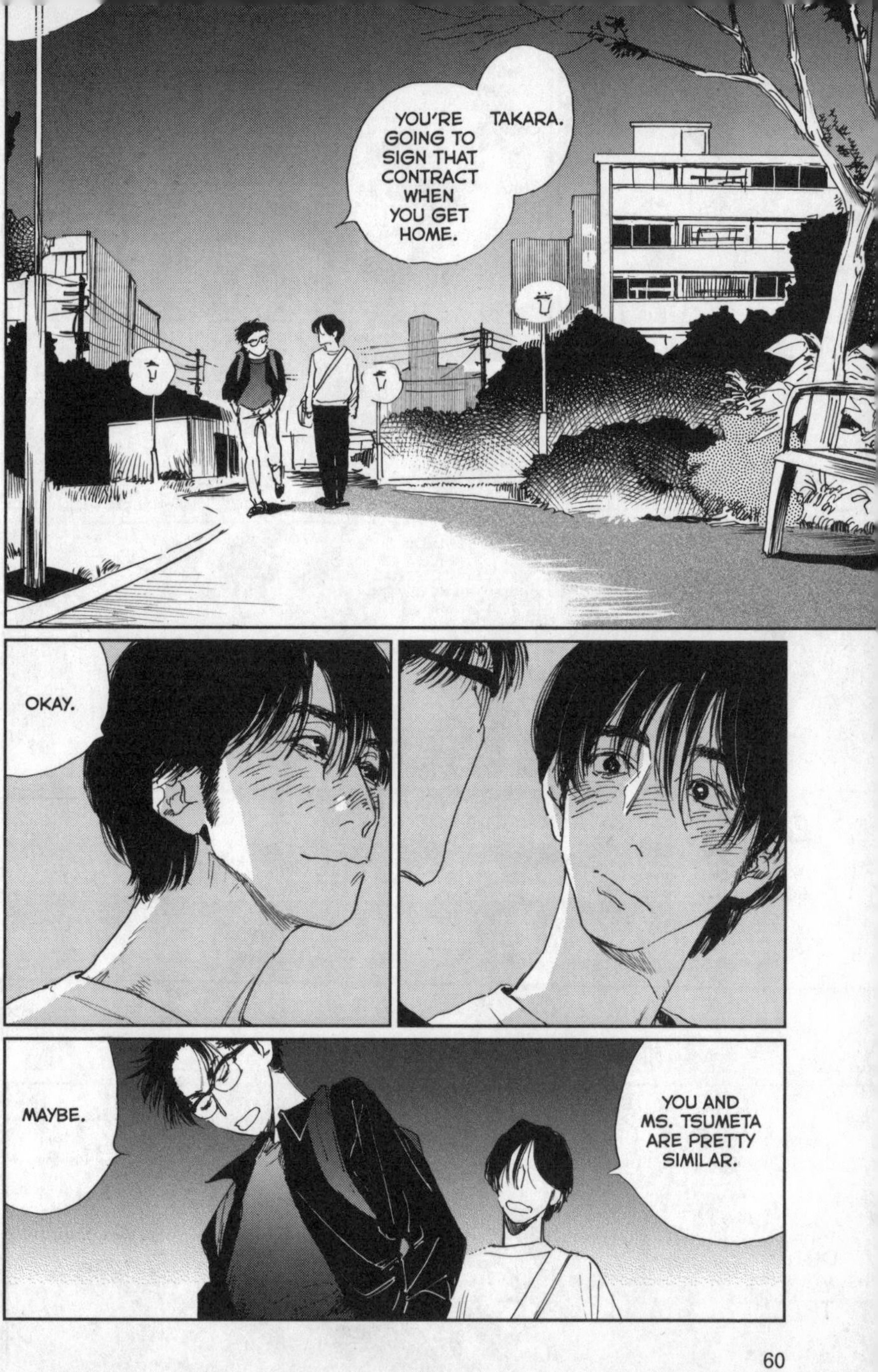
TAKARA.
YOU'RE GOING TO SIGN THAT CONTRACT WHEN YOU GET HOME.
OKAY.
YOU AND MS. TSUMETA ARE PRETTY SIMILAR.
MAYBE.

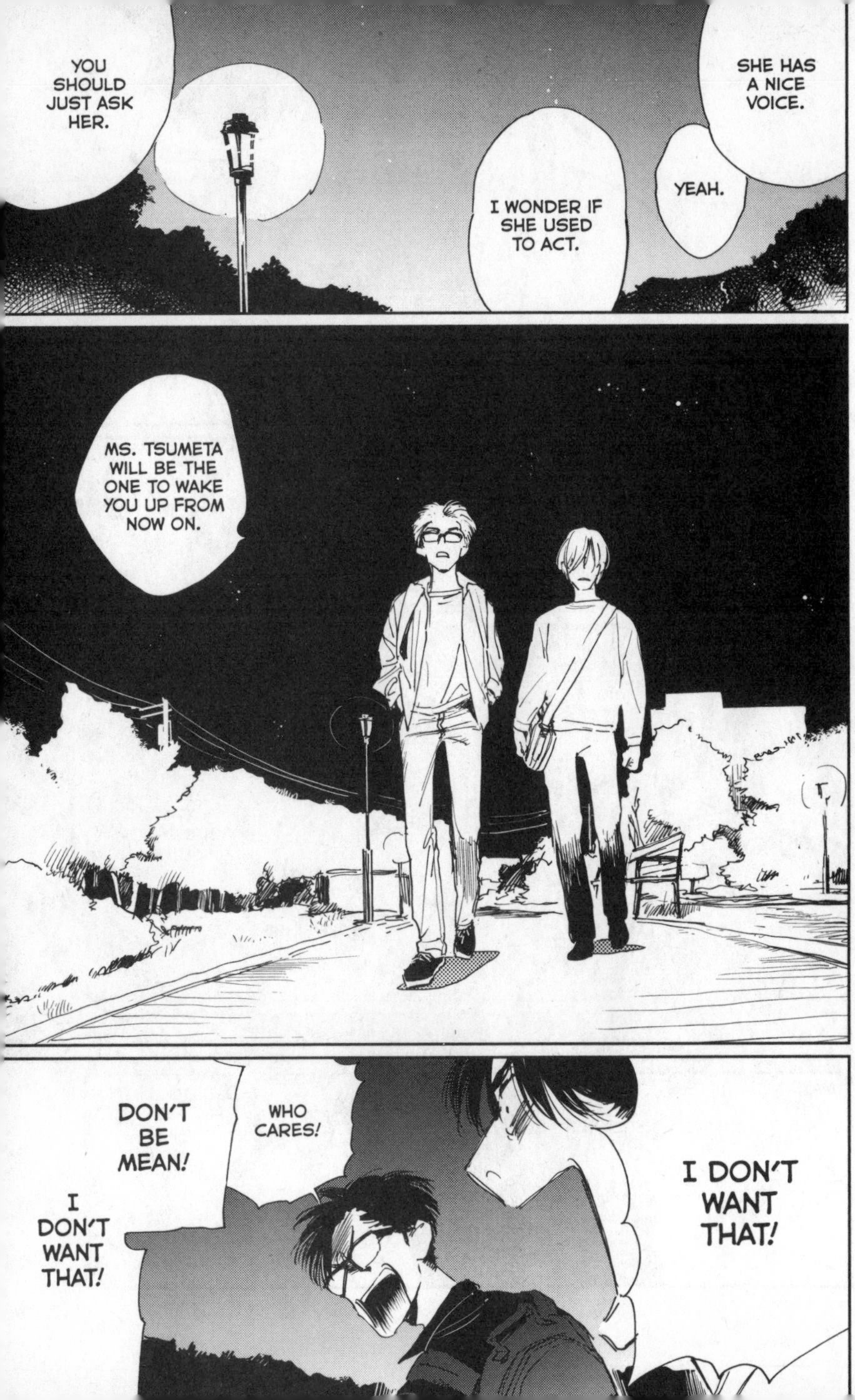
SHE HAS A NICE VOICE.
YEAH.
I WONDER IF SHE USED TO ACT.
YOU SHOULD JUST ASK HER.
MS. TSUMETA WILL BE THE ONE TO WAKE YOU UP FROM NOW ON.
I DON'T WANT THAT!
WHO CARES!
DON'T BE MEAN!
I DON'T WANT THAT!

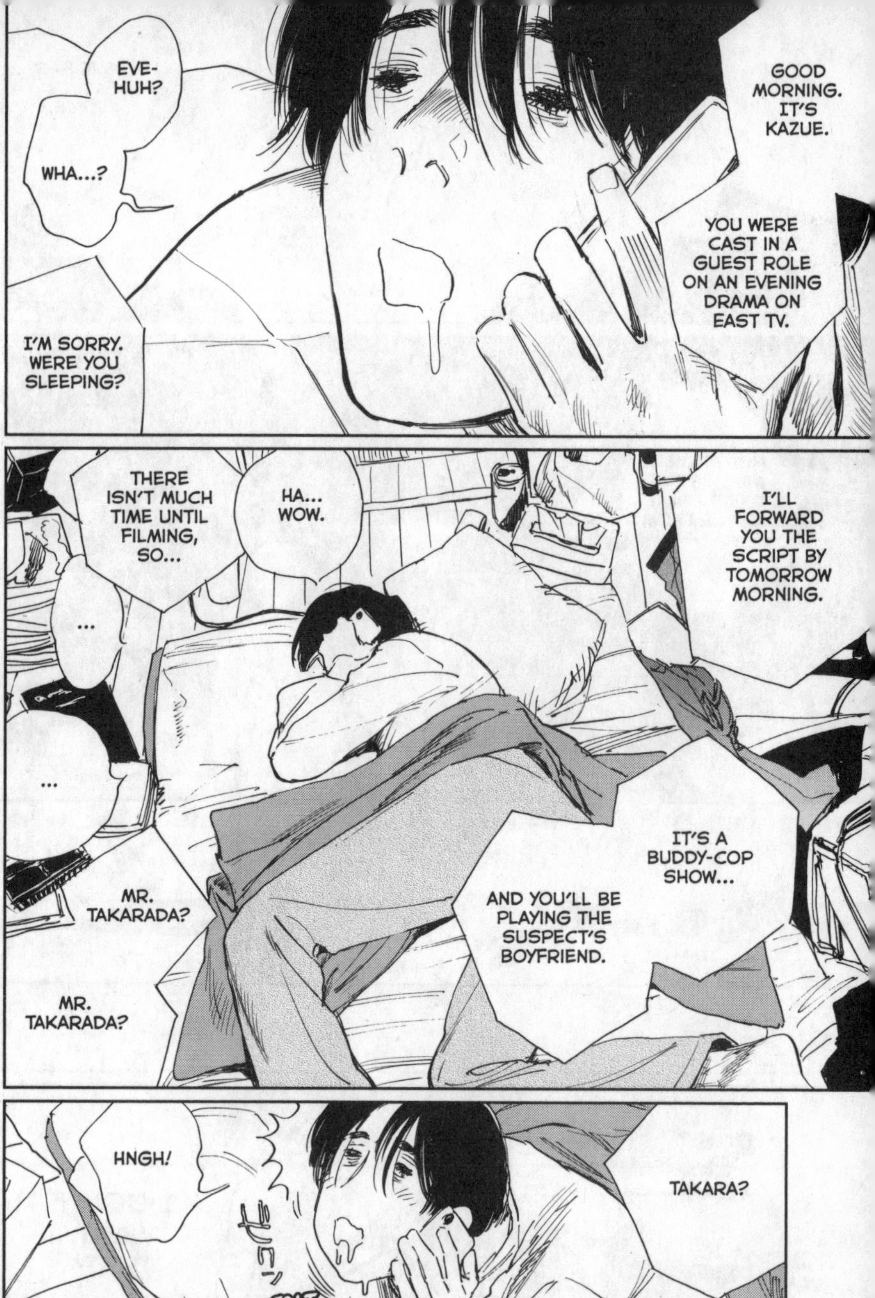
GOOD MORNING. IT'S KAZUE.
EVE-HUH?
WHA...?
YOU WERE CAST IN A GUEST ROLE ON AN EVENING DRAMA ON EAST TV.
I'M SORRY. WERE YOU SLEEPING?
I'LL FORWARD YOU THE SCRIPT BY TOMORROW MORNING.
HA... WOW.
THERE ISN'T MUCH TIME UNTIL FILMING, SO...
...
IT'S A BUDDY-COP SHOW...
AND YOU'LL BE PLAYING THE SUSPECT'S BOYFRIEND.
...
MR. TAKARADA?
MR. TAKARADA?
TAKARA?
HNGH!
JOLT

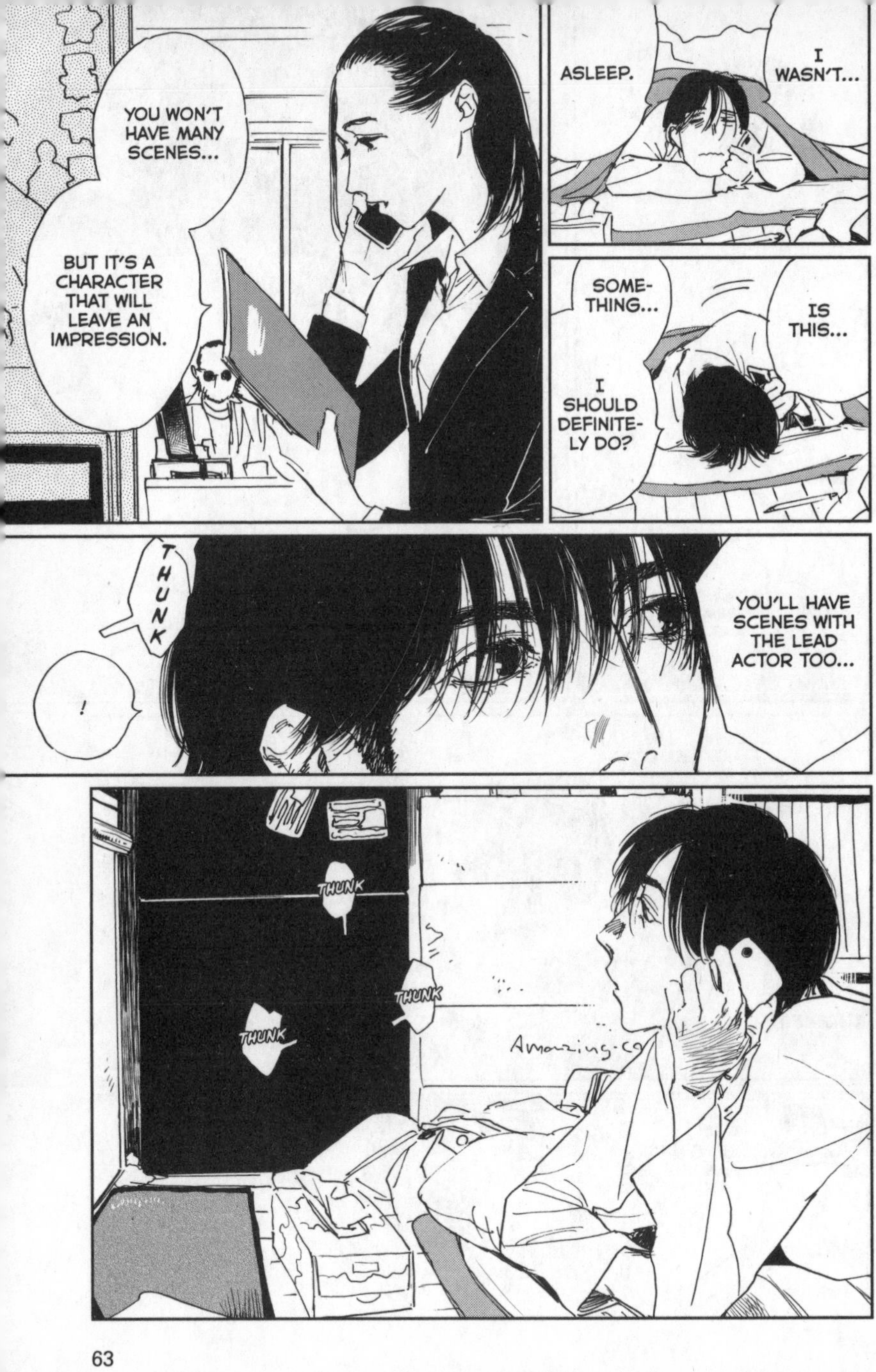
I WASN'T... ASLEEP.
IS THIS...
SOMETHING...
I SHOULD DEFINITELY DO?
YOU WON'T HAVE MANY SCENES...
BUT IT'S A CHARACTER THAT WILL LEAVE AN IMPRESSION.
YOU'LL HAVE SCENES WITH THE LEAD ACTOR TOO...
THUNK
!
THUNK
THUNK
THUNK

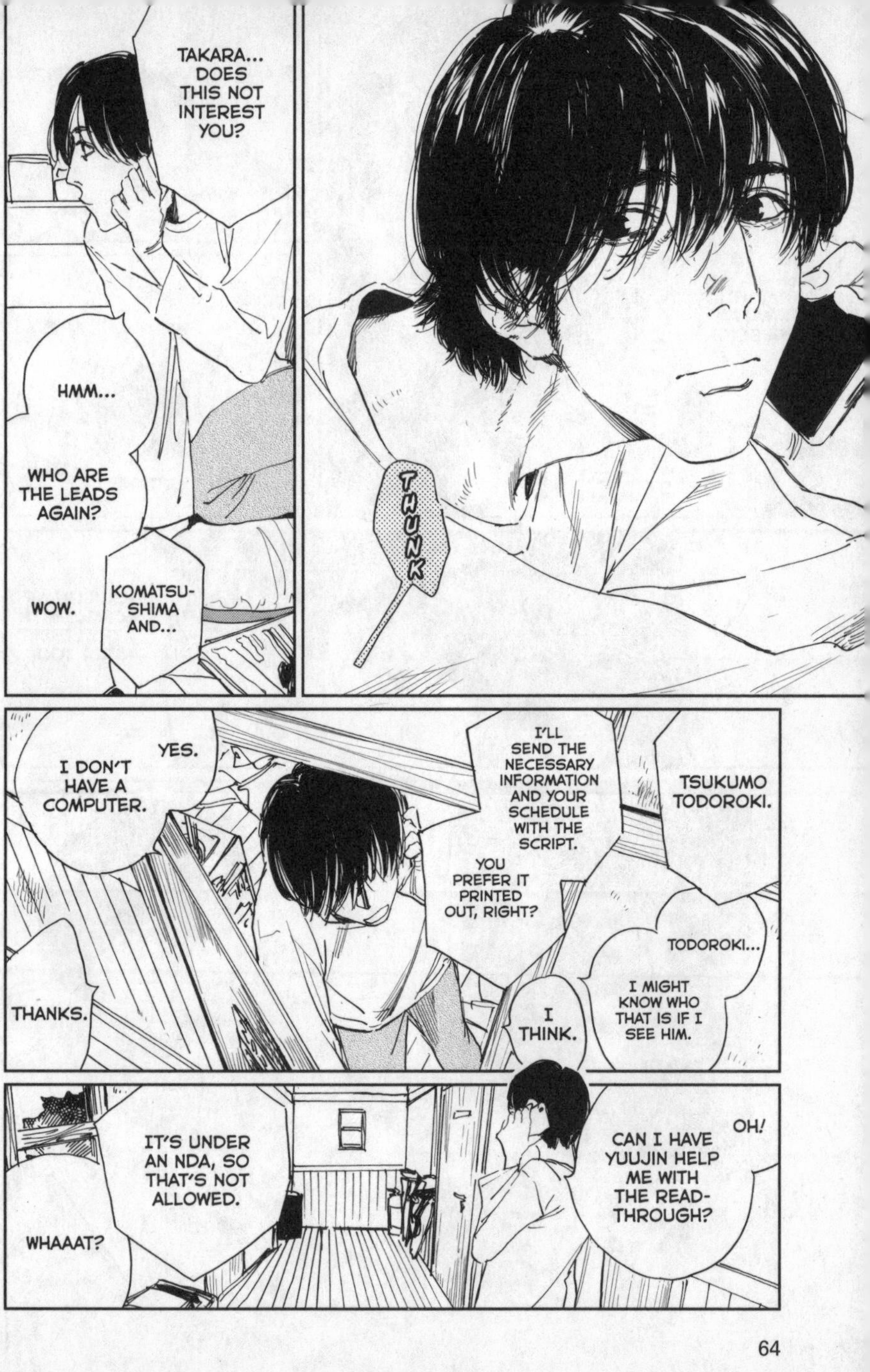
THUNK
TAKARA... DOES THIS NOT INTEREST YOU?
HMM...
WHO ARE THE LEADS AGAIN?
KOMATSU-SHIMA AND...
WOW.
TSUKUMO TODOROKI.
I'LL SEND THE NECESSARY INFORMATION AND YOUR SCHEDULE WITH THE SCRIPT.
YOU PREFER IT PRINTED OUT, RIGHT?
TODOROKI...
I MIGHT KNOW WHO THAT IS IF I SEE HIM.
I THINK.
YES.
I DON'T HAVE A COMPUTER.
THANKS.
OH!
CAN I HAVE YUUJIN HELP ME WITH THE READ-THROUGH?
IT'S UNDER AN NDA, SO THAT'S NOT ALLOWED.
WHAAAT?

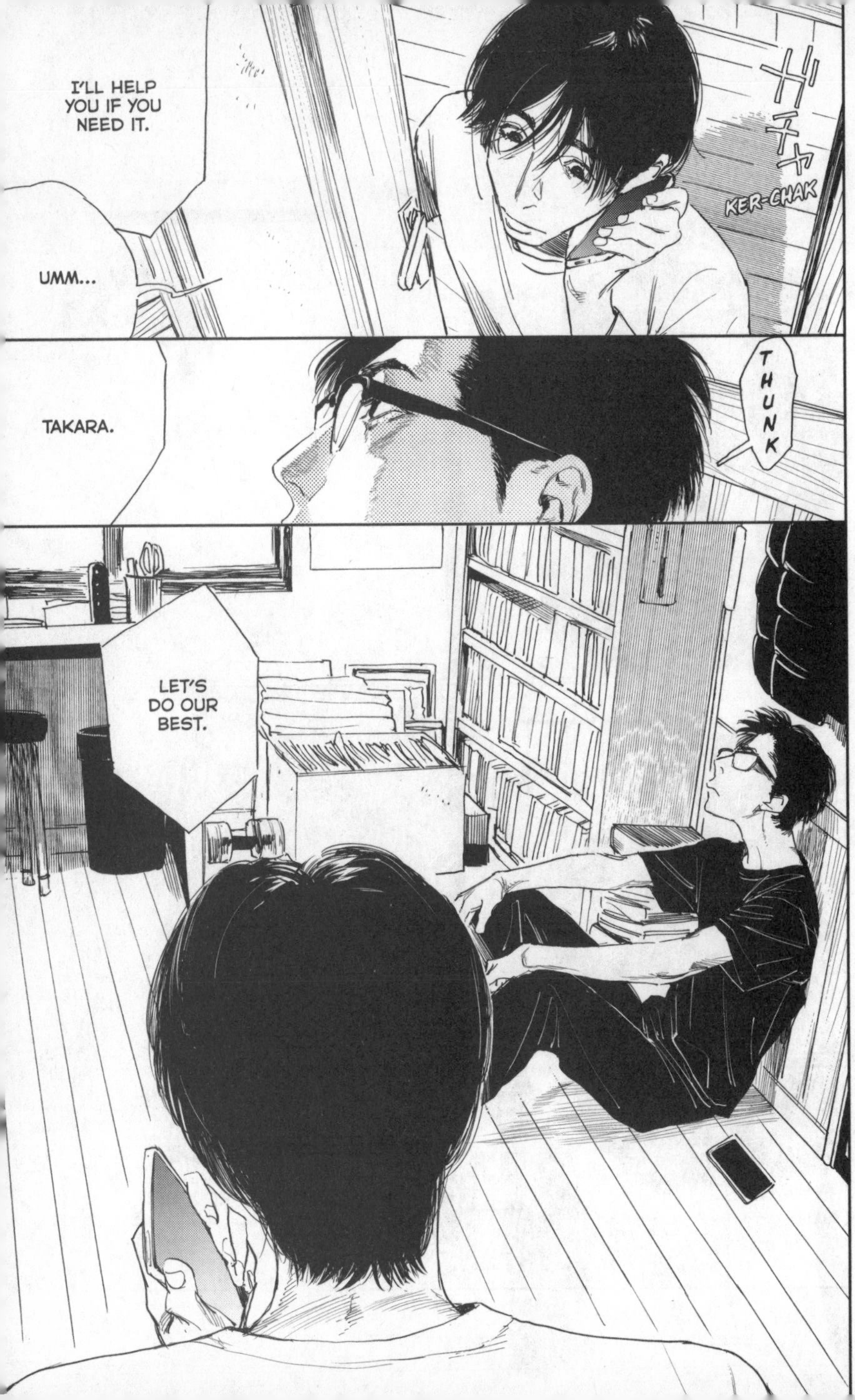
ガチャ
KER-CHAK
I'LL HELP YOU IF YOU NEED IT.
UMM...
THUNK
TAKARA.
LET'S DO OUR BEST.

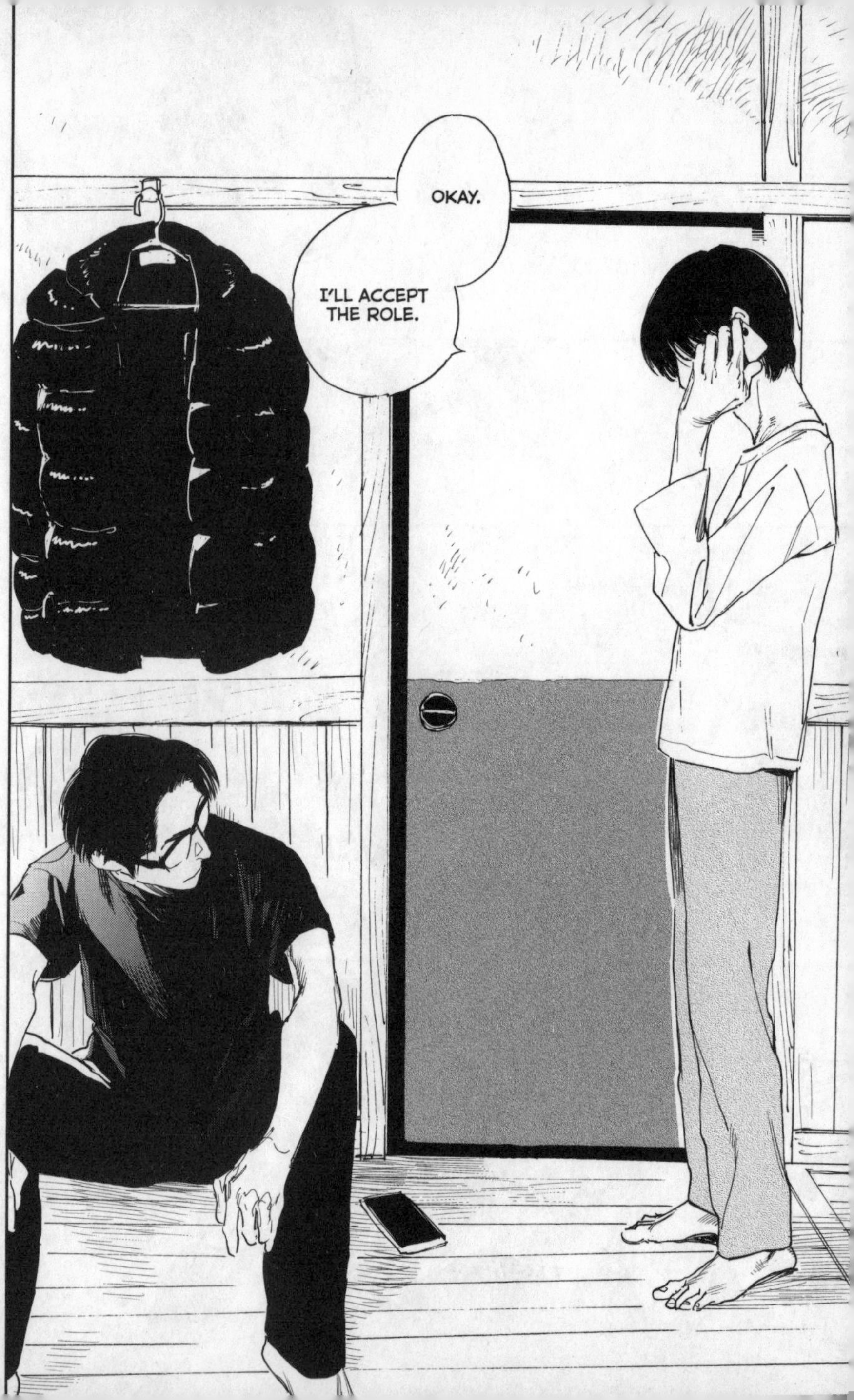
OKAY.
I'LL ACCEPT THE ROLE.

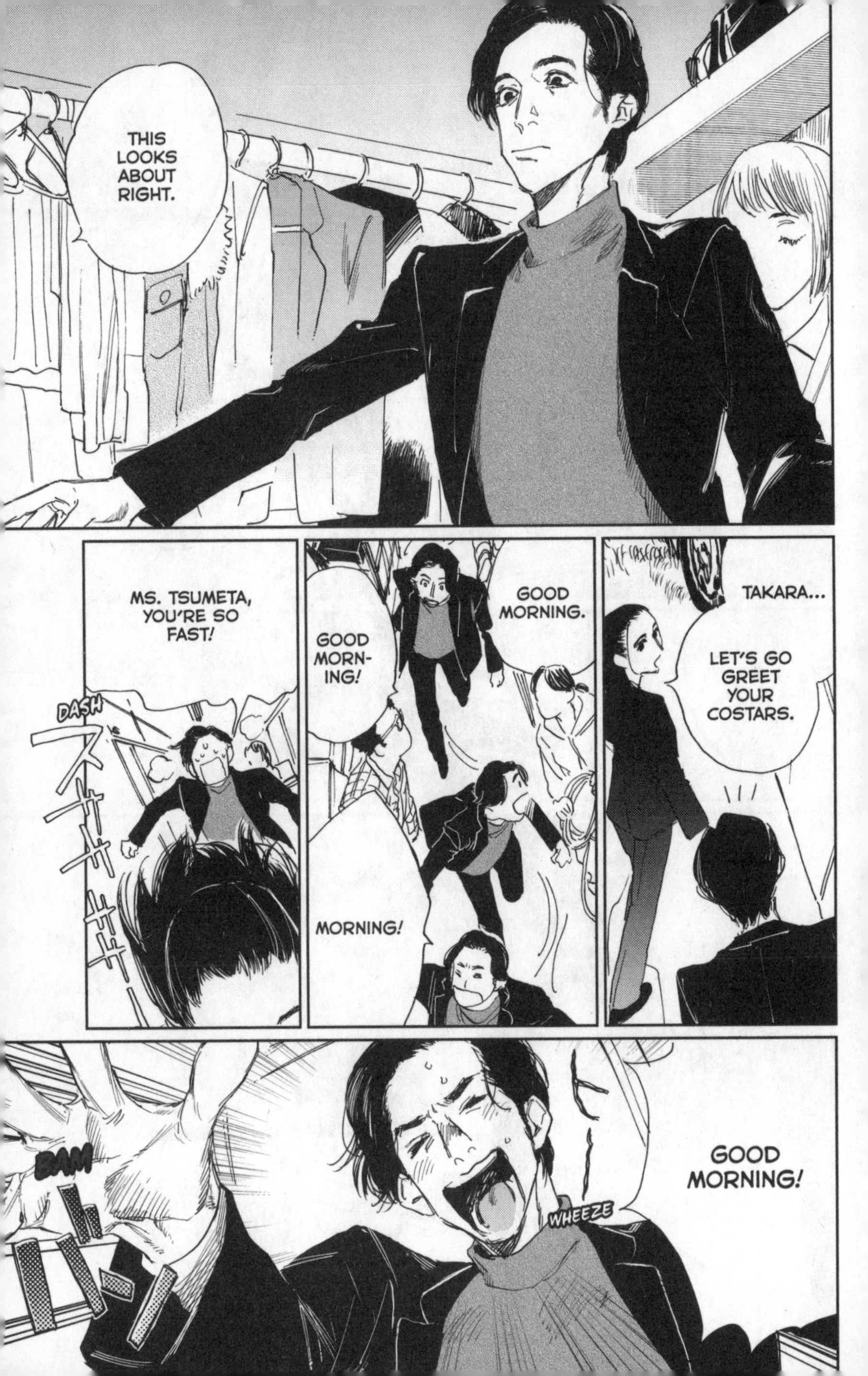
THIS LOOKS ABOUT RIGHT.
TAKARA...
LET'S GO GREET YOUR COSTARS.
GOOD MORNING.
GOOD MORN-ING!
MORNING!
MS. TSUMETA, YOU'RE SO FAST!
DASH
GOOD MORNING!
WHEEZE
BAM

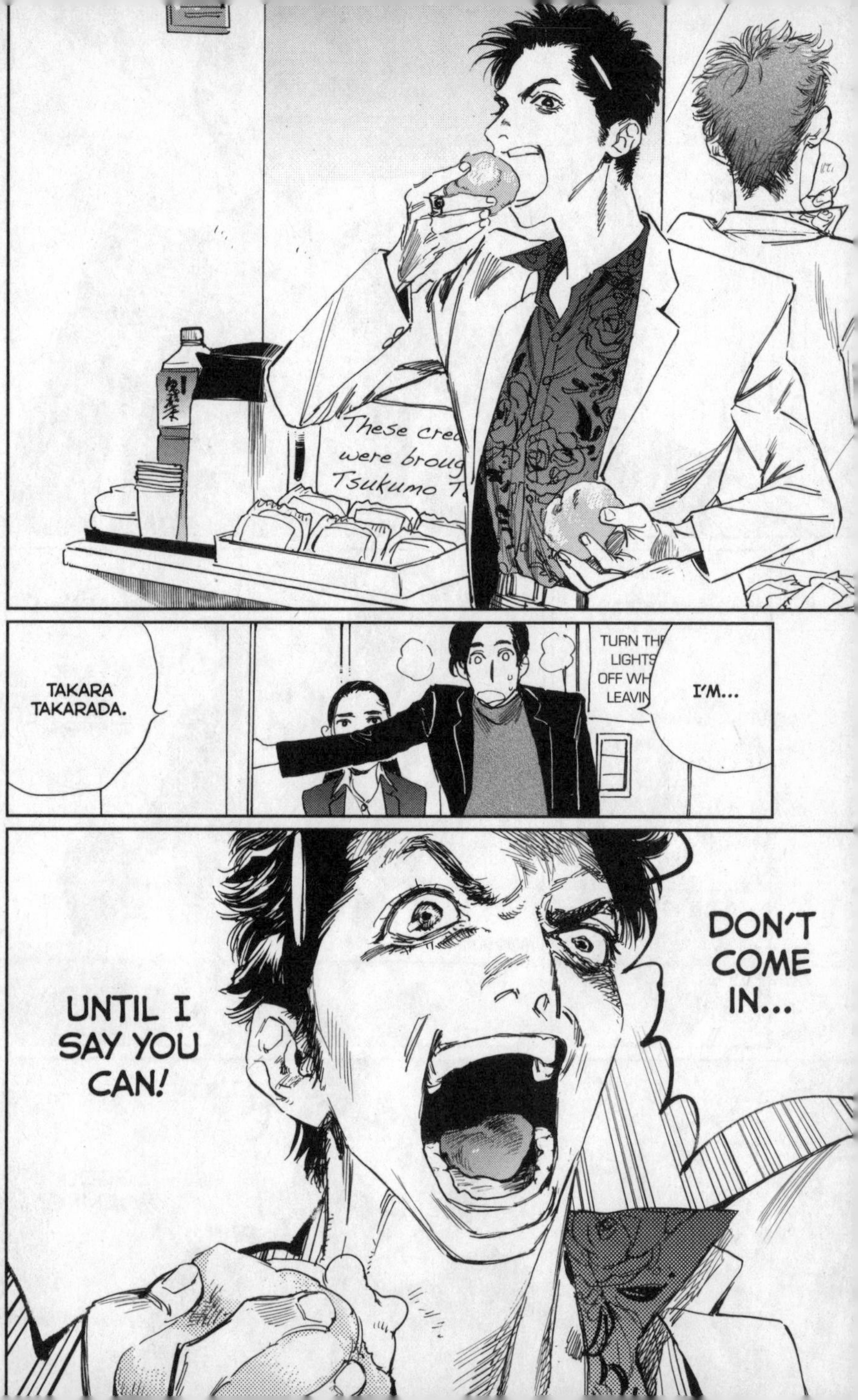
These cre
were broug
Tsukumo T
I'M...
TURN THE
LIGHTS
OFF WH
LEAVIN
TAKARA TAKARADA.
DON'T COME IN...
UNTIL I SAY YOU CAN!

DOUBLE

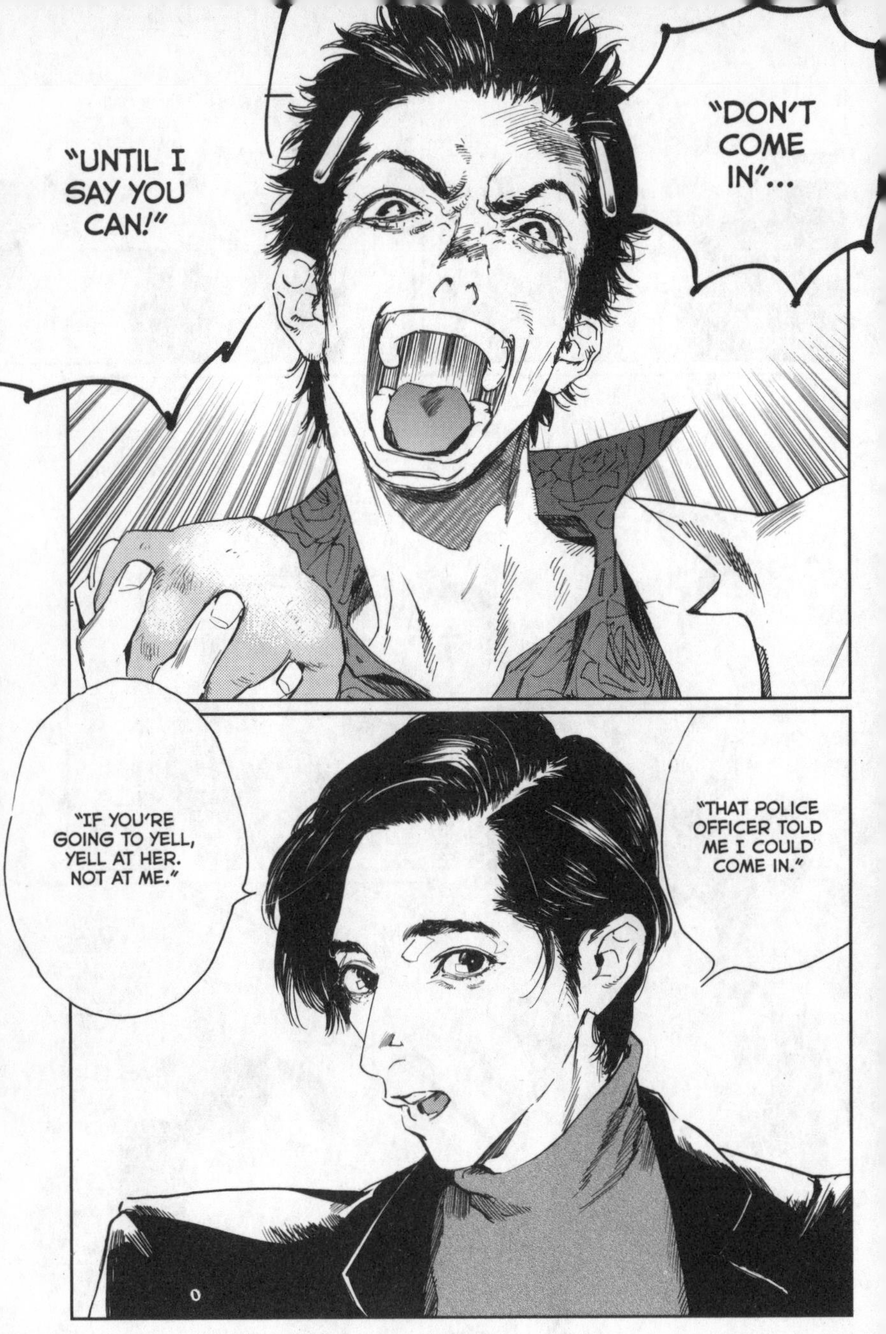
"DON'T COME IN"...
"UNTIL I SAY YOU CAN!"
"THAT POLICE OFFICER TOLD ME I COULD COME IN."
"IF YOU'RE GOING TO YELL, YELL AT HER. NOT AT ME."

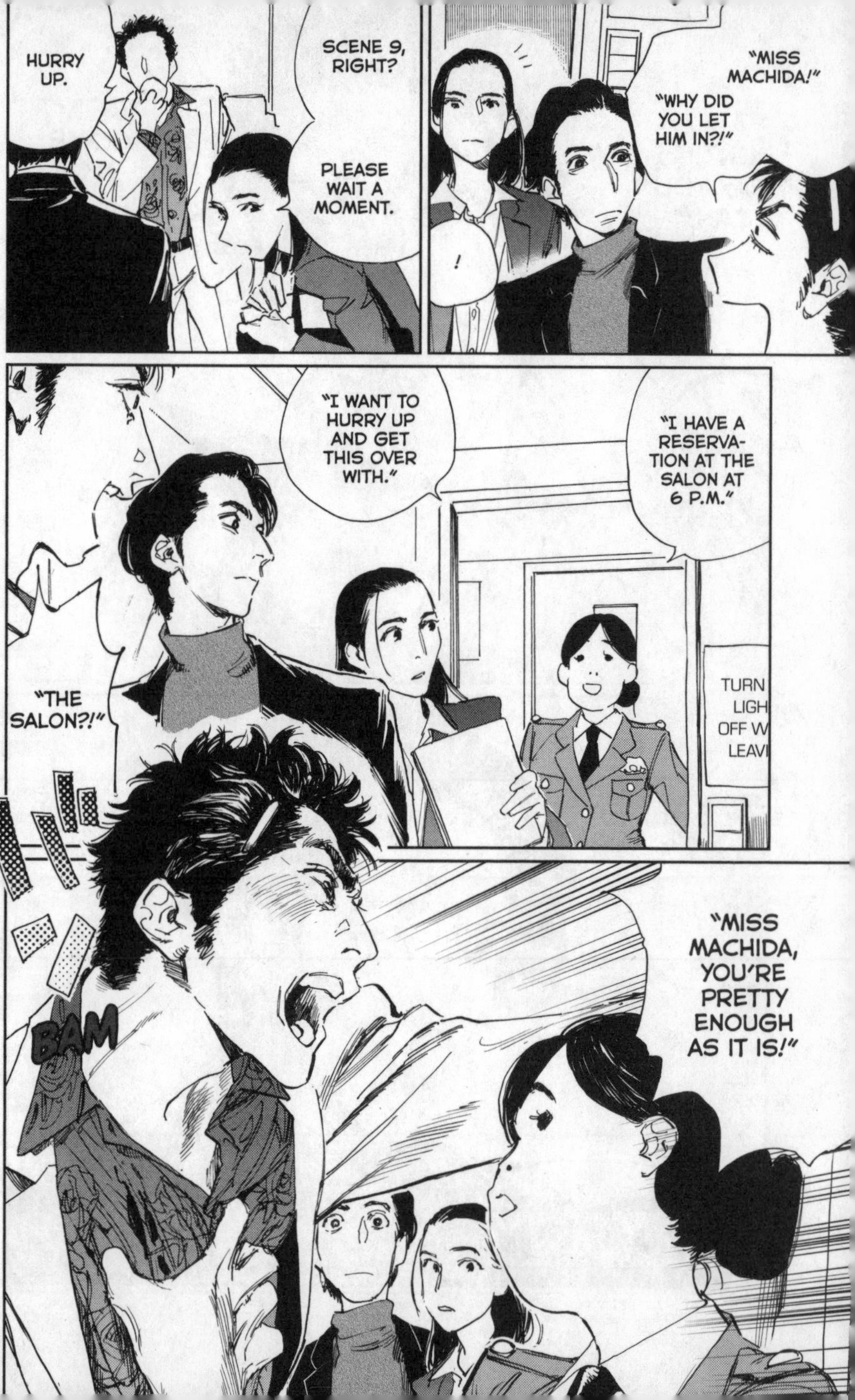
"MISS MACHIDA!"
"WHY DID YOU LET HIM IN?!"
!
SCENE 9, RIGHT?
HURRY UP.
PLEASE WAIT A MOMENT.
"I HAVE A RESERVATION AT THE SALON AT 6 P.M."
"I WANT TO HURRY UP AND GET THIS OVER WITH."
TURN
LIGH
OFF W
LEAVI
"THE SALON?!"
"MISS MACHIDA, YOU'RE PRETTY ENOUGH AS IT IS!"
BAM

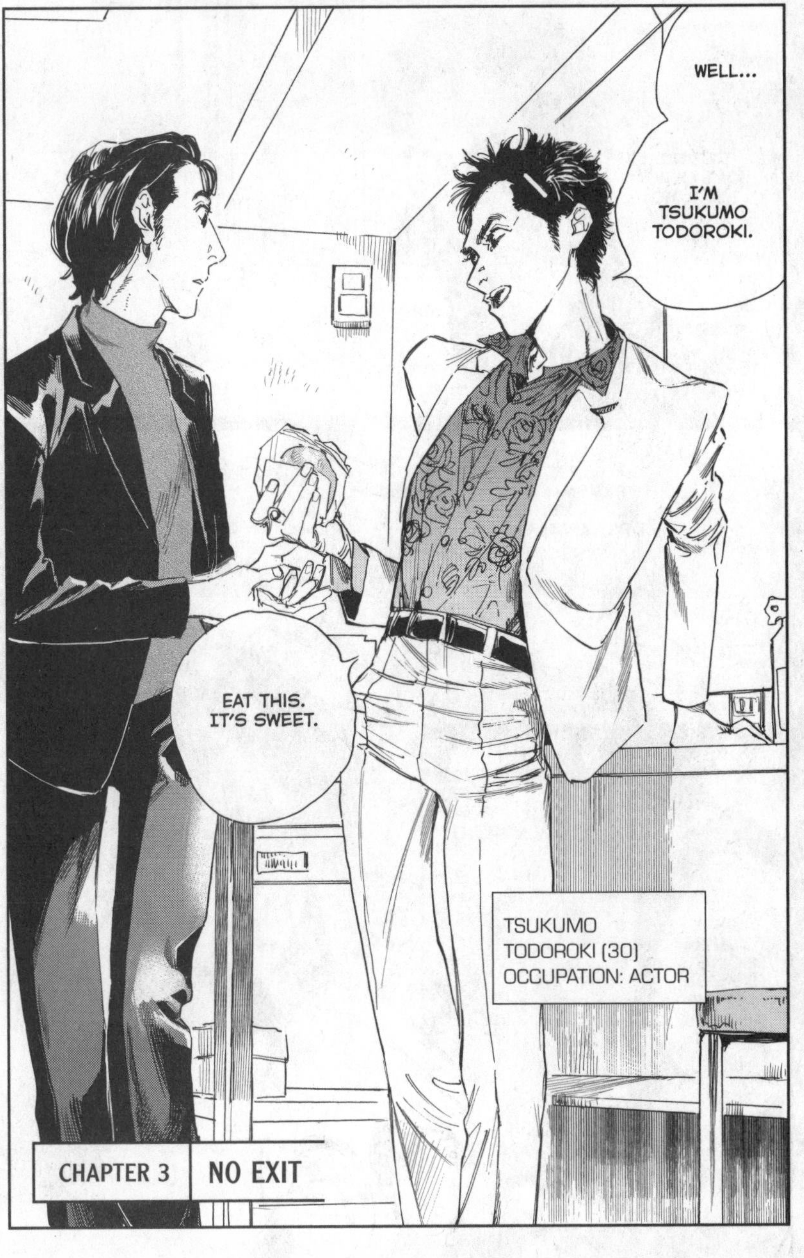
WELL...
I'M TSUKUMO TODOROKI.
EAT THIS. IT'S SWEET.
TSUKUMO TODOROKI (30) OCCUPATION: ACTOR
CHAPTER 3
NO EXIT

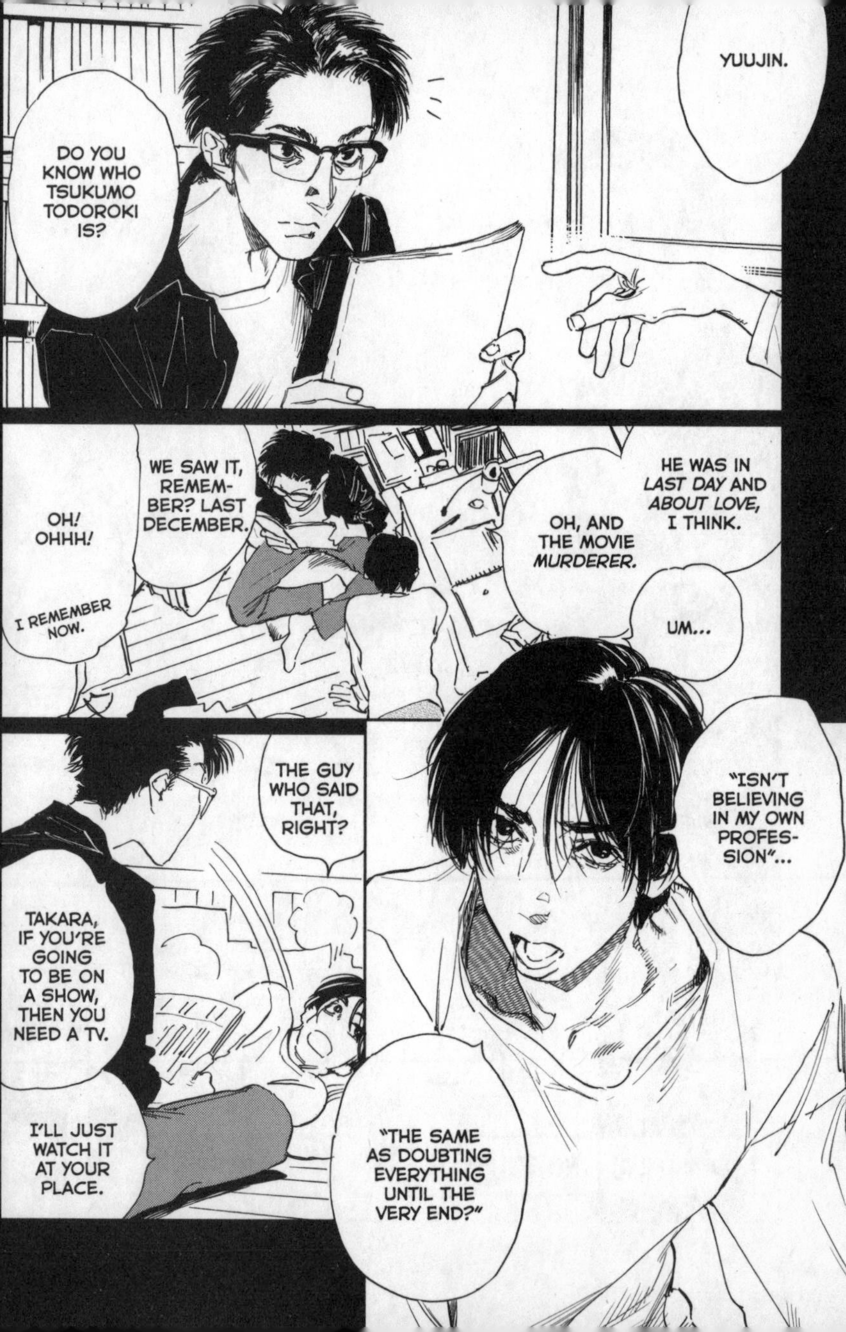
YUUJIN.
DO YOU KNOW WHO TSUKUMO TODOROKI IS?
HE WAS IN *LAST DAY* AND *ABOUT LOVE*, I THINK.
OH, AND THE MOVIE *MURDERER*.
WE SAW IT, REMEMBER? LAST DECEMBER.
OH! OHHH!
I REMEMBER NOW.
UM...
"ISN'T BELIEVING IN MY OWN PROFESSION"...
"THE SAME AS DOUBTING EVERYTHING UNTIL THE VERY END?"
THE GUY WHO SAID THAT, RIGHT?
TAKARA, IF YOU'RE GOING TO BE ON A SHOW, THEN YOU NEED A TV.
I'LL JUST WATCH IT AT YOUR PLACE.

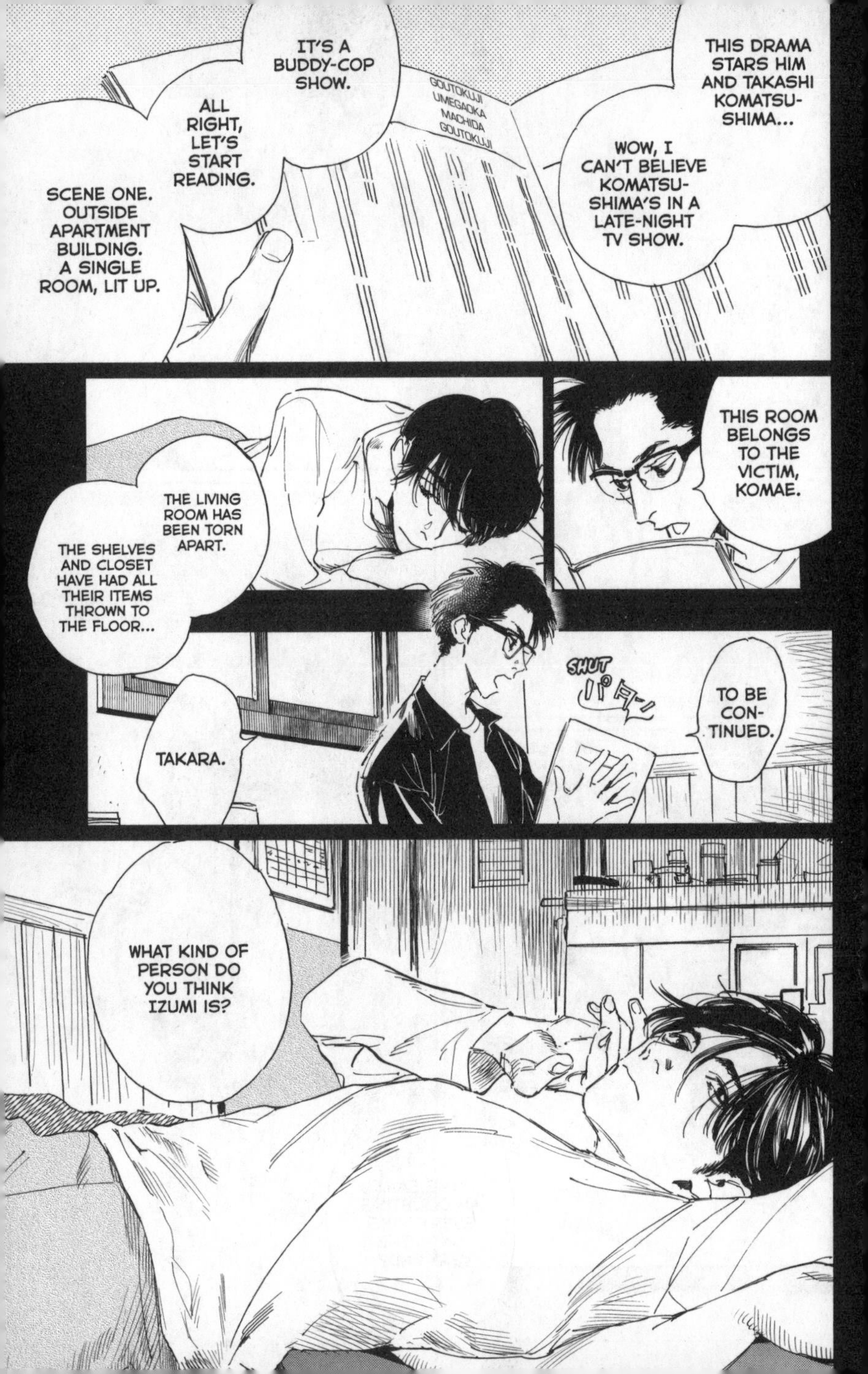
THIS DRAMA STARS HIM AND TAKASHI KOMATSU-SHIMA...
WOW, I CAN'T BELIEVE KOMATSU-SHIMA'S IN A LATE-NIGHT TV SHOW.
IT'S A BUDDY-COP SHOW.
GOUTOKUJI
UMEGAOKA
MACHIDA
GOUTOKUJI
ALL RIGHT, LET'S START READING.
SCENE ONE. OUTSIDE APARTMENT BUILDING. A SINGLE ROOM, LIT UP.
THIS ROOM BELONGS TO THE VICTIM, KOMAE.
THE LIVING ROOM HAS BEEN TORN APART.
THE SHELVES AND CLOSET HAVE HAD ALL THEIR ITEMS THROWN TO THE FLOOR...
TO BE CON-TINUED.
SHUT
TAKARA.
WHAT KIND OF PERSON DO YOU THINK IZUMI IS?

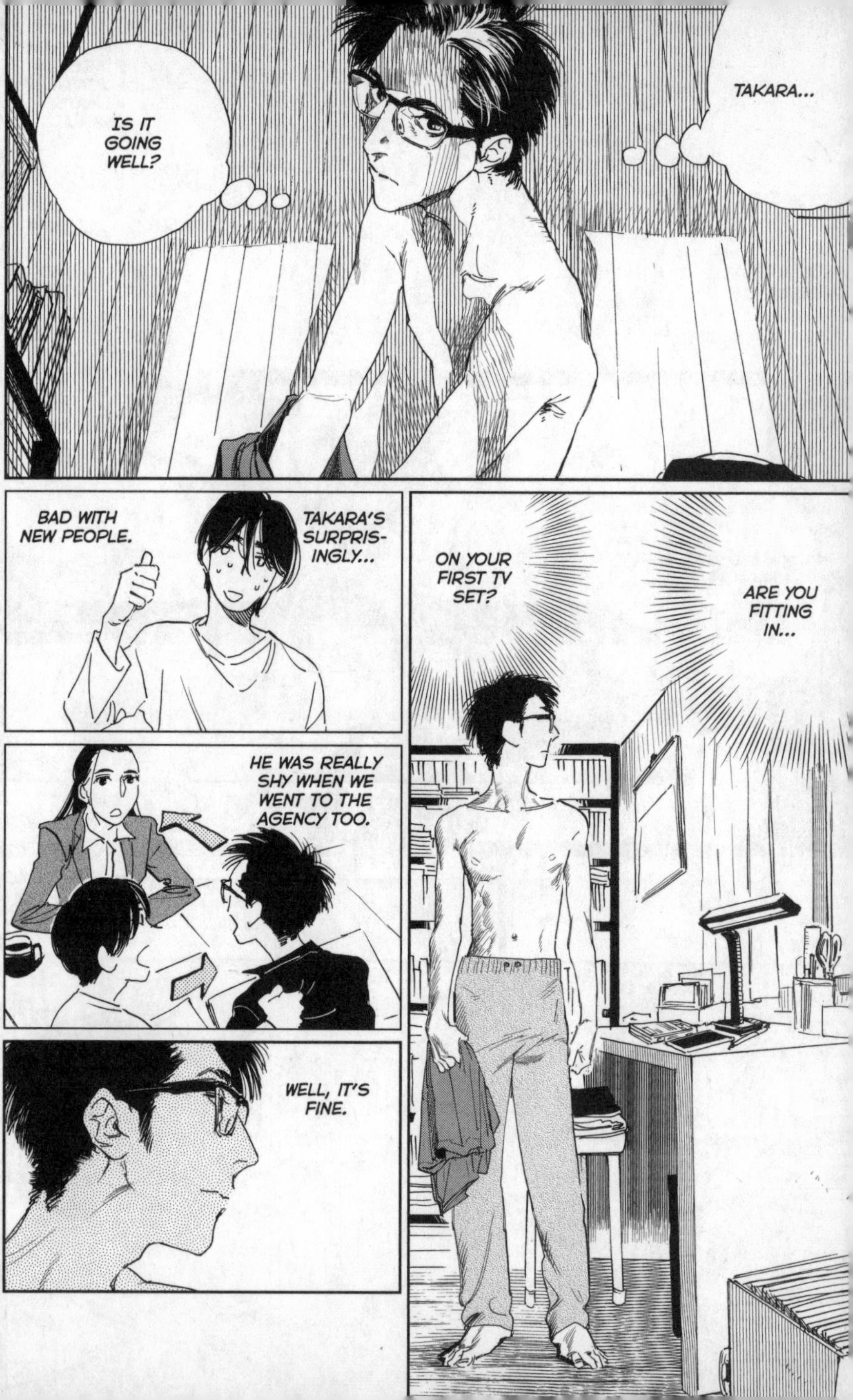
TAKARA...
IS IT GOING WELL?
ARE YOU FITTING IN...
ON YOUR FIRST TV SET?
TAKARA'S SURPRIS-INGLY...
BAD WITH NEW PEOPLE.
HE WAS REALLY SHY WHEN WE WENT TO THE AGENCY TOO.
WELL, IT'S FINE.

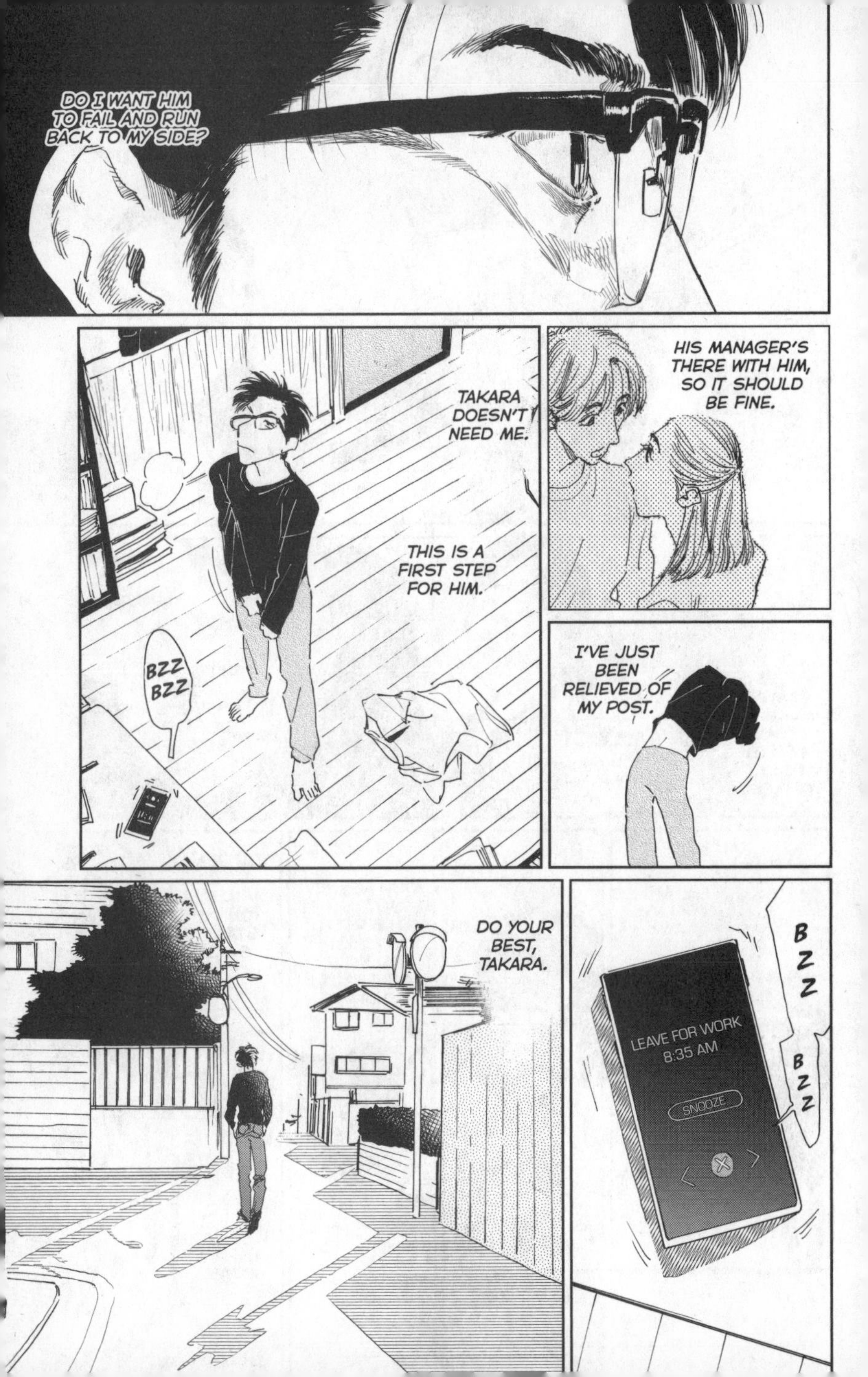
DO I WANT HIM TO FAIL AND RUN BACK TO MY SIDE?
HIS MANAGER'S THERE WITH HIM, SO IT SHOULD BE FINE.
I'VE JUST BEEN RELIEVED OF MY POST.
TAKARA DOESN'T NEED ME.
THIS IS A FIRST STEP FOR HIM.
BZZ BZZ
BZZ BZZ
LEAVE FOR WORK 8:35 AM
SNOOZE
DO YOUR BEST, TAKARA.

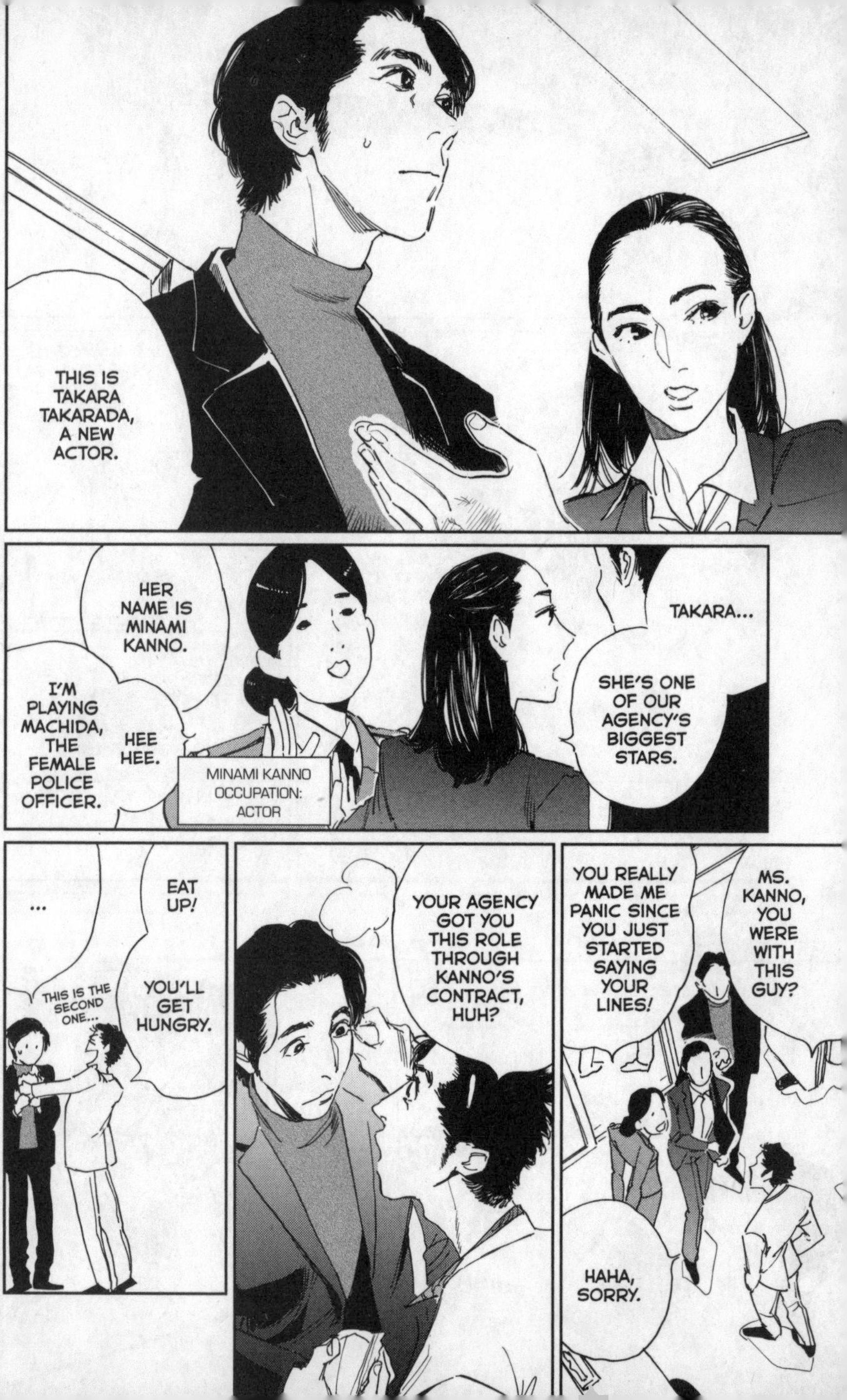
THIS IS TAKARA TAKARADA, A NEW ACTOR.
TAKARA...
SHE'S ONE OF OUR AGENCY'S BIGGEST STARS.
HER NAME IS MINAMI KANNO.
MINAMI KANNO OCCUPATION: ACTOR
HEE HEE.
I'M PLAYING MACHIDA, THE FEMALE POLICE OFFICER.
MS. KANNO, YOU WERE WITH THIS GUY?
YOU REALLY MADE ME PANIC SINCE YOU JUST STARTED SAYING YOUR LINES!
HAHA, SORRY.
YOUR AGENCY GOT YOU THIS ROLE THROUGH KANNO'S CONTRACT, HUH?
EAT UP!
...
YOU'LL GET HUNGRY.
THIS IS THE SECOND ONE...

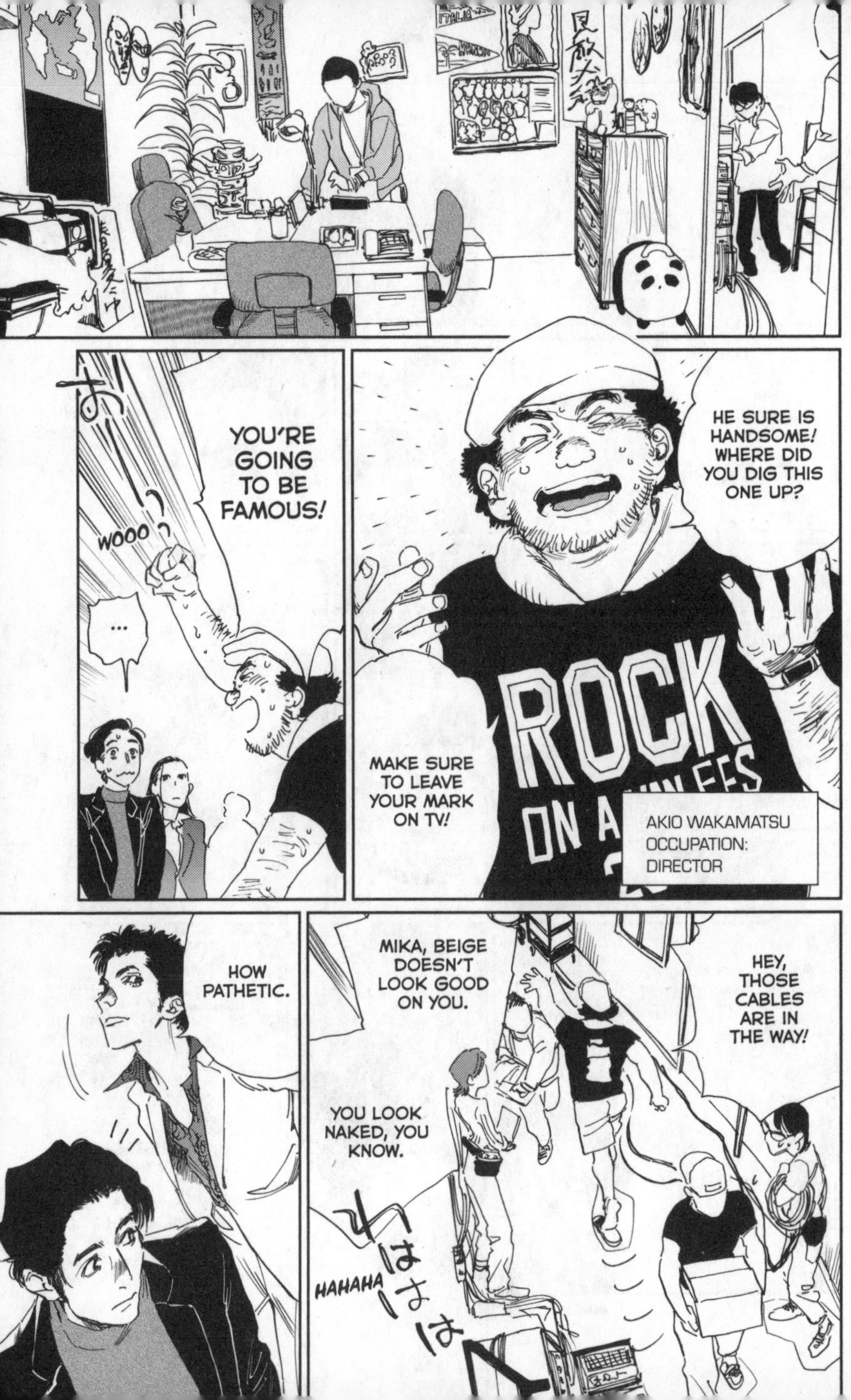
HE SURE IS HANDSOME! WHERE DID YOU DIG THIS ONE UP?
MAKE SURE TO LEAVE YOUR MARK ON TV!
AKIO WAKAMATSU
OCCUPATION:
DIRECTOR
YOU'RE GOING TO BE FAMOUS!
WOOO
...
HEY, THOSE CABLES ARE IN THE WAY!
MIKA, BEIGE DOESN'T LOOK GOOD ON YOU.
YOU LOOK NAKED, YOU KNOW.
HAHAHA
HOW PATHETIC.

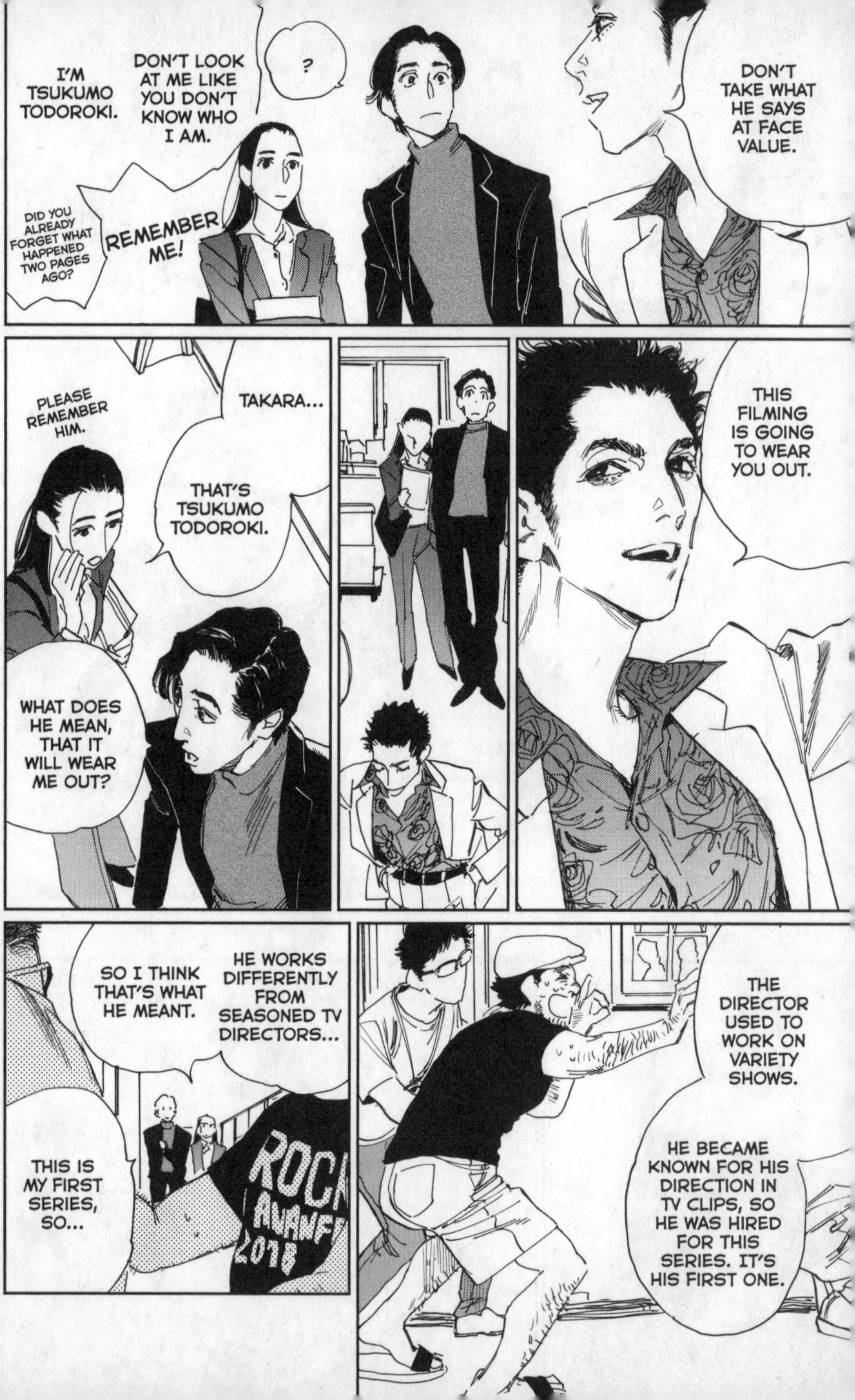
DON'T TAKE WHAT HE SAYS AT FACE VALUE.
?
DON'T LOOK AT ME LIKE YOU DON'T KNOW WHO I AM.
I'M TSUKUMO TODOROKI.
REMEMBER ME!
DID YOU ALREADY FORGET WHAT HAPPENED TWO PAGES AGO?
THIS FILMING IS GOING TO WEAR YOU OUT.
TAKARA...
THAT'S TSUKUMO TODOROKI.
PLEASE REMEMBER HIM.
WHAT DOES HE MEAN, THAT IT WILL WEAR ME OUT?
THE DIRECTOR USED TO WORK ON VARIETY SHOWS.
HE BECAME KNOWN FOR HIS DIRECTION IN TV CLIPS, SO HE WAS HIRED FOR THIS SERIES. IT'S HIS FIRST ONE.
HE WORKS DIFFERENTLY FROM SEASONED TV DIRECTORS...
SO I THINK THAT'S WHAT HE MEANT.
THIS IS MY FIRST SERIES, SO...

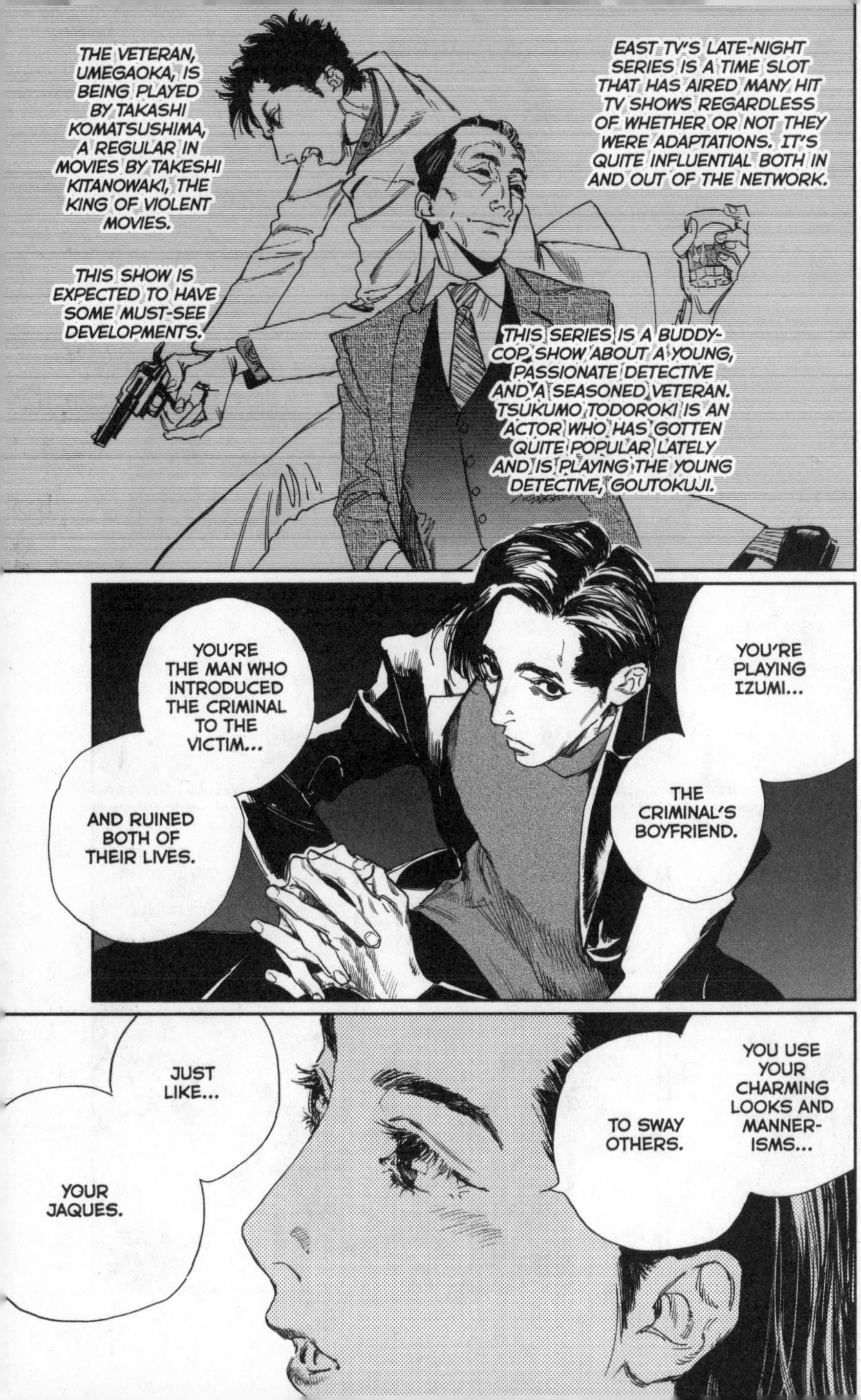
EAST TV'S LATE-NIGHT SERIES IS A TIME SLOT THAT HAS AIRED MANY HIT TV SHOWS REGARDLESS OF WHETHER OR NOT THEY WERE ADAPTATIONS. IT'S QUITE INFLUENTIAL BOTH IN AND OUT OF THE NETWORK.
THIS SERIES IS A BUDDY-COP SHOW ABOUT A YOUNG, PASSIONATE DETECTIVE AND A SEASONED VETERAN. TSUKUMO TODOROKI IS AN ACTOR WHO HAS GOTTEN QUITE POPULAR LATELY AND IS PLAYING THE YOUNG DETECTIVE, GOUTOKUJI.
THE VETERAN, UMEGAOKA, IS BEING PLAYED BY TAKASHI KOMATSUSHIMA, A REGULAR IN MOVIES BY TAKESHI KITANOWAKI, THE KING OF VIOLENT MOVIES.
THIS SHOW IS EXPECTED TO HAVE SOME MUST-SEE DEVELOPMENTS.
YOU'RE PLAYING IZUMI...
THE CRIMINAL'S BOYFRIEND.
YOU'RE THE MAN WHO INTRODUCED THE CRIMINAL TO THE VICTIM...
AND RUINED BOTH OF THEIR LIVES.
YOU USE YOUR CHARMING LOOKS AND MANNER-ISMS...
TO SWAY OTHERS.
JUST LIKE...
YOUR JAQUES.

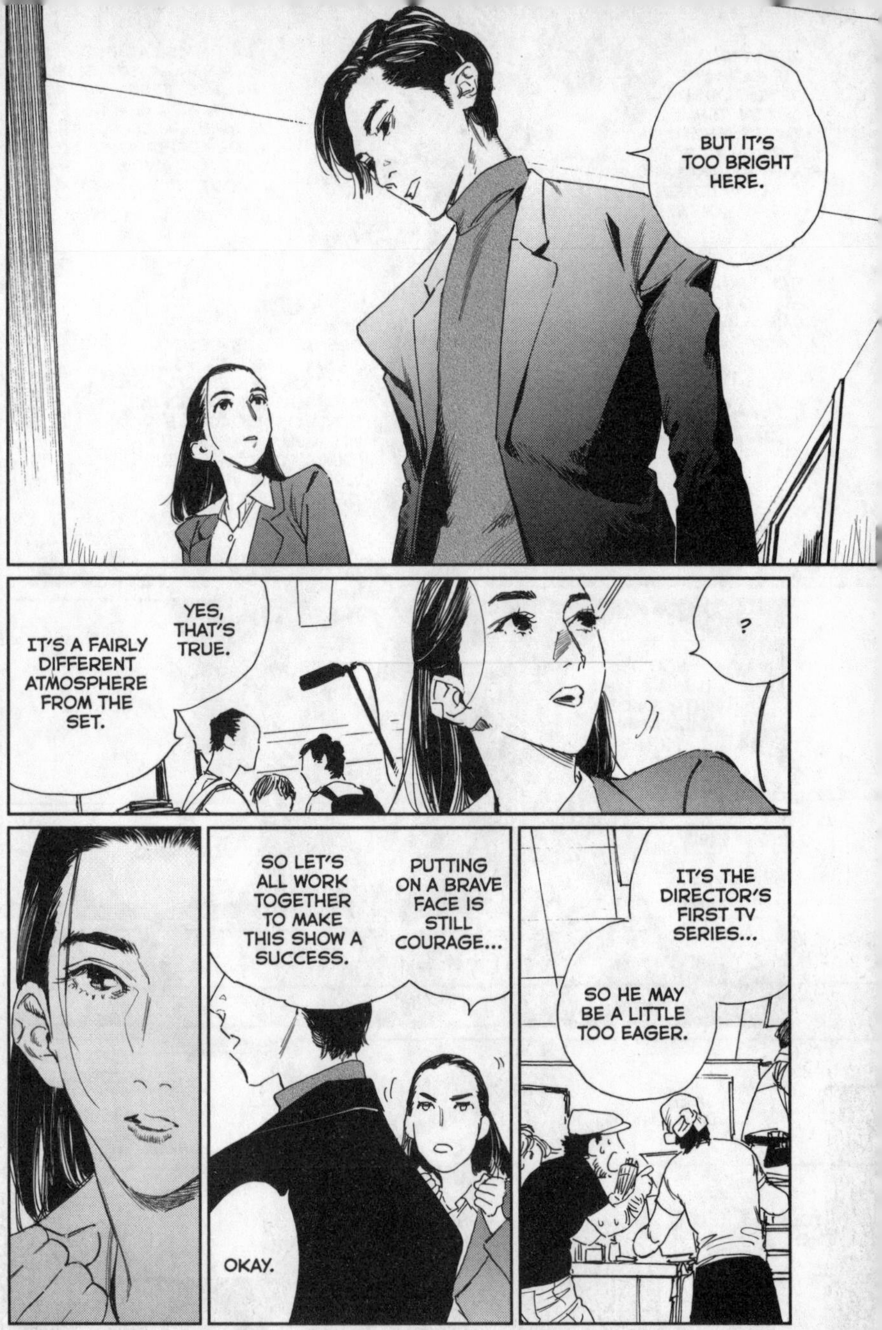
BUT IT'S TOO BRIGHT HERE.
?
YES, THAT'S TRUE.
IT'S A FAIRLY DIFFERENT ATMOSPHERE FROM THE SET.
IT'S THE DIRECTOR'S FIRST TV SERIES...
SO HE MAY BE A LITTLE TOO EAGER.
PUTTING ON A BRAVE FACE IS STILL COURAGE...
SO LET'S ALL WORK TOGETHER TO MAKE THIS SHOW A SUCCESS.
OKAY.

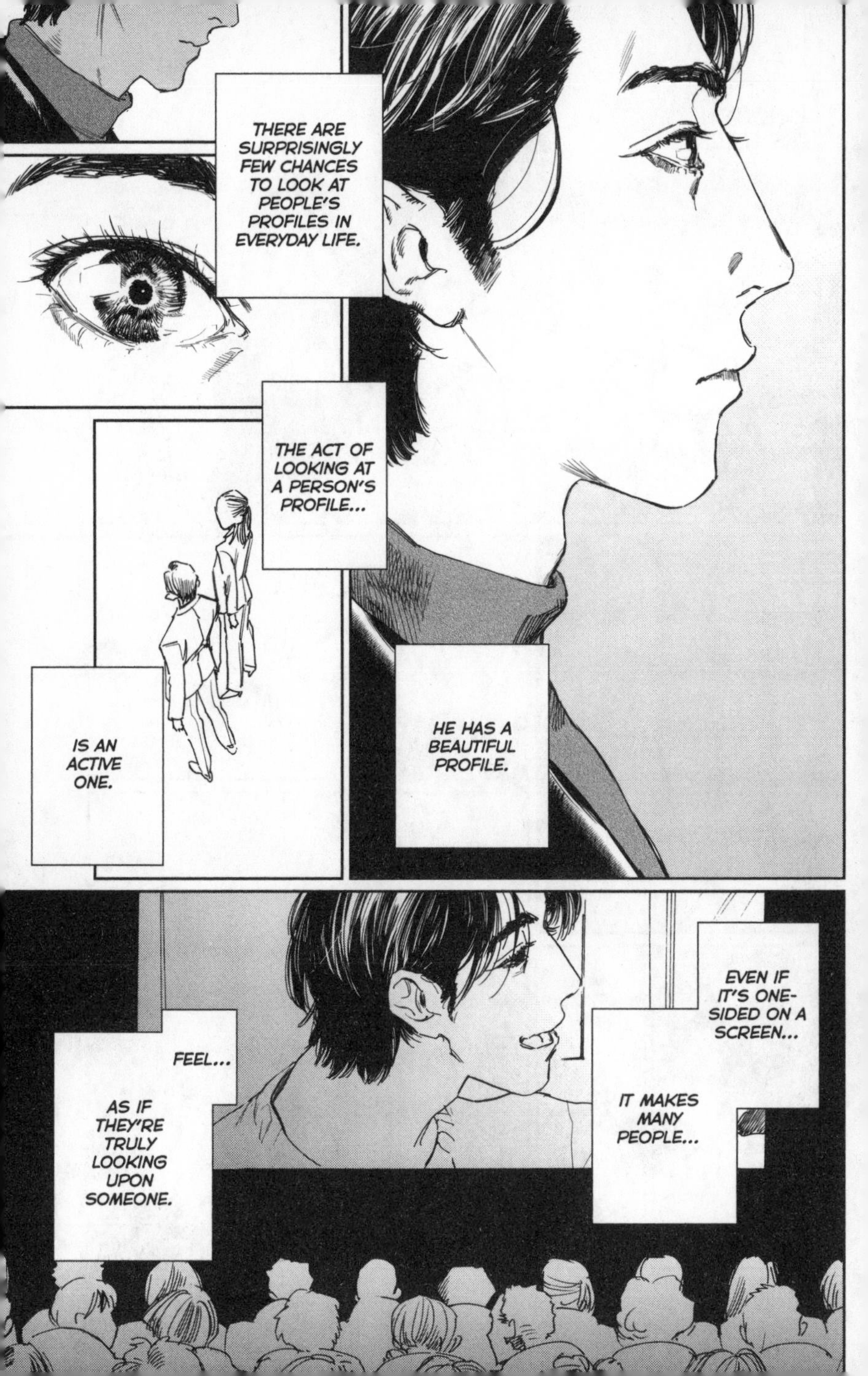
THERE ARE SURPRISINGLY FEW CHANCES TO LOOK AT PEOPLE'S PROFILES IN EVERYDAY LIFE.
THE ACT OF LOOKING AT A PERSON'S PROFILE...
IS AN ACTIVE ONE.
HE HAS A BEAUTIFUL PROFILE.
EVEN IF IT'S ONE-SIDED ON A SCREEN...
IT MAKES MANY PEOPLE...
FEEL...
AS IF THEY'RE TRULY LOOKING UPON SOMEONE.

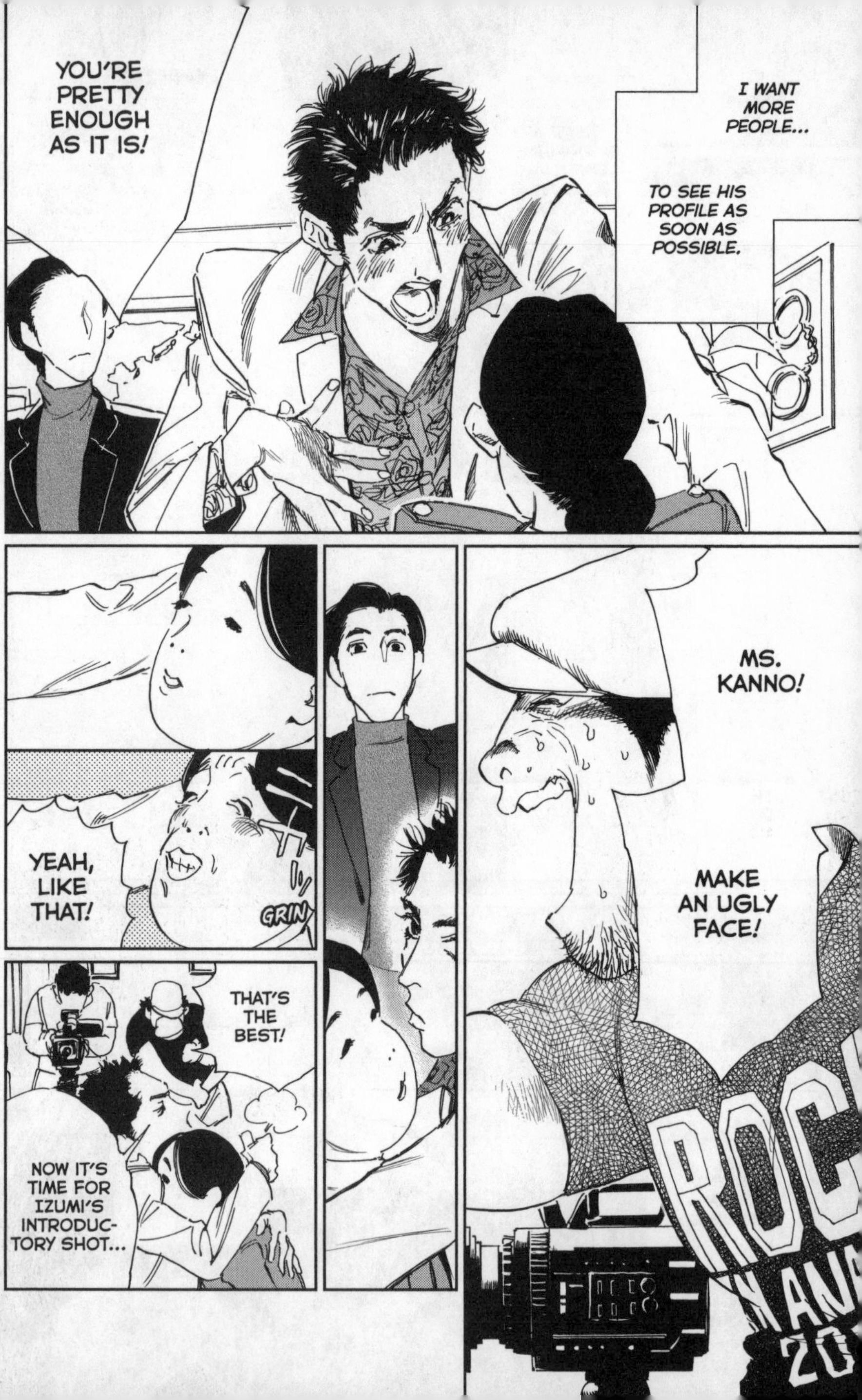
I WANT MORE PEOPLE...
TO SEE HIS PROFILE AS SOON AS POSSIBLE.
YOU'RE PRETTY ENOUGH AS IT IS!
MS. KANNO!
MAKE AN UGLY FACE!
YEAH, LIKE THAT!
GRIN
THAT'S THE BEST!
NOW IT'S TIME FOR IZUMI'S INTRODUCTORY SHOT...

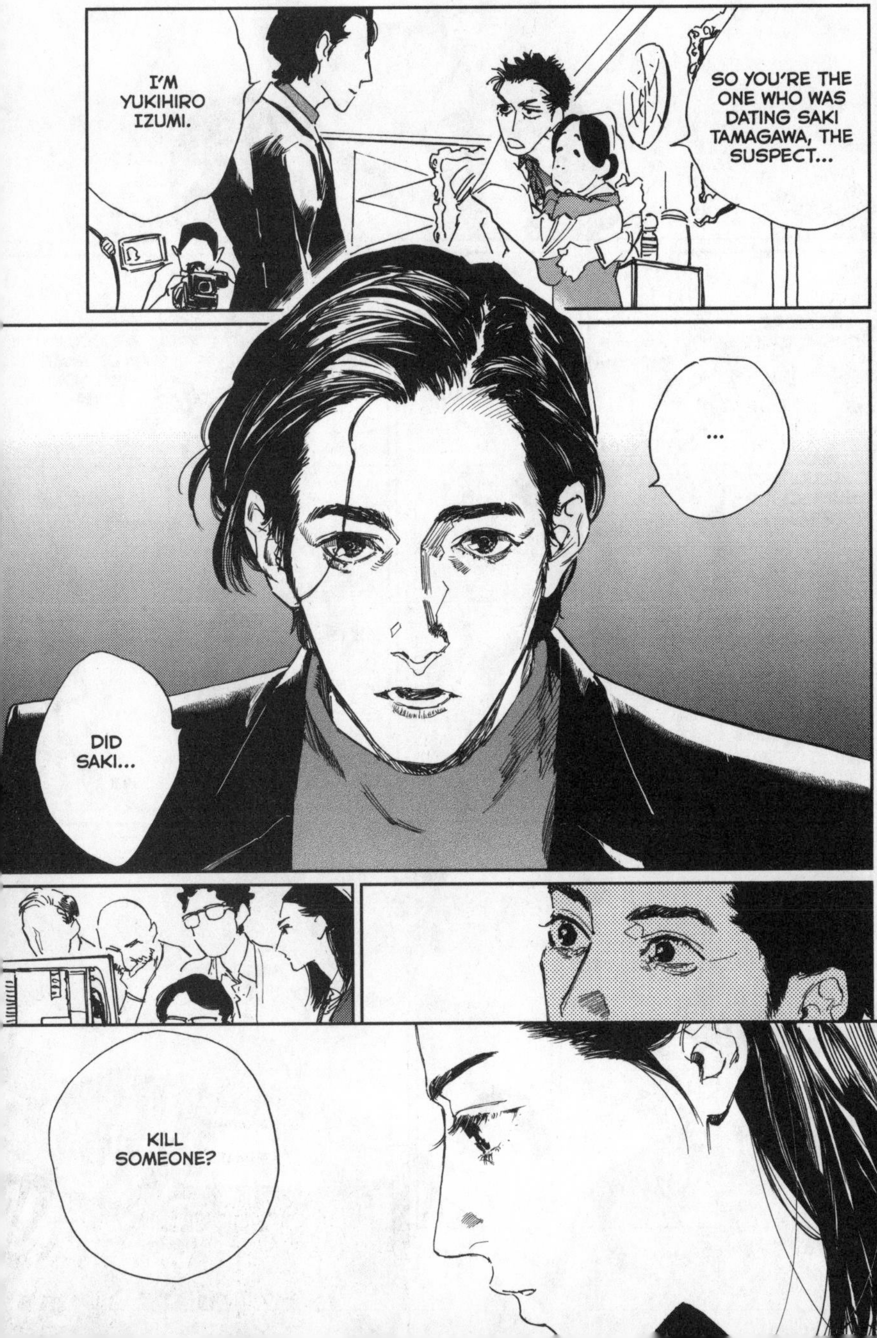
SO YOU'RE THE ONE WHO WAS DATING SAKI TAMAGAWA, THE SUSPECT...
I'M YUKIHIRO IZUMI.
...
DID SAKI...
KILL SOMEONE?

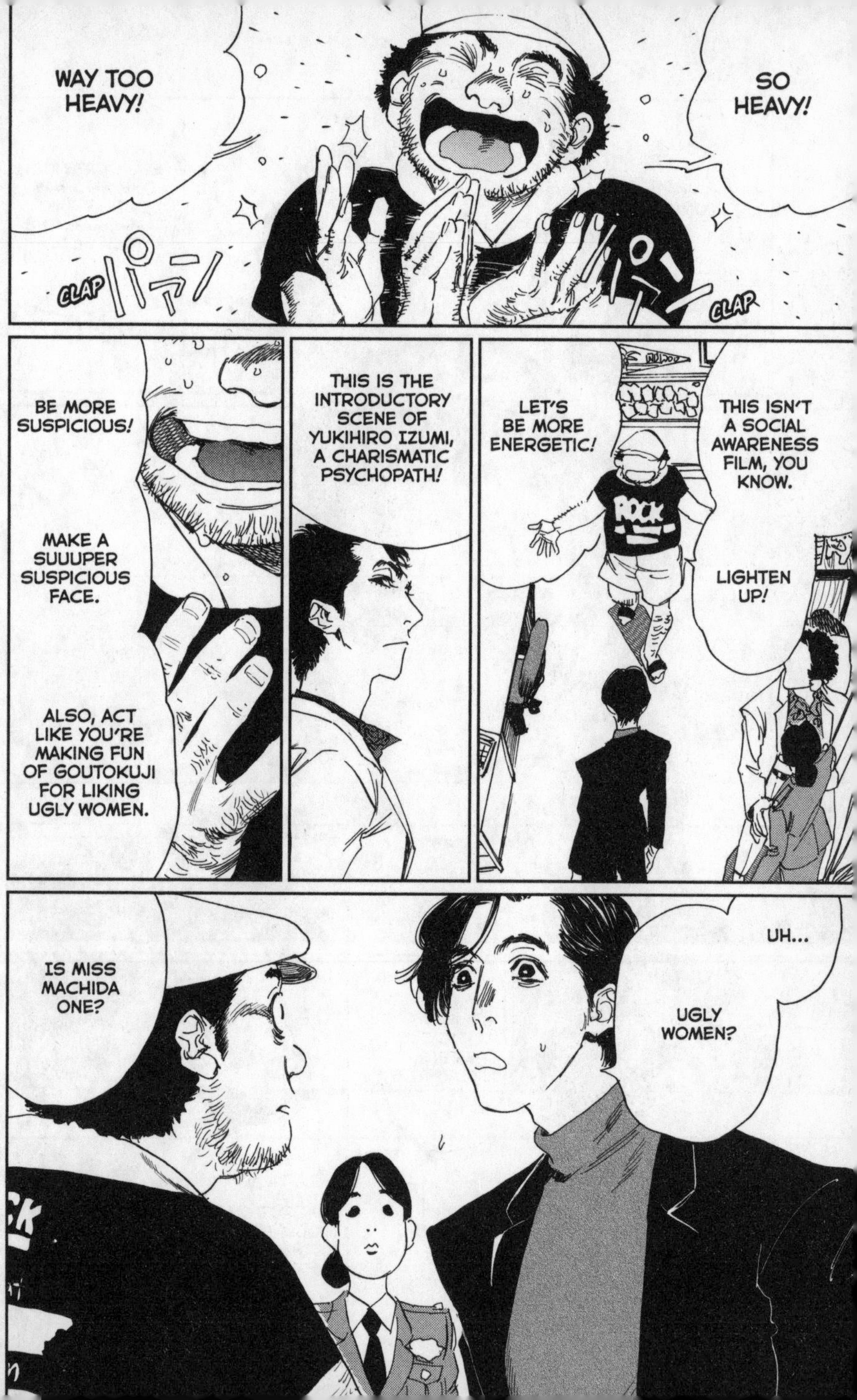
SO HEAVY!
WAY TOO HEAVY!
CLAP
CLAP
THIS ISN'T A SOCIAL AWARENESS FILM, YOU KNOW.
LIGHTEN UP!
LET'S BE MORE ENERGETIC!
THIS IS THE INTRODUCTORY SCENE OF YUKIHIRO IZUMI, A CHARISMATIC PSYCHOPATH!
BE MORE SUSPICIOUS!
MAKE A SUUUPER SUSPICIOUS FACE.
ALSO, ACT LIKE YOU'RE MAKING FUN OF GOUTOKUJI FOR LIKING UGLY WOMEN.
UH...
UGLY WOMEN?
IS MISS MACHIDA ONE?

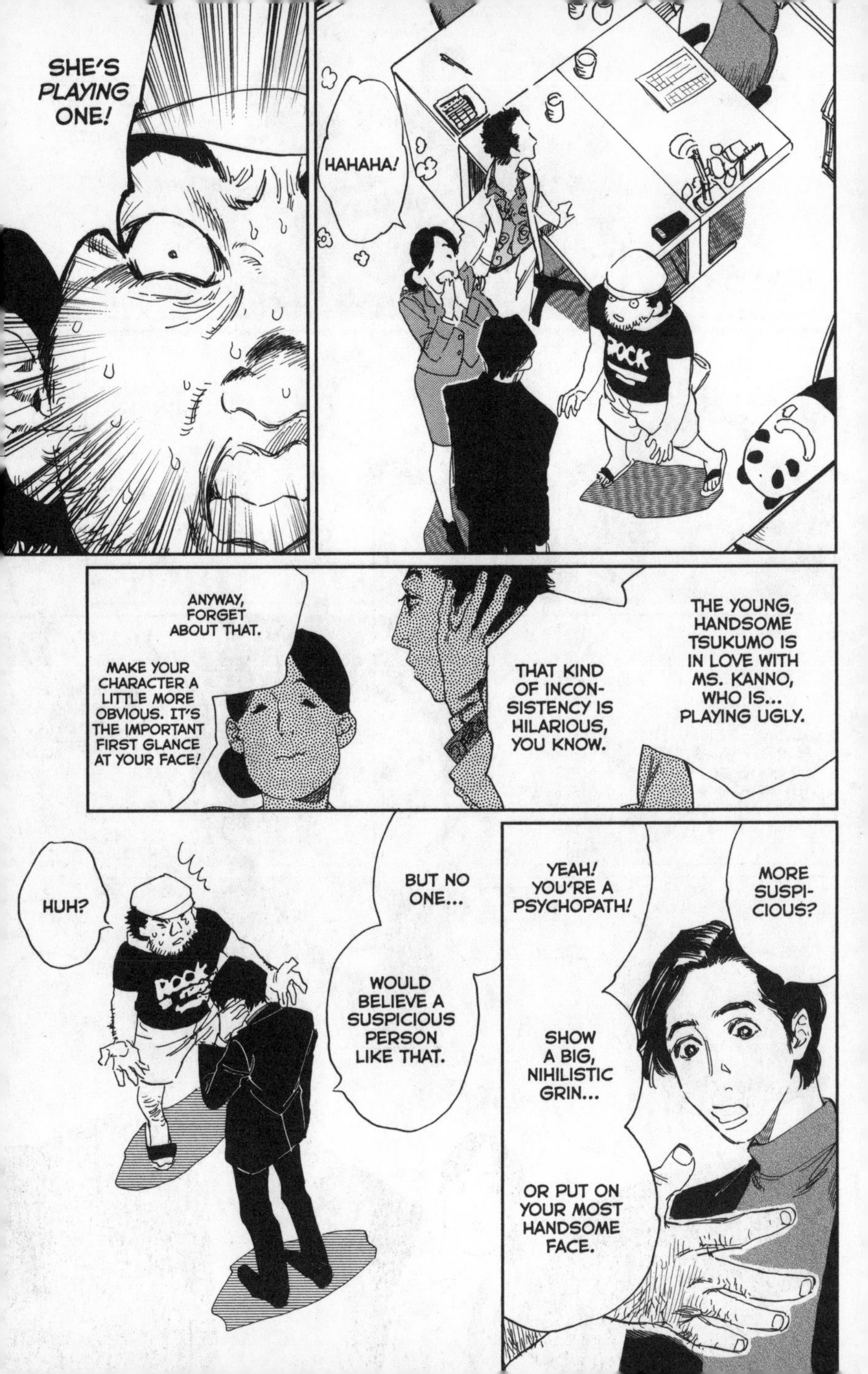
HAHAHA!
SHE'S PLAYING ONE!
THE YOUNG, HANDSOME TSUKUMO IS IN LOVE WITH MS. KANNO, WHO IS... PLAYING UGLY.
THAT KIND OF INCON-SISTENCY IS HILARIOUS, YOU KNOW.
ANYWAY, FORGET ABOUT THAT.
MAKE YOUR CHARACTER A LITTLE MORE OBVIOUS. IT'S THE IMPORTANT FIRST GLANCE AT YOUR FACE!
MORE SUSPI-CIOUS?
YEAH! YOU'RE A PSYCHOPATH!
SHOW A BIG, NIHILISTIC GRIN...
OR PUT ON YOUR MOST HANDSOME FACE.
BUT NO ONE...
WOULD BELIEVE A SUSPICIOUS PERSON LIKE THAT.
HUH?

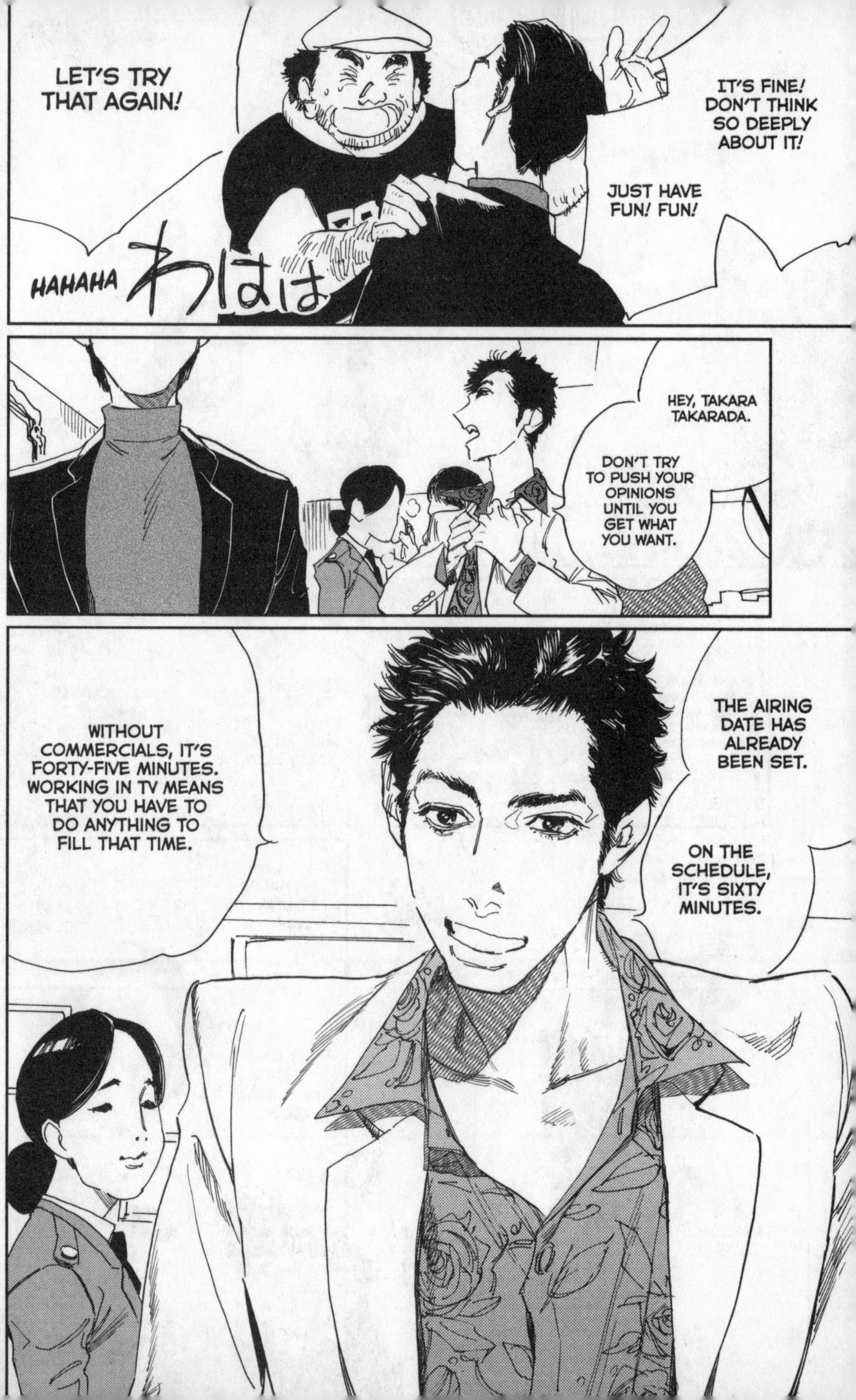
IT'S FINE! DON'T THINK SO DEEPLY ABOUT IT!
JUST HAVE FUN! FUN!
LET'S TRY THAT AGAIN!
HAHAHA わはは
HEY, TAKARA TAKARADA.
DON'T TRY TO PUSH YOUR OPINIONS UNTIL YOU GET WHAT YOU WANT.
THE AIRING DATE HAS ALREADY BEEN SET.
ON THE SCHEDULE, IT'S SIXTY MINUTES.
WITHOUT COMMERCIALS, IT'S FORTY-FIVE MINUTES. WORKING IN TV MEANS THAT YOU HAVE TO DO ANYTHING TO FILL THAT TIME.

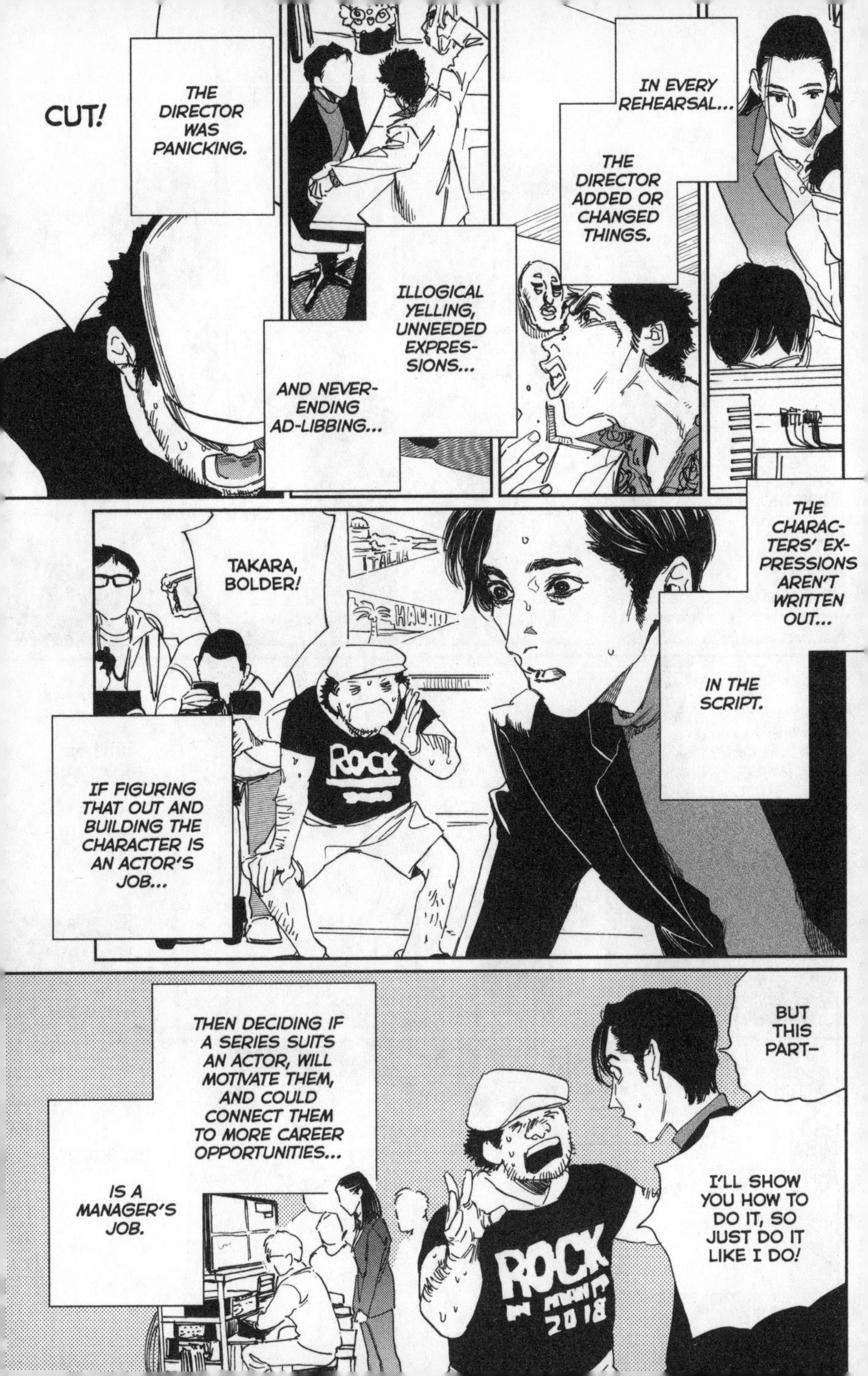
IN EVERY REHEARSAL...
THE DIRECTOR ADDED OR CHANGED THINGS.
ILLOGICAL YELLING, UNNEEDED EXPRES-SIONS...
AND NEVER-ENDING AD-LIBBING...
CUT!
THE DIRECTOR WAS PANICKING.
THE CHARAC-TERS' EX-PRESSIONS AREN'T WRITTEN OUT...
IN THE SCRIPT.
TAKARA, BOLDER!
ITALIA
HAWAII
ROCK
IF FIGURING THAT OUT AND BUILDING THE CHARACTER IS AN ACTOR'S JOB...
BUT THIS PART—
I'LL SHOW YOU HOW TO DO IT, SO JUST DO IT LIKE I DO!
ROCK 2018
THEN DECIDING IF A SERIES SUITS AN ACTOR, WILL MOTIVATE THEM, AND COULD CONNECT THEM TO MORE CAREER OPPORTUNITIES...
IS A MANAGER'S JOB.

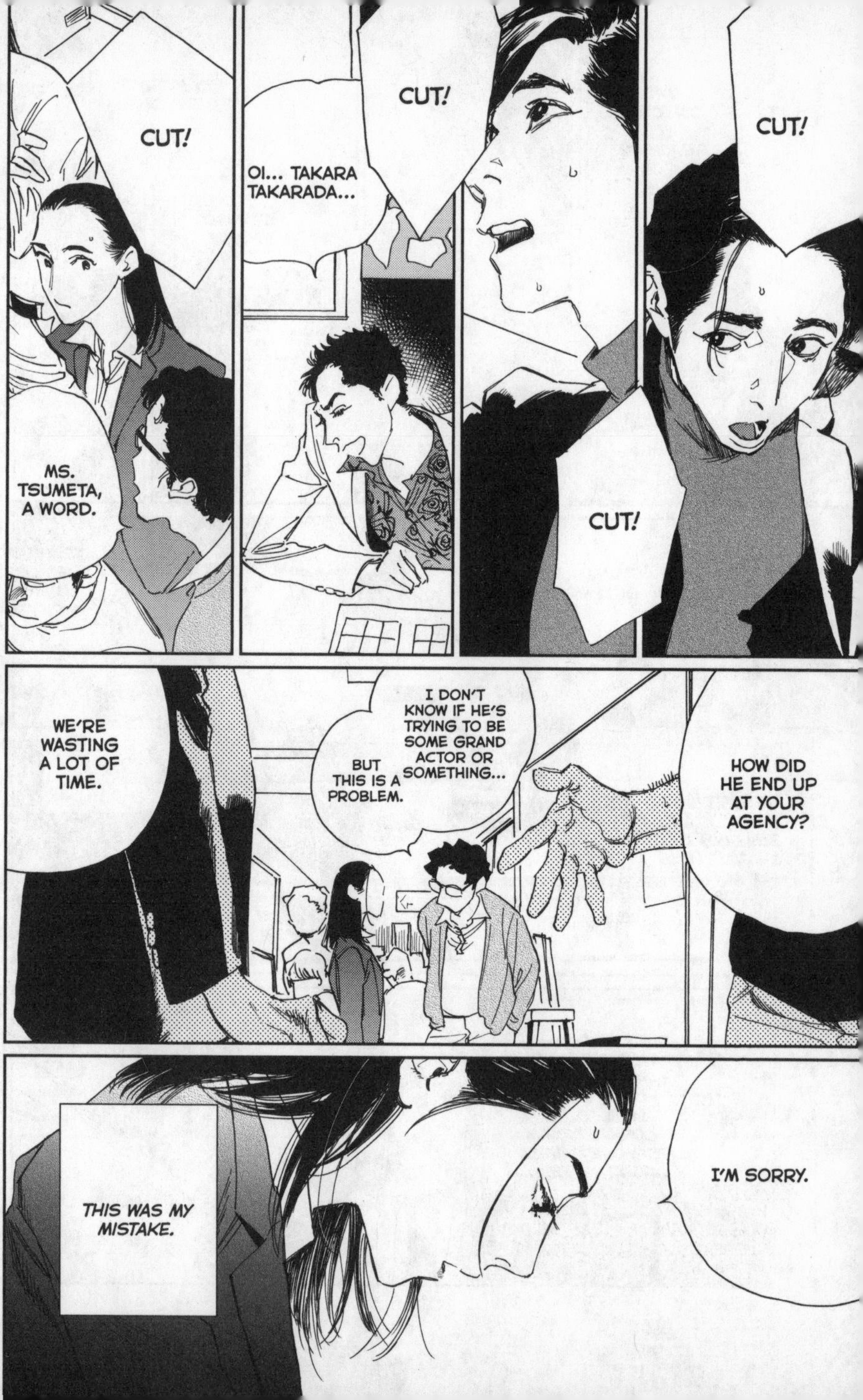
CUT!
CUT!
CUT!
OI... TAKARA TAKARADA...
CUT!
MS. TSUMETA, A WORD.
HOW DID HE END UP AT YOUR AGENCY?
I DON'T KNOW IF HE'S TRYING TO BE SOME GRAND ACTOR OR SOMETHING...
BUT THIS IS A PROBLEM.
WE'RE WASTING A LOT OF TIME.
I'M SORRY.
THIS WAS MY MISTAKE.

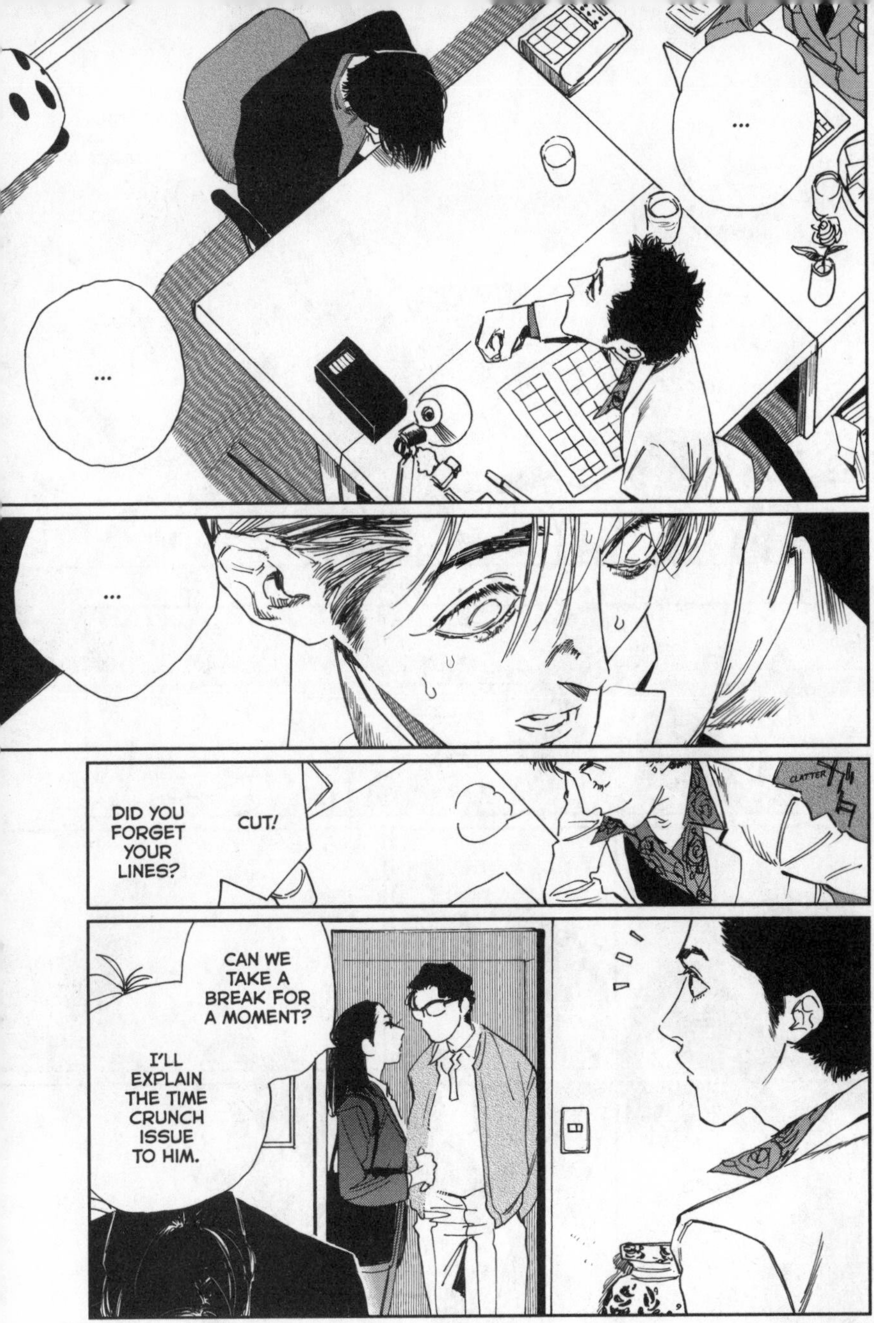
...
...
...
CLATTER
CUT!
DID YOU FORGET YOUR LINES?
CAN WE TAKE A BREAK FOR A MOMENT?
I'LL EXPLAIN THE TIME CRUNCH ISSUE TO HIM.

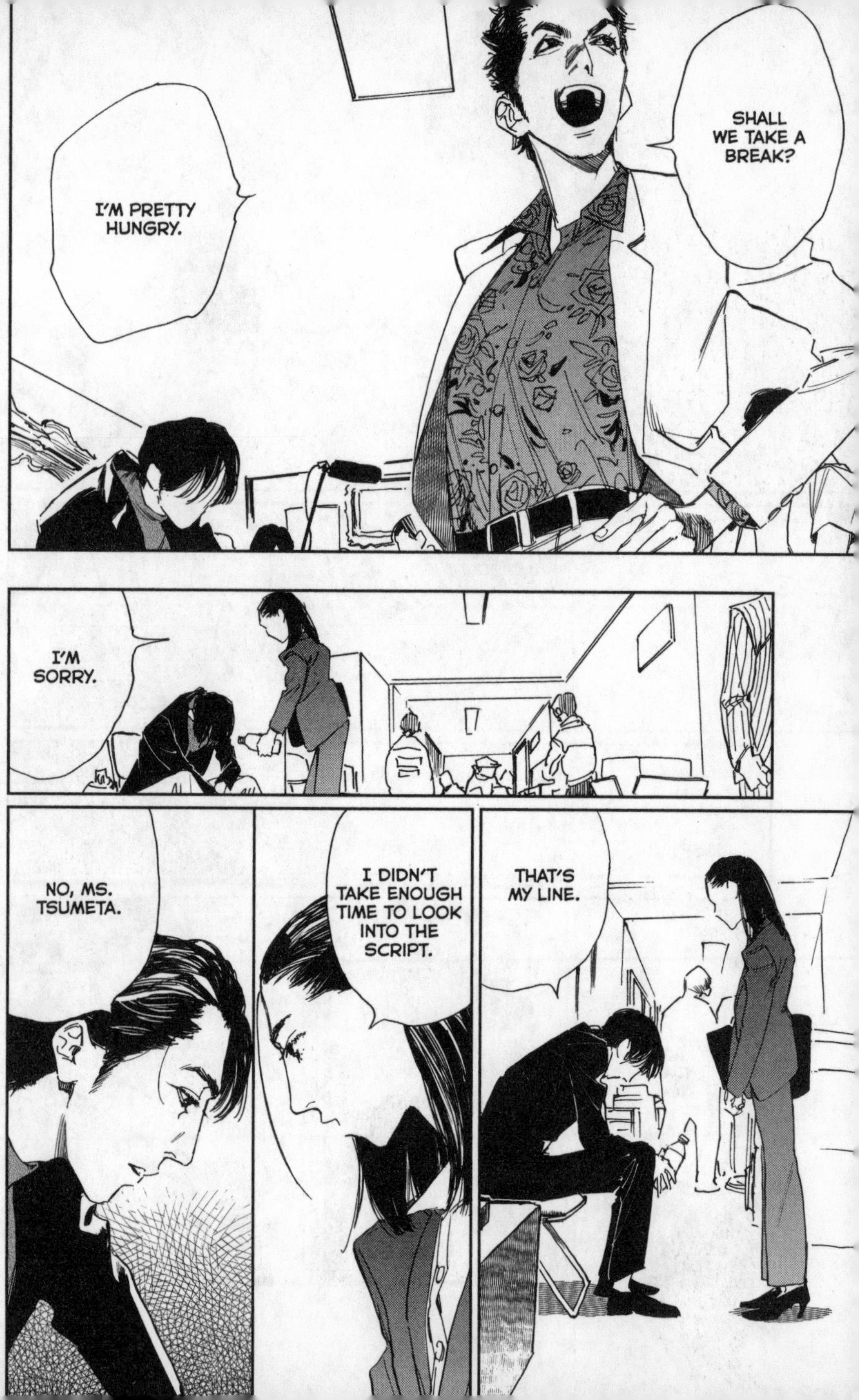
SHALL WE TAKE A BREAK?
I'M PRETTY HUNGRY.
I'M SORRY.
THAT'S MY LINE.
I DIDN'T TAKE ENOUGH TIME TO LOOK INTO THE SCRIPT.
NO, MS. TSUMETA.

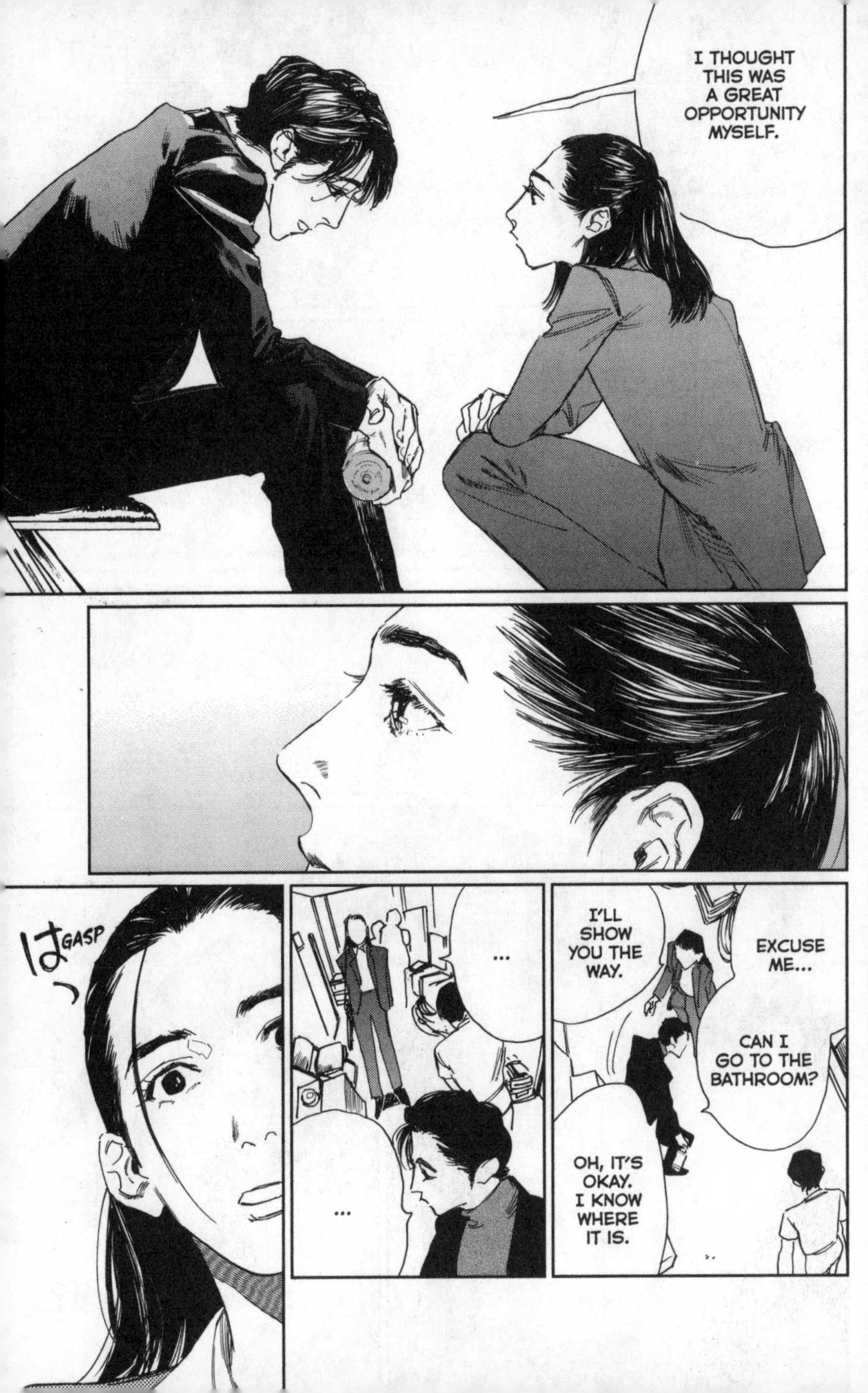
I THOUGHT THIS WAS A GREAT OPPORTUNITY MYSELF.
EXCUSE ME...
CAN I GO TO THE BATHROOM?
I'LL SHOW YOU THE WAY.
OH, IT'S OKAY. I KNOW WHERE IT IS.
...
...
は GASP

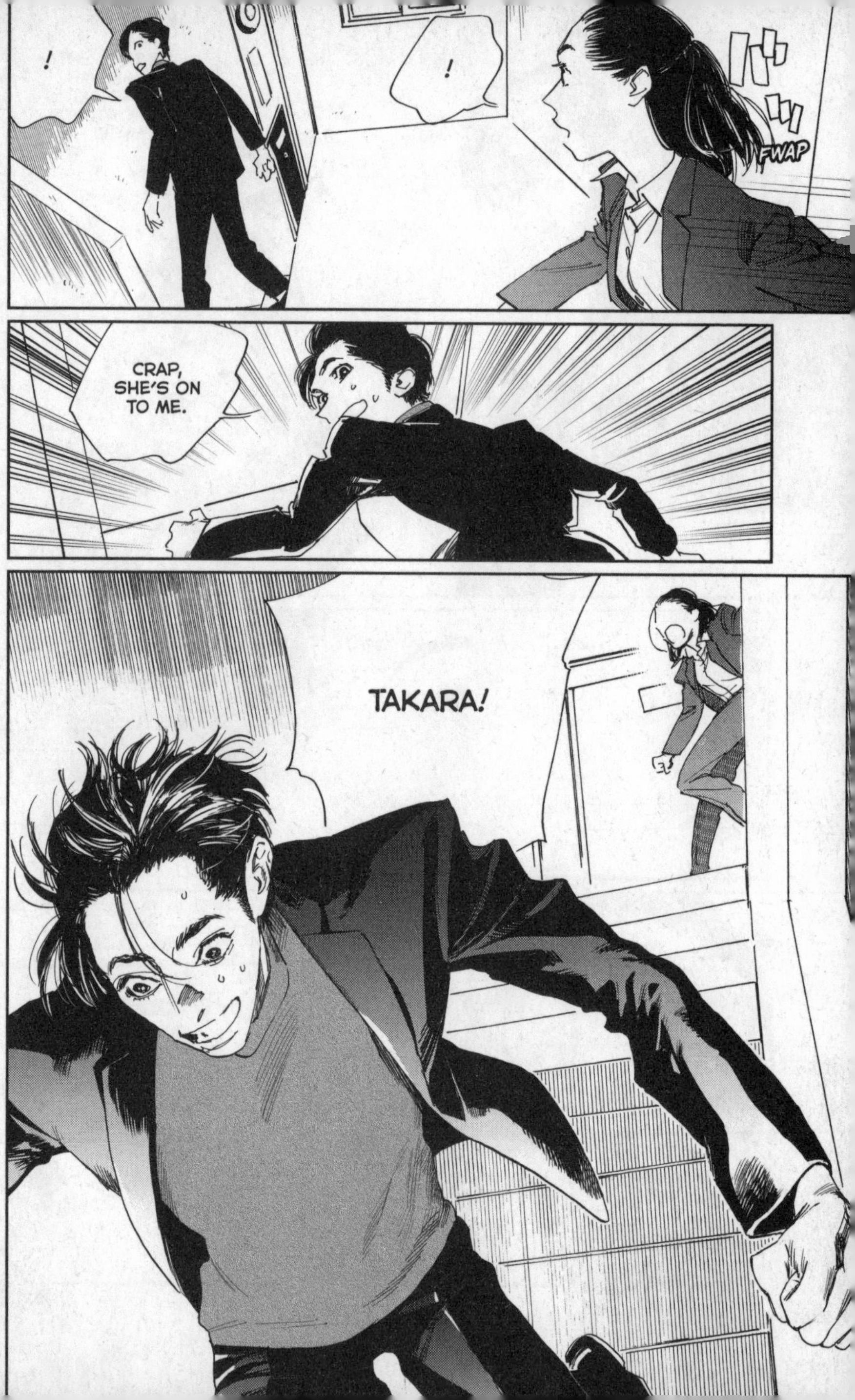
FWAP
!
!
CRAP, SHE'S ON TO ME.
TAKARA!

DOUBLE

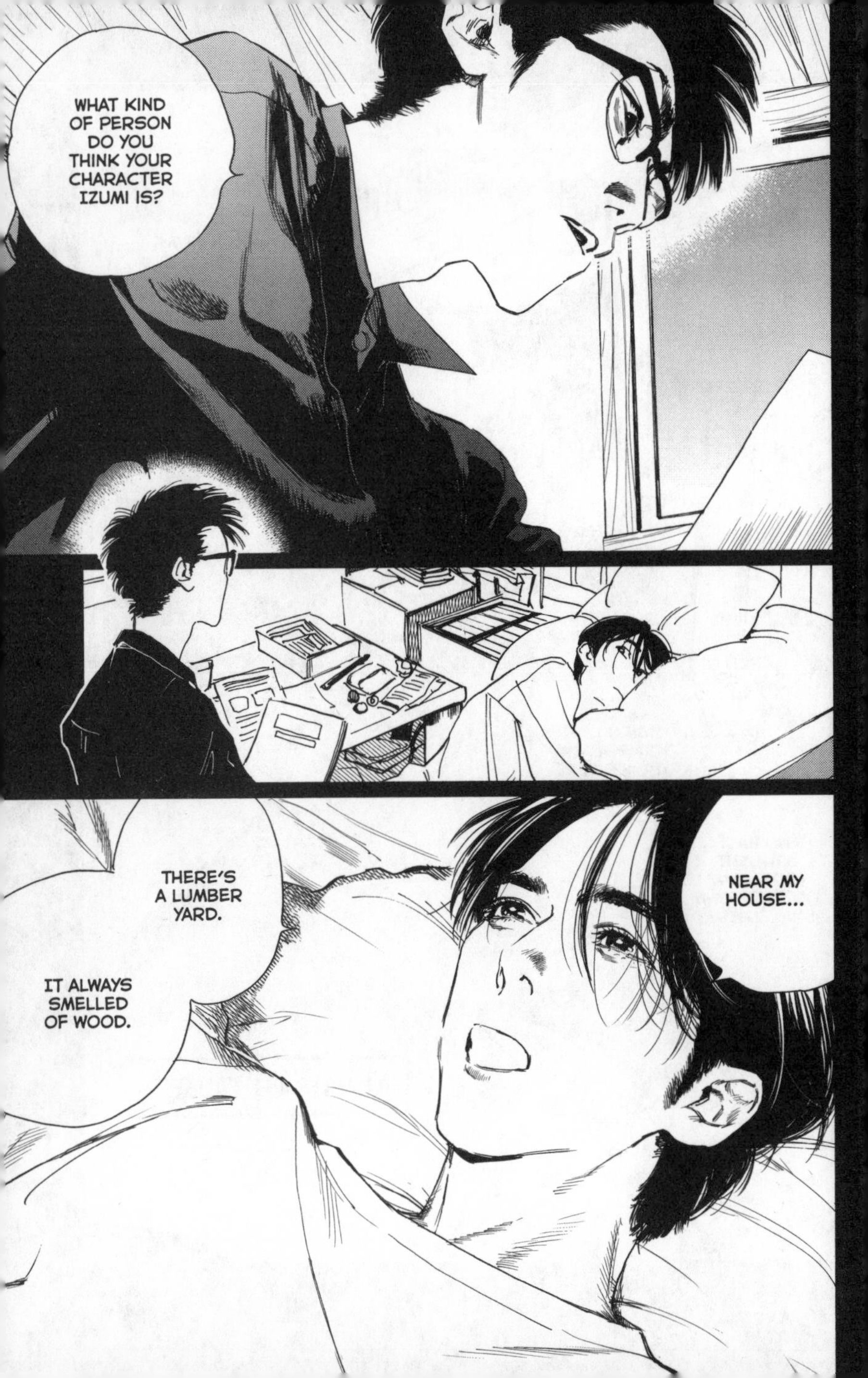
WHAT KIND OF PERSON DO YOU THINK YOUR CHARACTER IZUMI IS?
NEAR MY HOUSE...
THERE'S A LUMBER YARD.
IT ALWAYS SMELLED OF WOOD.

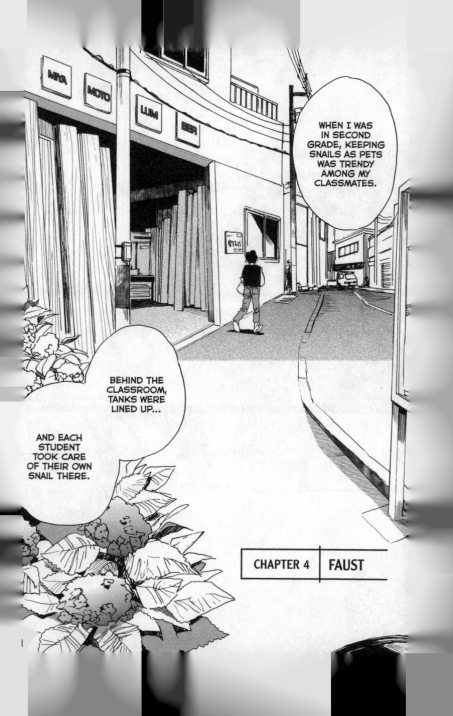

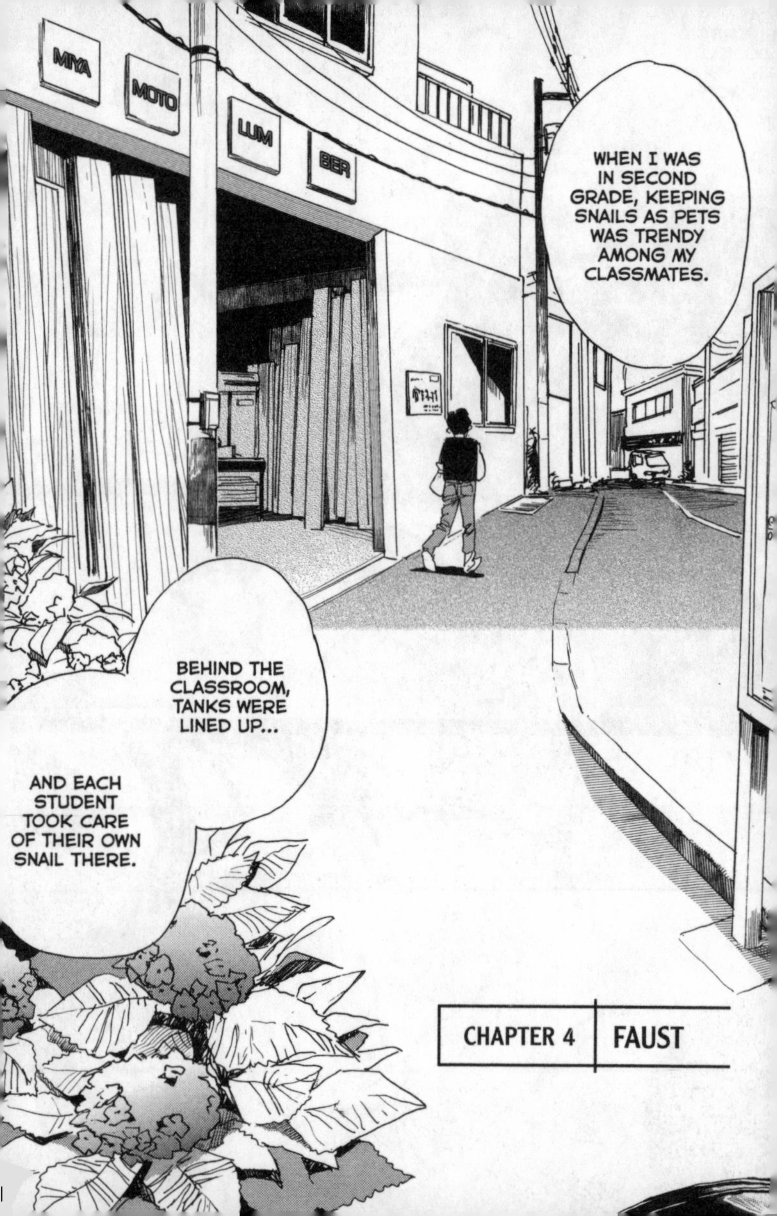
WHEN I WAS IN SECOND GRADE, KEEPING SNAILS AS PETS WAS TRENDY AMONG MY CLASSMATES.
MIYA MOTO LUM BER
BEHIND THE CLASSROOM, TANKS WERE LINED UP...
AND EACH STUDENT TOOK CARE OF THEIR OWN SNAIL THERE.
CHAPTER 4 FAUST

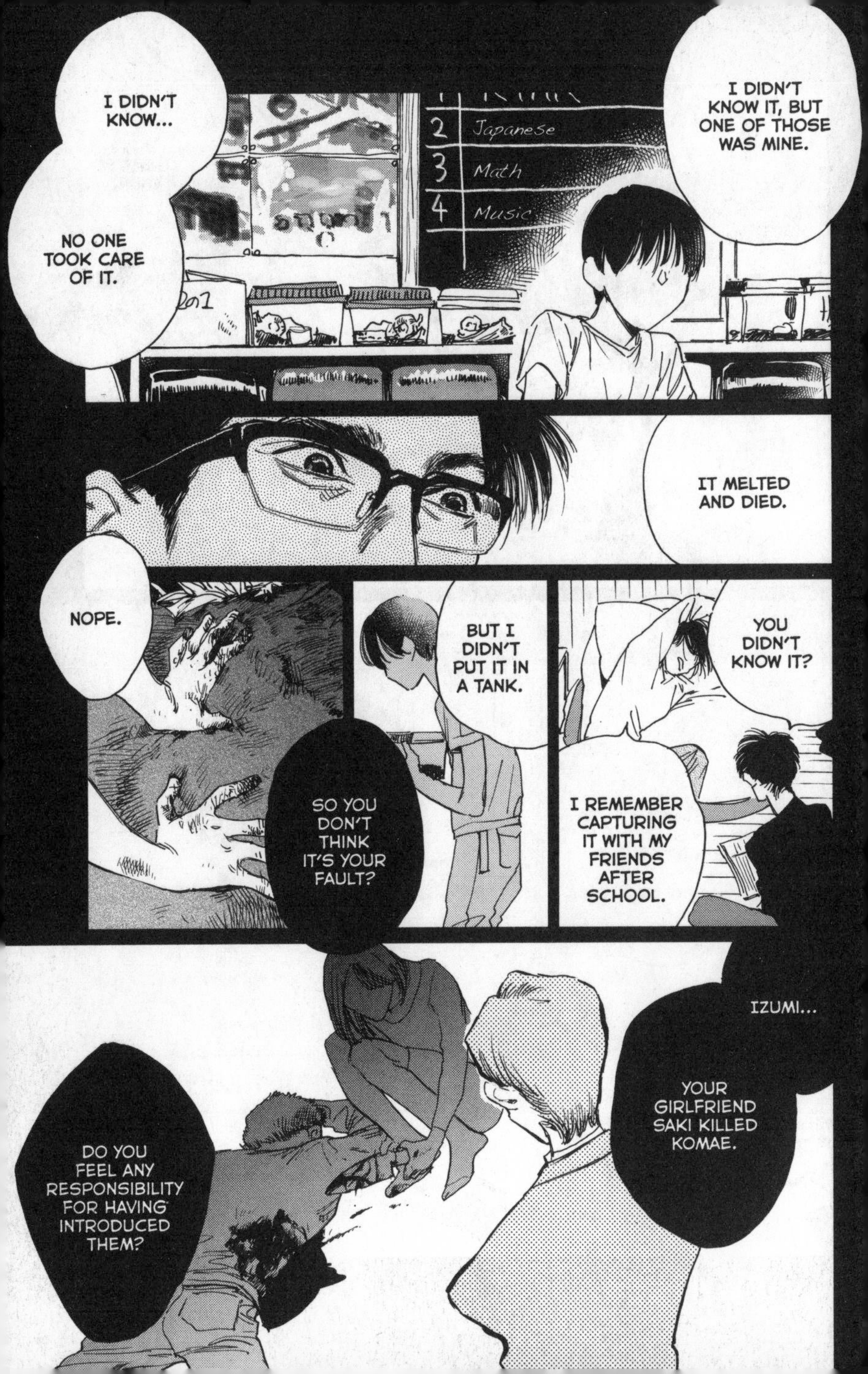
I DIDN'T KNOW IT, BUT ONE OF THOSE WAS MINE.
I DIDN'T KNOW...
NO ONE TOOK CARE OF IT.
2 Japanese
3 Math
4 Music
IT MELTED AND DIED.
YOU DIDN'T KNOW IT?
I REMEMBER CAPTURING IT WITH MY FRIENDS AFTER SCHOOL.
BUT I DIDN'T PUT IT IN A TANK.
SO YOU DON'T THINK IT'S YOUR FAULT?
NOPE.
IZUMI...
YOUR GIRLFRIEND SAKI KILLED KOMAE.
DO YOU FEEL ANY RESPONSIBILITY FOR HAVING INTRODUCED THEM?

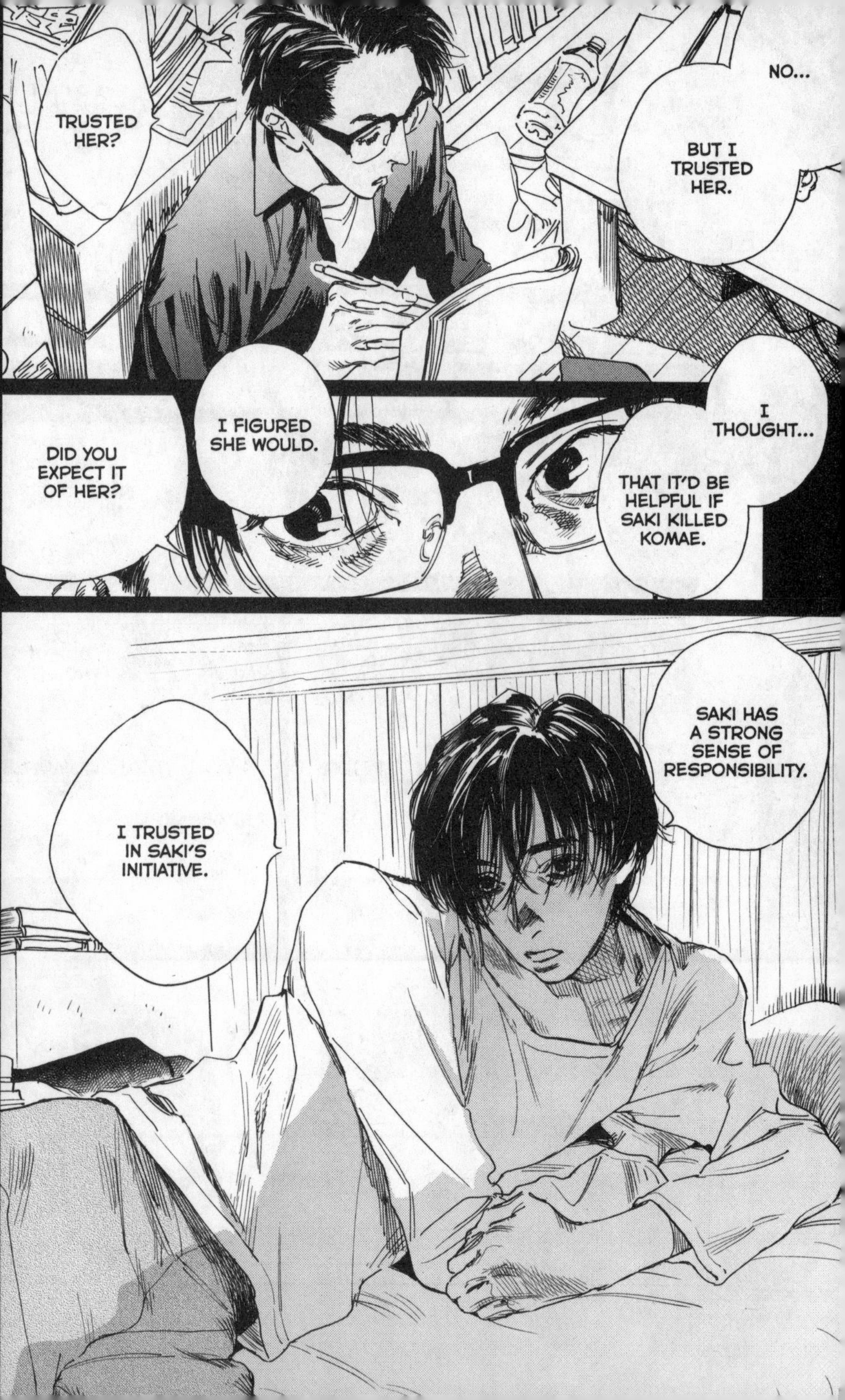
NO...
BUT I TRUSTED HER.
TRUSTED HER?
I THOUGHT...
THAT IT'D BE HELPFUL IF SAKI KILLED KOMAE.
I FIGURED SHE WOULD.
DID YOU EXPECT IT OF HER?
SAKI HAS A STRONG SENSE OF RESPONSIBILITY.
I TRUSTED IN SAKI'S INITIATIVE.

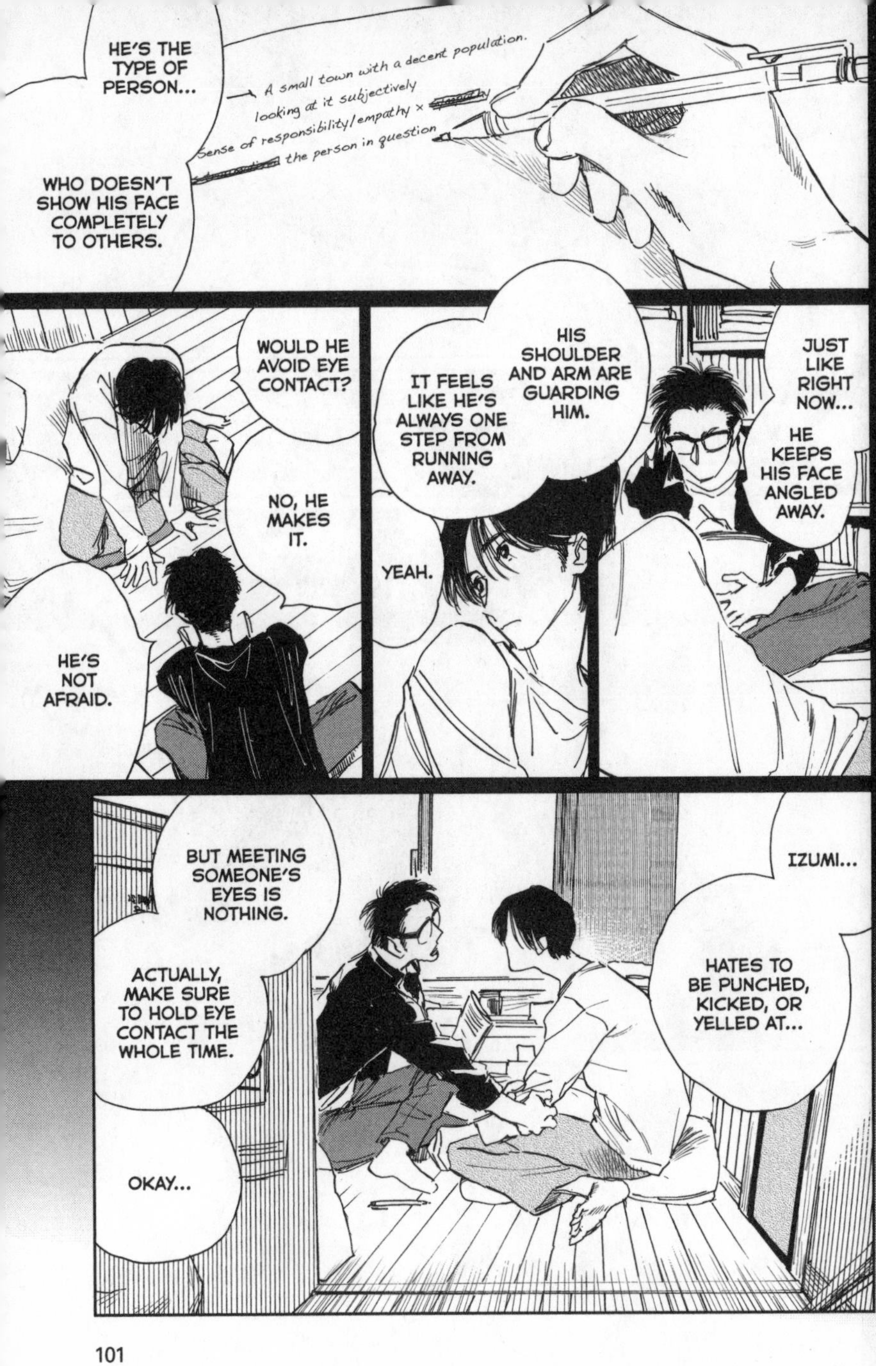
HE'S THE TYPE OF PERSON...
A small town with a decent population.
looking at it subjectively
Sense of responsibility/empathy ×
the person in question
WHO DOESN'T SHOW HIS FACE COMPLETELY TO OTHERS.
JUST LIKE RIGHT NOW...
HE KEEPS HIS FACE ANGLED AWAY.
HIS SHOULDER AND ARM ARE GUARDING HIM.
IT FEELS LIKE HE'S ALWAYS ONE STEP FROM RUNNING AWAY.
YEAH.
WOULD HE AVOID EYE CONTACT?
NO, HE MAKES IT.
HE'S NOT AFRAID.
IZUMI...
HATES TO BE PUNCHED, KICKED, OR YELLED AT...
BUT MEETING SOMEONE'S EYES IS NOTHING.
ACTUALLY, MAKE SURE TO HOLD EYE CONTACT THE WHOLE TIME.
OKAY...

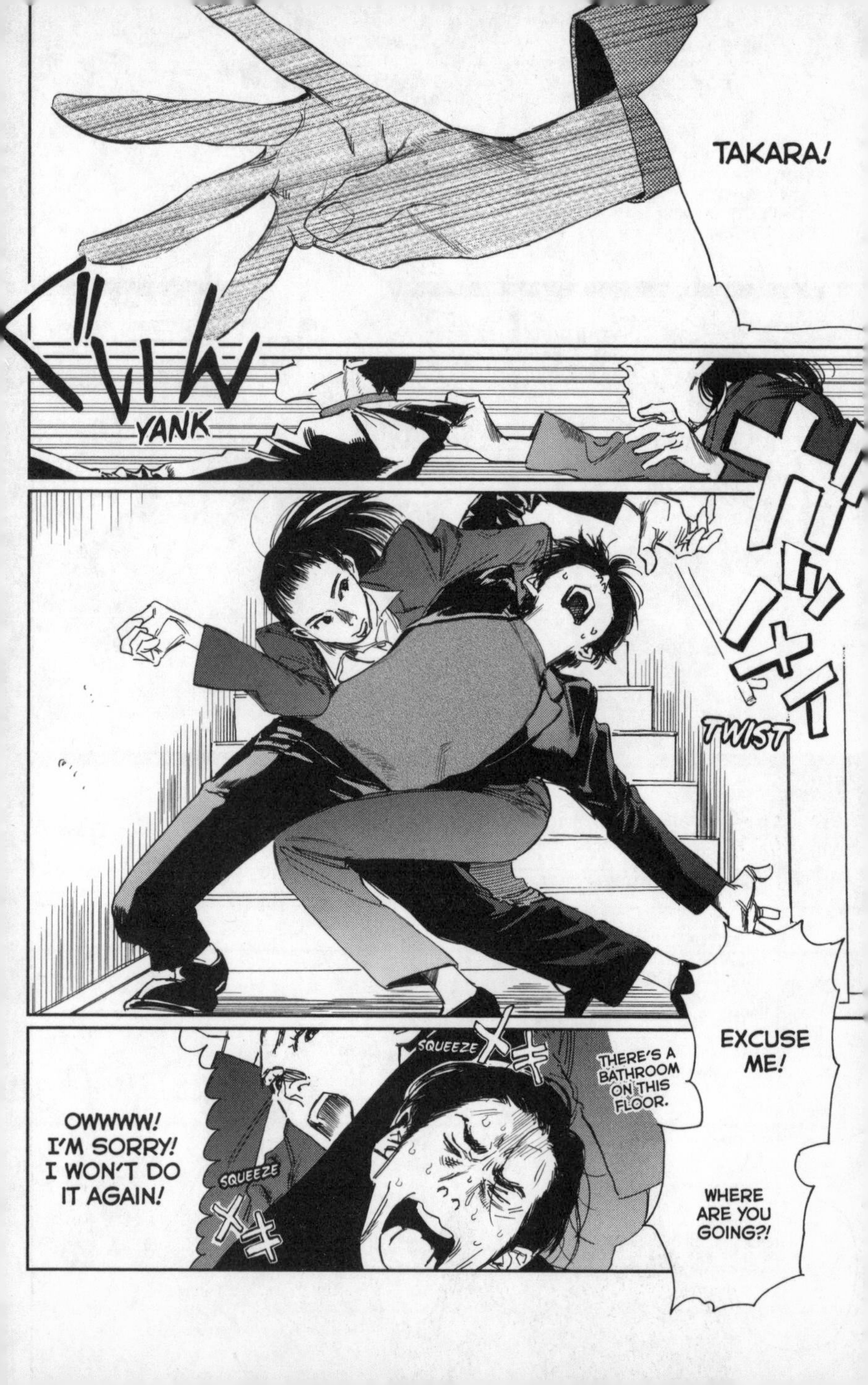
TAKARA!
YANK
TWIST
EXCUSE ME!
WHERE ARE YOU GOING?!
THERE'S A BATHROOM ON THIS FLOOR.
SQUEEZE
OWWWW! I'M SORRY! I WON'T DO IT AGAIN!
SQUEEZE

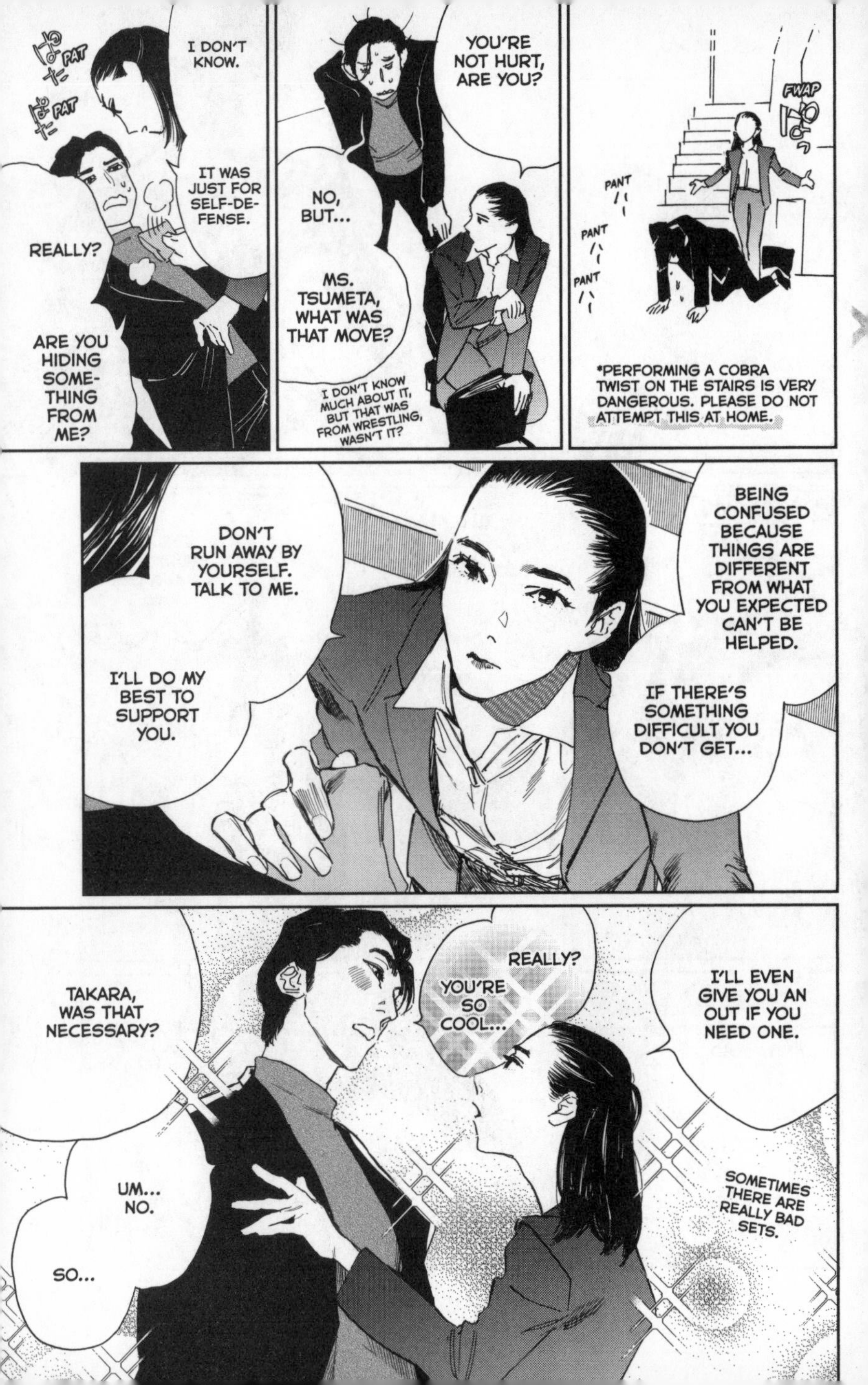
FWAP
PANT
PANT
PANT
*PERFORMING A COBRA TWIST ON THE STAIRS IS VERY DANGEROUS. PLEASE DO NOT ATTEMPT THIS AT HOME.
YOU'RE NOT HURT, ARE YOU?
NO, BUT...
MS. TSUMETA, WHAT WAS THAT MOVE?
I DON'T KNOW MUCH ABOUT IT, BUT THAT WAS FROM WRESTLING, WASN'T IT?
PAT
PAT
I DON'T KNOW.
IT WAS JUST FOR SELF-DEFENSE.
REALLY?
ARE YOU HIDING SOMETHING FROM ME?
BEING CONFUSED BECAUSE THINGS ARE DIFFERENT FROM WHAT YOU EXPECTED CAN'T BE HELPED.
IF THERE'S SOMETHING DIFFICULT YOU DON'T GET...
DON'T RUN AWAY BY YOURSELF. TALK TO ME.
I'LL DO MY BEST TO SUPPORT YOU.
I'LL EVEN GIVE YOU AN OUT IF YOU NEED ONE.
SOMETIMES THERE ARE REALLY BAD SETS.
REALLY?
YOU'RE SO COOL...
TAKARA, WAS THAT NECESSARY?
UM... NO.
SO...

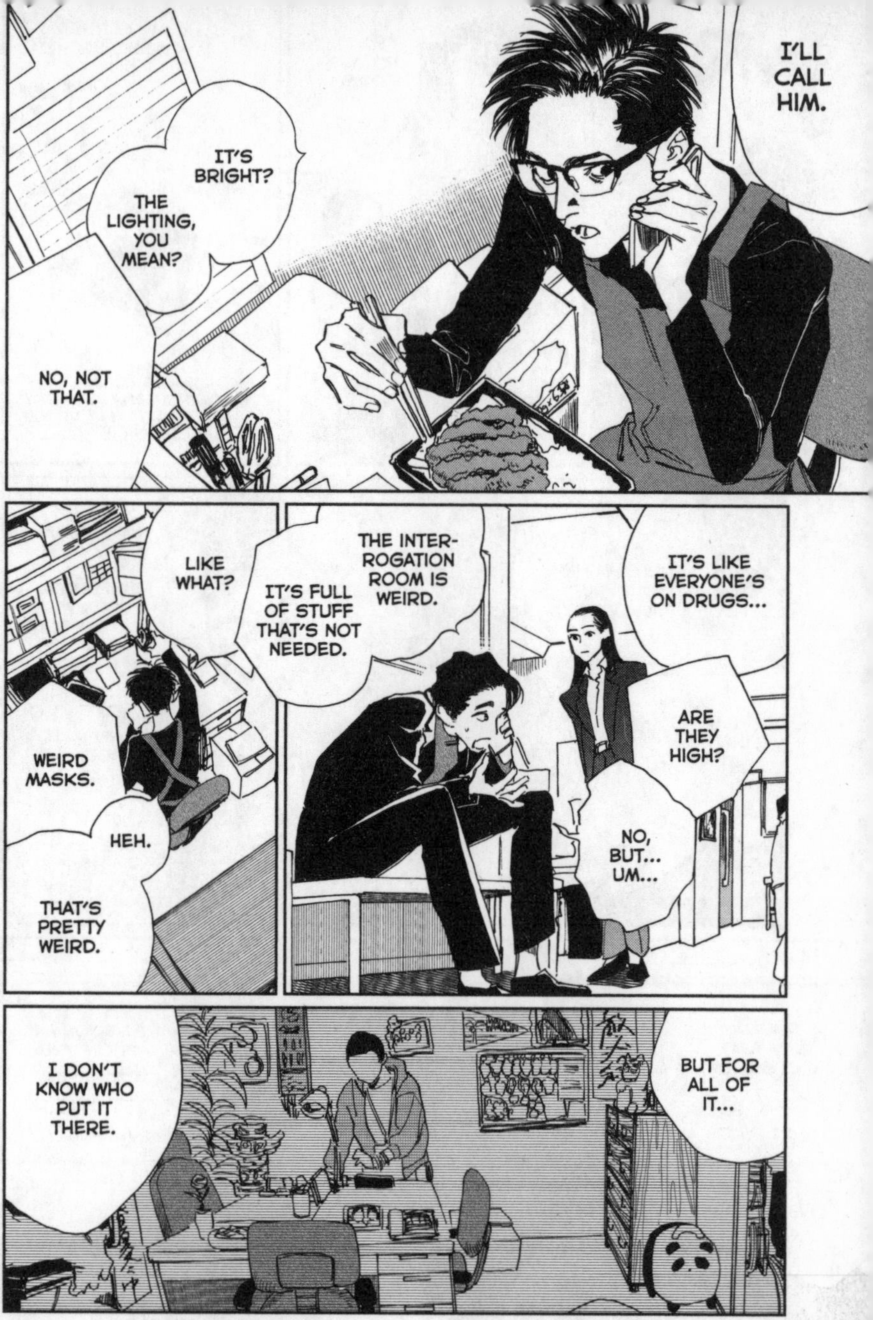
I'LL CALL HIM.
IT'S BRIGHT?
THE LIGHTING, YOU MEAN?
NO, NOT THAT.
IT'S LIKE EVERYONE'S ON DRUGS...
ARE THEY HIGH?
NO, BUT... UM...
THE INTERROGATION ROOM IS WEIRD.
IT'S FULL OF STUFF THAT'S NOT NEEDED.
LIKE WHAT?
WEIRD MASKS.
HEH.
THAT'S PRETTY WEIRD.
BUT FOR ALL OF IT...
I DON'T KNOW WHO PUT IT THERE.

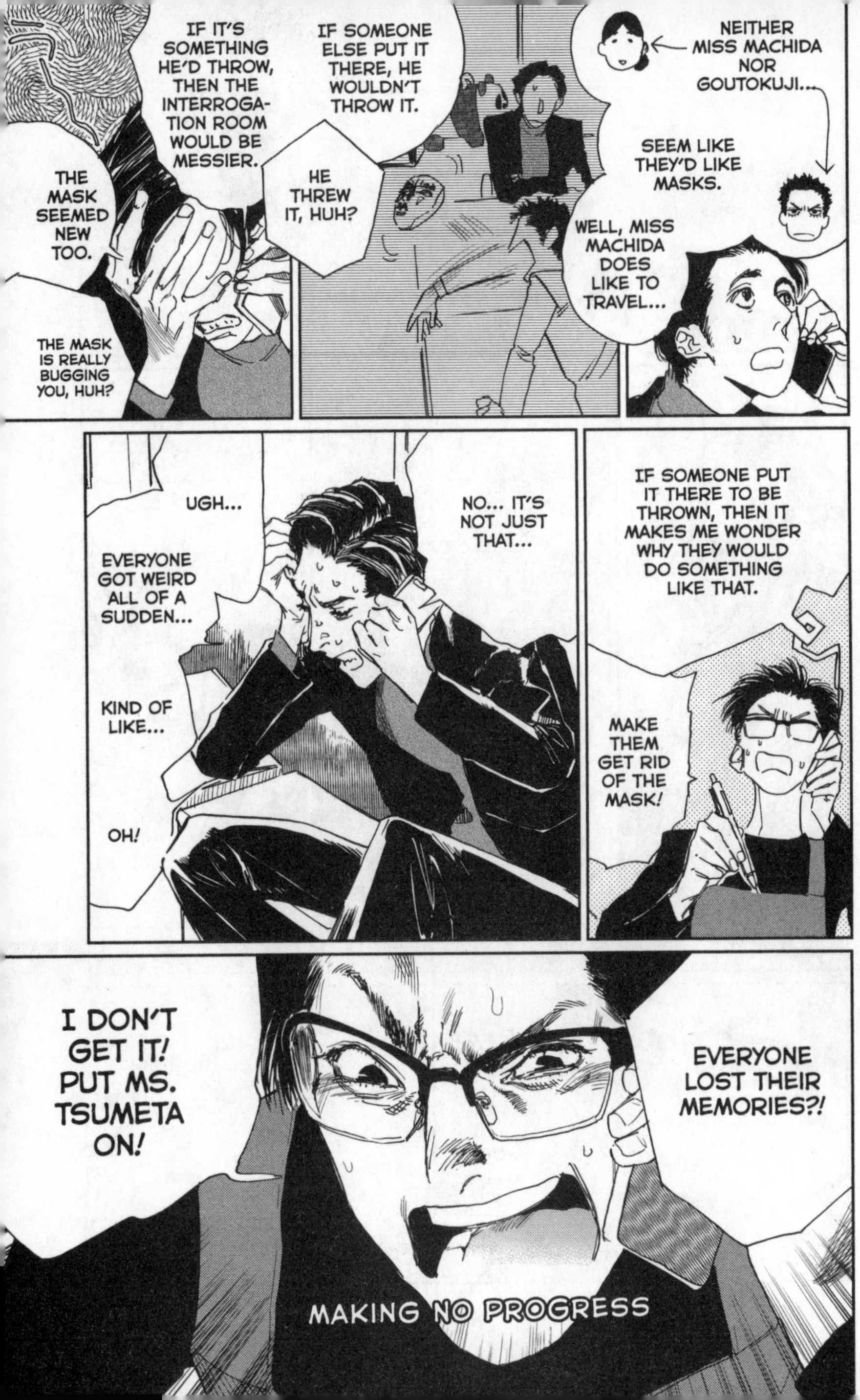
NEITHER MISS MACHIDA NOR GOUTOKUJI...
SEEM LIKE THEY'D LIKE MASKS.
WELL, MISS MACHIDA DOES LIKE TO TRAVEL...
IF SOMEONE ELSE PUT IT THERE, HE WOULDN'T THROW IT.
HE THREW IT, HUH?
IF IT'S SOMETHING HE'D THROW, THEN THE INTERROGATION ROOM WOULD BE MESSIER.
THE MASK SEEMED NEW TOO.
THE MASK IS REALLY BUGGING YOU, HUH?
IF SOMEONE PUT IT THERE TO BE THROWN, THEN IT MAKES ME WONDER WHY THEY WOULD DO SOMETHING LIKE THAT.
MAKE THEM GET RID OF THE MASK!
NO... IT'S NOT JUST THAT...
UGH...
EVERYONE GOT WEIRD ALL OF A SUDDEN...
KIND OF LIKE...
OH!
EVERYONE LOST THEIR MEMORIES?!
I DON'T GET IT! PUT MS. TSUMETA ON!
MAKING NO PROGRESS

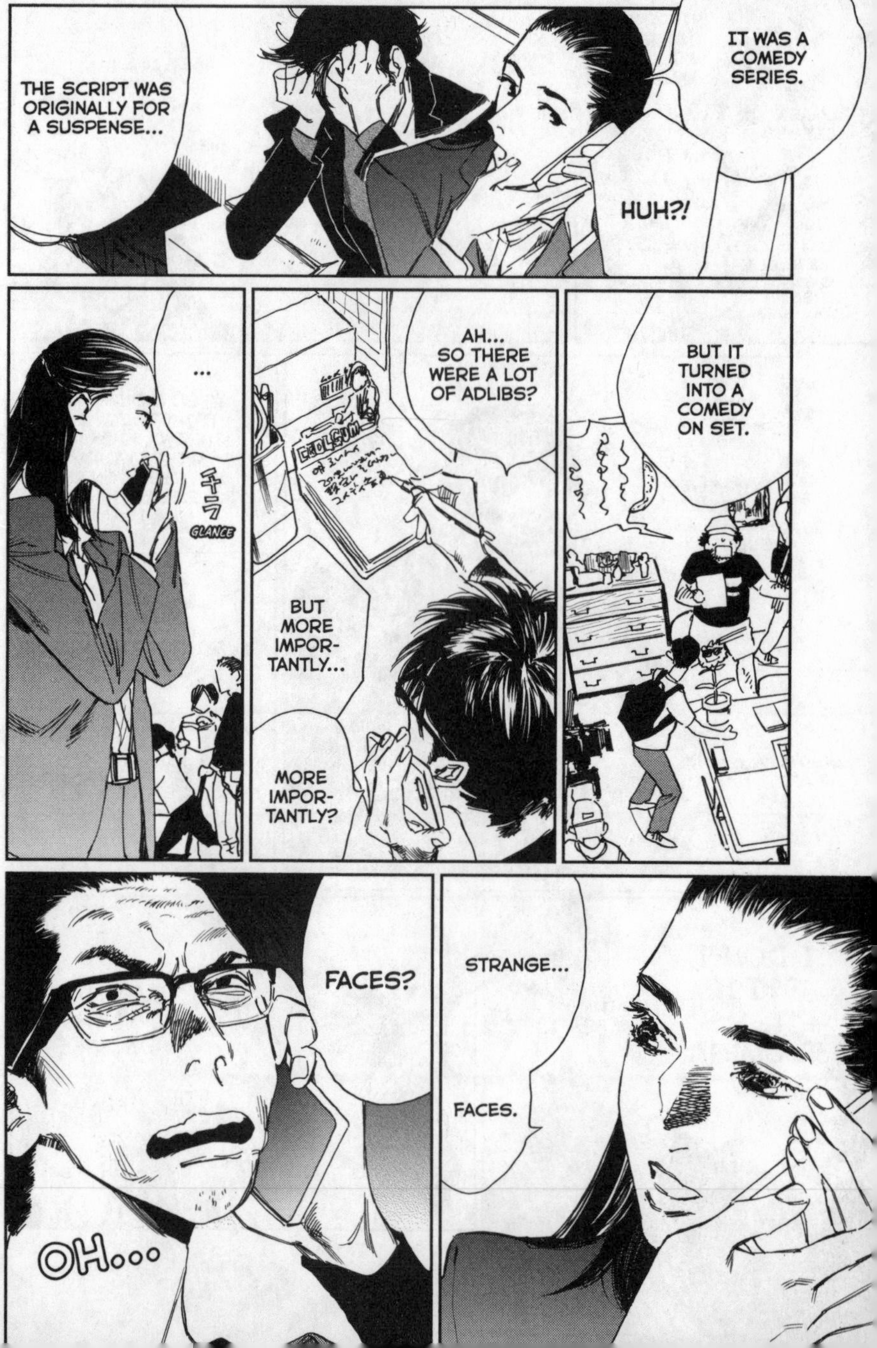
IT WAS A COMEDY SERIES.
HUH?!
THE SCRIPT WAS ORIGINALLY FOR A SUSPENSE...
BUT IT TURNED INTO A COMEDY ON SET.
AH... SO THERE WERE A LOT OF ADLIBS?
BUT MORE IMPORTANTLY...
MORE IMPORTANTLY?
...
チラ
GLANCE
STRANGE...
FACES.
FACES?
OH...

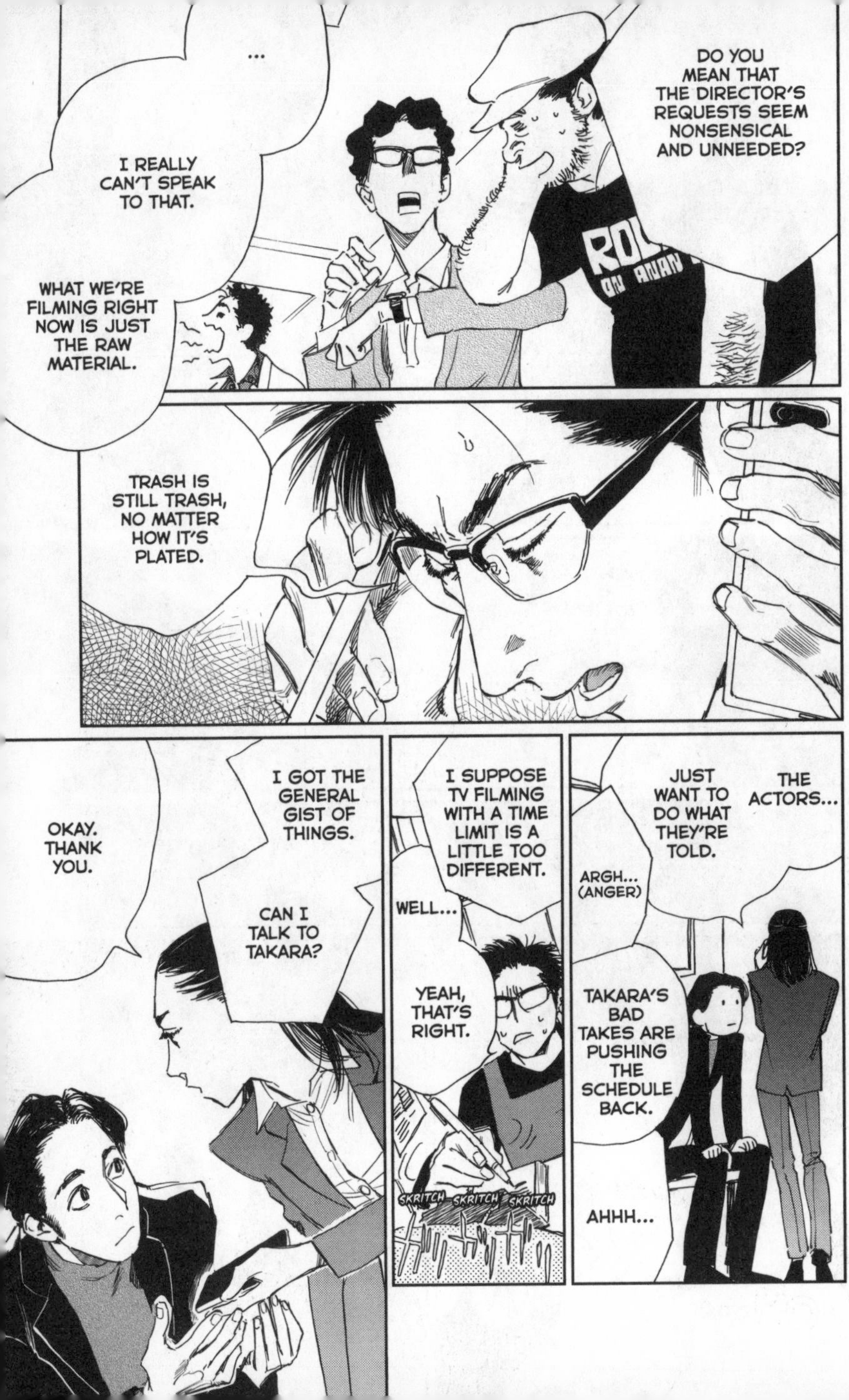
DO YOU MEAN THAT THE DIRECTOR'S REQUESTS SEEM NONSENSICAL AND UNNEEDED?
...
I REALLY CAN'T SPEAK TO THAT.
WHAT WE'RE FILMING RIGHT NOW IS JUST THE RAW MATERIAL.
TRASH IS STILL TRASH, NO MATTER HOW IT'S PLATED.
THE ACTORS...
JUST WANT TO DO WHAT THEY'RE TOLD.
ARGH... (ANGER)
TAKARA'S BAD TAKES ARE PUSHING THE SCHEDULE BACK.
AHHH...
I SUPPOSE TV FILMING WITH A TIME LIMIT IS A LITTLE TOO DIFFERENT.
WELL...
YEAH, THAT'S RIGHT.
SKRITCH SKRITCH SKRITCH
I GOT THE GENERAL GIST OF THINGS.
OKAY. THANK YOU.
CAN I TALK TO TAKARA?

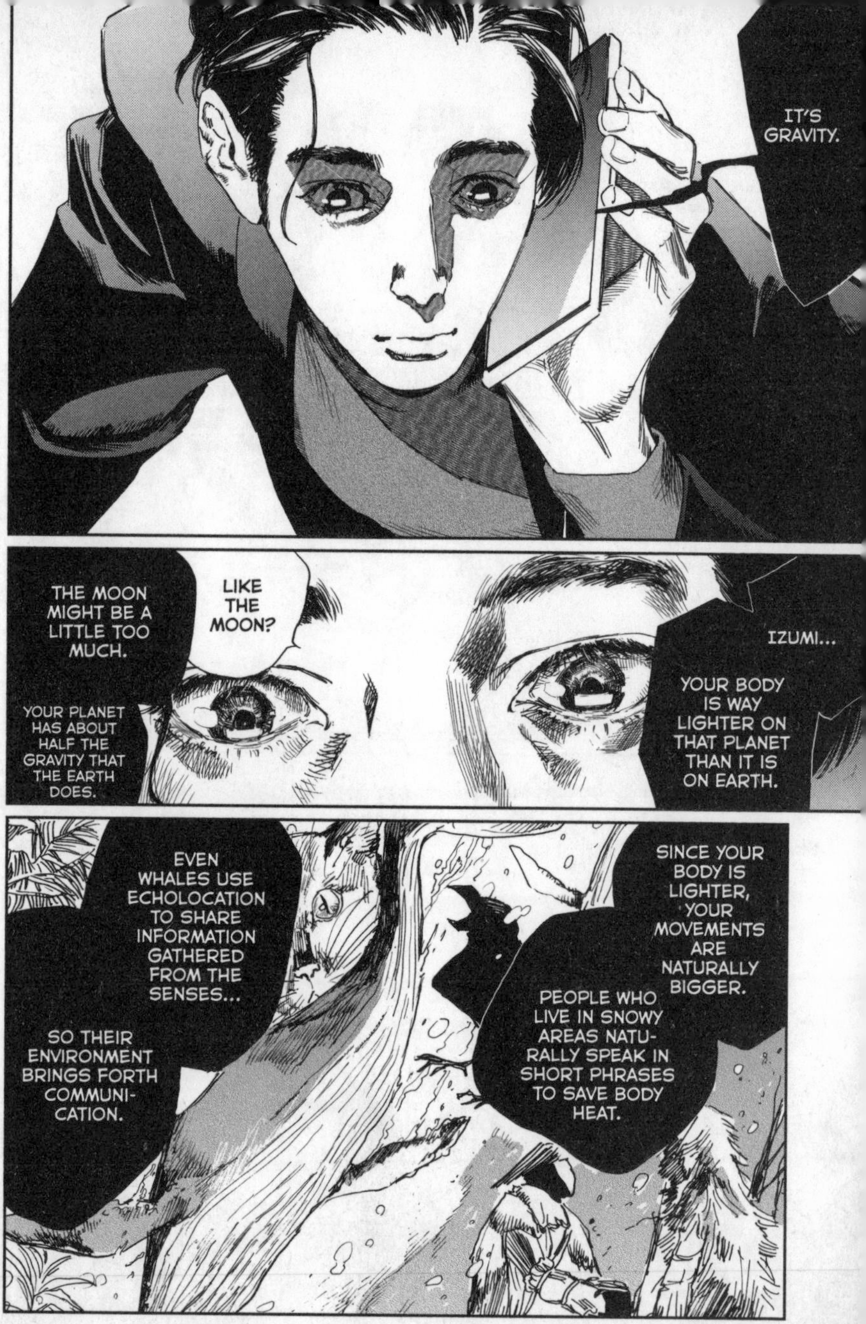
IT'S GRAVITY.
IZUMI...
YOUR BODY IS WAY LIGHTER ON THAT PLANET THAN IT IS ON EARTH.
LIKE THE MOON?
THE MOON MIGHT BE A LITTLE TOO MUCH.
YOUR PLANET HAS ABOUT HALF THE GRAVITY THAT THE EARTH DOES.
SINCE YOUR BODY IS LIGHTER, YOUR MOVEMENTS ARE NATURALLY BIGGER.
PEOPLE WHO LIVE IN SNOWY AREAS NATURALLY SPEAK IN SHORT PHRASES TO SAVE BODY HEAT.
EVEN WHALES USE ECHOLOCATION TO SHARE INFORMATION GATHERED FROM THE SENSES...
SO THEIR ENVIRONMENT BRINGS FORTH COMMUNICATION.

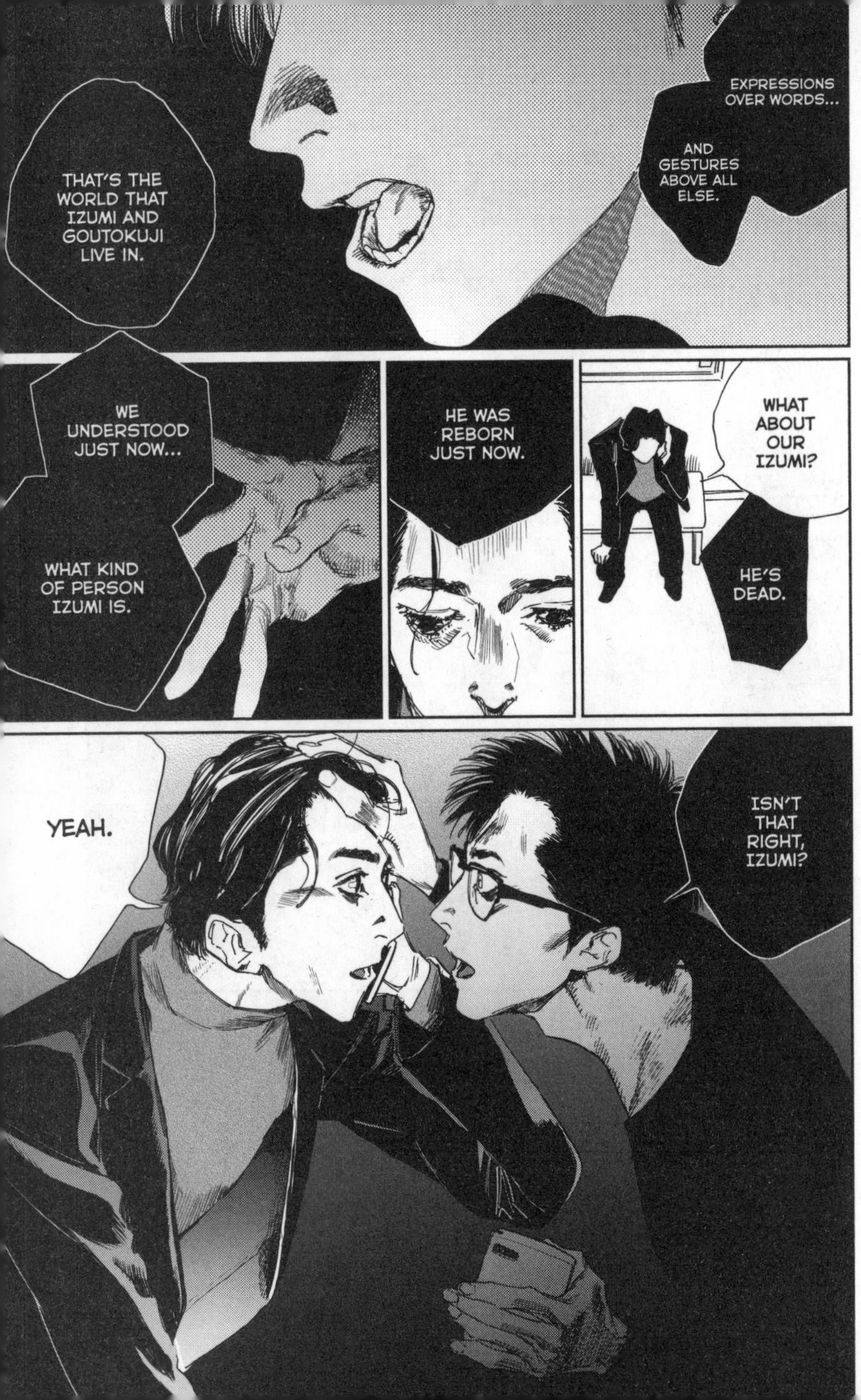
EXPRESSIONS OVER WORDS...
AND GESTURES ABOVE ALL ELSE.
THAT'S THE WORLD THAT IZUMI AND GOUTOKUJI LIVE IN.
WHAT ABOUT OUR IZUMI?
HE'S DEAD.
HE WAS REBORN JUST NOW.
WE UNDERSTOOD JUST NOW...
WHAT KIND OF PERSON IZUMI IS.
ISN'T THAT RIGHT, IZUMI?
YEAH.

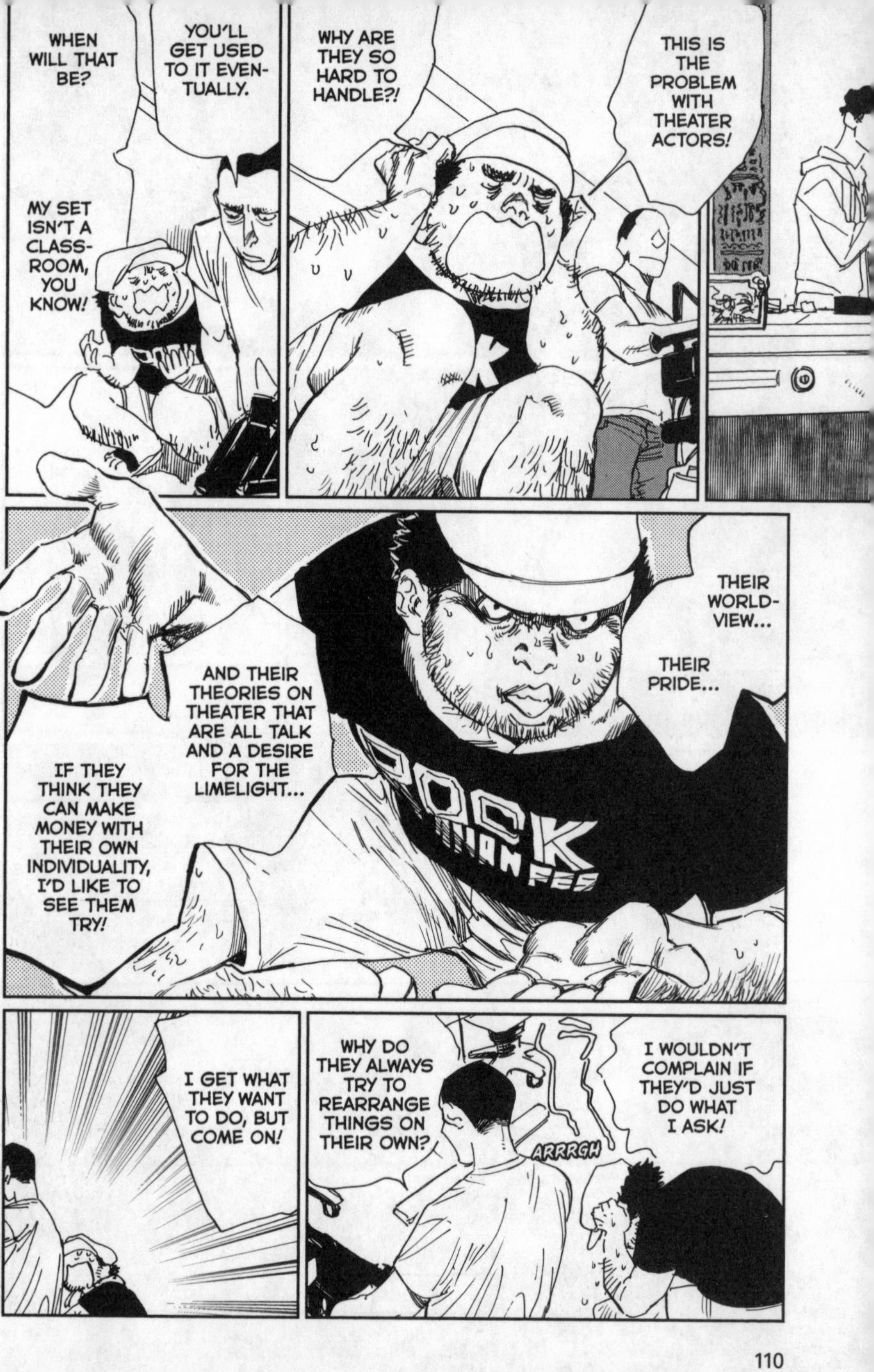
THIS IS THE PROBLEM WITH THEATER ACTORS!
WHY ARE THEY SO HARD TO HANDLE?!
YOU'LL GET USED TO IT EVEN-TUALLY.
WHEN WILL THAT BE?
MY SET ISN'T A CLASS-ROOM, YOU KNOW!
THEIR WORLD-VIEW...
THEIR PRIDE...
AND THEIR THEORIES ON THEATER THAT ARE ALL TALK AND A DESIRE FOR THE LIMELIGHT...
IF THEY THINK THEY CAN MAKE MONEY WITH THEIR OWN INDIVIDUALITY, I'D LIKE TO SEE THEM TRY!
I WOULDN'T COMPLAIN IF THEY'D JUST DO WHAT I ASK!
ARRRGH
WHY DO THEY ALWAYS TRY TO REARRANGE THINGS ON THEIR OWN?
I GET WHAT THEY WANT TO DO, BUT COME ON!

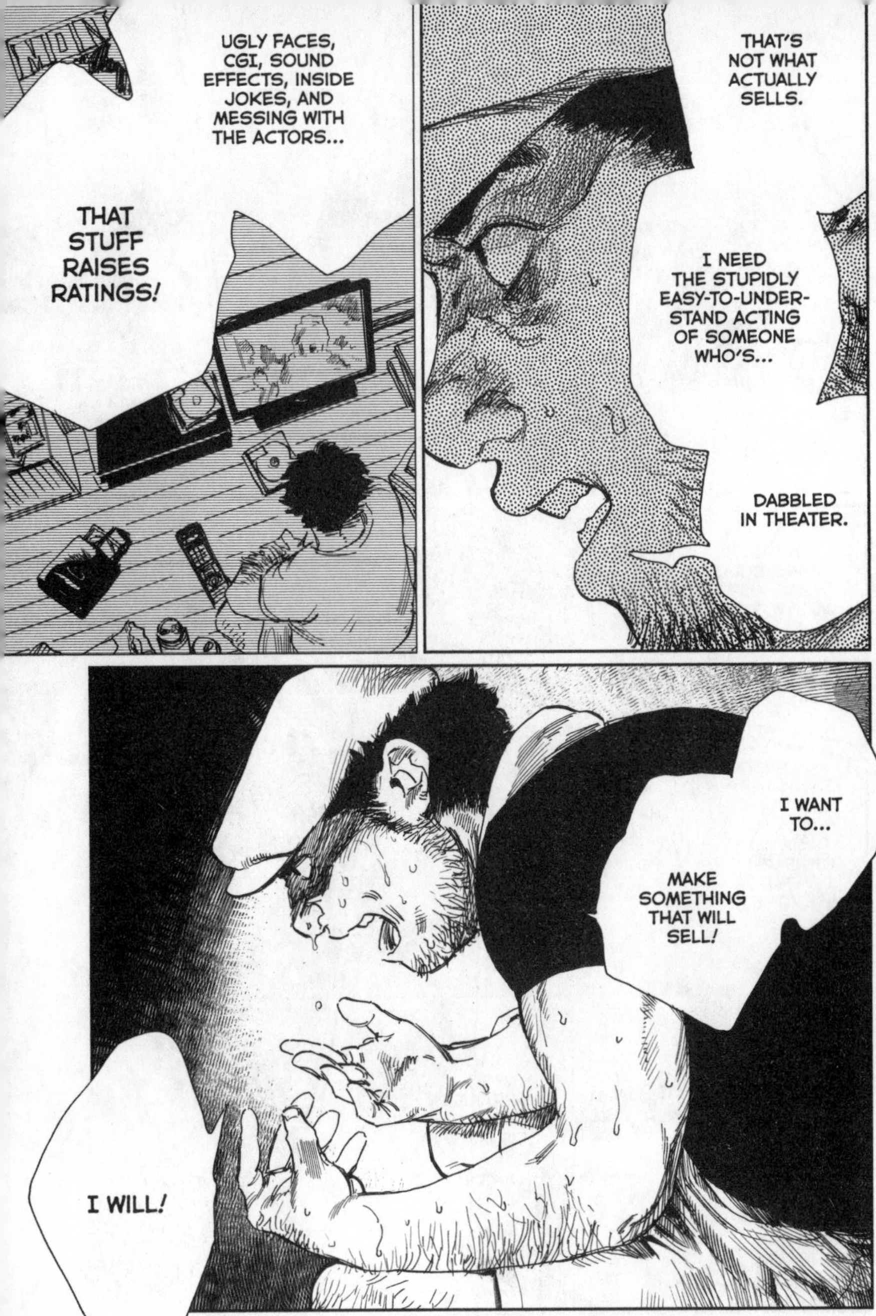
THAT'S NOT WHAT ACTUALLY SELLS.
I NEED THE STUPIDLY EASY-TO-UNDER-STAND ACTING OF SOMEONE WHO'S...
DABBLED IN THEATER.
UGLY FACES, CGI, SOUND EFFECTS, INSIDE JOKES, AND MESSING WITH THE ACTORS...
THAT STUFF RAISES RATINGS!
I WANT TO...
MAKE SOMETHING THAT WILL SELL!
I WILL!

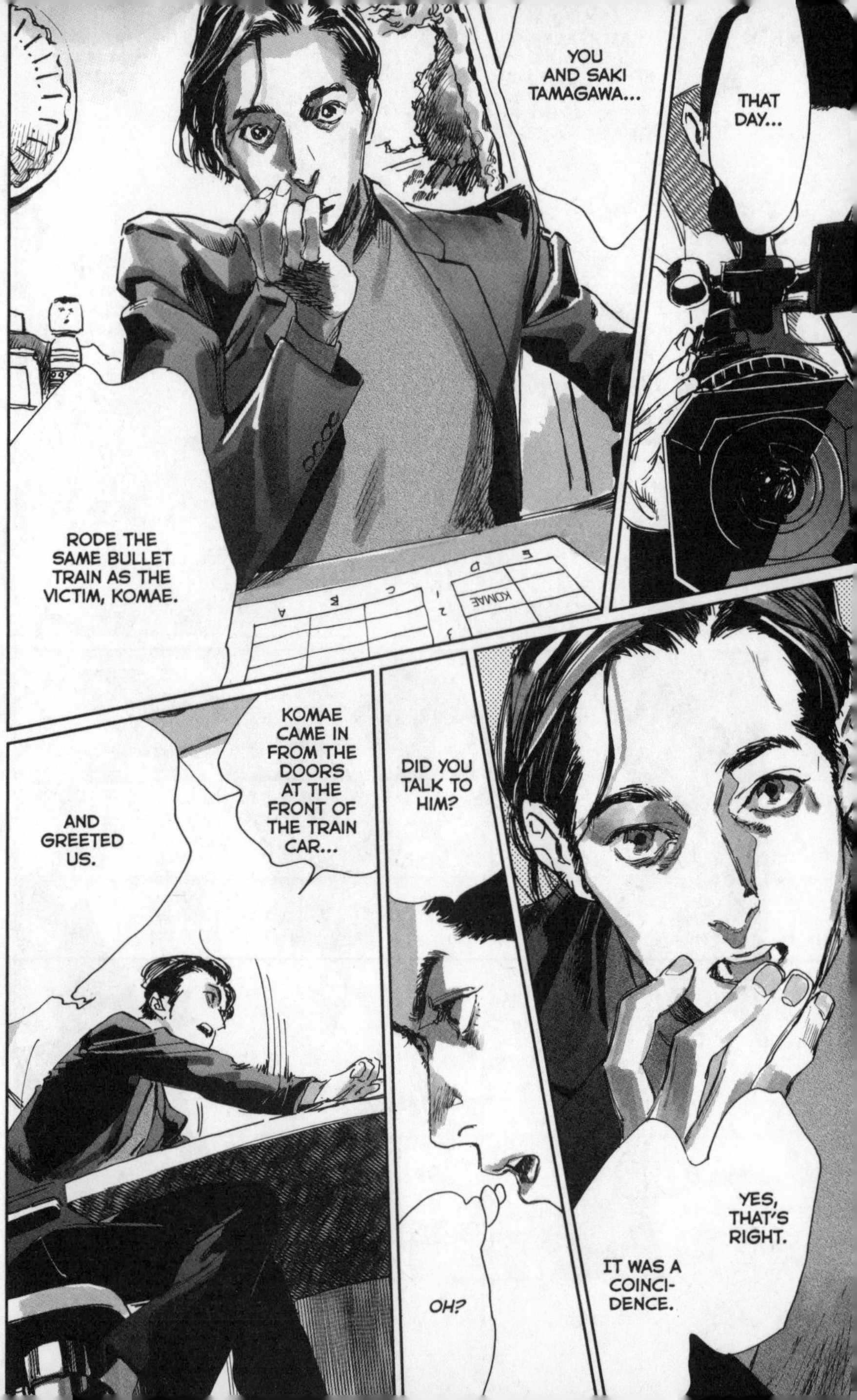
THAT DAY...
YOU AND SAKI TAMAGAWA...
RODE THE SAME BULLET TRAIN AS THE VICTIM, KOMAE.
YES, THAT'S RIGHT.
IT WAS A COINCIDENCE.
DID YOU TALK TO HIM?
OH?
KOMAE CAME IN FROM THE DOORS AT THE FRONT OF THE TRAIN CAR...
AND GREETED US.

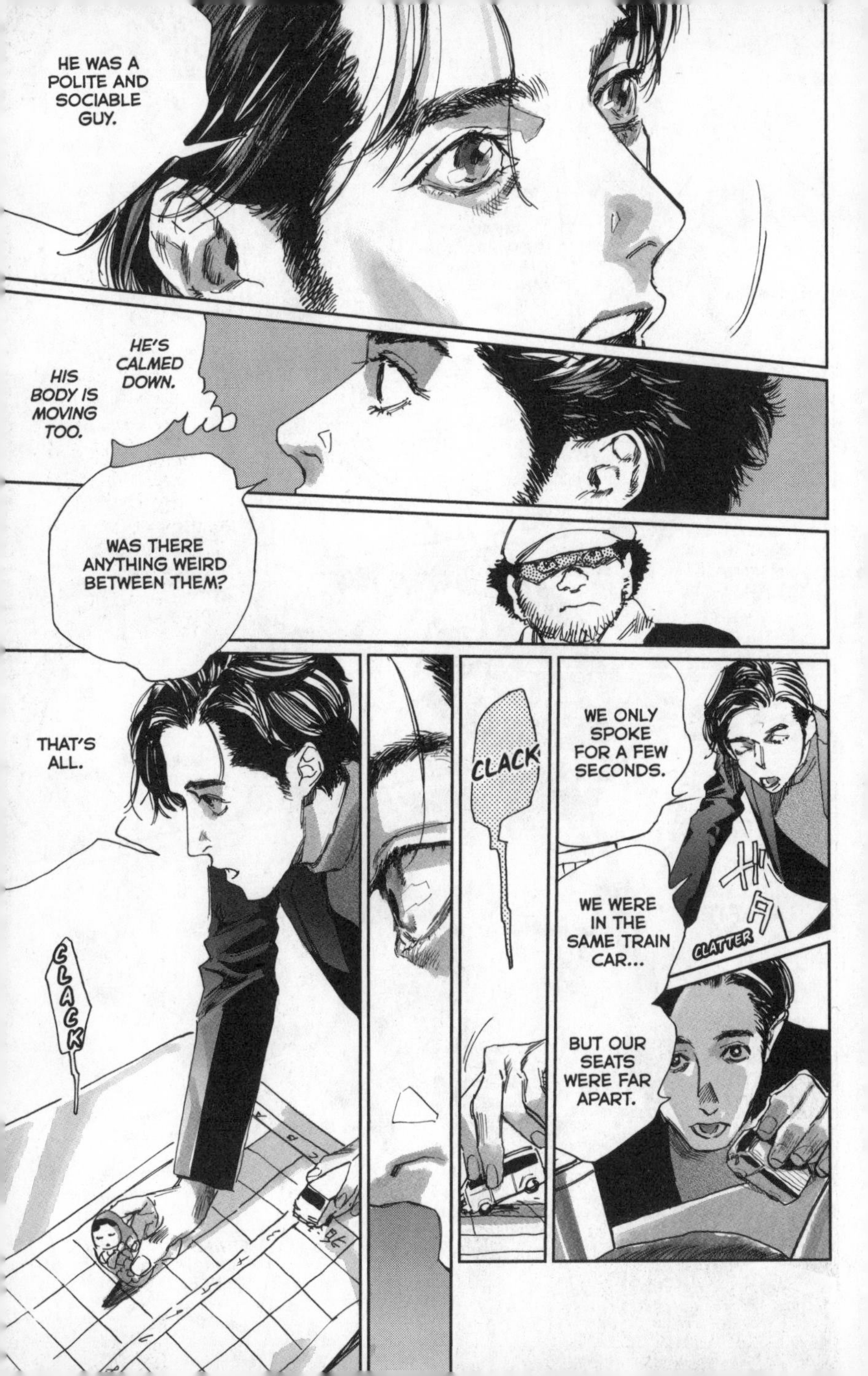
HE WAS A POLITE AND SOCIABLE GUY.
HE'S CALMED DOWN.
HIS BODY IS MOVING TOO.
WAS THERE ANYTHING WEIRD BETWEEN THEM?
WE ONLY SPOKE FOR A FEW SECONDS.
CLATTER
WE WERE IN THE SAME TRAIN CAR...
BUT OUR SEATS WERE FAR APART.
CLACK
THAT'S ALL.
CLACK

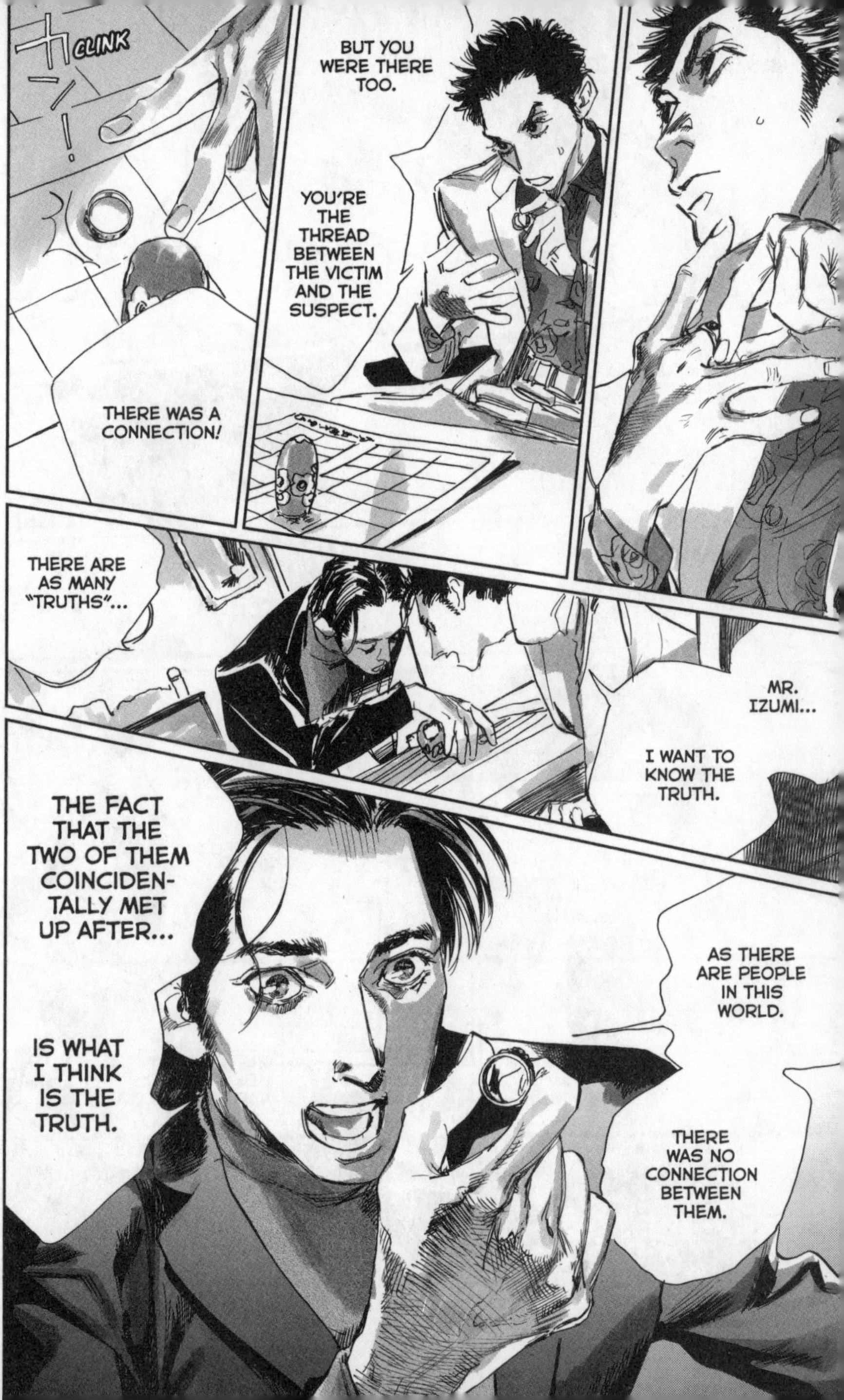
BUT YOU WERE THERE TOO.
YOU'RE THE THREAD BETWEEN THE VICTIM AND THE SUSPECT.
CLINK
THERE WAS A CONNECTION!
MR. IZUMI...
I WANT TO KNOW THE TRUTH.
THERE ARE AS MANY "TRUTHS"...
AS THERE ARE PEOPLE IN THIS WORLD.
THERE WAS NO CONNECTION BETWEEN THEM.
THE FACT THAT THE TWO OF THEM COINCIDEN-TALLY MET UP AFTER...
IS WHAT I THINK IS THE TRUTH.

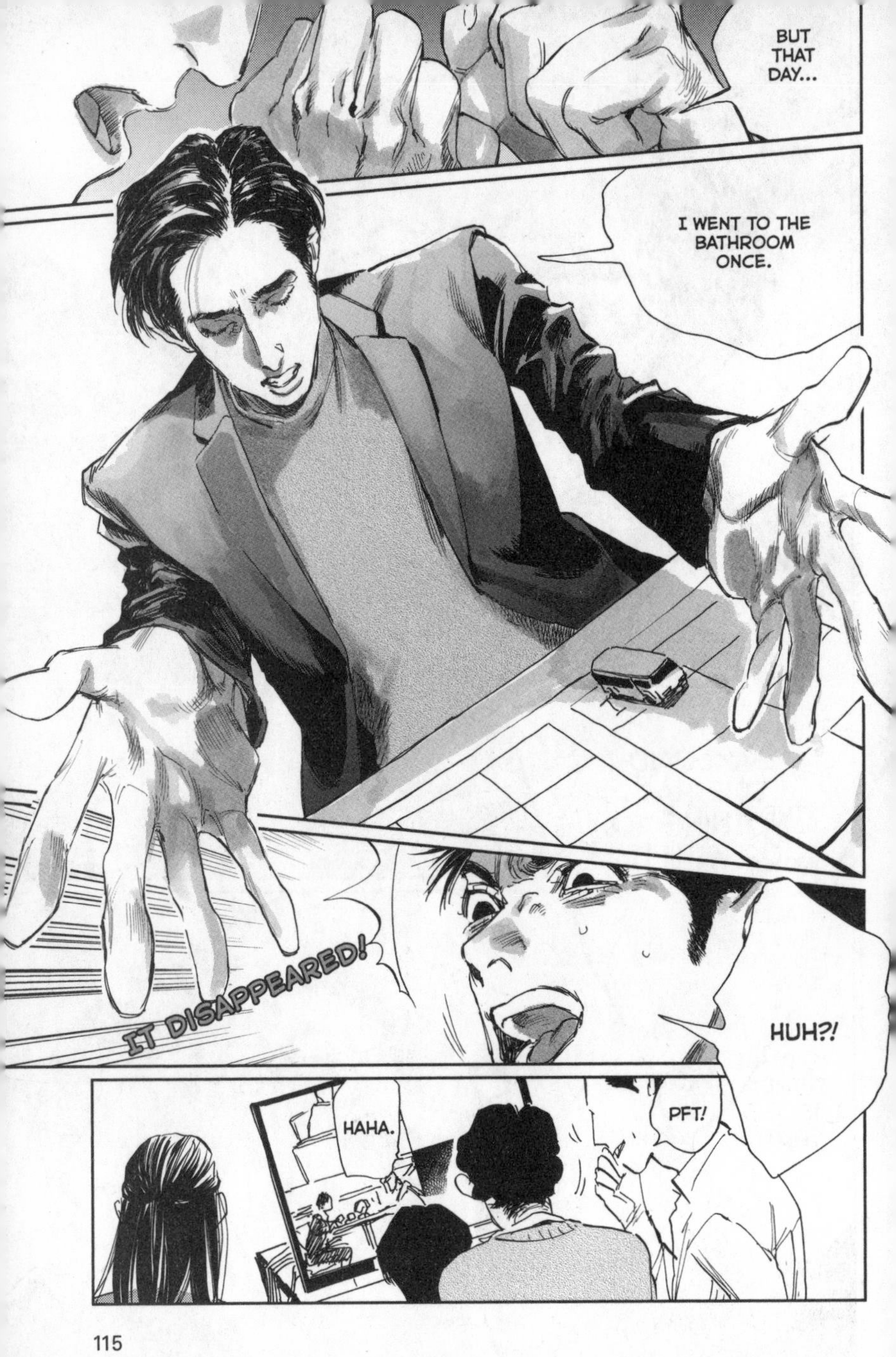
BUT THAT DAY...
I WENT TO THE BATHROOM ONCE.
IT DISAPPEARED!
HUH?!
PFT!
HAHA.

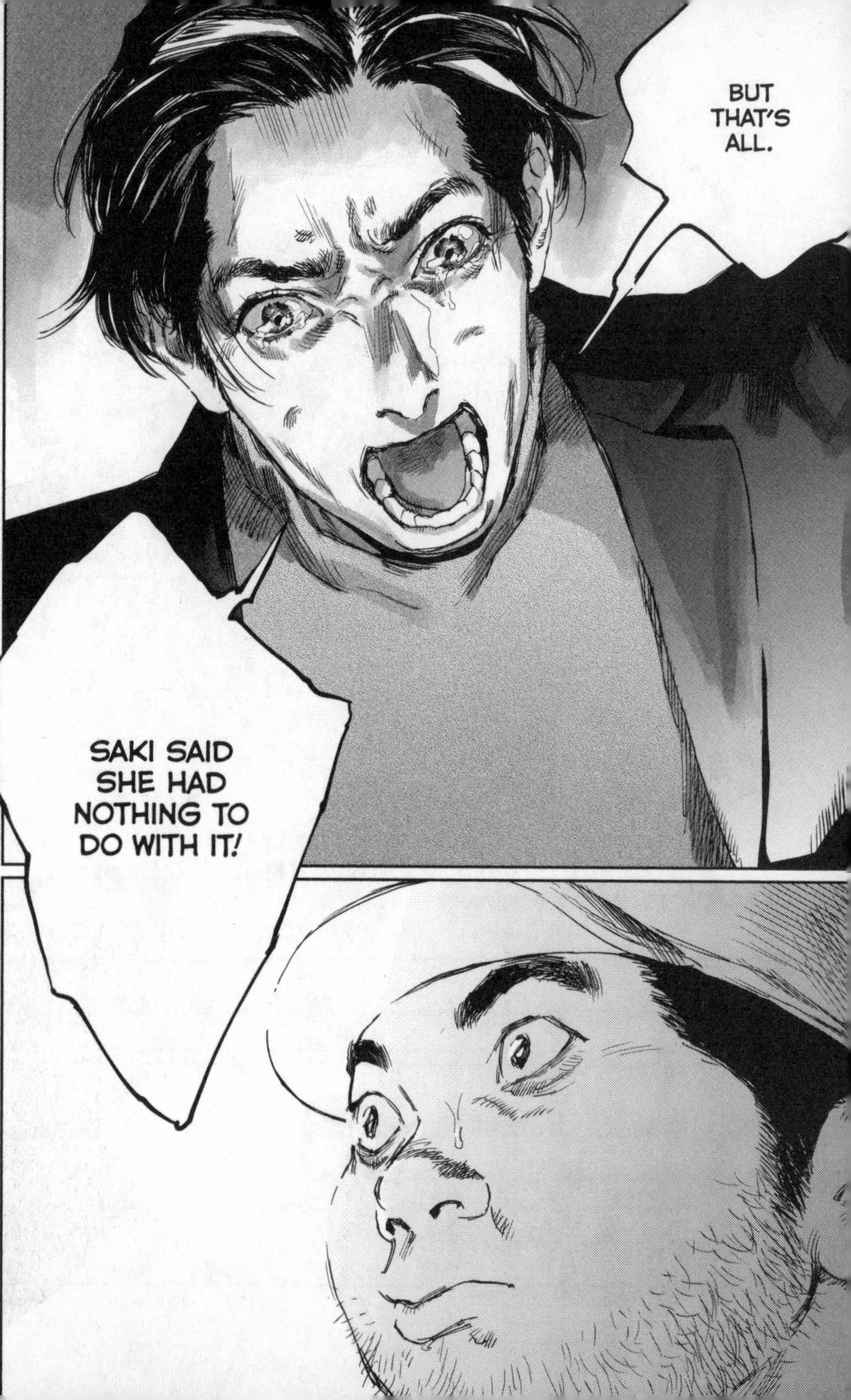
BUT THAT'S ALL.
SAKI SAID SHE HAD NOTHING TO DO WITH IT!

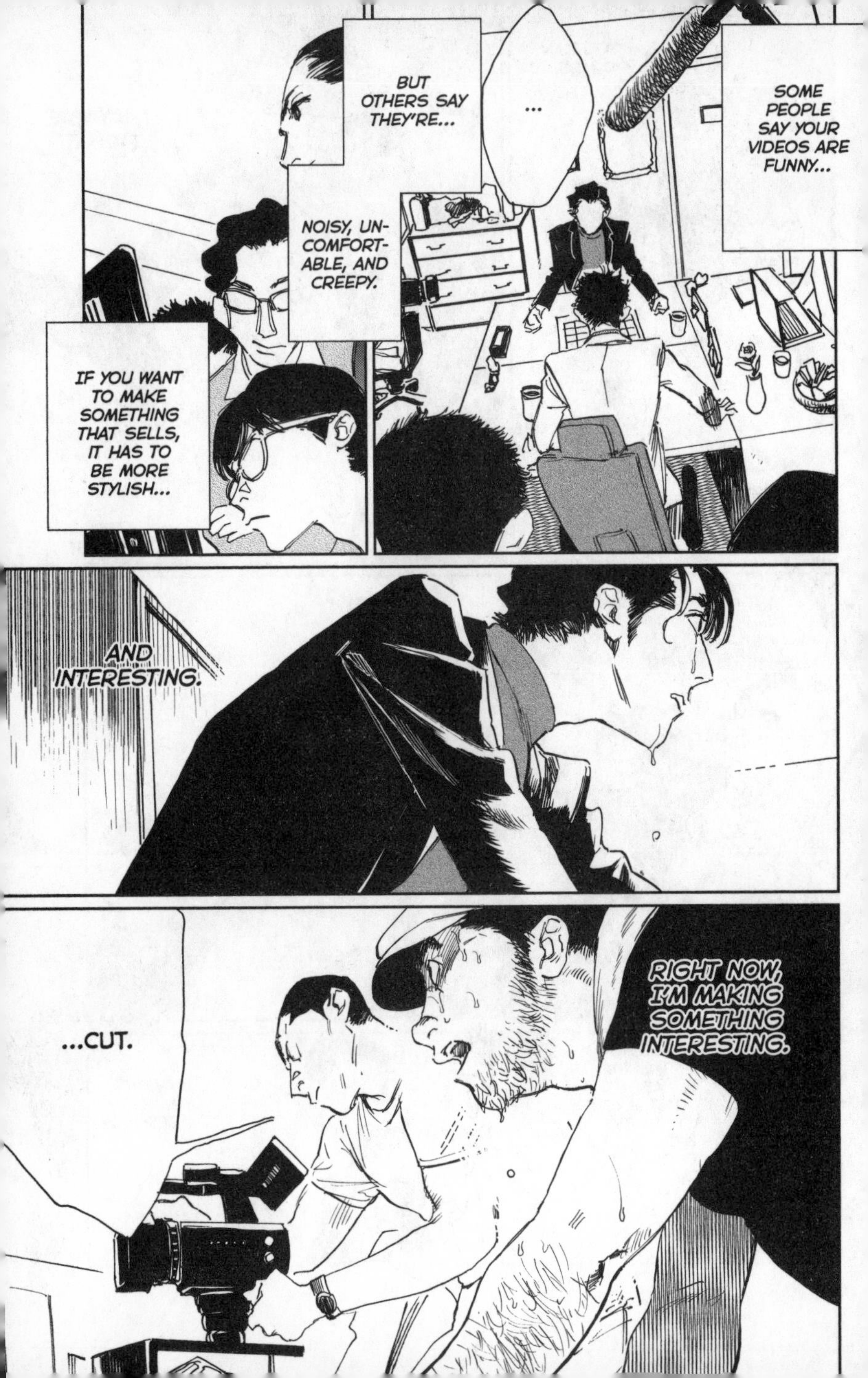
SOME PEOPLE SAY YOUR VIDEOS ARE FUNNY...
...
BUT OTHERS SAY THEY'RE...
NOISY, UN-COMFORTABLE, AND CREEPY.
IF YOU WANT TO MAKE SOMETHING THAT SELLS, IT HAS TO BE MORE STYLISH...
AND INTERESTING.
RIGHT NOW, I'M MAKING SOMETHING INTERESTING.
...CUT.

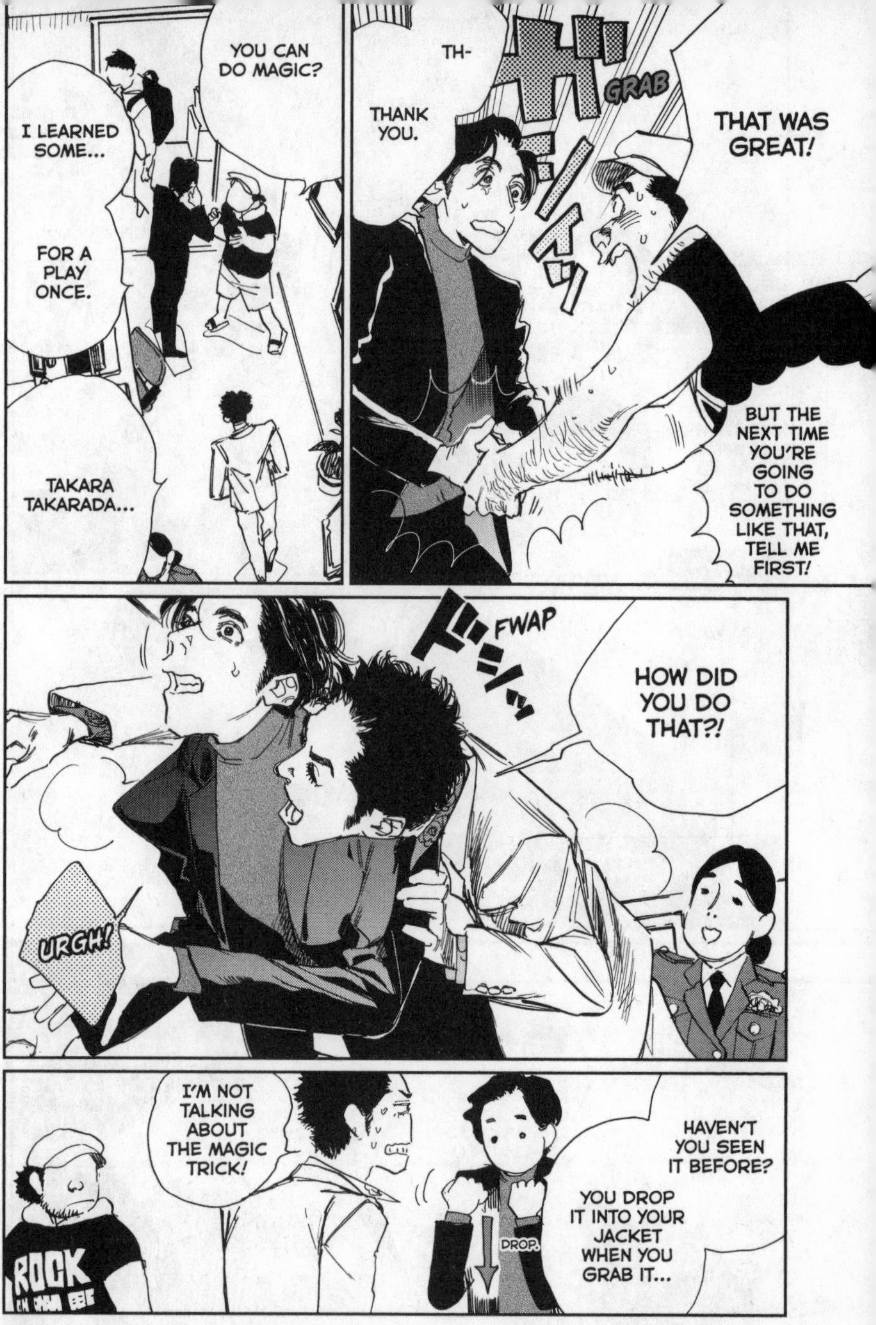
GRAB
THAT WAS GREAT!
TH-
THANK YOU.
BUT THE NEXT TIME YOU'RE GOING TO DO SOMETHING LIKE THAT, TELL ME FIRST!
YOU CAN DO MAGIC?
I LEARNED SOME...
FOR A PLAY ONCE.
TAKARA TAKARADA...
FWAP
HOW DID YOU DO THAT?!
URGH!
HAVEN'T YOU SEEN IT BEFORE?
YOU DROP IT INTO YOUR JACKET WHEN YOU GRAB IT...
DROP.
I'M NOT TALKING ABOUT THE MAGIC TRICK!
ROCK

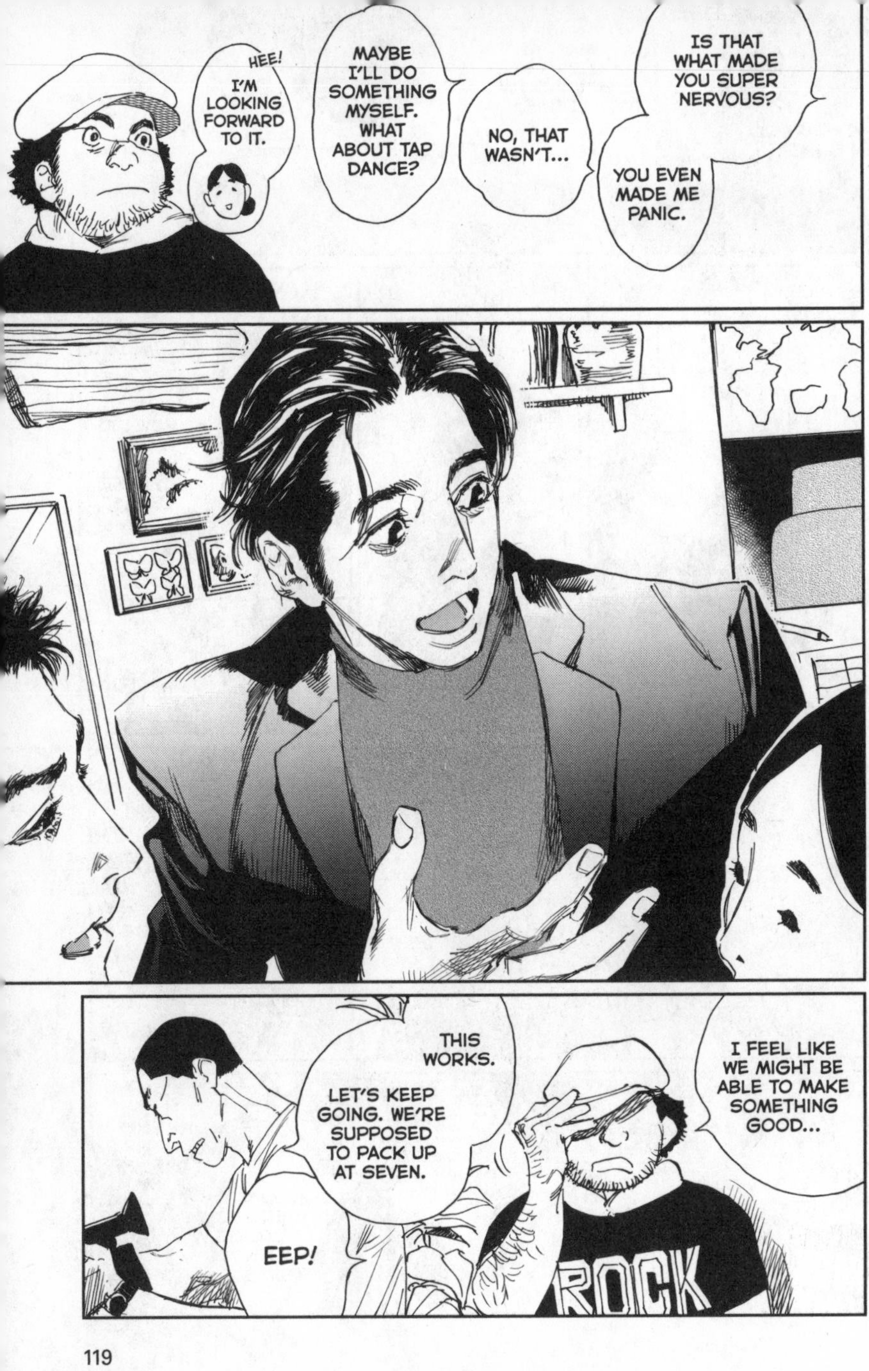
IS THAT WHAT MADE YOU SUPER NERVOUS?
YOU EVEN MADE ME PANIC.
NO, THAT WASN'T...
MAYBE I'LL DO SOMETHING MYSELF. WHAT ABOUT TAP DANCE?
HEE!
I'M LOOKING FORWARD TO IT.
I FEEL LIKE WE MIGHT BE ABLE TO MAKE SOMETHING GOOD...
THIS WORKS.
LET'S KEEP GOING. WE'RE SUPPOSED TO PACK UP AT SEVEN.
ROCK
EEP!

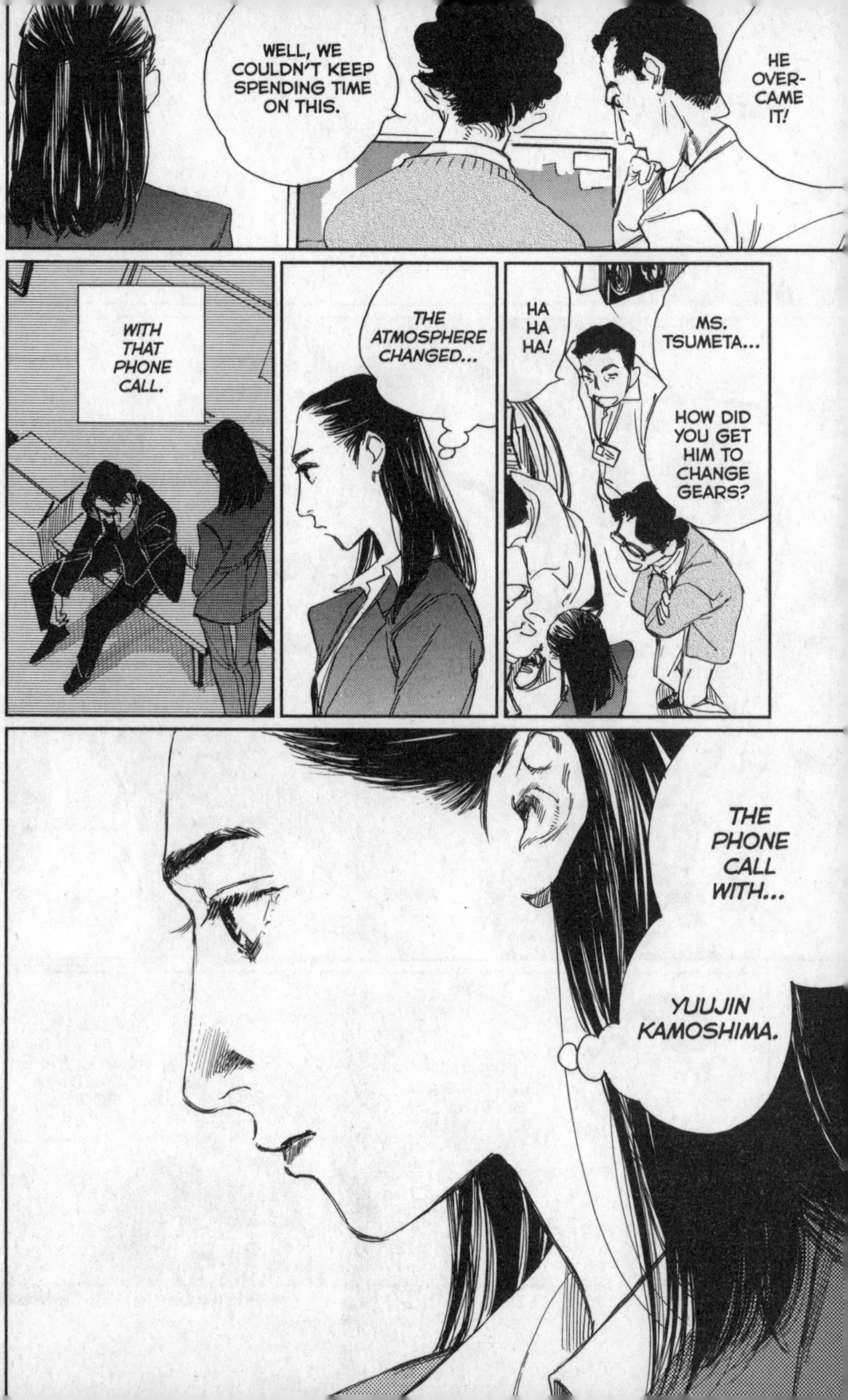
HE OVER-CAME IT!
WELL, WE COULDN'T KEEP SPENDING TIME ON THIS.
MS. TSUMETA...
HA HA HA!
HOW DID YOU GET HIM TO CHANGE GEARS?
THE ATMOSPHERE CHANGED...
WITH THAT PHONE CALL.
THE PHONE CALL WITH...
YUUJIN KAMOSHIMA.

DOUBLE

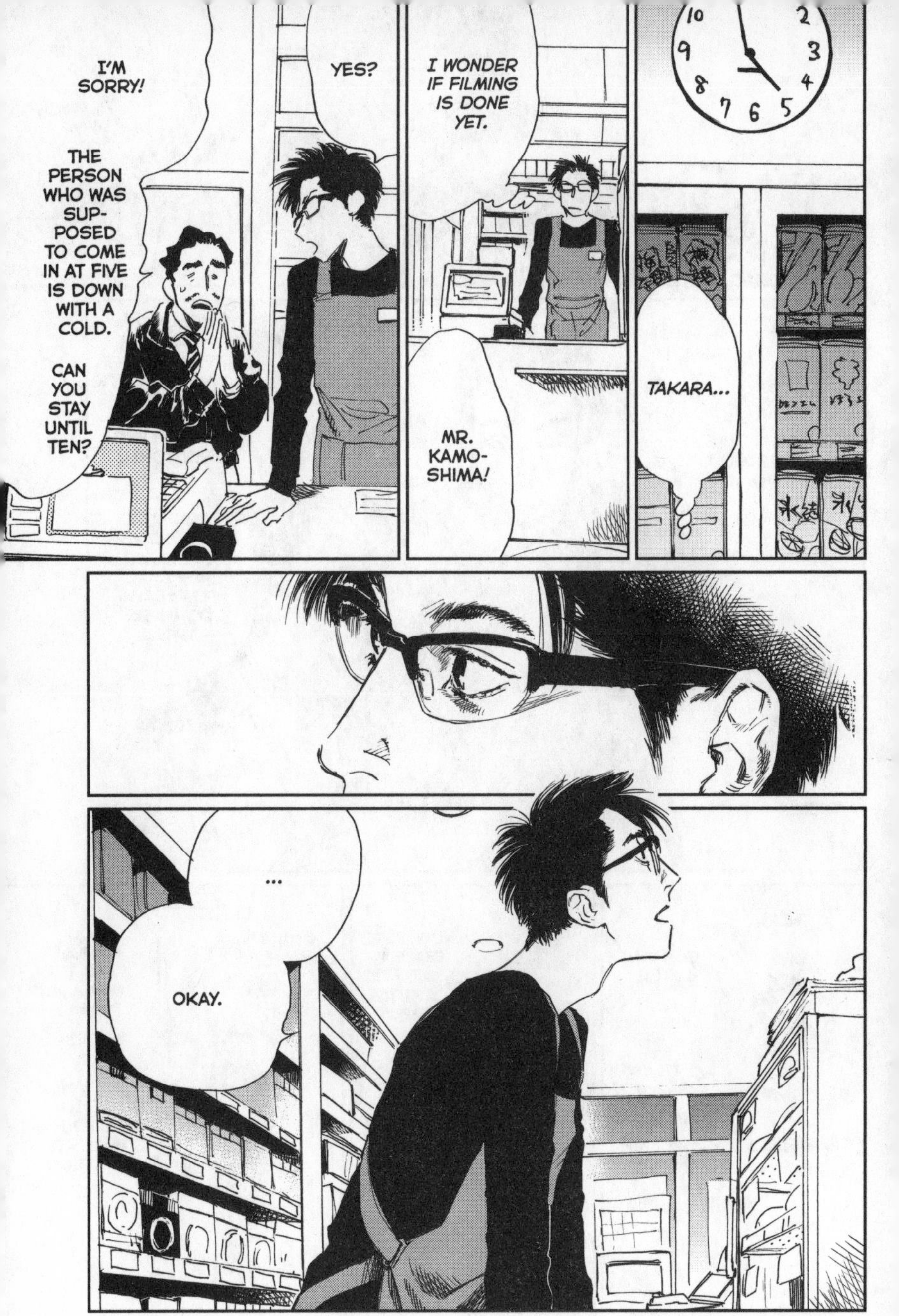
TAKARA...
I WONDER IF FILMING IS DONE YET.
MR. KAMOSHIMA!
YES?
I'M SORRY!
THE PERSON WHO WAS SUPPOSED TO COME IN AT FIVE IS DOWN WITH A COLD.
CAN YOU STAY UNTIL TEN?
...
OKAY.

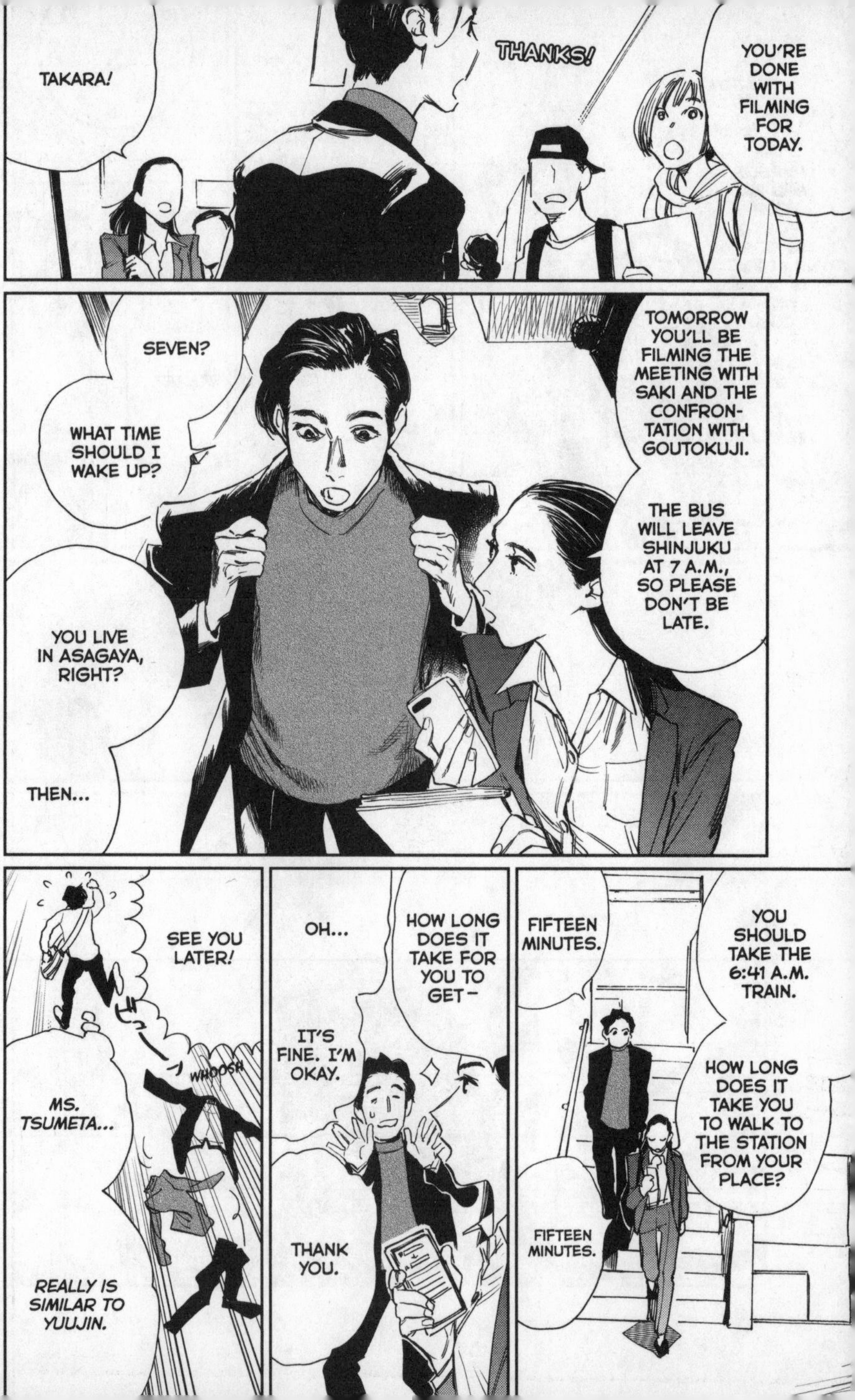
YOU'RE DONE WITH FILMING FOR TODAY.
THANKS!
TAKARA!
TOMORROW YOU'LL BE FILMING THE MEETING WITH SAKI AND THE CONFRONTATION WITH GOUTOKUJI.
THE BUS WILL LEAVE SHINJUKU AT 7 A.M., SO PLEASE DON'T BE LATE.
SEVEN?
WHAT TIME SHOULD I WAKE UP?
YOU LIVE IN ASAGAYA, RIGHT?
THEN...
YOU SHOULD TAKE THE 6:41 A.M. TRAIN.
FIFTEEN MINUTES.
HOW LONG DOES IT TAKE YOU TO WALK TO THE STATION FROM YOUR PLACE?
FIFTEEN MINUTES.
HOW LONG DOES IT TAKE FOR YOU TO GET–
OH...
IT'S FINE. I'M OKAY.
THANK YOU.
SEE YOU LATER!
WHOOSH
MS. TSUMETA...
REALLY IS SIMILAR TO YUUJIN.

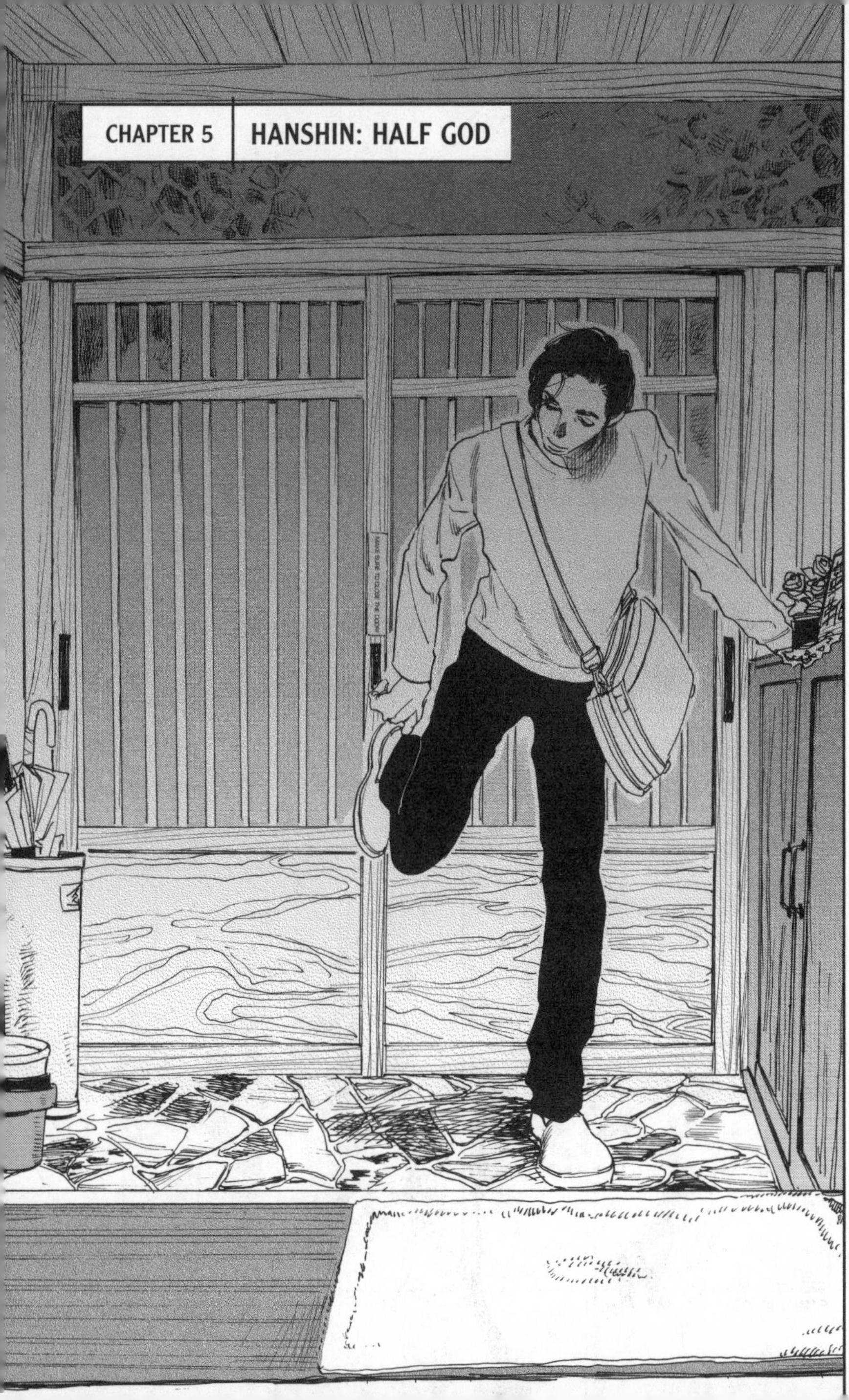
CHAPTER 5 HANSHIN: HALF GOD
MAKE SURE TO CLOSE THE DOOR!

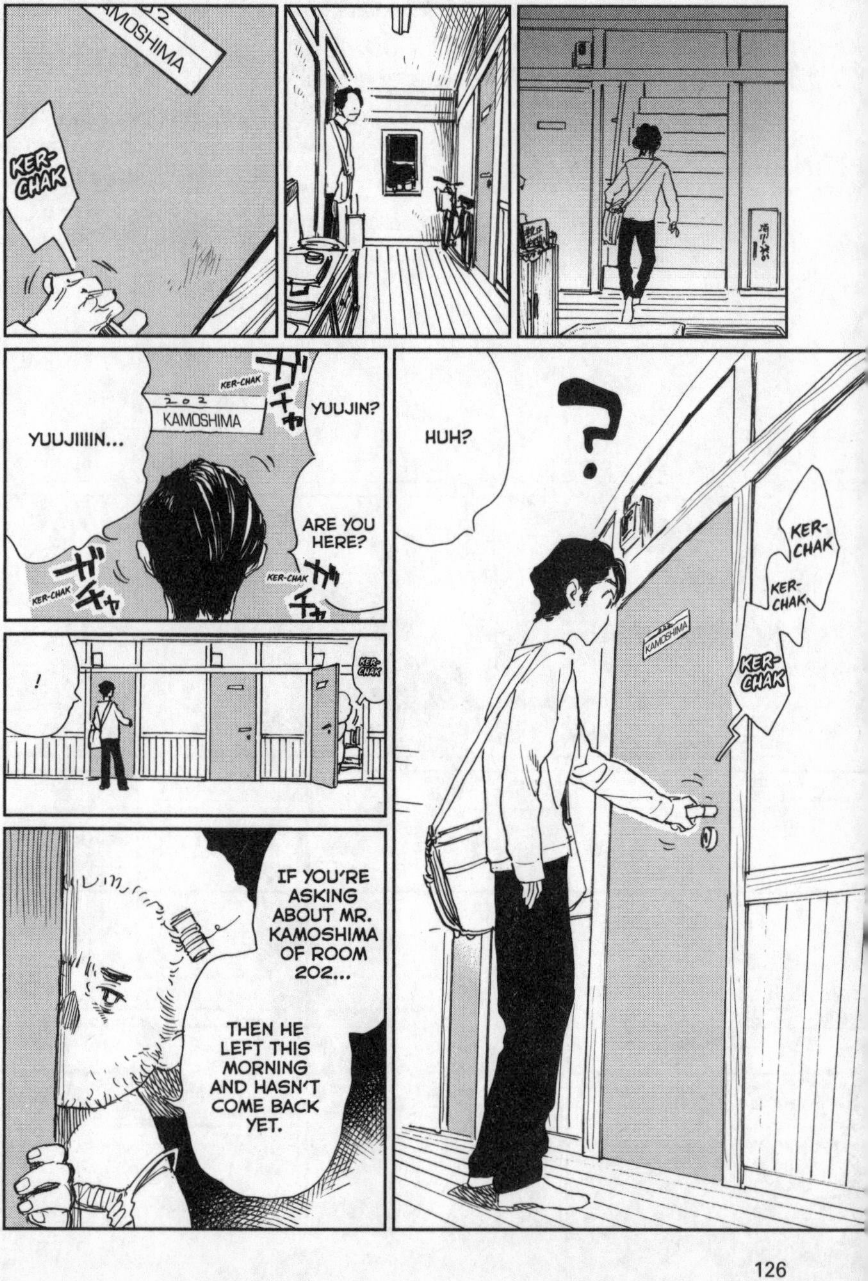
KER-CHAK
HUH?
?
KAMOSHIMA
KER-CHAK
KER-CHAK
KER-CHAK
ガチャ
KER-CHAK
202
KAMOSHIMA
YUUJIN?
ARE YOU HERE?
YUUJIIIIN...
ガチャ
KER-CHAK
ガチャ
KER-CHAK
KER-CHAK
!
IF YOU'RE ASKING ABOUT MR. KAMOSHIMA OF ROOM 202...
THEN HE LEFT THIS MORNING AND HASN'T COME BACK YET.

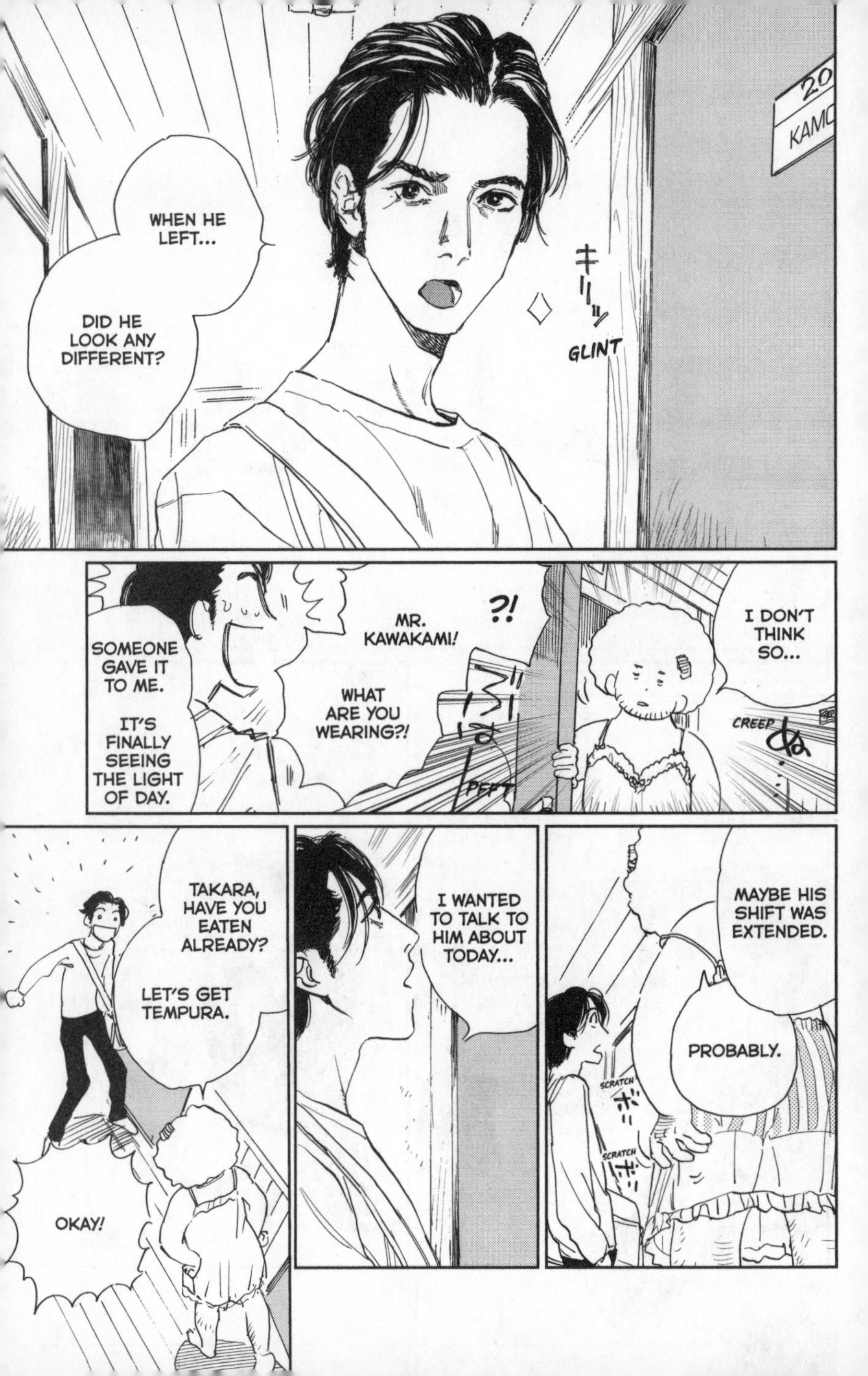
20
KAMO
WHEN HE LEFT...
DID HE LOOK ANY DIFFERENT?
GLINT
I DON'T THINK SO...
CREEP
?!
MR. KAWAKAMI!
WHAT ARE YOU WEARING?!
PFFT
SOMEONE GAVE IT TO ME.
IT'S FINALLY SEEING THE LIGHT OF DAY.
MAYBE HIS SHIFT WAS EXTENDED.
PROBABLY.
SCRATCH
SCRATCH
I WANTED TO TALK TO HIM ABOUT TODAY...
TAKARA, HAVE YOU EATEN ALREADY?
LET'S GET TEMPURA.
OKAY!

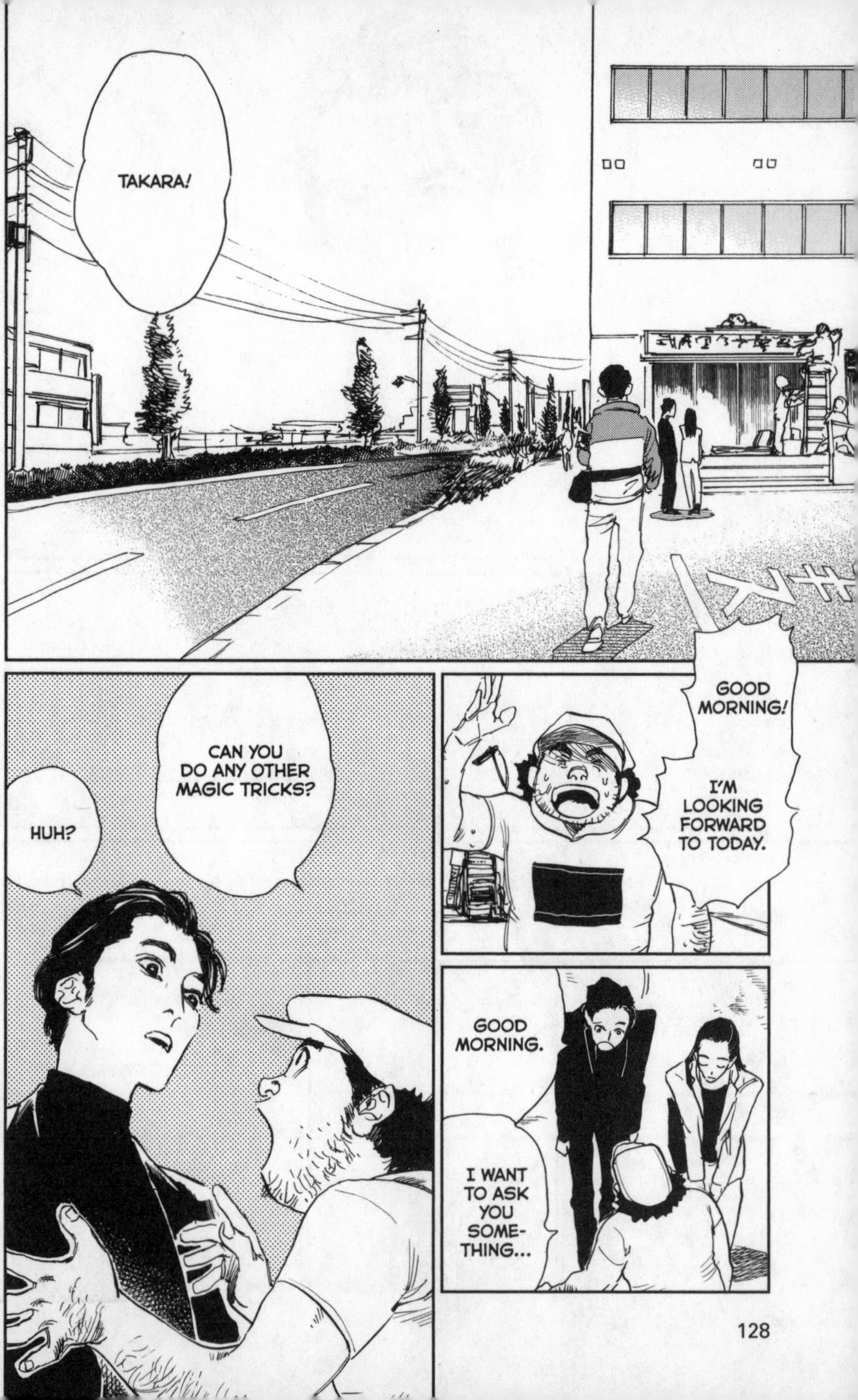
TAKARA!
GOOD MORNING!
I'M LOOKING FORWARD TO TODAY.
GOOD MORNING.
I WANT TO ASK YOU SOME-THING...
CAN YOU DO ANY OTHER MAGIC TRICKS?
HUH?

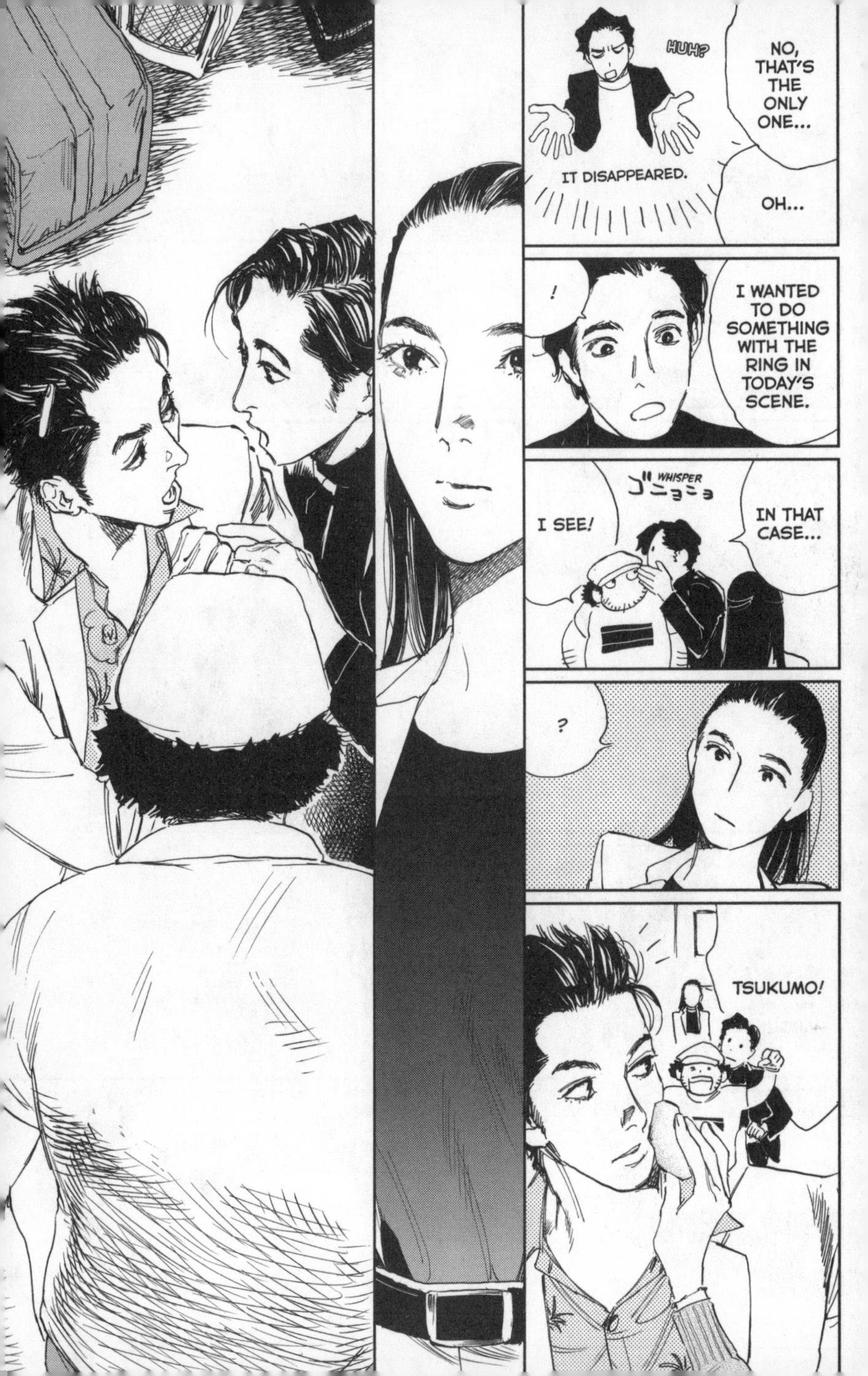
NO, THAT'S THE ONLY ONE...
HUH?
IT DISAPPEARED.
OH...
I WANTED TO DO SOMETHING WITH THE RING IN TODAY'S SCENE.
!
IN THAT CASE...
WHISPER ゴニョニョ
I SEE!
?
TSUKUMO!

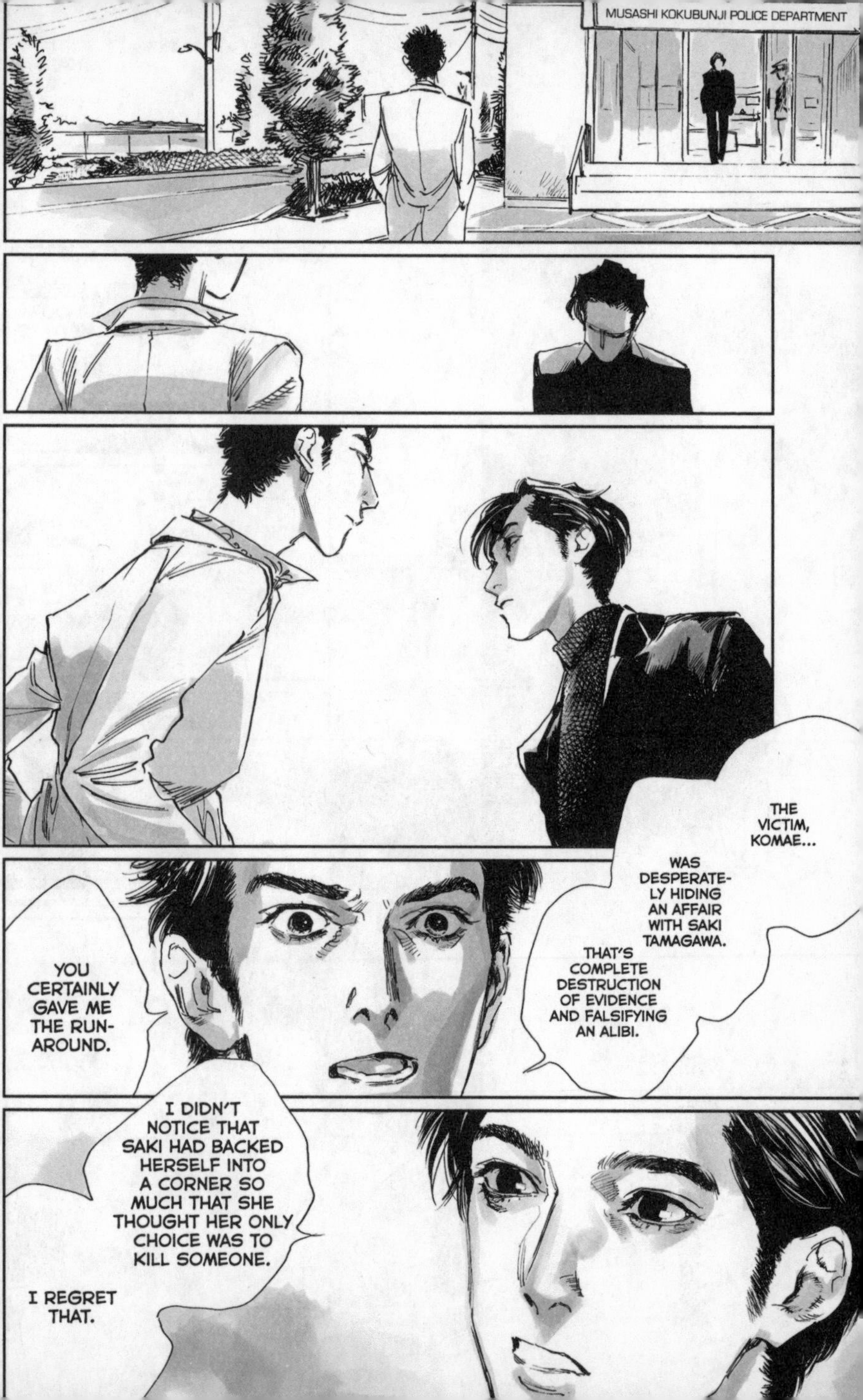
MUSASHI KOKUBUNJI POLICE DEPARTMENT
THE VICTIM, KOMAE...
WAS DESPERATE-LY HIDING AN AFFAIR WITH SAKI TAMAGAWA.
THAT'S COMPLETE DESTRUCTION OF EVIDENCE AND FALSIFYING AN ALIBI.
YOU CERTAINLY GAVE ME THE RUN-AROUND.
I DIDN'T NOTICE THAT SAKI HAD BACKED HERSELF INTO A CORNER SO MUCH THAT SHE THOUGHT HER ONLY CHOICE WAS TO KILL SOMEONE.
I REGRET THAT.

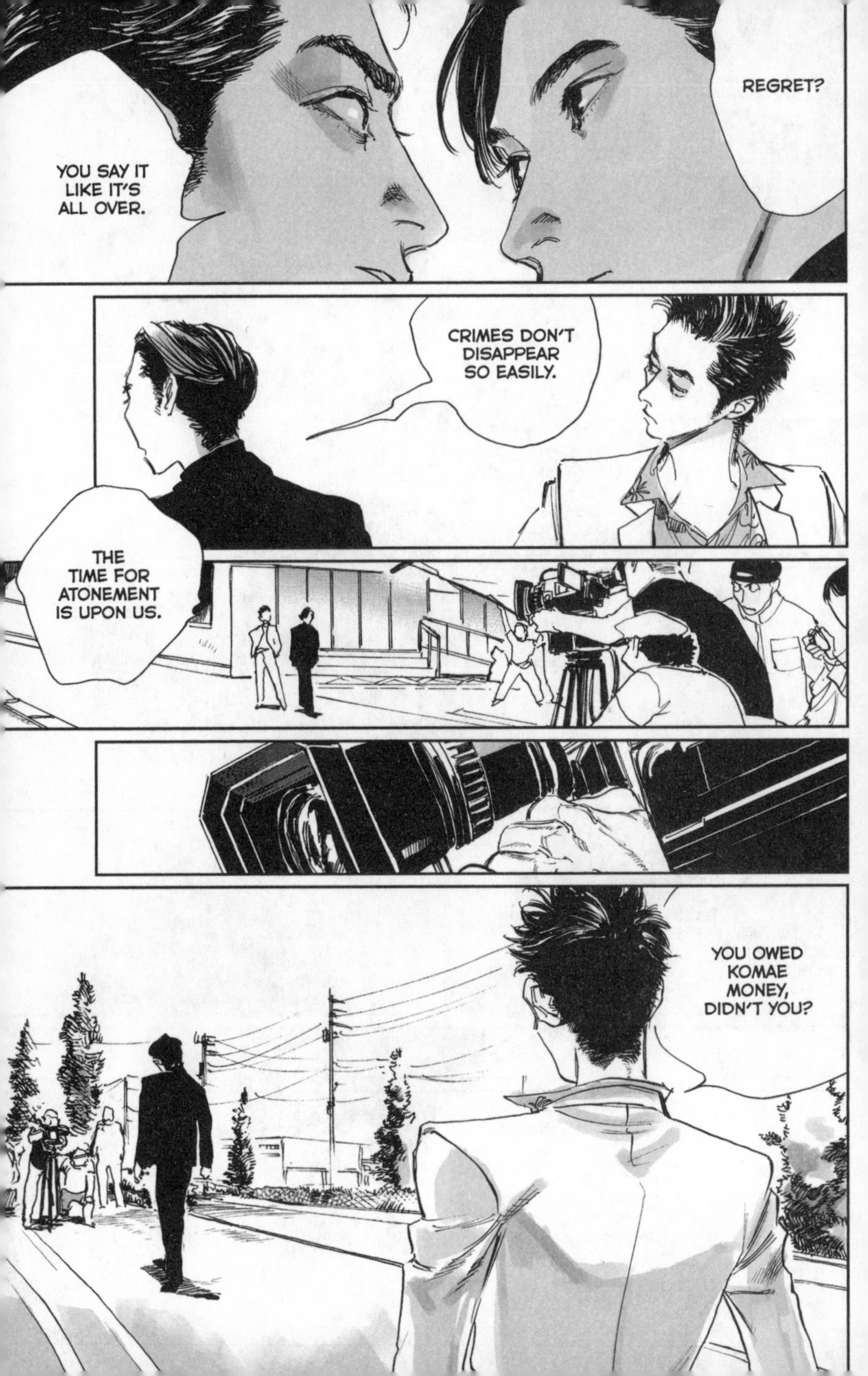
REGRET?
YOU SAY IT LIKE IT'S ALL OVER.
CRIMES DON'T DISAPPEAR SO EASILY.
THE TIME FOR ATONEMENT IS UPON US.
YOU OWED KOMAE MONEY, DIDN'T YOU?

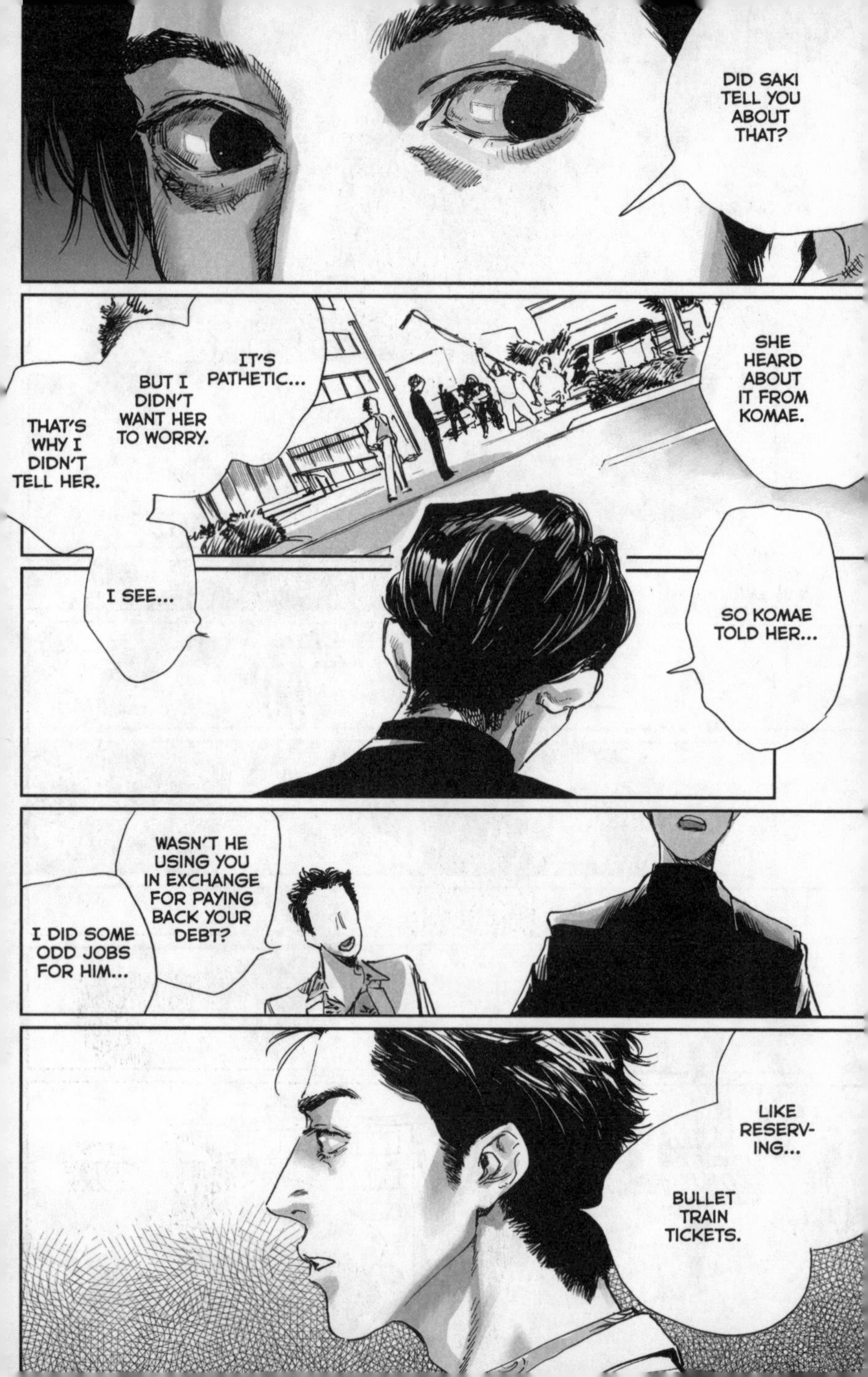
DID SAKI TELL YOU ABOUT THAT?
SHE HEARD ABOUT IT FROM KOMAE.
IT'S PATHETIC...
BUT I DIDN'T WANT HER TO WORRY.
THAT'S WHY I DIDN'T TELL HER.
SO KOMAE TOLD HER...
I SEE...
WASN'T HE USING YOU IN EXCHANGE FOR PAYING BACK YOUR DEBT?
I DID SOME ODD JOBS FOR HIM...
LIKE RESERV-ING...
BULLET TRAIN TICKETS.

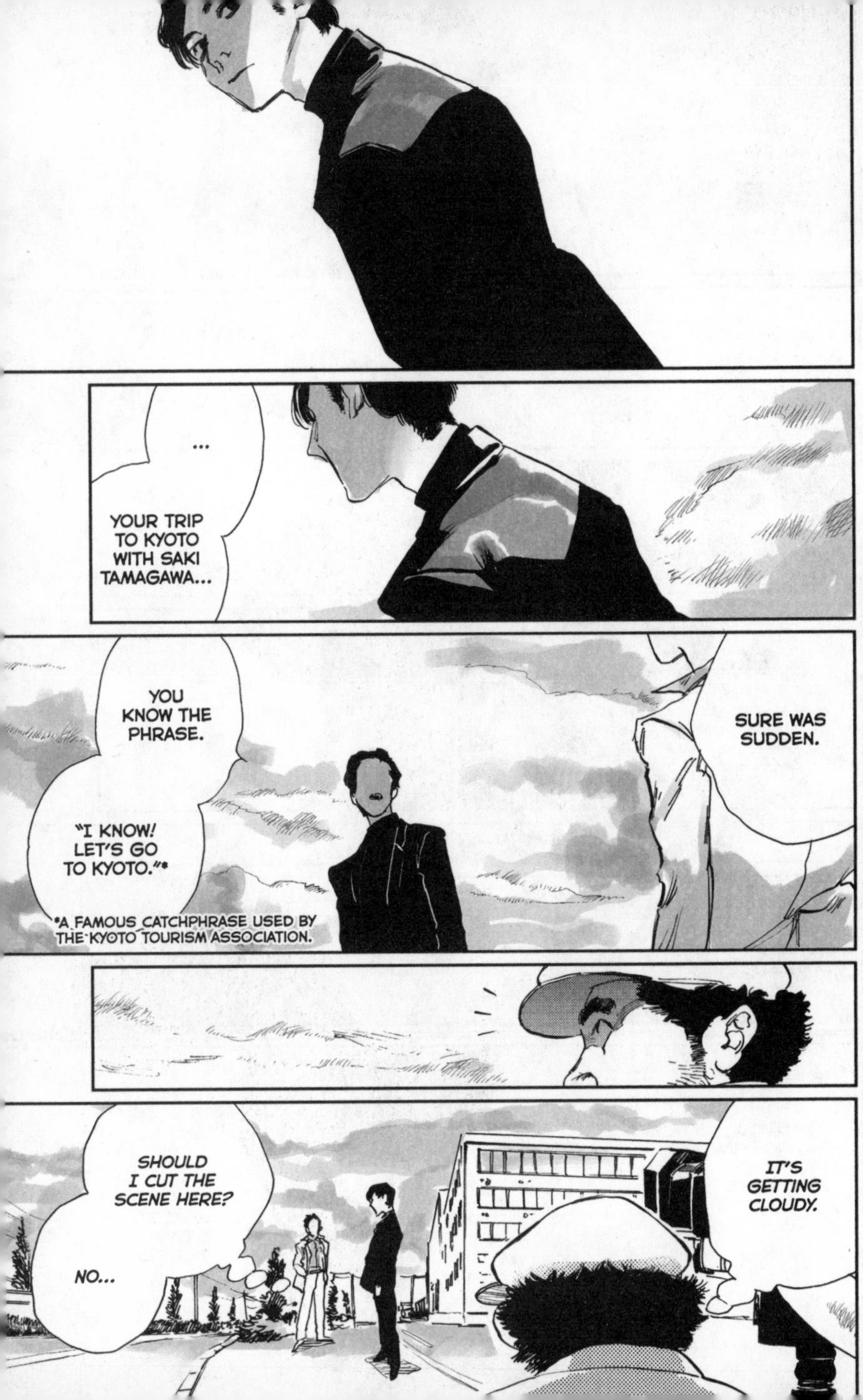
...
YOUR TRIP TO KYOTO WITH SAKI TAMAGAWA...
SURE WAS SUDDEN.
YOU KNOW THE PHRASE.
"I KNOW! LET'S GO TO KYOTO."*
*A FAMOUS CATCHPHRASE USED BY THE KYOTO TOURISM ASSOCIATION.
IT'S GETTING CLOUDY.
SHOULD I CUT THE SCENE HERE?
NO...

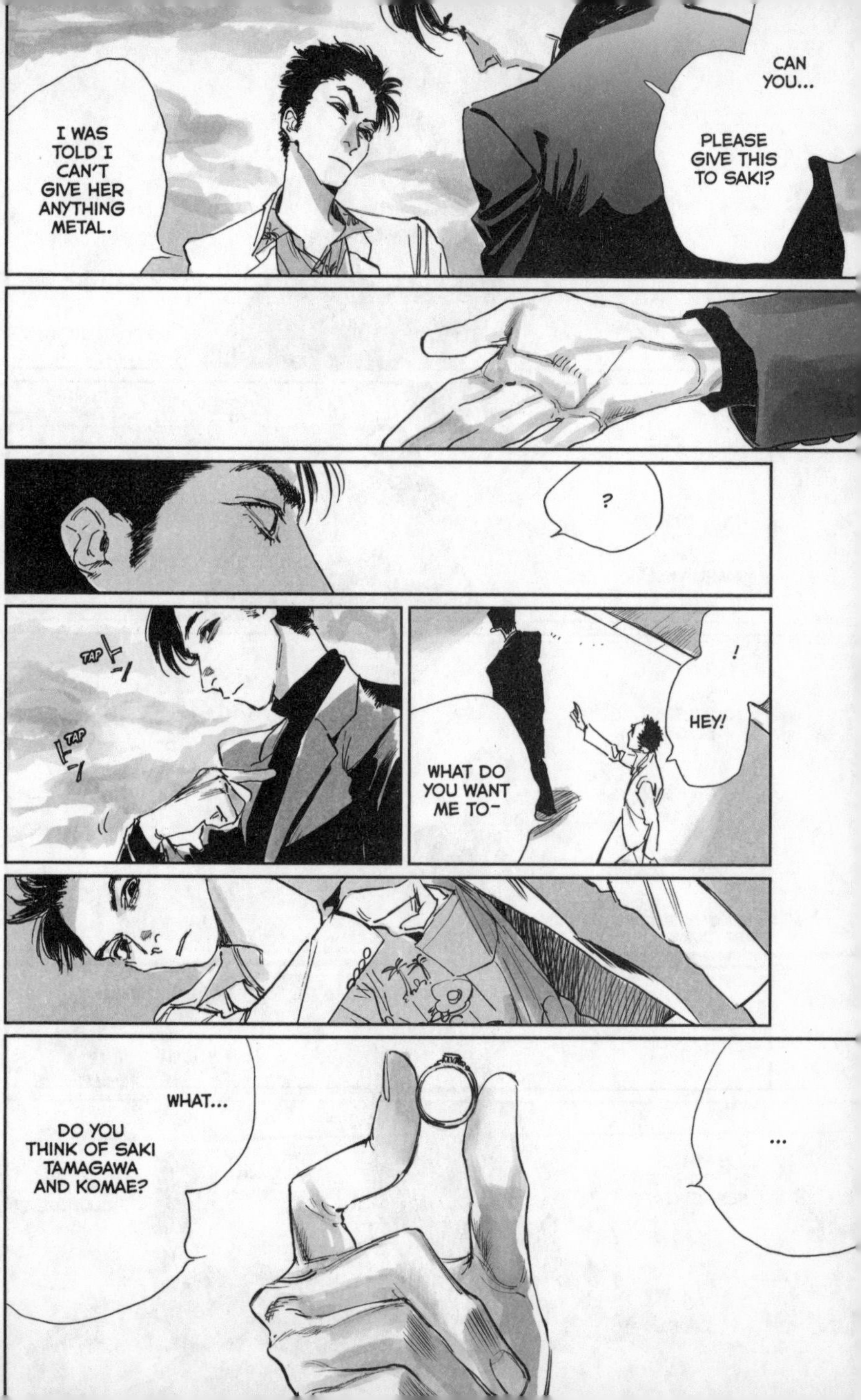
CAN YOU...
PLEASE GIVE THIS TO SAKI?
I WAS TOLD I CAN'T GIVE HER ANYTHING METAL.
?
!
HEY!
WHAT DO YOU WANT ME TO–
TAP
TAP
...
WHAT...
DO YOU THINK OF SAKI TAMAGAWA AND KOMAE?

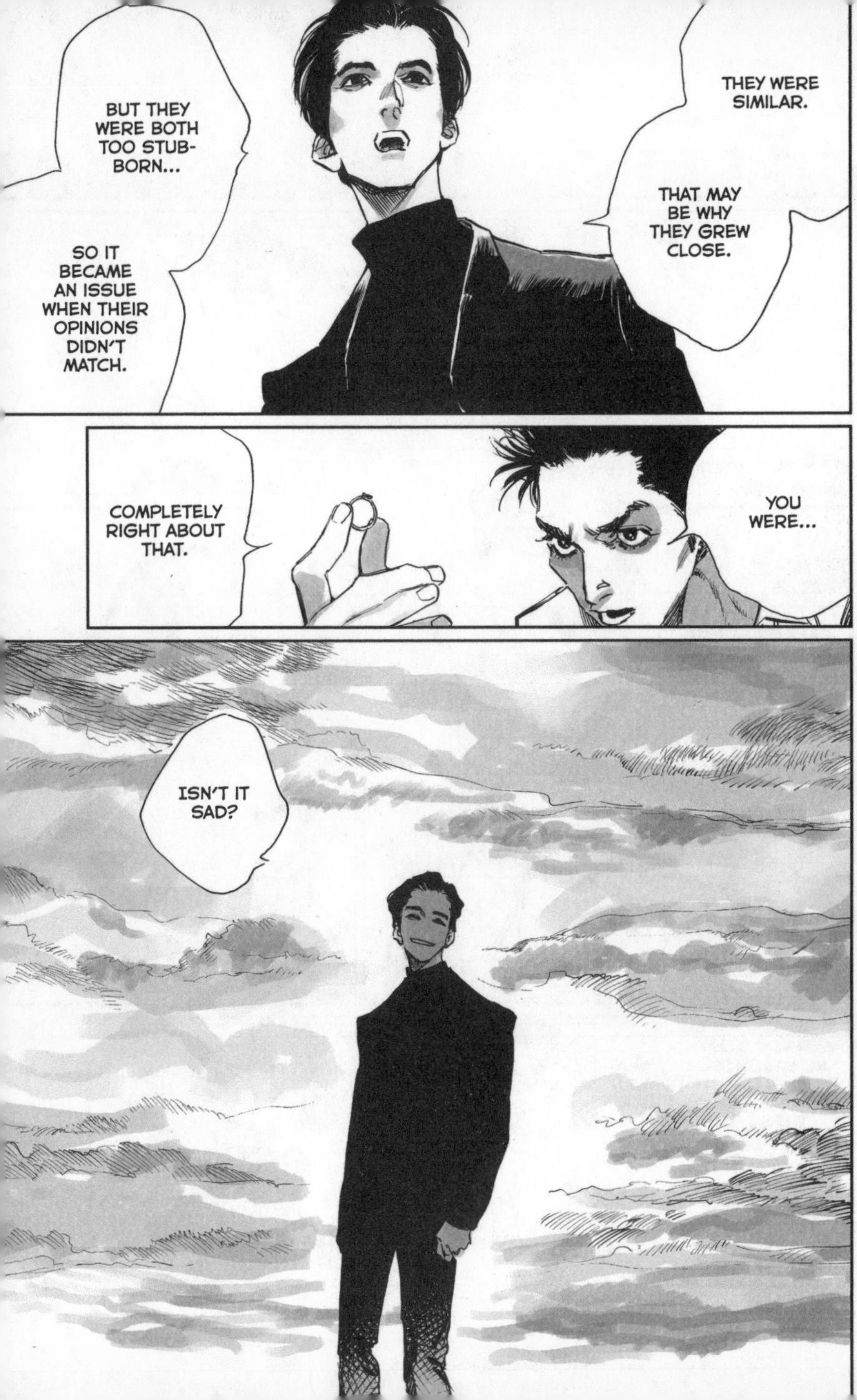
THEY WERE SIMILAR.
THAT MAY BE WHY THEY GREW CLOSE.
BUT THEY WERE BOTH TOO STUB-BORN...
SO IT BECAME AN ISSUE WHEN THEIR OPINIONS DIDN'T MATCH.
YOU WERE...
COMPLETELY RIGHT ABOUT THAT.
ISN'T IT SAD?

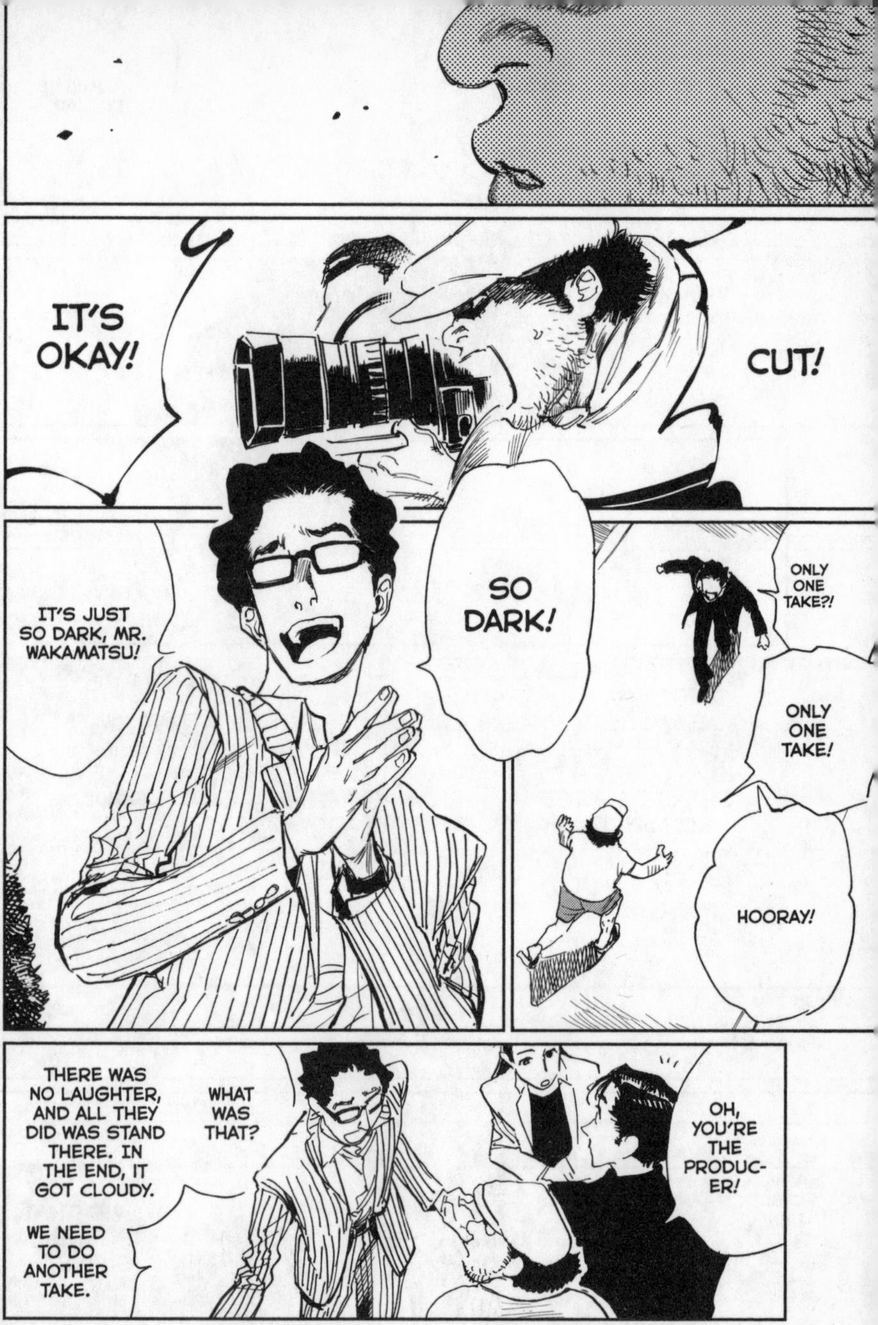
CUT!
IT'S OKAY!
ONLY ONE TAKE?!
ONLY ONE TAKE!
HOORAY!
SO DARK!
IT'S JUST SO DARK, MR. WAKAMATSU!
OH, YOU'RE THE PRODUC-ER!
WHAT WAS THAT?
THERE WAS NO LAUGHTER, AND ALL THEY DID WAS STAND THERE. IN THE END, IT GOT CLOUDY.
WE NEED TO DO ANOTHER TAKE.

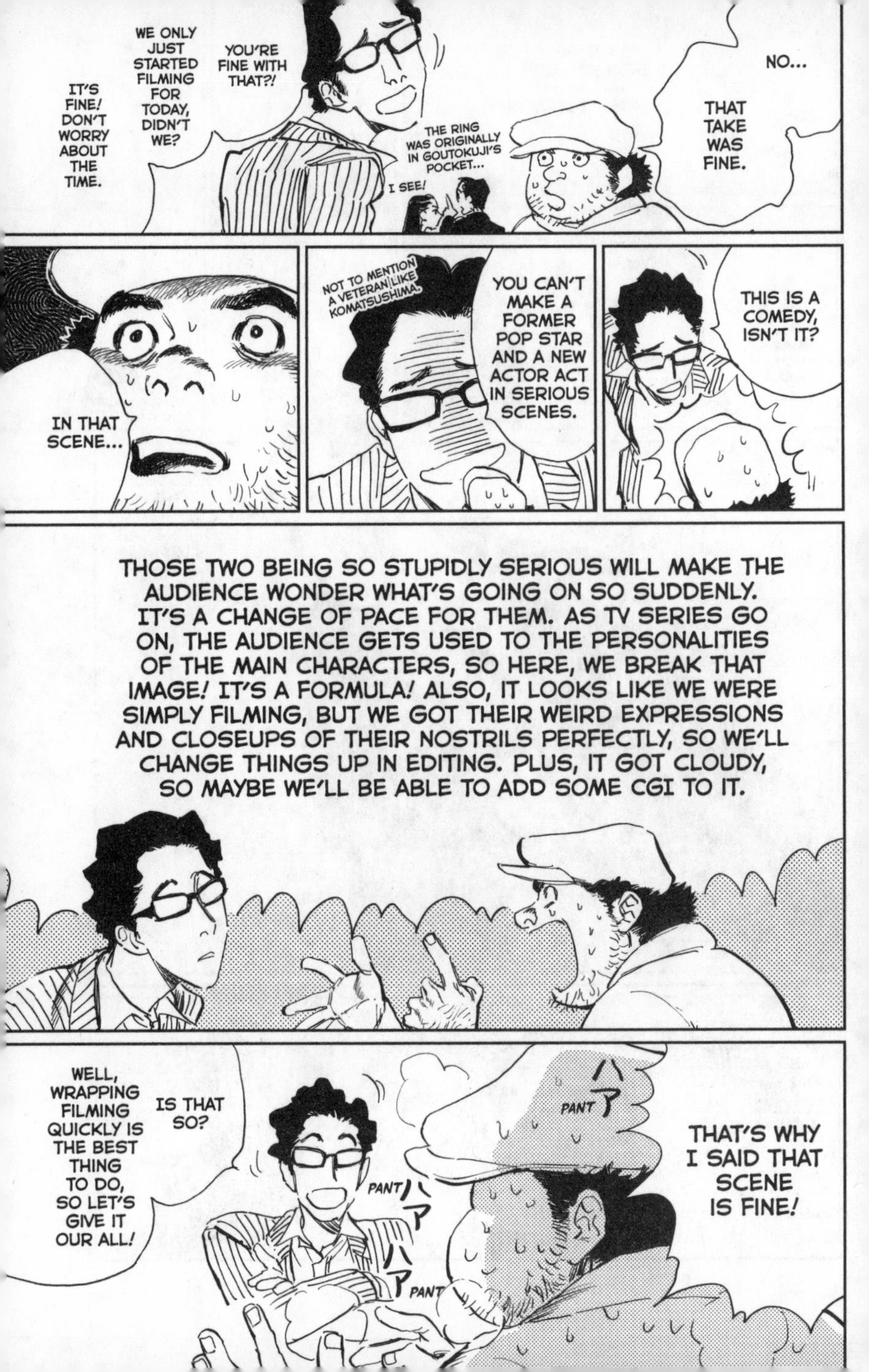
NO...
THAT TAKE WAS FINE.
THE RING WAS ORIGINALLY IN GOUTOKUJI'S POCKET...
I SEE!
YOU'RE FINE WITH THAT?!
WE ONLY JUST STARTED FILMING FOR TODAY, DIDN'T WE?
IT'S FINE! DON'T WORRY ABOUT THE TIME.
THIS IS A COMEDY, ISN'T IT?
YOU CAN'T MAKE A FORMER POP STAR AND A NEW ACTOR ACT IN SERIOUS SCENES.
NOT TO MENTION A VETERAN LIKE KOMATSUSHIMA.
IN THAT SCENE...
THOSE TWO BEING SO STUPIDLY SERIOUS WILL MAKE THE AUDIENCE WONDER WHAT'S GOING ON SO SUDDENLY. IT'S A CHANGE OF PACE FOR THEM. AS TV SERIES GO ON, THE AUDIENCE GETS USED TO THE PERSONALITIES OF THE MAIN CHARACTERS, SO HERE, WE BREAK THAT IMAGE! IT'S A FORMULA! ALSO, IT LOOKS LIKE WE WERE SIMPLY FILMING, BUT WE GOT THEIR WEIRD EXPRESSIONS AND CLOSEUPS OF THEIR NOSTRILS PERFECTLY, SO WE'LL CHANGE THINGS UP IN EDITING. PLUS, IT GOT CLOUDY, SO MAYBE WE'LL BE ABLE TO ADD SOME CGI TO IT.
THAT'S WHY I SAID THAT SCENE IS FINE!
PANT
PANT
PANT
IS THAT SO?
WELL, WRAPPING FILMING QUICKLY IS THE BEST THING TO DO, SO LET'S GIVE IT OUR ALL!

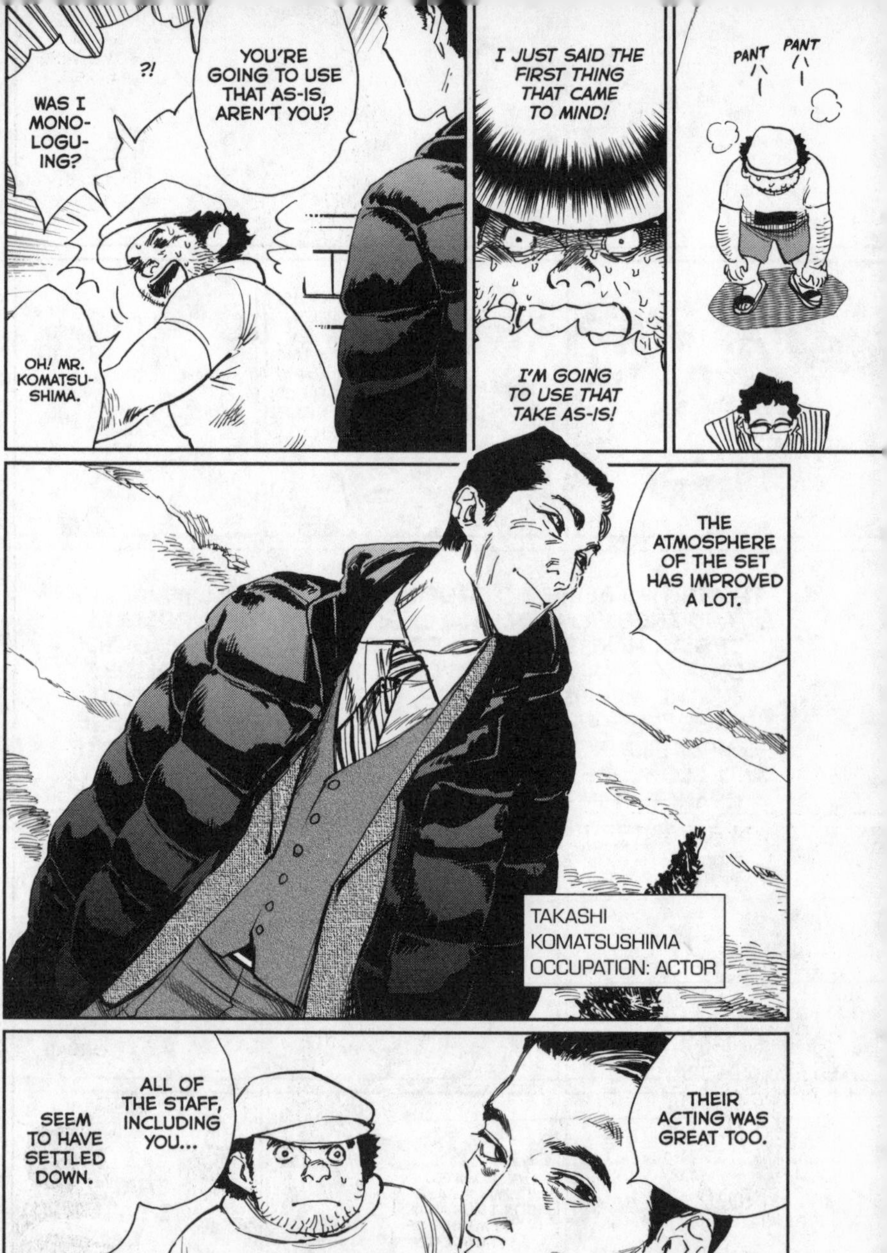
PANT PANT
I JUST SAID THE FIRST THING THAT CAME TO MIND!
I'M GOING TO USE THAT TAKE AS-IS!
YOU'RE GOING TO USE THAT AS-IS, AREN'T YOU?
?!
WAS I MONO-LOGU-ING?
OH! MR. KOMATSU-SHIMA.
THE ATMOSPHERE OF THE SET HAS IMPROVED A LOT.
TAKASHI KOMATSUSHIMA
OCCUPATION: ACTOR
THEIR ACTING WAS GREAT TOO.
ALL OF THE STAFF, INCLUDING YOU...
SEEM TO HAVE SETTLED DOWN.

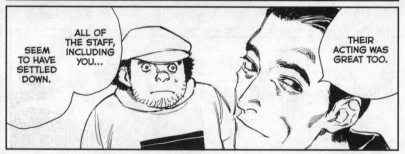

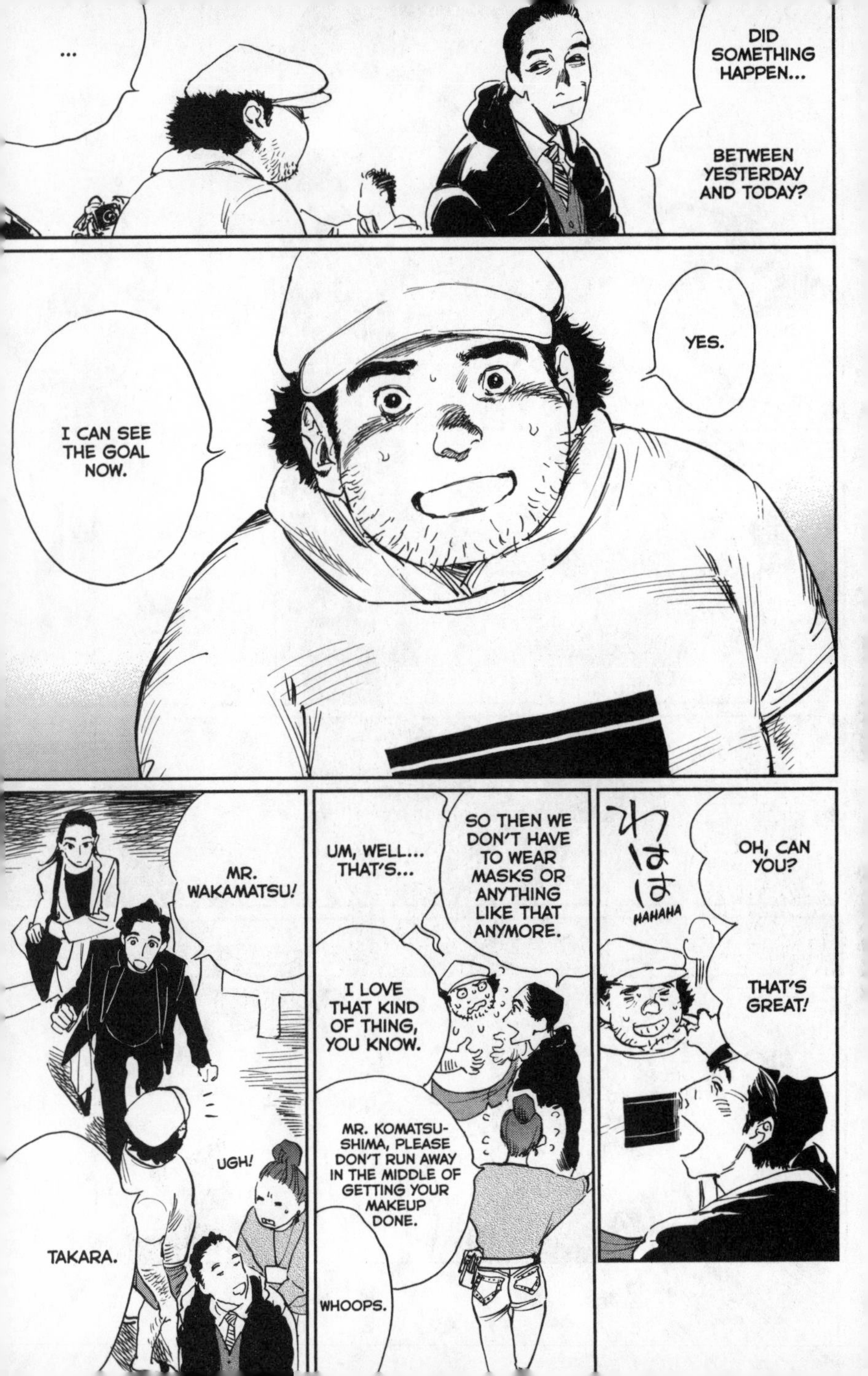
DID SOMETHING HAPPEN...
BETWEEN YESTERDAY AND TODAY?
...
YES.
I CAN SEE THE GOAL NOW.
OH, CAN YOU?
わはは
HAHAHA
THAT'S GREAT!
SO THEN WE DON'T HAVE TO WEAR MASKS OR ANYTHING LIKE THAT ANYMORE.
UM, WELL... THAT'S...
I LOVE THAT KIND OF THING, YOU KNOW.
MR. KOMATSU-SHIMA, PLEASE DON'T RUN AWAY IN THE MIDDLE OF GETTING YOUR MAKEUP DONE.
WHOOPS.
MR. WAKAMATSU!
UGH!
TAKARA.

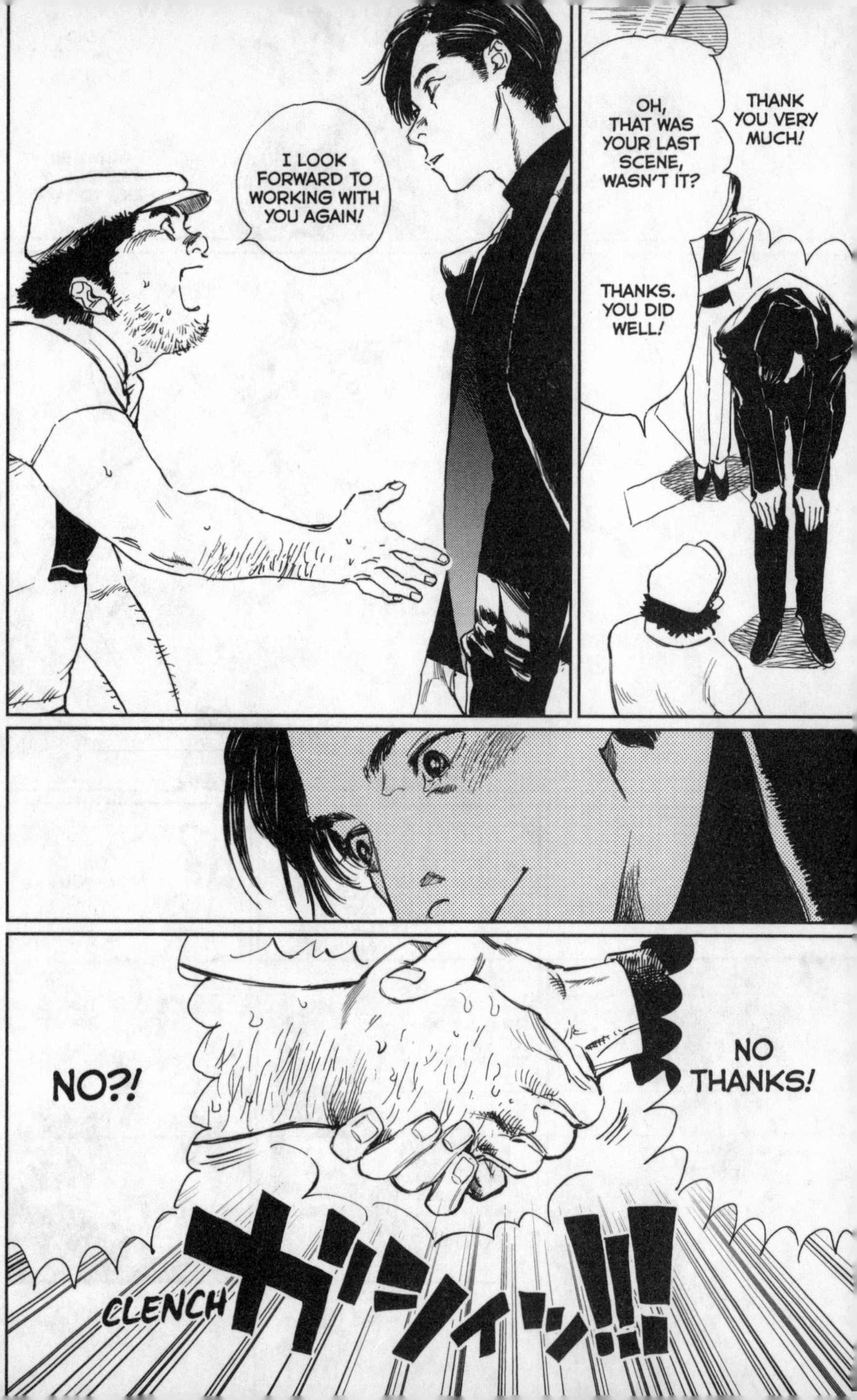
THANK YOU VERY MUCH!
OH, THAT WAS YOUR LAST SCENE, WASN'T IT?
THANKS. YOU DID WELL!
I LOOK FORWARD TO WORKING WITH YOU AGAIN!
NO THANKS!
NO?!
ガシィッ!!
CLENCH

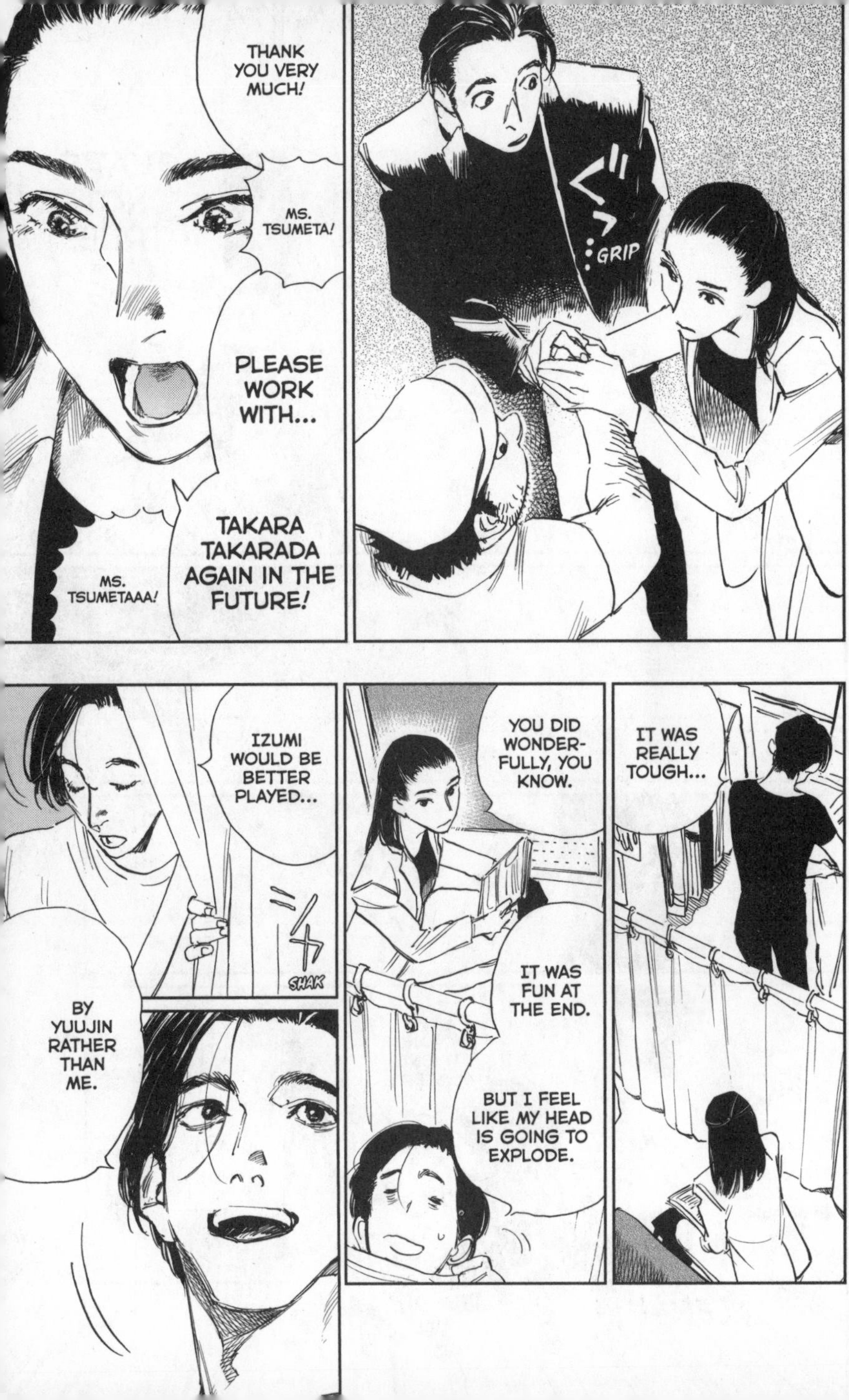
GRIP
THANK YOU VERY MUCH!
MS. TSUMETA!
PLEASE WORK WITH...
TAKARA TAKARADA AGAIN IN THE FUTURE!
MS. TSUMETAAA!
IT WAS REALLY TOUGH...
YOU DID WONDER-FULLY, YOU KNOW.
IT WAS FUN AT THE END.
BUT I FEEL LIKE MY HEAD IS GOING TO EXPLODE.
IZUMI WOULD BE BETTER PLAYED...
SHAK
BY YUUJIN RATHER THAN ME.

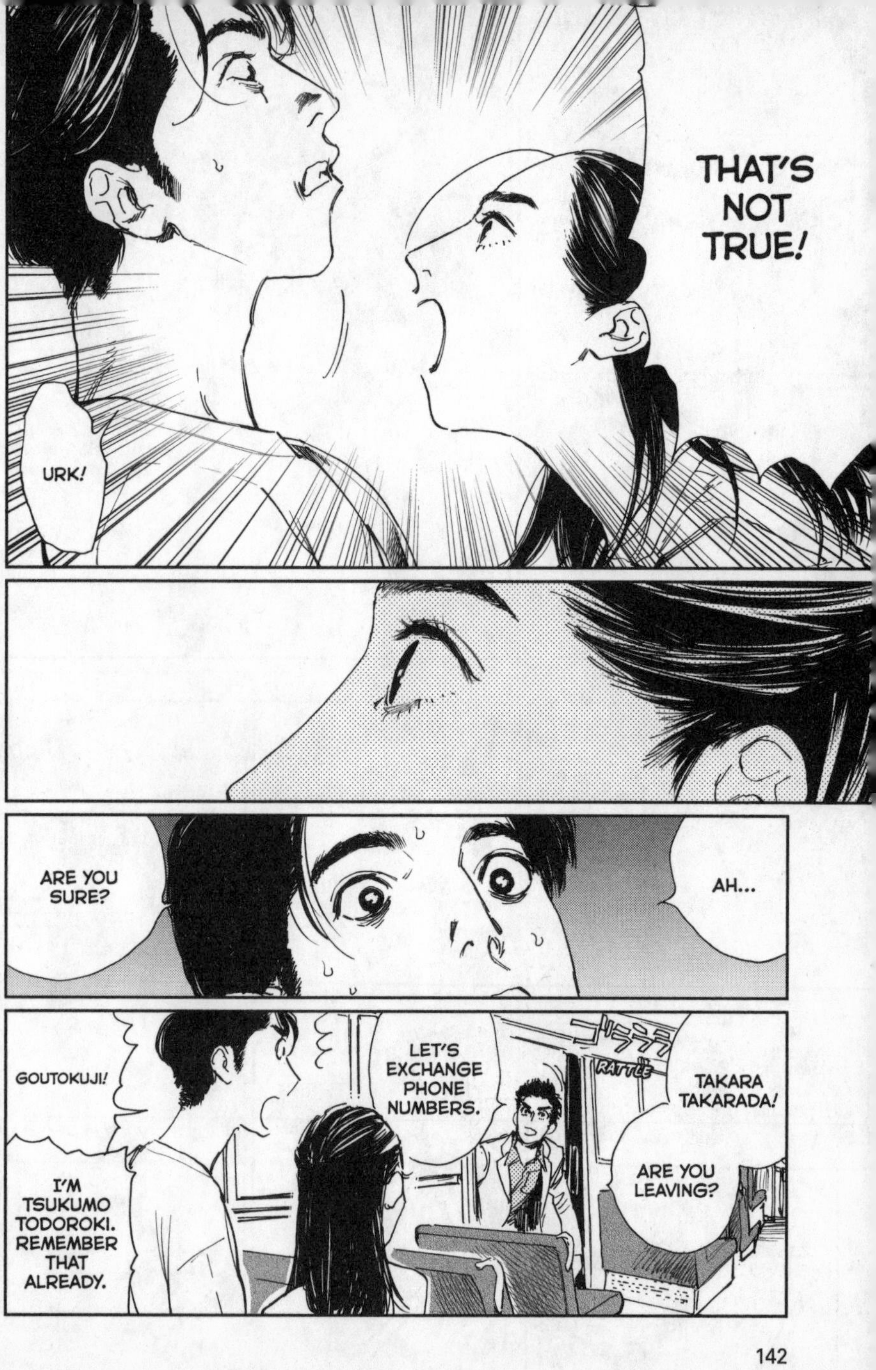
THAT'S NOT TRUE!
URK!
AH...
ARE YOU SURE?
TAKARA TAKARADA!
ARE YOU LEAVING?
RATTLE
LET'S EXCHANGE PHONE NUMBERS.
GOUTOKUJI!
I'M TSUKUMO TODOROKI. REMEMBER THAT ALREADY.

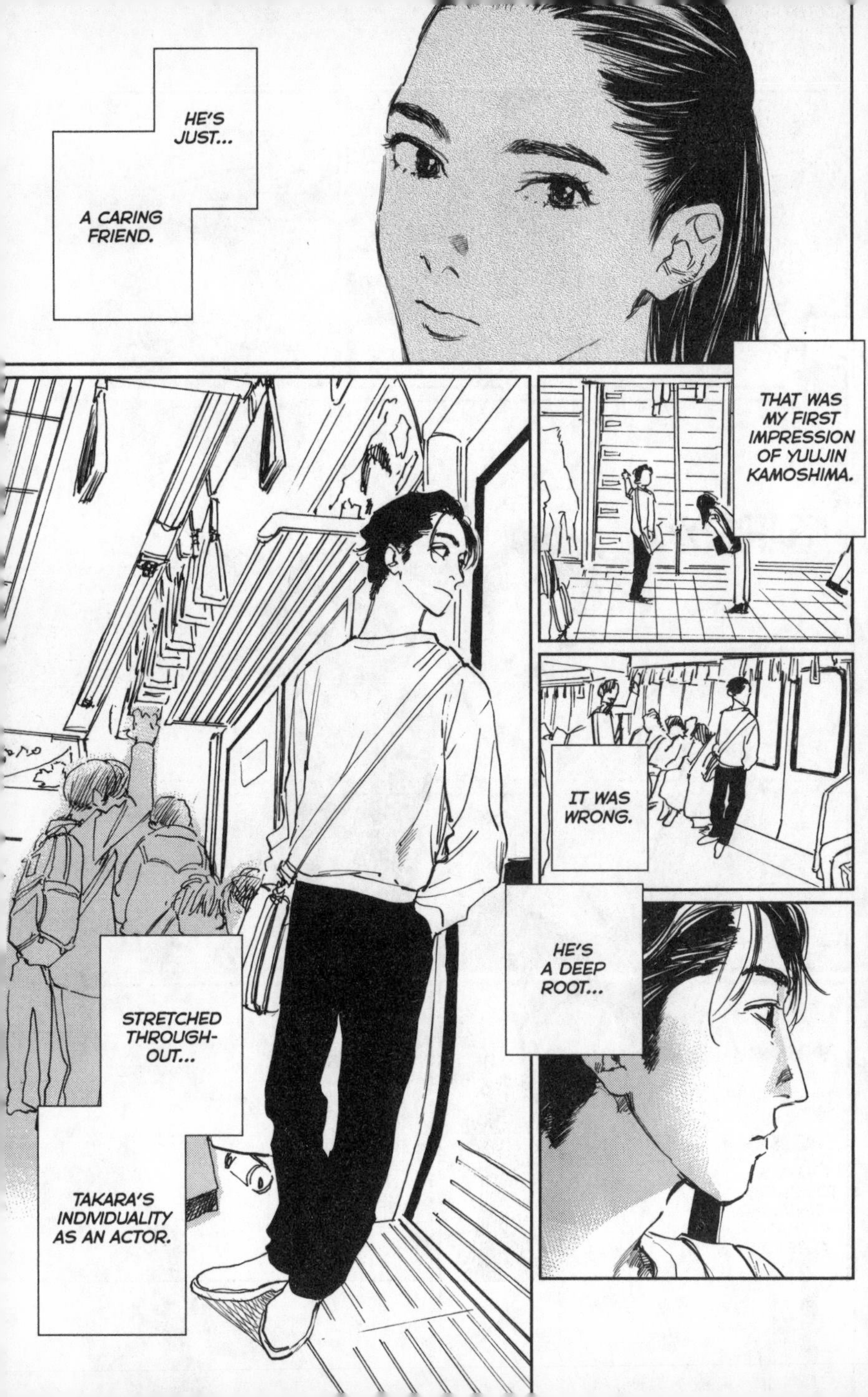
HE'S JUST...
A CARING FRIEND.
THAT WAS MY FIRST IMPRESSION OF YUUJIN KAMOSHIMA.
IT WAS WRONG.
HE'S A DEEP ROOT...
STRETCHED THROUGH-OUT...
TAKARA'S INDIVIDUALITY AS AN ACTOR.

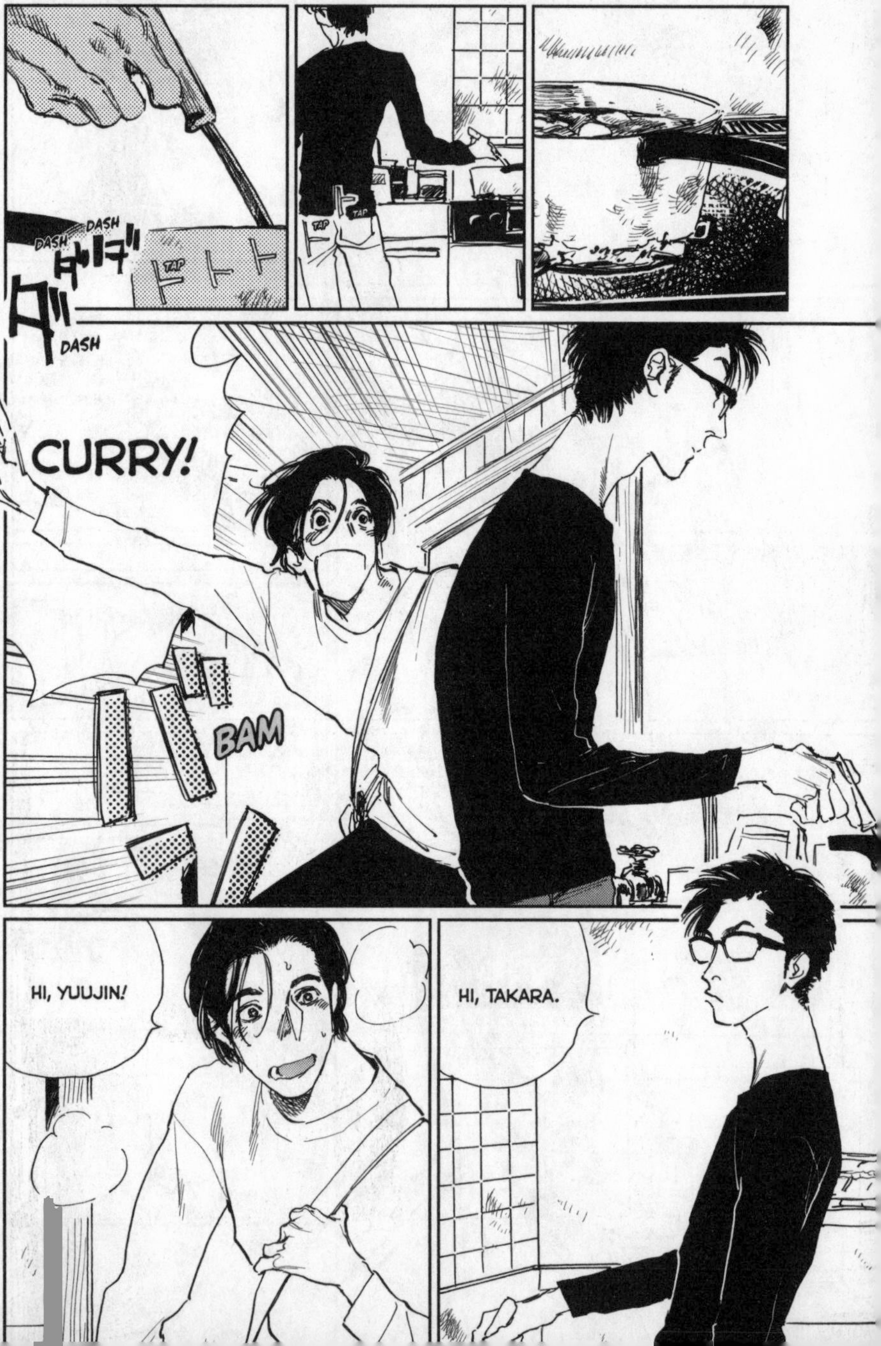
TAP
TAP
DASH
DASH
TAP
DASH
CURRY!
BAM
HI, TAKARA.
HI, YUUJIN!

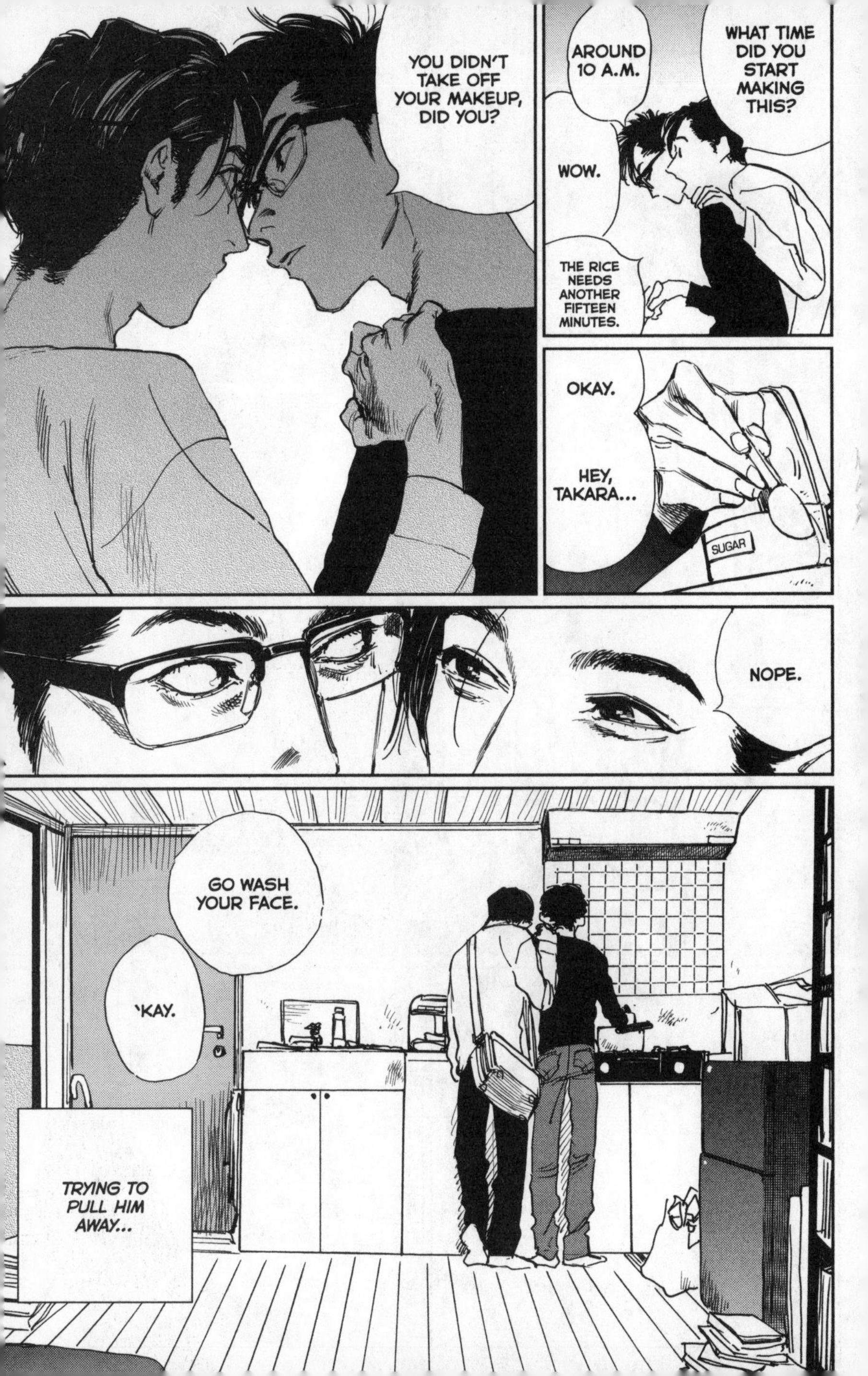
WHAT TIME DID YOU START MAKING THIS?
AROUND 10 A.M.
WOW.
THE RICE NEEDS ANOTHER FIFTEEN MINUTES.
OKAY.
HEY, TAKARA...
SUGAR
YOU DIDN'T TAKE OFF YOUR MAKEUP, DID YOU?
NOPE.
GO WASH YOUR FACE.
'KAY.
TRYING TO PULL HIM AWAY...

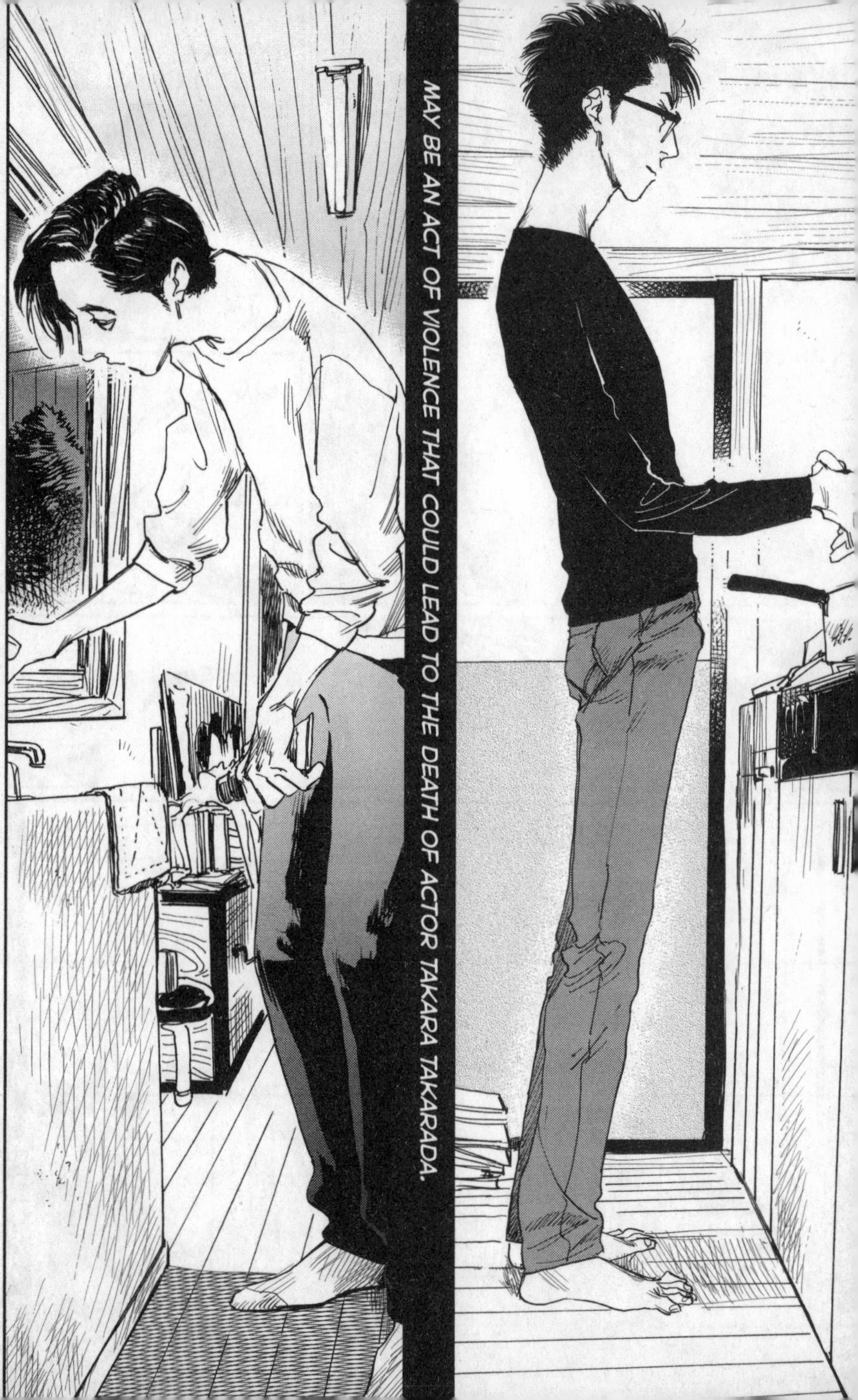
MAY BE AN ACT OF VIOLENCE THAT COULD LEAD TO THE DEATH OF ACTOR TAKARA TAKARADA.

DOUBLE

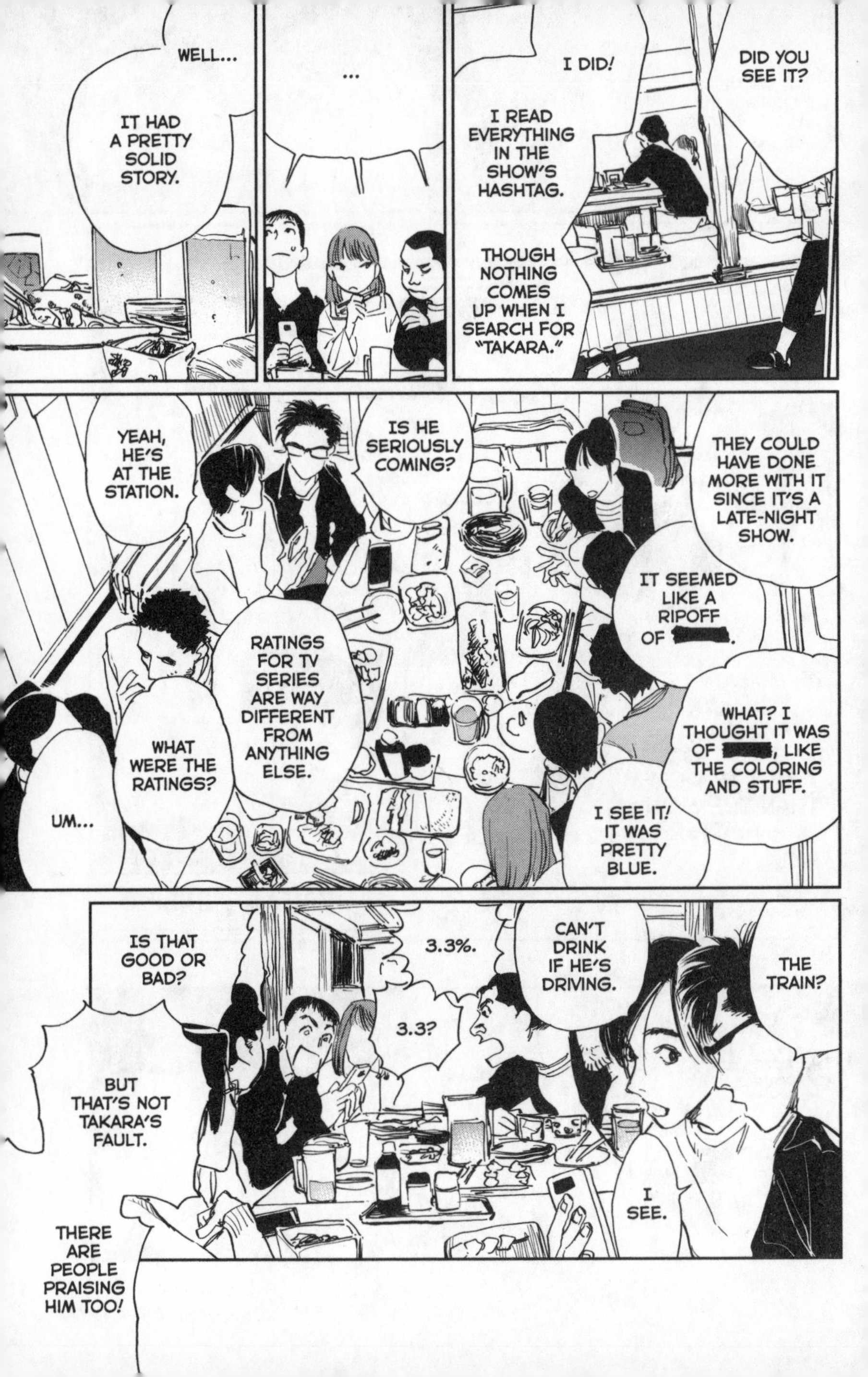
DID YOU SEE IT?
I DID!
I READ EVERYTHING IN THE SHOW'S HASHTAG.
THOUGH NOTHING COMES UP WHEN I SEARCH FOR "TAKARA."
...
WELL...
IT HAD A PRETTY SOLID STORY.
THEY COULD HAVE DONE MORE WITH IT SINCE IT'S A LATE-NIGHT SHOW.
IT SEEMED LIKE A RIPOFF OF [redacted].
WHAT? I THOUGHT IT WAS OF [redacted], LIKE THE COLORING AND STUFF.
I SEE IT! IT WAS PRETTY BLUE.
IS HE SERIOUSLY COMING?
YEAH, HE'S AT THE STATION.
RATINGS FOR TV SERIES ARE WAY DIFFERENT FROM ANYTHING ELSE.
WHAT WERE THE RATINGS?
UM...
THE TRAIN?
CAN'T DRINK IF HE'S DRIVING.
I SEE.
3.3%.
3.3?
IS THAT GOOD OR BAD?
BUT THAT'S NOT TAKARA'S FAULT.
THERE ARE PEOPLE PRAISING HIM TOO!

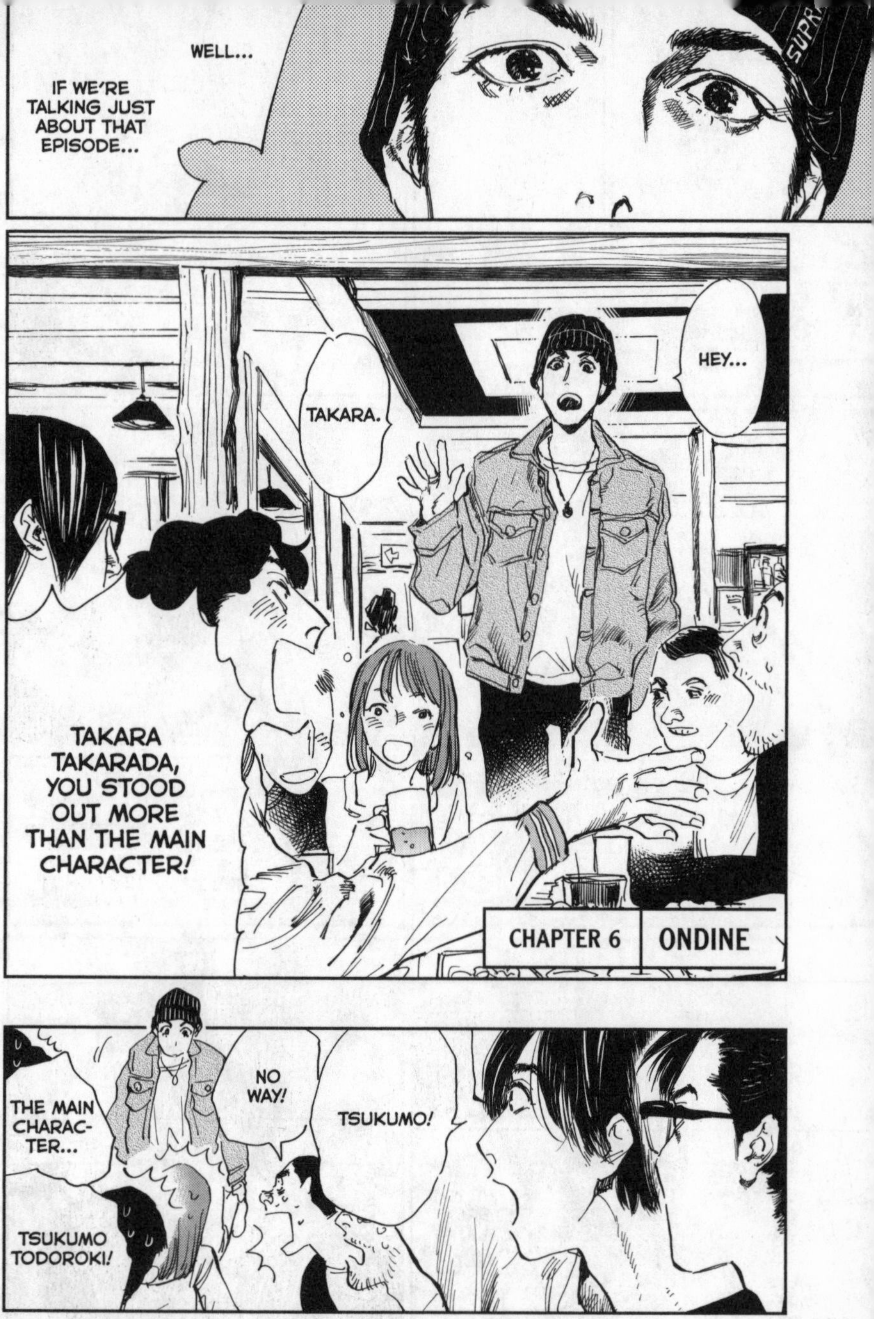
WELL...
IF WE'RE TALKING JUST ABOUT THAT EPISODE...
HEY...
TAKARA.
TAKARA TAKARADA, YOU STOOD OUT MORE THAN THE MAIN CHARACTER!
CHAPTER 6
ONDINE
TSUKUMO!
NO WAY!
THE MAIN CHARACTER...
TSUKUMO TODOROKI!

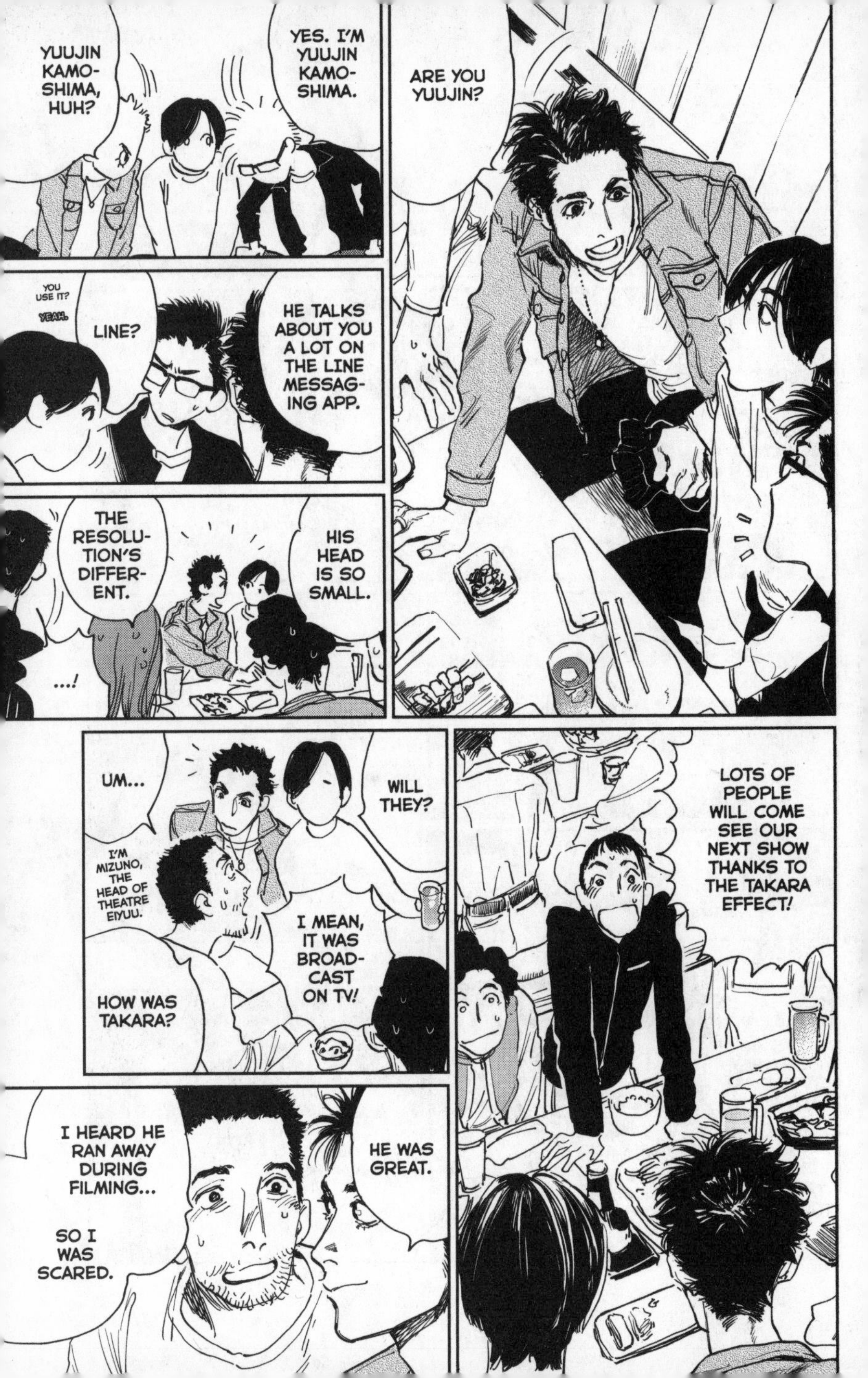
ARE YOU YUUJIN?
YES. I'M YUUJIN KAMOSHIMA.
YUUJIN KAMOSHIMA, HUH?
HE TALKS ABOUT YOU A LOT ON THE LINE MESSAGING APP.
LINE?
YOU USE IT?
YEAH.
HIS HEAD IS SO SMALL.
THE RESOLUTION'S DIFFERENT.
...!
LOTS OF PEOPLE WILL COME SEE OUR NEXT SHOW THANKS TO THE TAKARA EFFECT!
WILL THEY?
UM...
I'M MIZUNO, THE HEAD OF THEATRE EIYUU.
I MEAN, IT WAS BROADCAST ON TV!
HOW WAS TAKARA?
HE WAS GREAT.
I HEARD HE RAN AWAY DURING FILMING...
SO I WAS SCARED.

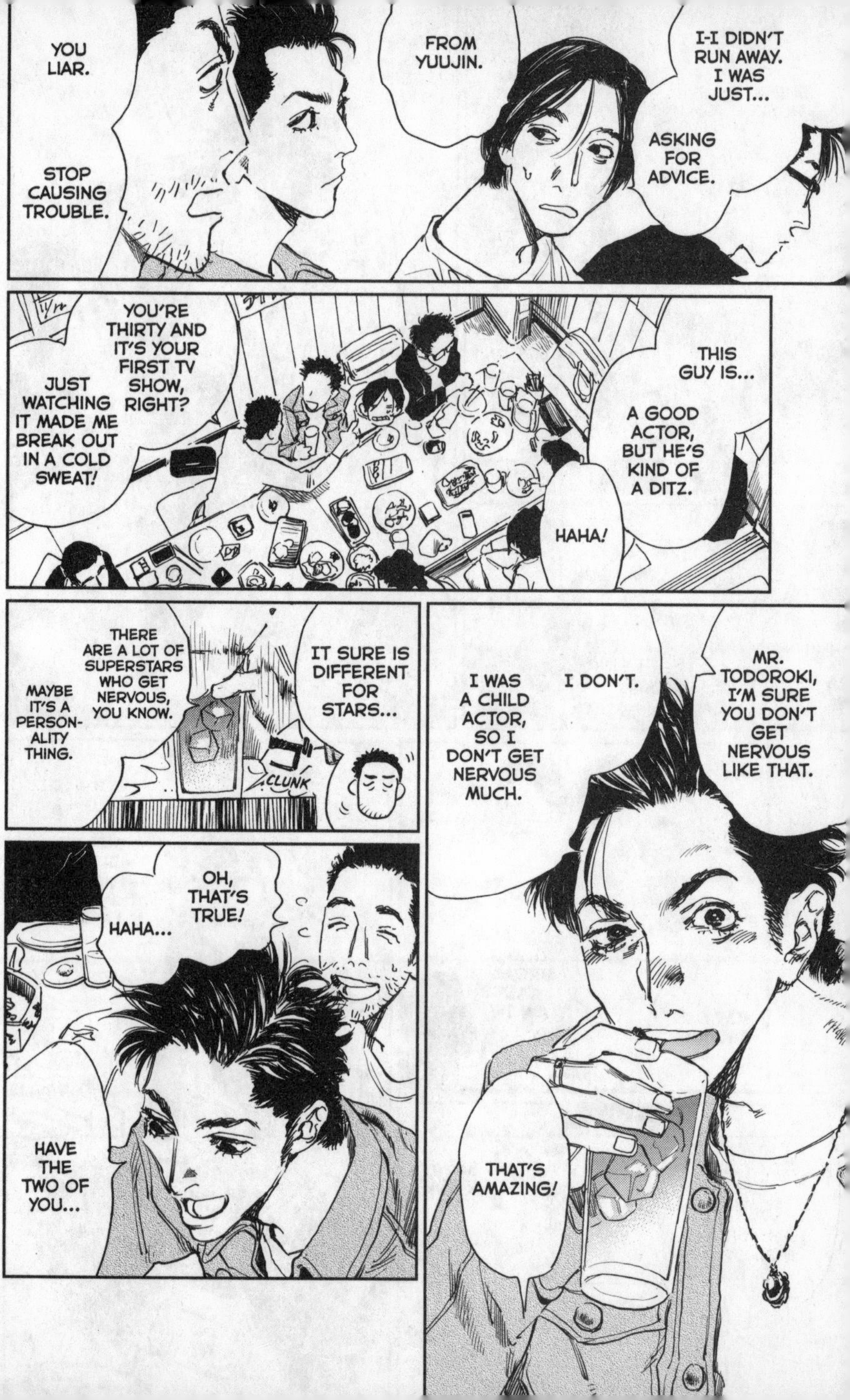
I-I DIDN'T RUN AWAY. I WAS JUST...
ASKING FOR ADVICE.
FROM YUUJIN.
YOU LIAR.
STOP CAUSING TROUBLE.
THIS GUY IS...
A GOOD ACTOR, BUT HE'S KIND OF A DITZ.
HAHA!
YOU'RE THIRTY AND IT'S YOUR FIRST TV SHOW, RIGHT?
JUST WATCHING IT MADE ME BREAK OUT IN A COLD SWEAT!
MR. TODOROKI, I'M SURE YOU DON'T GET NERVOUS LIKE THAT.
I DON'T.
I WAS A CHILD ACTOR, SO I DON'T GET NERVOUS MUCH.
THAT'S AMAZING!
IT SURE IS DIFFERENT FOR STARS...
THERE ARE A LOT OF SUPERSTARS WHO GET NERVOUS, YOU KNOW.
MAYBE IT'S A PERSONALITY THING.
CLUNK
OH, THAT'S TRUE!
HAHA...
HAVE THE TWO OF YOU...

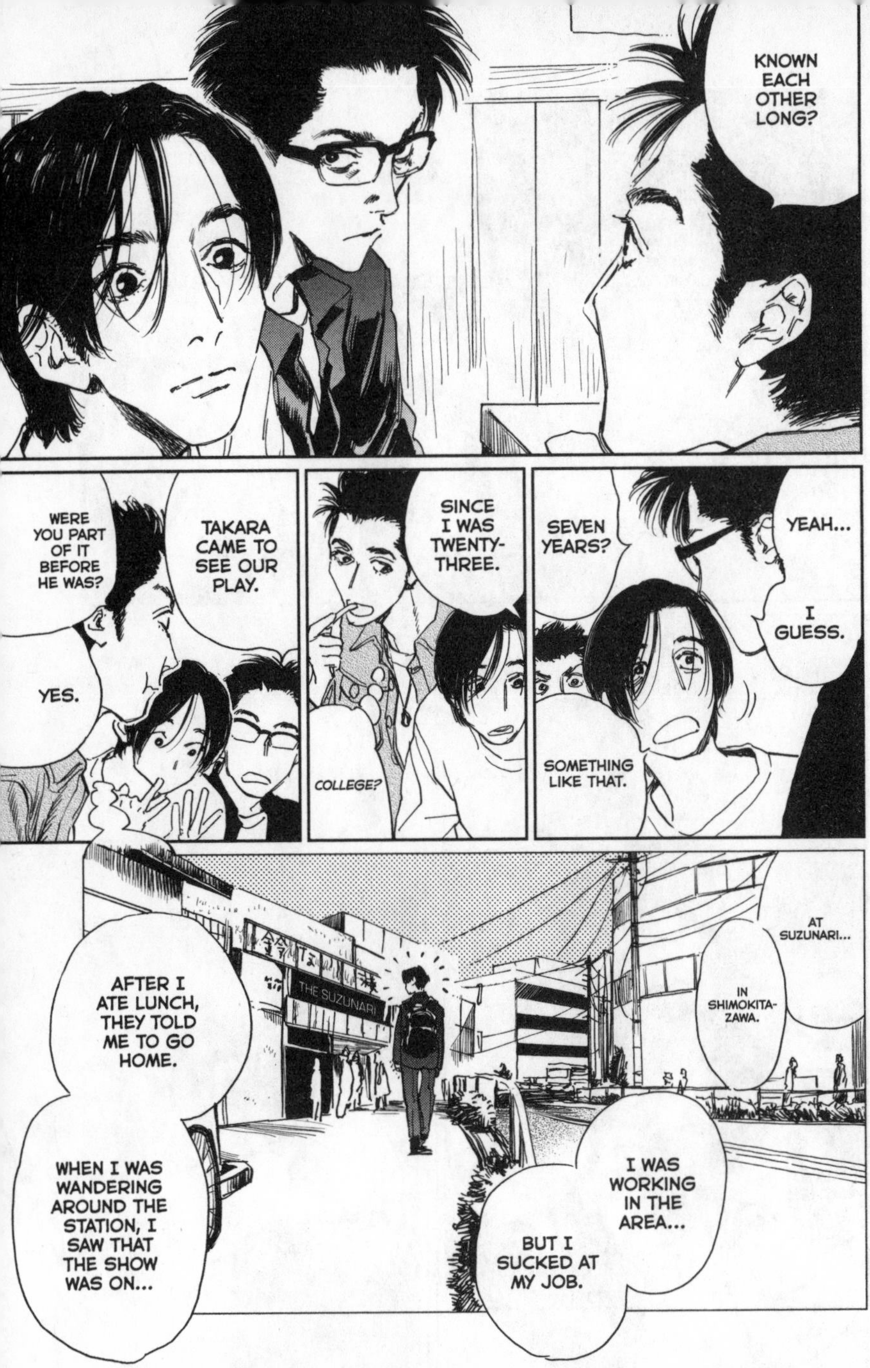
KNOWN EACH OTHER LONG?
YEAH... I GUESS.
SEVEN YEARS?
SOMETHING LIKE THAT.
SINCE I WAS TWENTY-THREE.
COLLEGE?
TAKARA CAME TO SEE OUR PLAY.
WERE YOU PART OF IT BEFORE HE WAS?
YES.
AT SUZUNARI...
IN SHIMOKITA-ZAWA.
THE SUZUNARI
I WAS WORKING IN THE AREA...
BUT I SUCKED AT MY JOB.
AFTER I ATE LUNCH, THEY TOLD ME TO GO HOME.
WHEN I WAS WANDERING AROUND THE STATION, I SAW THAT THE SHOW WAS ON...

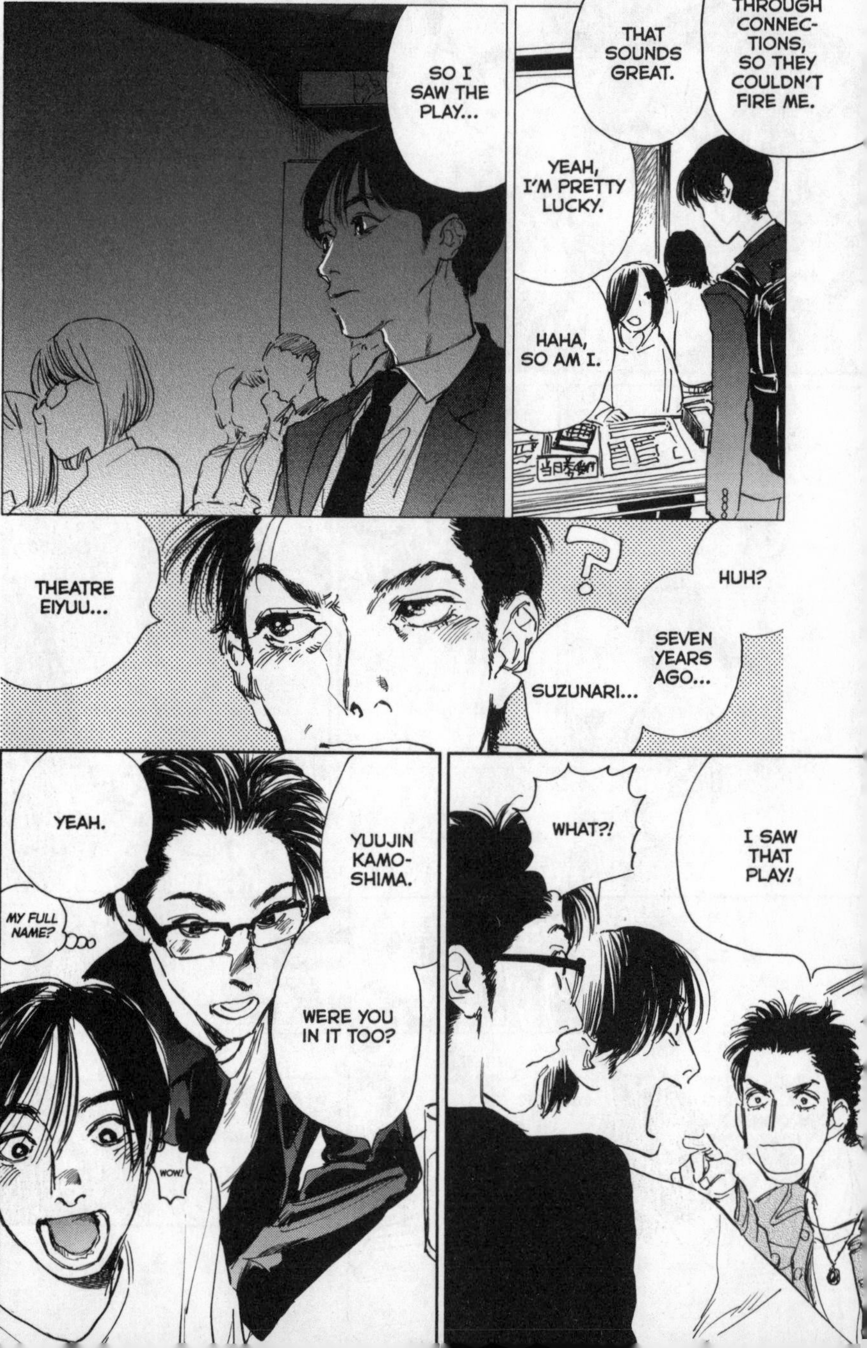
I GOT THE JOB THROUGH CONNEC-TIONS, SO THEY COULDN'T FIRE ME.
THAT SOUNDS GREAT.
YEAH, I'M PRETTY LUCKY.
HAHA, SO AM I.
SO I SAW THE PLAY...
HUH?
SEVEN YEARS AGO...
SUZUNARI...
THEATRE EIYUU...
I SAW THAT PLAY!
WHAT?!
YUUJIN KAMO-SHIMA.
YEAH.
MY FULL NAME?
WERE YOU IN IT TOO?
WOW!

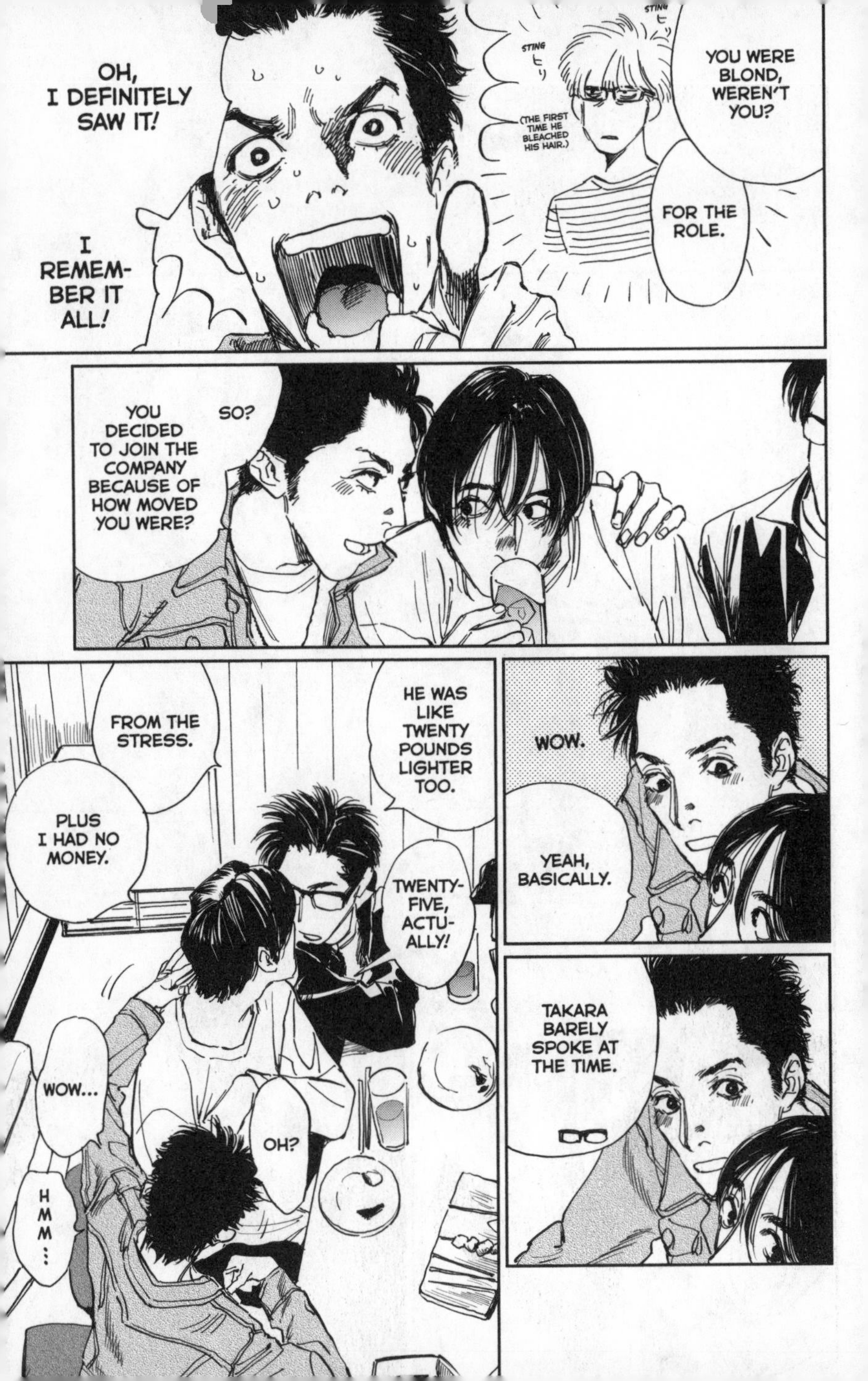

YOU WERE BLOND, WEREN'T YOU?
FOR THE ROLE.
STING
STING
(THE FIRST TIME HE BLEACHED HIS HAIR.)
OH, I DEFINITELY SAW IT!
I REMEMBER IT ALL!
SO?
YOU DECIDED TO JOIN THE COMPANY BECAUSE OF HOW MOVED YOU WERE?
WOW.
YEAH, BASICALLY.
TAKARA BARELY SPOKE AT THE TIME.
HE WAS LIKE TWENTY POUNDS LIGHTER TOO.
FROM THE STRESS.
PLUS I HAD NO MONEY.
TWENTY-FIVE, ACTUALLY!
OH?
WOW...
HMM...

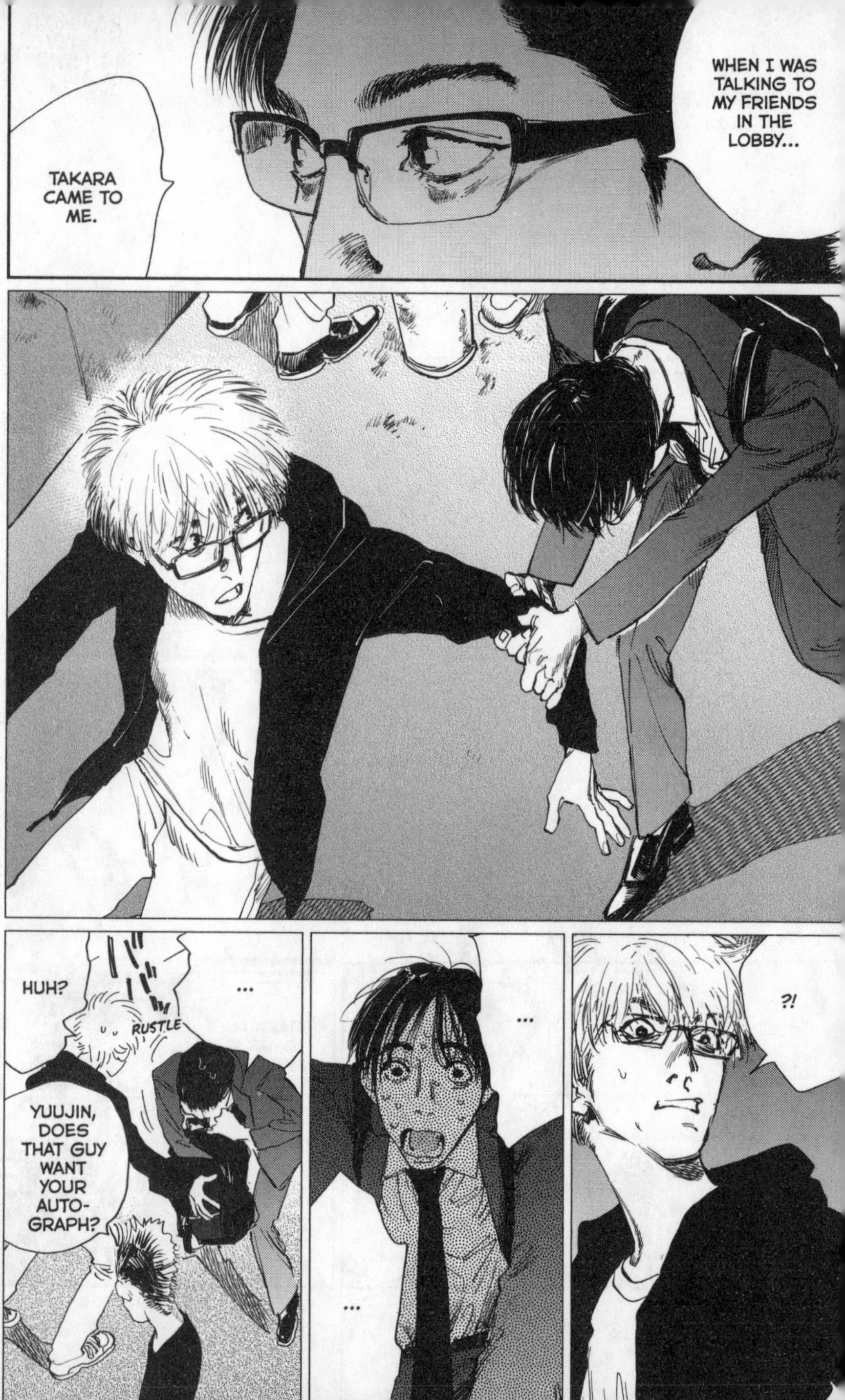
WHEN I WAS TALKING TO MY FRIENDS IN THE LOBBY...
TAKARA CAME TO ME.
?!
...
...
...
...
HUH?
RUSTLE
YUUJIN, DOES THAT GUY WANT YOUR AUTO-GRAPH?

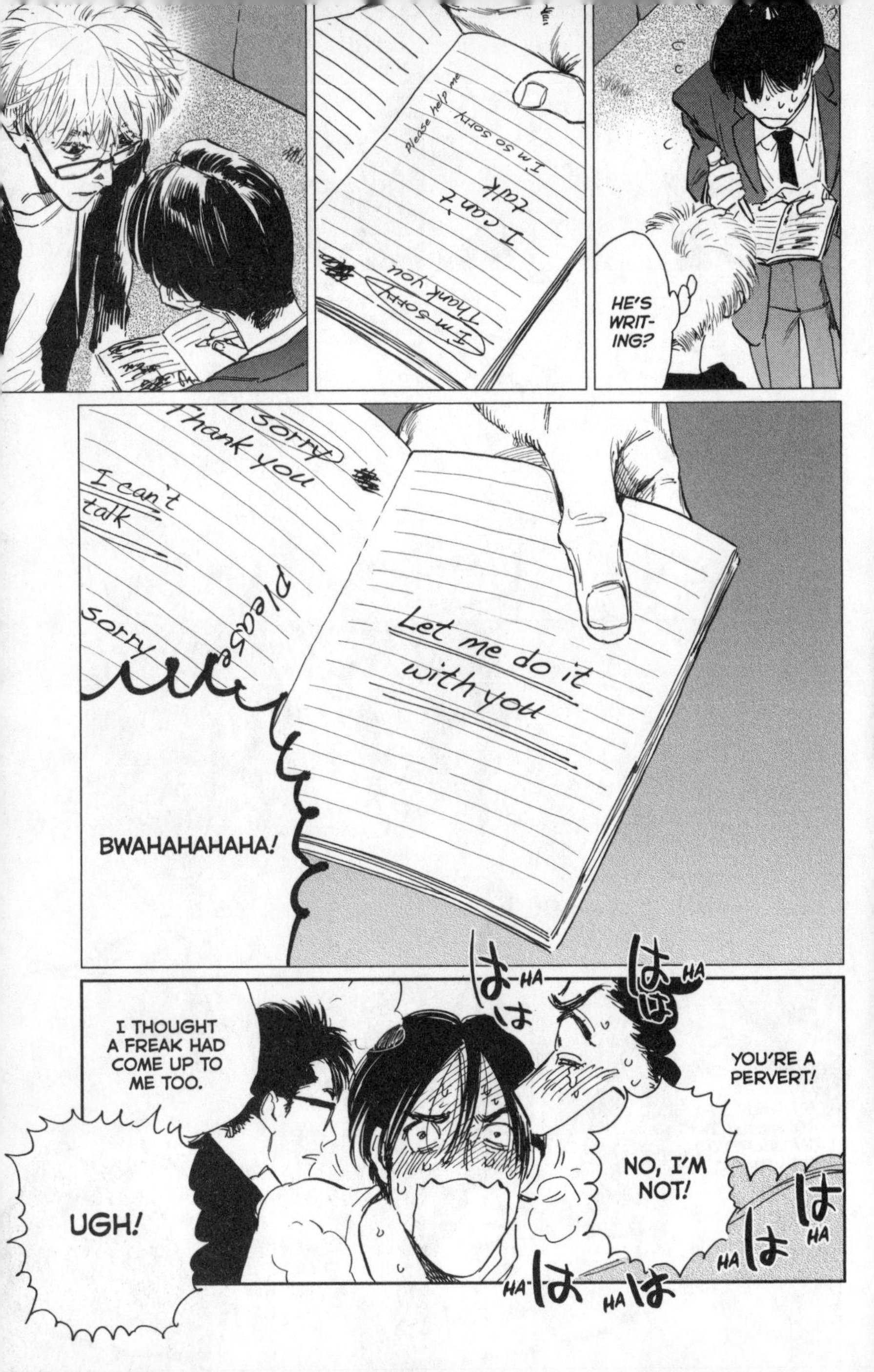
HE'S WRITING?
I'm sorry
Thank you
I can't talk
I'm so sorry
please help me
Let me do it with you
Thank you
I can't talk
Please
sorry
BWAHAHAHAHA!
は HA
は HA
YOU'RE A PERVERT!
NO, I'M NOT!
は HA
は HA
は HA
は HA
I THOUGHT A FREAK HAD COME UP TO ME TOO.
UGH!

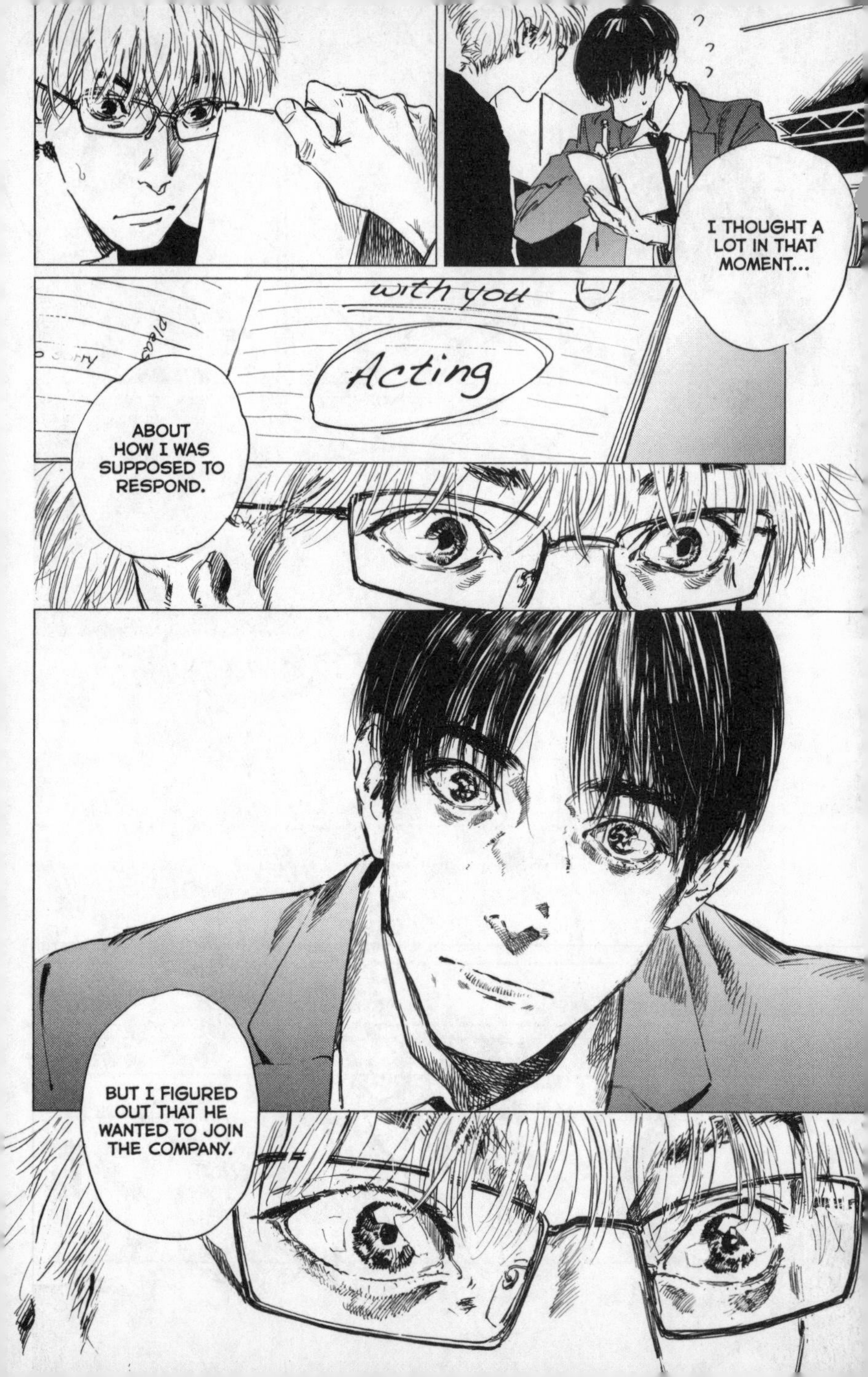

I THOUGHT A LOT IN THAT MOMENT...
with you
Acting
ABOUT HOW I WAS SUPPOSED TO RESPOND.
BUT I FIGURED OUT THAT HE WANTED TO JOIN THE COMPANY.

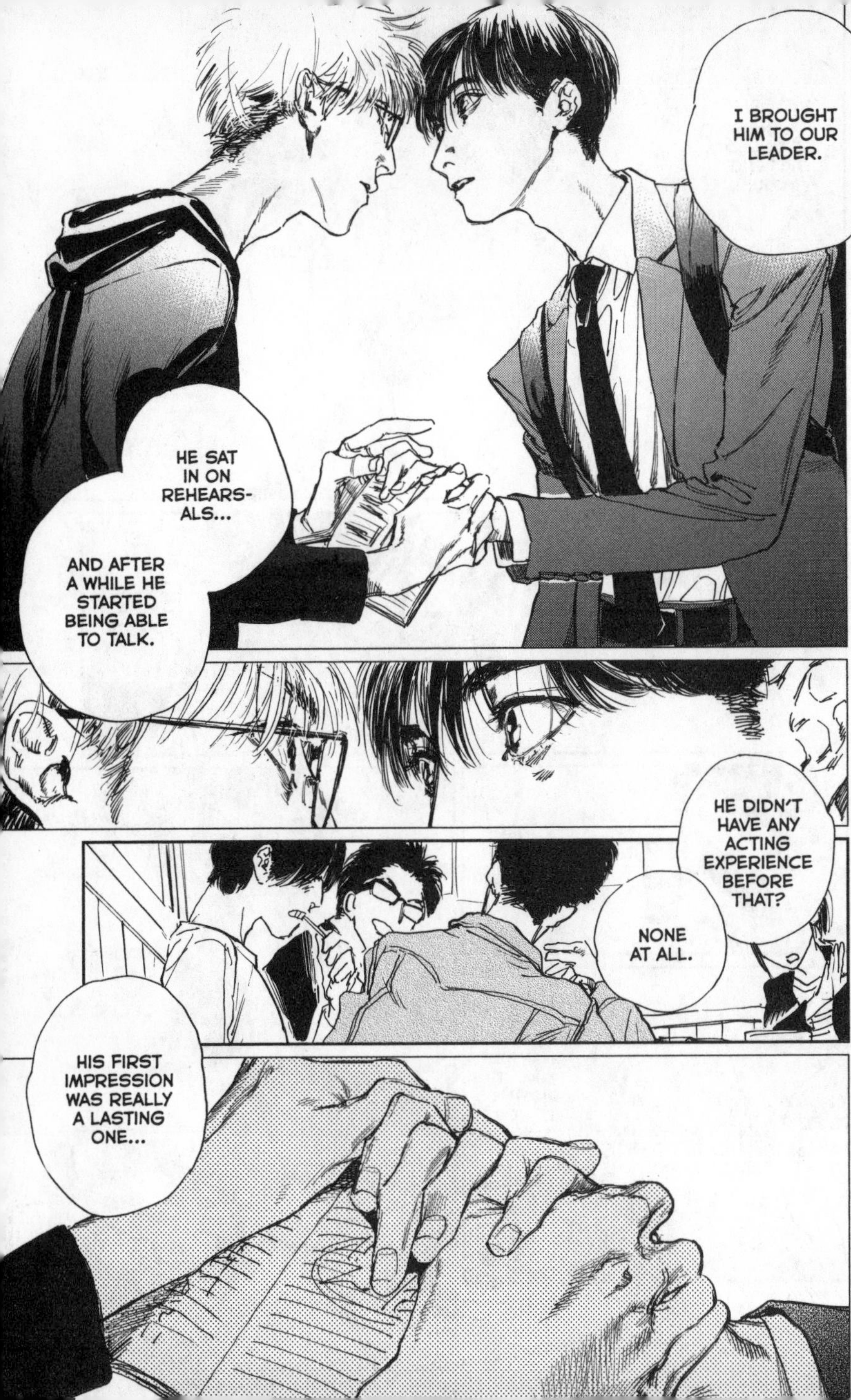
I BROUGHT HIM TO OUR LEADER.
HE SAT IN ON REHEARS-ALS...
AND AFTER A WHILE HE STARTED BEING ABLE TO TALK.
HE DIDN'T HAVE ANY ACTING EXPERIENCE BEFORE THAT?
NONE AT ALL.
HIS FIRST IMPRESSION WAS REALLY A LASTING ONE...

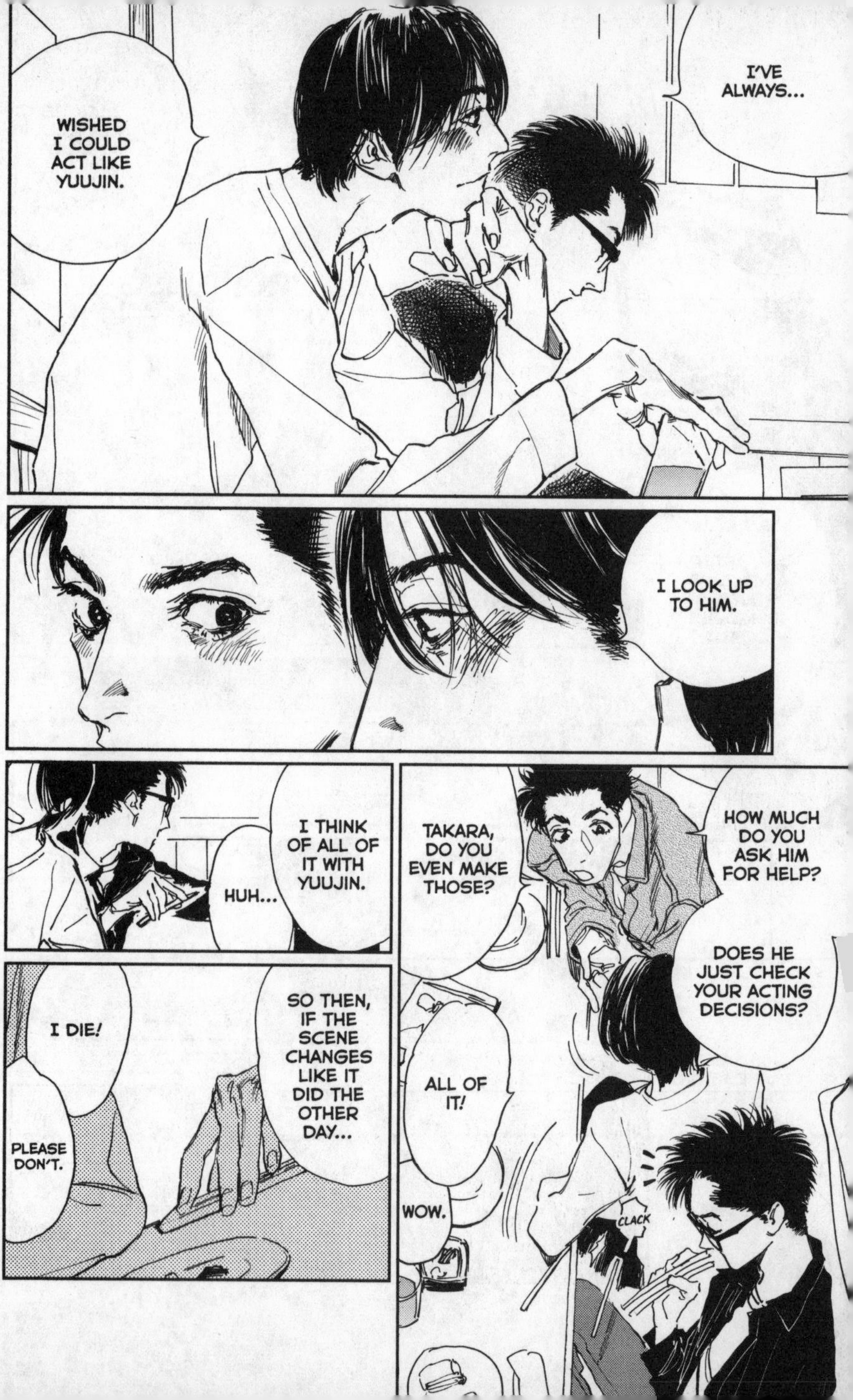
I'VE ALWAYS...
WISHED I COULD ACT LIKE YUUJIN.
I LOOK UP TO HIM.
HOW MUCH DO YOU ASK HIM FOR HELP?
TAKARA, DO YOU EVEN MAKE THOSE?
DOES HE JUST CHECK YOUR ACTING DECISIONS?
ALL OF IT!
CLACK
WOW.
I THINK OF ALL OF IT WITH YUUJIN.
HUH...
SO THEN, IF THE SCENE CHANGES LIKE IT DID THE OTHER DAY...
I DIE!
PLEASE DON'T.

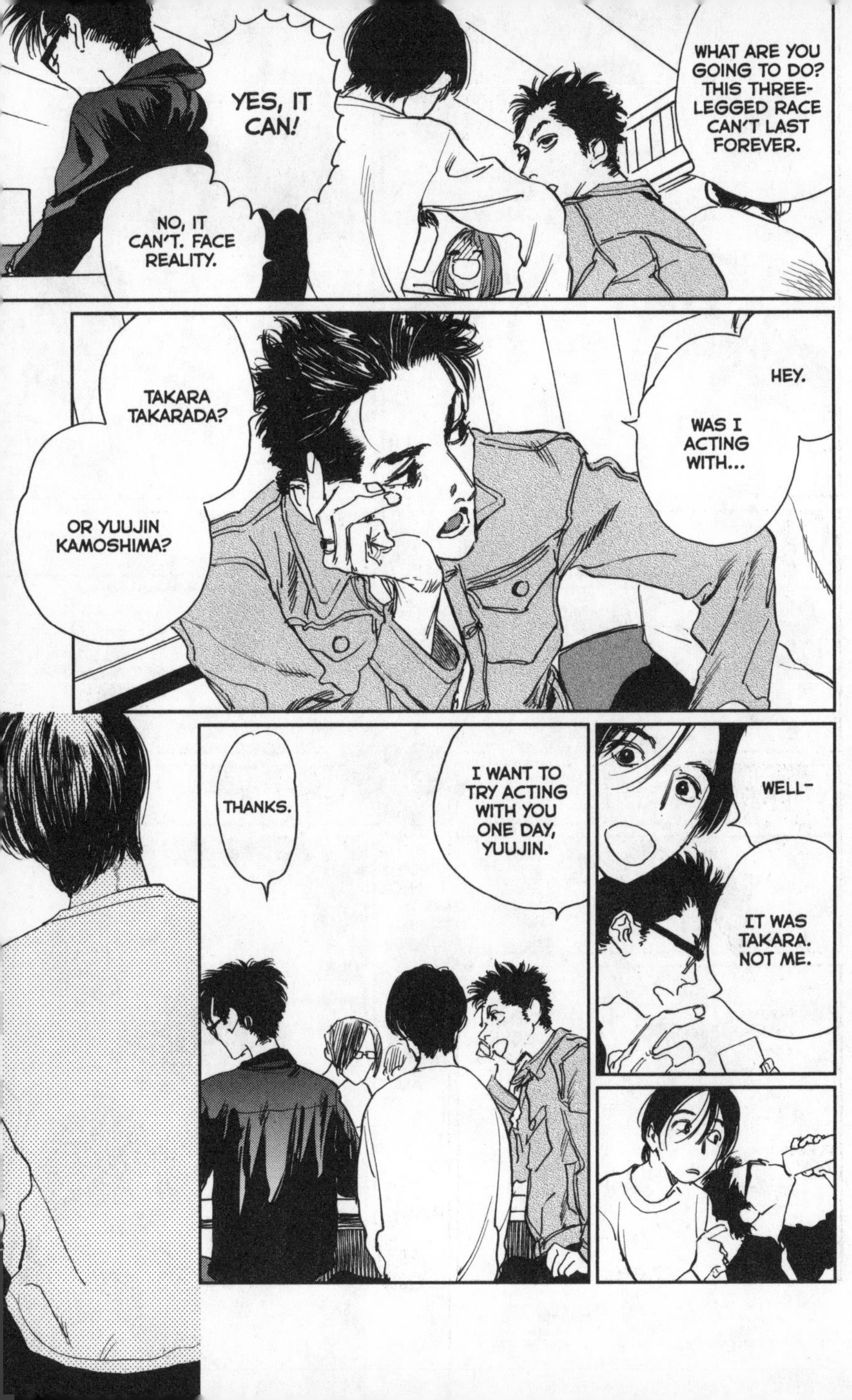
WHAT ARE YOU GOING TO DO? THIS THREE-LEGGED RACE CAN'T LAST FOREVER.
YES, IT CAN!
NO, IT CAN'T. FACE REALITY.
HEY.
WAS I ACTING WITH...
TAKARA TAKARADA?
OR YUUJIN KAMOSHIMA?
WELL-
IT WAS TAKARA. NOT ME.
I WANT TO TRY ACTING WITH YOU ONE DAY, YUUJIN.
THANKS.

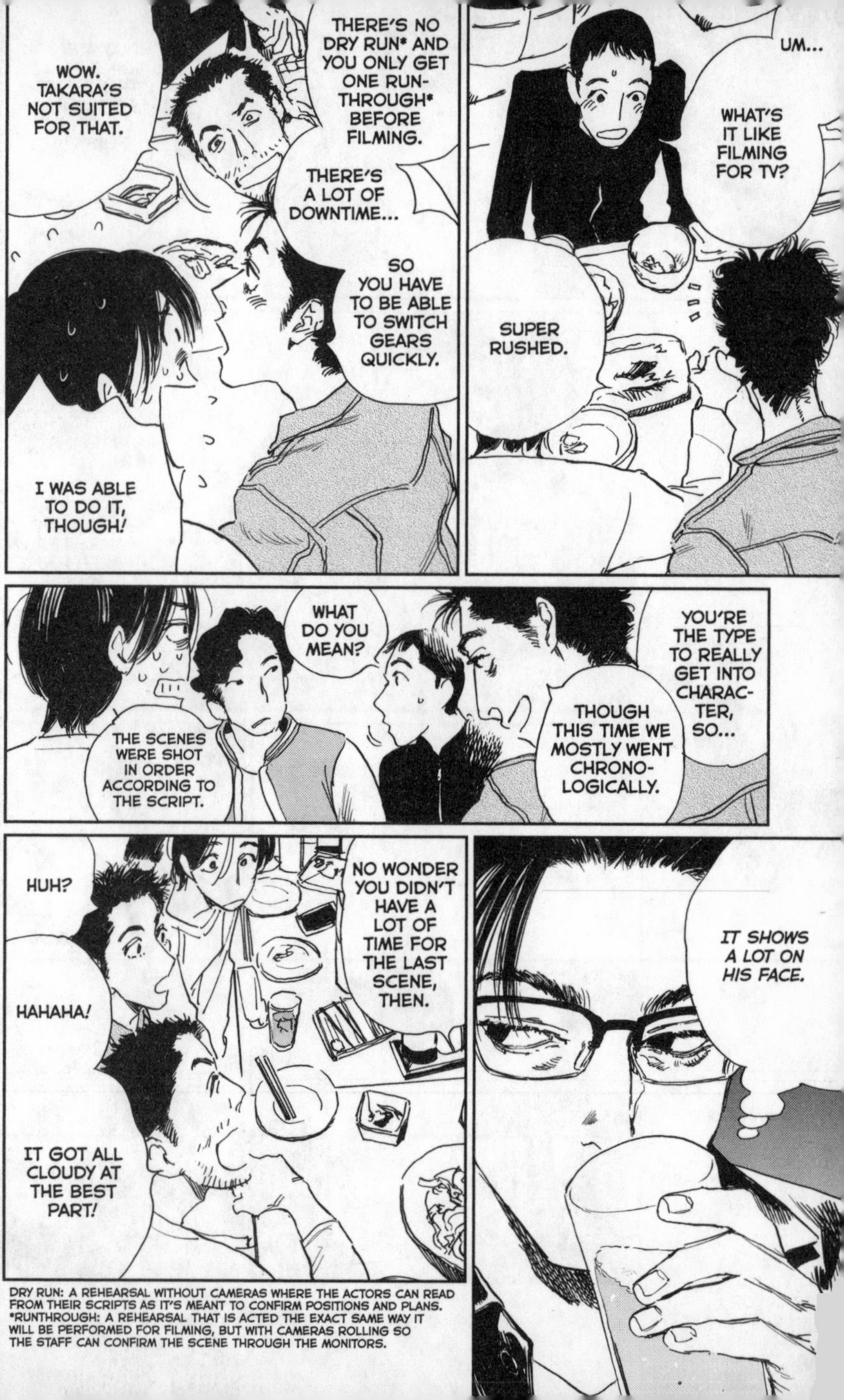
UM...
WHAT'S IT LIKE FILMING FOR TV?
SUPER RUSHED.
THERE'S NO DRY RUN* AND YOU ONLY GET ONE RUN-THROUGH* BEFORE FILMING.
THERE'S A LOT OF DOWNTIME...
SO YOU HAVE TO BE ABLE TO SWITCH GEARS QUICKLY.
WOW. TAKARA'S NOT SUITED FOR THAT.
I WAS ABLE TO DO IT, THOUGH!
YOU'RE THE TYPE TO REALLY GET INTO CHARAC-TER, SO...
THOUGH THIS TIME WE MOSTLY WENT CHRONO-LOGICALLY.
WHAT DO YOU MEAN?
THE SCENES WERE SHOT IN ORDER ACCORDING TO THE SCRIPT.
IT SHOWS A LOT ON HIS FACE.
NO WONDER YOU DIDN'T HAVE A LOT OF TIME FOR THE LAST SCENE, THEN.
HUH?
HAHAHA!
IT GOT ALL CLOUDY AT THE BEST PART!

DRY RUN: A REHEARSAL WITHOUT CAMERAS WHERE THE ACTORS CAN READ FROM THEIR SCRIPTS AS IT'S MEANT TO CONFIRM POSITIONS AND PLANS.
*RUNTHROUGH: A REHEARSAL THAT IS ACTED THE EXACT SAME WAY IT WILL BE PERFORMED FOR FILMING, BUT WITH CAMERAS ROLLING SO THE STAFF CAN CONFIRM THE SCENE THROUGH THE MONITORS.

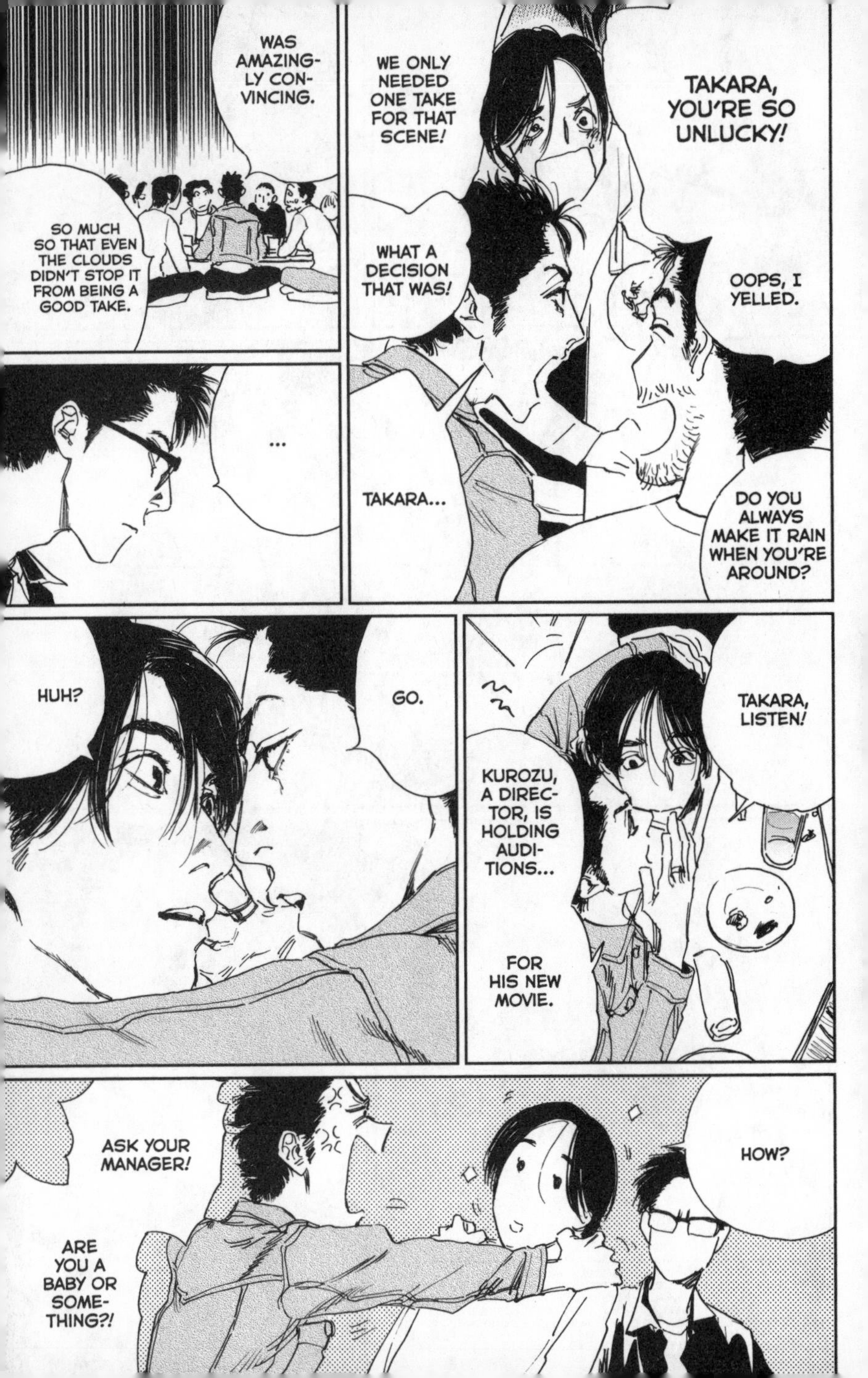
TAKARA, YOU'RE SO UNLUCKY!
WE ONLY NEEDED ONE TAKE FOR THAT SCENE!
OOPS, I YELLED.
WHAT A DECISION THAT WAS!
DO YOU ALWAYS MAKE IT RAIN WHEN YOU'RE AROUND?
TAKARA...
WAS AMAZING-LY CON-VINCING.
SO MUCH SO THAT EVEN THE CLOUDS DIDN'T STOP IT FROM BEING A GOOD TAKE.
...
TAKARA, LISTEN!
KUROZU, A DIREC-TOR, IS HOLDING AUDI-TIONS...
FOR HIS NEW MOVIE.
GO.
HUH?
HOW?
ASK YOUR MANAGER!
ARE YOU A BABY OR SOME-THING?!

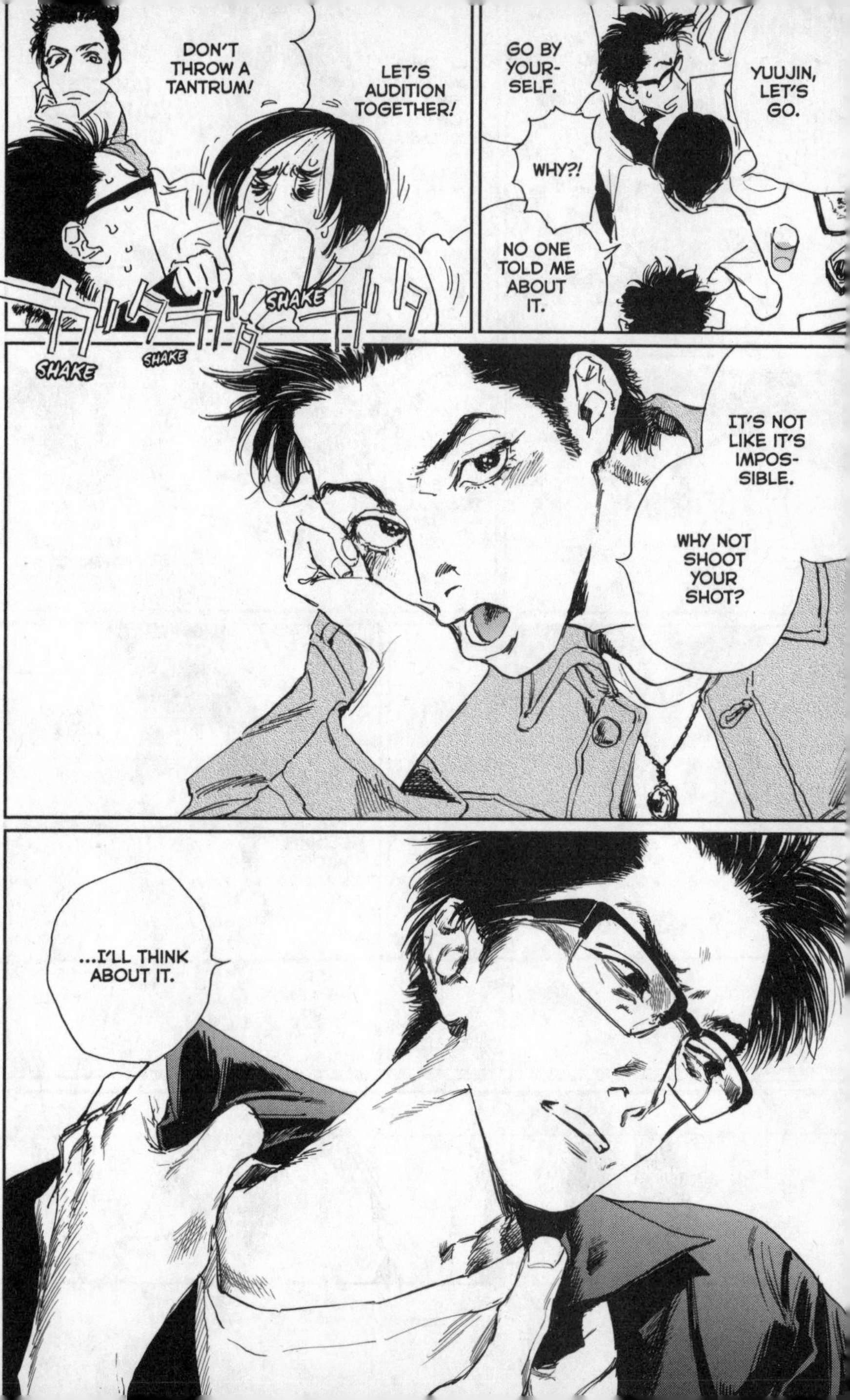
YUUJIN, LET'S GO.
GO BY YOURSELF.
WHY?!
NO ONE TOLD ME ABOUT IT.
LET'S AUDITION TOGETHER!
DON'T THROW A TANTRUM!
SHAKE
SHAKE
SHAKE
IT'S NOT LIKE IT'S IMPOSSIBLE.
WHY NOT SHOOT YOUR SHOT?
...I'LL THINK ABOUT IT.

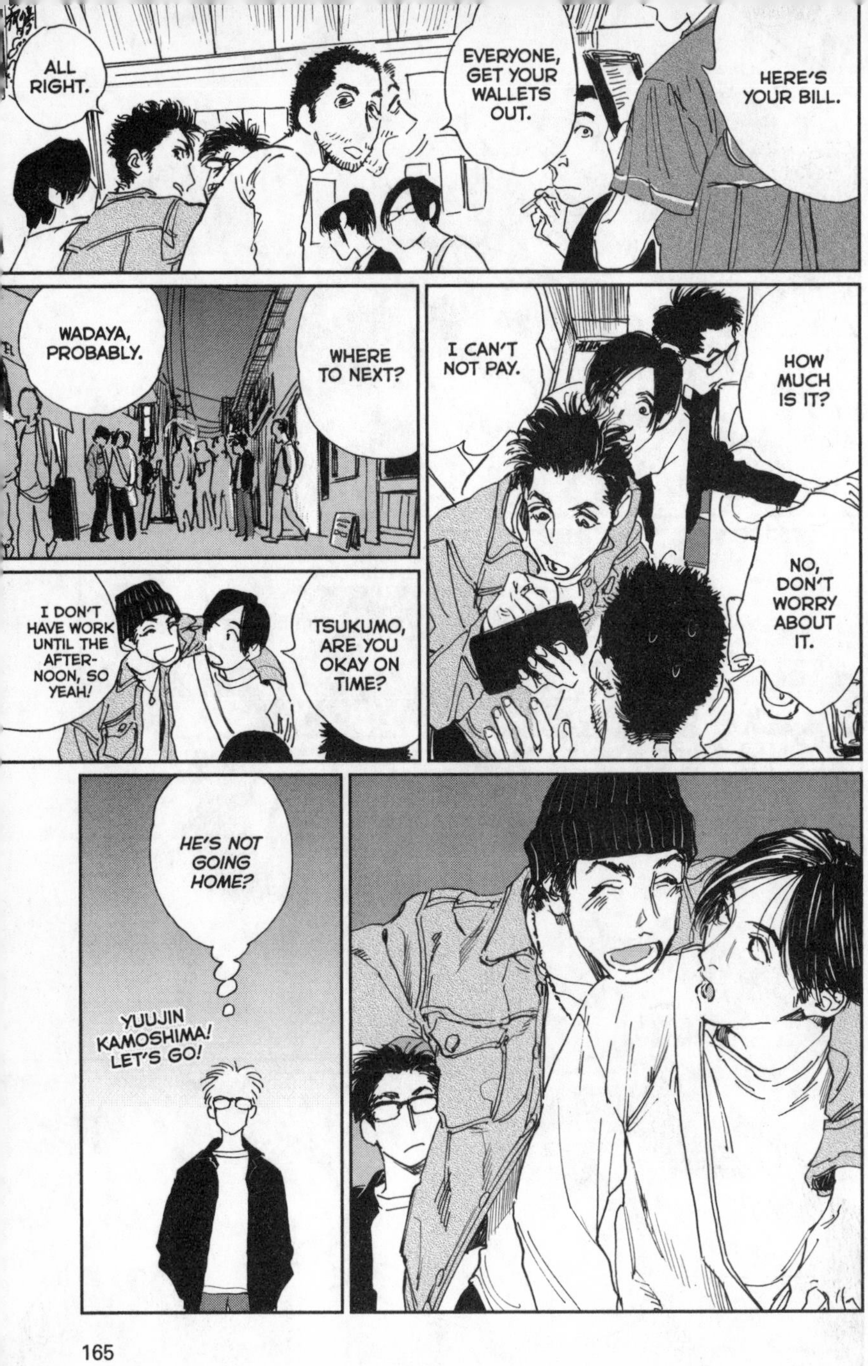
HERE'S YOUR BILL.
EVERYONE, GET YOUR WALLETS OUT.
ALL RIGHT.
HOW MUCH IS IT?
I CAN'T NOT PAY.
NO, DON'T WORRY ABOUT IT.
WHERE TO NEXT?
WADAYA, PROBABLY.
TSUKUMO, ARE YOU OKAY ON TIME?
I DON'T HAVE WORK UNTIL THE AFTER-NOON, SO YEAH!
HE'S NOT GOING HOME?
YUUJIN KAMOSHIMA! LET'S GO!

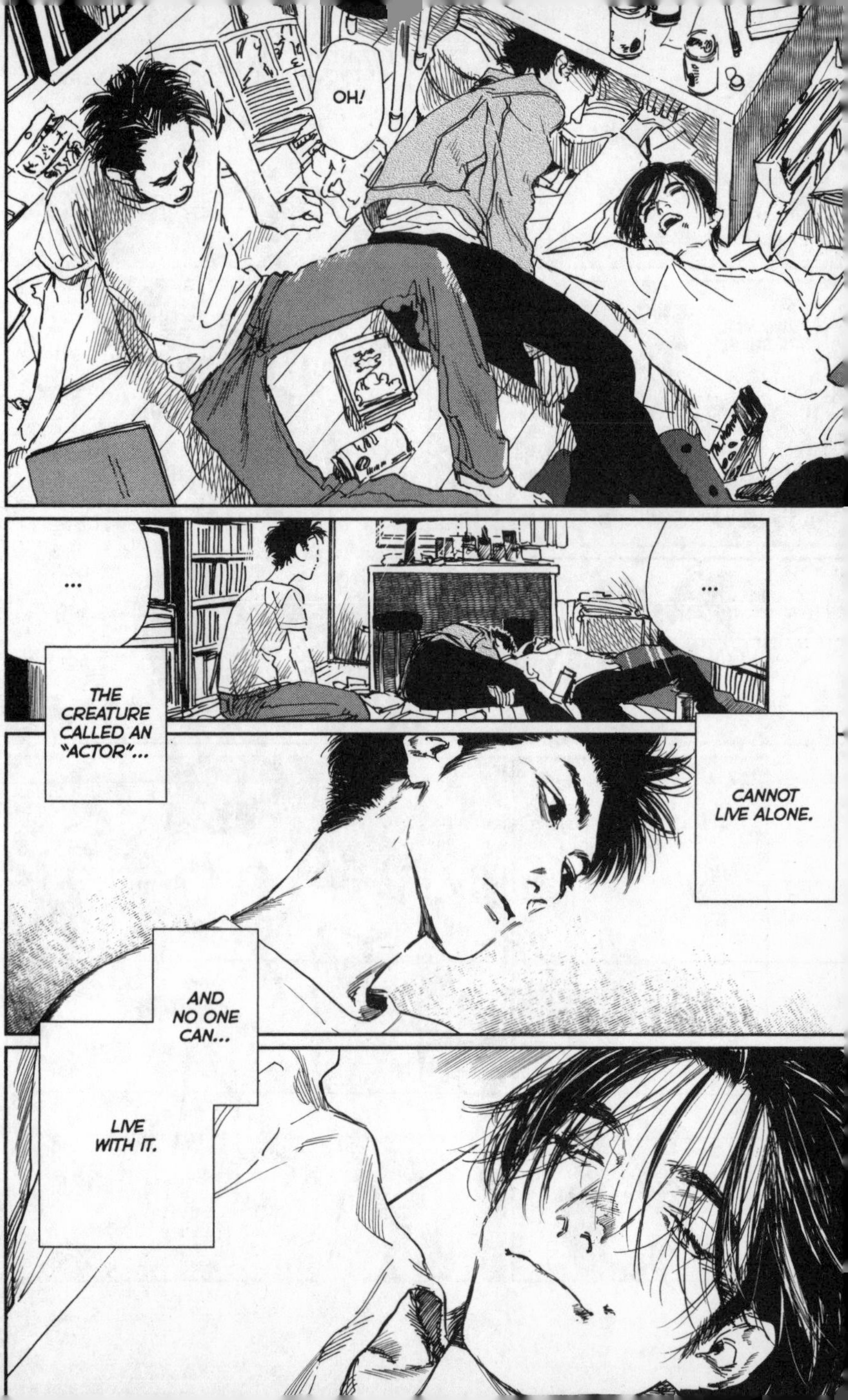
OH!
...
...
THE CREATURE CALLED AN "ACTOR"...
CANNOT LIVE ALONE.
AND NO ONE CAN...
LIVE WITH IT.

DOUBLE VOL. 1 COMPLETE

CONTINUED IN VOL. 2

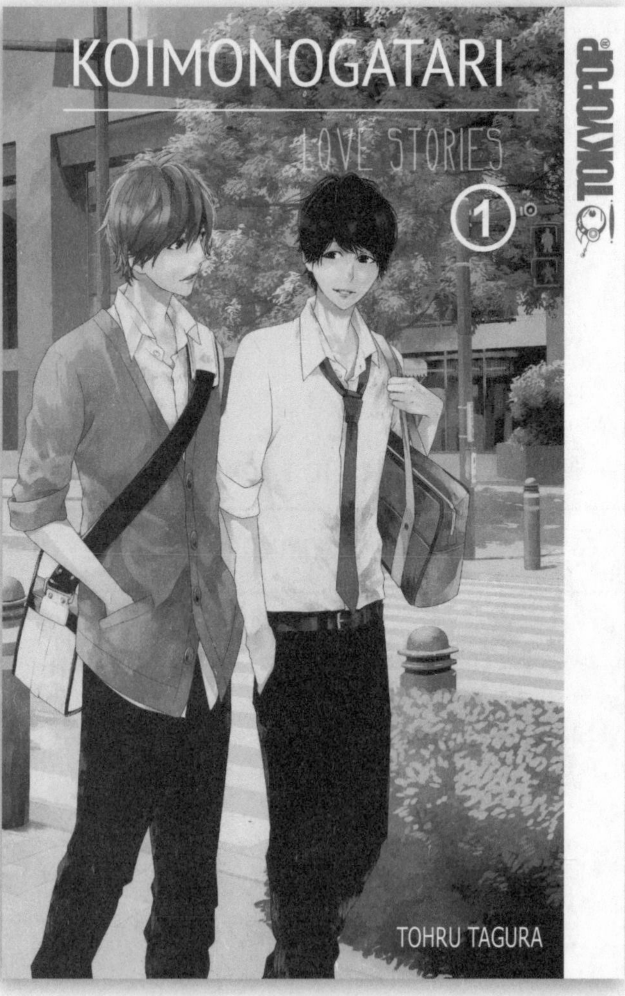
KOIMONOGATARI
LOVE STORIES
1
TOKYOPOP
TOHRU TAGURA

KOIMONOGATARI: LOVE STORIES, VOLUME 1

Tohru Tagura

LOVE x LOVE

When Yuiji accidentally overhears his classmate Yamato confessing to another friend that he's gay, his perspective shifts. Seeing Yamato in a new light, Yuiji does his best not to let prejudice color his view, but he still finds himself overthinking his classmates' interactions now. He especially notices the way Yamato looks at one particular boy: Yuiji's own best friend. Even though he tells himself he shouldn't get involved, Yuiji finds he just can't help it; watching Yamato's one-sided love draws him in a way he never expected. At first, it's empathy, knowing that the boy Yamato has his sights on is definitely straight and has no idea. But as his own friendship with Yamato develops and the two of them grow closer through a mutual study group, Yuiji comes to truly care about Yamato as a person, regardless of his sexuality. He only wants Yamato to be happy, and to be able to express his true self.

TOKYOPOP

LAUGHING UNDER THE CLOUDS, VOLUME 1
KarakaraKemuri

FANTASY

Under the curse of Orochi, the great demon serpent reborn every 300 years, Japan has been shrouded in clouds for as long as anyone can remember... The era of the samurai is at an end, and carrying swords has been outlawed. To combat the rising crime rates, an inescapable prison was built in the middle of Lake Biwa. When brothers Tenka, Soramaru and Chutaro Kumo are hired to capture and transport offenders to their final lodgings in this prison, they unexpectedly find themselves faced with a greater destiny than any of them could have imagined.

OUR NOT-SO-LONELY PLANET TRAVEL GUIDE, VOLUME 1

Mone Sorai

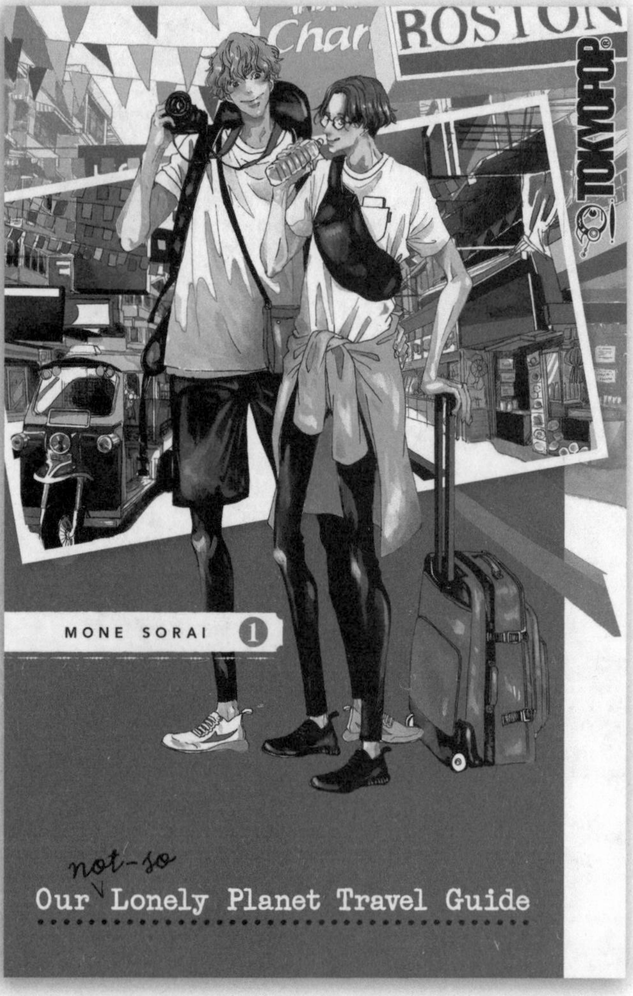
TOKYOPOP
MONE SORAI 1
Our not-so Lonely Planet Travel Guide

LOVE-x-LOVE

Super serious Asahi Suzumura and laidback, easygoing Mitsuki Sayama might seem like an odd couple, but they made a deal; they'll vacation around the world and when they get back to Japan, they'll get married. As they travel from country to country, the different people, cultures and cuisine they encounter begin to bring them closer together. After all they're not just learning about the world, but about themselves too.

TOKYOPOP

GLASS SYNDROME
Eiko Ariki

Glass Syndrome

by EIKO ARIKI

Class president Nijou is a talented athlete, popular honor student... and a total people-pleaser who can't stop living up to others' smothering expectations of him. When his teacher asks him to check on Toomi, a classmate who's stopped coming to school, that chance meeting leads to an unexpected connection that neither young man expects. Toomi sees right through his diligent facade, and Nijou can't forget the cool comfort of Toomi's undemanding touch.

But when Nijou discovers the reason behind Toomi's frequent absences — that he's been working as an online cam "girl" — he doesn't know how to react. How can he bring up what he knows? And how will it change their relationship?

OSSAN IDOL! VOLUME 1

Ichika Kino & Mochiko Mochida

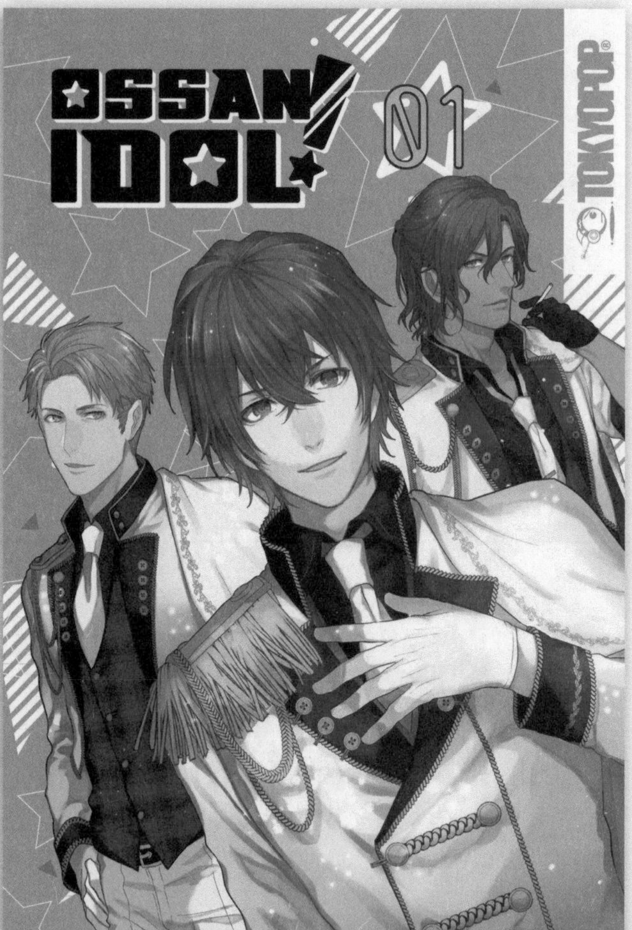
OSSAN IDOL!
01
TOKYOPOP
ICHIKA KINO • MOCHIKO MOCHIDA

IDOL

Miroku Osaki is 36 years old, unemployed, and unhappy. Having been bullied in his childhood and even into his adult life, he became a shut-in after being unfairly laid off. For a long time, the only thing that brought him joy was online gaming. Then, he tried the popular "Let's Try Dancing!" karaoke style. It was addicting... and transformative! Inspired by his new hobby, Miroku decides to turn his life around. He begins singing karaoke and going to the gym, where he meets Yoichi, the director of an entertainment company who encourages Miroku to pursue his dreams. Miroku only wanted to be good at the game he loves, but when he accidentally uploads a clip of himself singing and dancing, it goes viral! Can he really become an idol, even at his age? Suddenly, it doesn't seem so impossible!

TOKYOPOP

A GENTLE NOBLE'S VACATION RECOMMENDATION, VOLUME 1

Misaki, Momochi & Sando

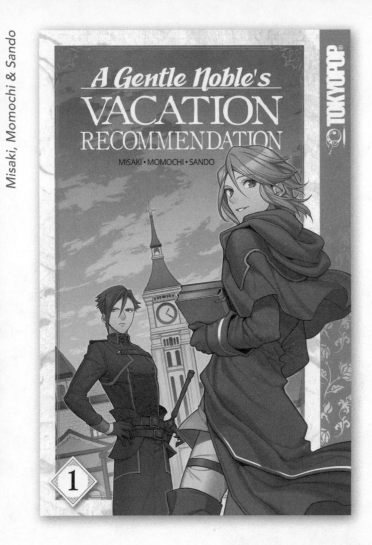

A Gentle Noble's
VACATION
RECOMMENDATION

MISAKI • MOMOCHI • SANDO

1

FANTASY

When Lizel mysteriously finds himself in a city that bears odd similarities to his own but clearly isn't, he quickly comes to terms with the unlikely truth: this is an entirely different world. Even so, laid-back Lizel isn't the type to panic. He immediately sets out to learn more about this strange place, and to help him do so, hires a seasoned adventurer named Gil as his tour guide and protector. Until he's able to find a way home, Lizel figures this is a perfect opportunity to explore a new way of life adventuring as part of a guild. After all, he's sure he'll go home eventually... might as well enjoy the otherworldly vacation for now!

STOP

THIS IS THE BACK OF THE BOOK!

How do you read manga-style? It's simple! Let's practice -- just start in the top right panel and follow the numbers below!

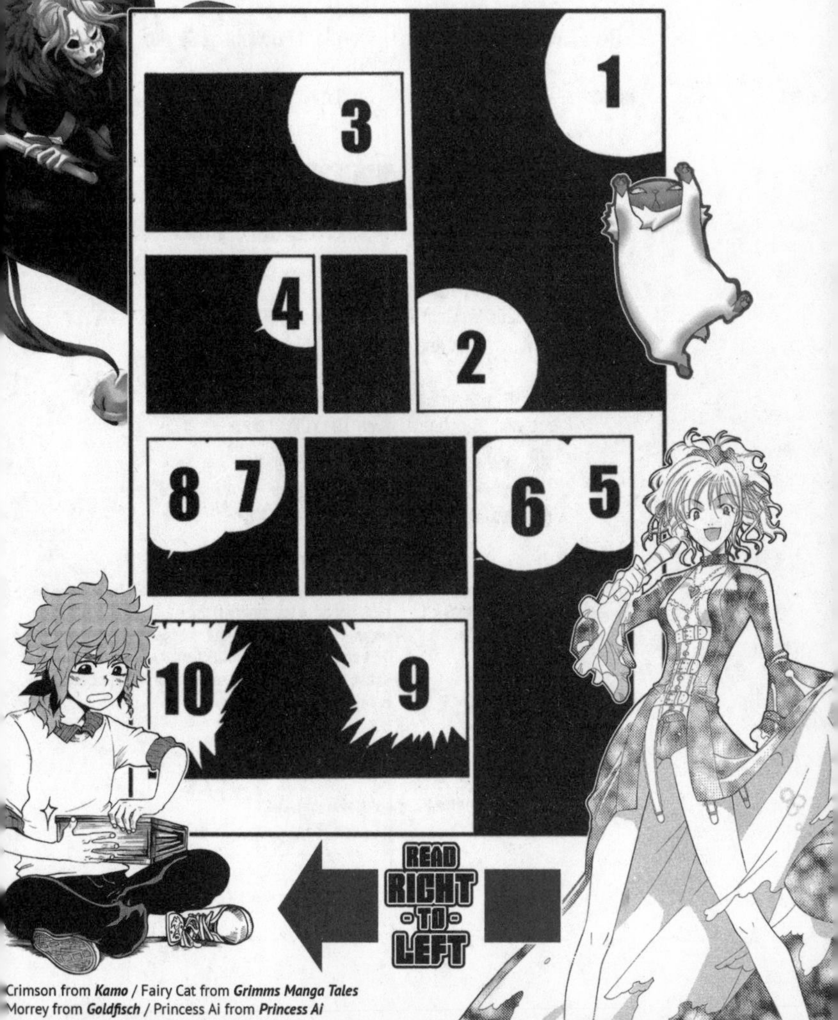

1
2
3
4
5
6
7
8
9
10
READ
RIGHT
-TO-
LEFT

Crimson from ***Kamo*** / Fairy Cat from ***Grimms Manga Tales***
Morrey from ***Goldfisch*** / Princess Ai from ***Princess Ai***

Double, Volume 1
Manga by Ayako Noda

Editor - Lena Atanassova
Translator - Massiel Gutierrez
Copy Editor - Tina Tseng
Quality Check - Daichi Nemoto
Proofreader - Katie Kimura
Graphic Designer - Sol DeLeo
Editorial Associate - Janae Young
Retouching and Lettering - Vibrraant Publishing Studio
Licensing Specialist - Arika Yanaka
Editor-in-Chief & Publisher - Stu Levy

A  Manga

TOKYOPOP and 🐸 are trademarks or registered trademarks of TOKYOPOP Inc.

TOKYOPOP Inc.
5200 W. Century Blvd. Suite 705
Los Angeles, 90045

E-mail: info@TOKYOPOP.com
Come visit us online at www.TOKYOPOP.com

f www.facebook.com/TOKYOPOP
🐦 www.twitter.com/TOKYOPOP
📷 www.instagram.com/TOKYOPOP

ISBN: 978-1-4278-6907-4

First TOKYOPOP Printing: November 2021
Printed in CANADA